POLITICAL PARTIES AND PRIMARIES IN KENTUCKY

POLITICAL PARTIES AND PRIMARIES IN KENTUCKY

Penny M. Miller
Malcolm E. Jewell

THE UNIVERSITY PRESS OF KENTUCKY

Scholarly publisher for the Commonwealth,
serving Bellarmine College, Berea College, Centre
College of Kentucky, Eastern Kentucky University,
The Filson Club, Georgetown College, Kentucky
Historical Society, Kentucky State University,
Morehead State University, Transylvania University,
University of Kentucky, University of Louisville,
and Western Kentucky University.

Editorial and Sales Offices: Lexington, Kentucky 40506-0336

Library of Congress Cataloging-in-Publication Data

Miller, Penny M., 1943-
Political parties and primaries in Kentucky / Penny M. Miller,
Malcom E. Jewell.

p. cm.
Includes bibliographical references (p.
ISBN 0-8131-1753-4
1. Political parties—Kentucky. 2. Primaries—Kentucky.
I. Jewell, Malcolm Edwin, 1928- . II. Title.
JK2295.K43M55 1990 89-70690
324.5'4'09769—dc20

This book is printed on acid-free paper meeting
the requirements he American National Standard
for Permanence of Paper for Printed Library Materials.
♾

CONTENTS

TABLES

FIGURES

ACKNOWLEDGMENTS

A LARGE number of persons were helpful in our research and should be acknowledged collectively or individually. First are nearly a thousand persons active in Democratic gubernatorial primary campaigns (1979 to 1987) who filled out lengthy questionnaires, some of them on two occasions.

We interviewed a number of candidates and campaign leaders in the 1987 Democratic primaries, as well as party leaders in both parties. We assume that they prefer their assistance to be acknowledged anonymously.

We gained valuable insights into the Kentucky politics and particularly the 1987 primaries from reporters who had covered politics and primaries firsthand: Bob Johnson, Ferrell Wellman, Al Cross, Tom Loftus, Cindy Rugeley, John Winn Miller, Jack Brammer, Jacqueline Duke, Mary Ann Roser, and Carol Marie Cropper. For coverage of the 1987 primaries and general elections we relied heavily on the excellent coverage by these and other reporters in the *Courier-Journal* and the *Lexington Herald-Leader*. Our chapter on campaign finance makes extensive use of the excellent series of articles written by Richard Whitt and R.G. Dunlop in October 1987 in the *Courier-Journal*.

We have made use of research that one or both of us carried out with other political scientists at the University of Kentucky. Phillip Roeder collaborated on a study of party alignments in Kentucky. Lee Sigelman, Michael Baer, and Phillip Roeder collaborated on a study of voting and nonvoing in the state. Lee Sigelman collaborated on previous publications of political activists. We very much appreciate their contributions. We also benefited from the excellent data collections of the Kentucky Survey Research Center.

Some of the material in chapters 3 and 5 has been published (with Lee Sigelman) in two earlier articles: "Reconsidering a Typology of Incentives among Campaign Activists: A Research Note," *Western Political Quarterly* 40 (1987): 519-26, reprinted by permission of the University of Utah, copyright holder; and "Divisive Primaries and Party Activists: Kentucky, 1979 and 1983," *Journal of Politics* 50 (1988): 459-70, also reprinted by permission.

1

KENTUCKY IN A NATIONAL PERSPECTIVE

THE AMERICAN political and electoral system is characterized by diversity and change. Every state is different, with its own unique political history, traditions, leaders, and partisan loyalties. Political scientists often use the term *political culture* to define the dominant beliefs and attitudes in a state that are shaped by its political history (Patterson, 1968; Rosenthal and Moakley, 1984). Kentucky has its own style of politics, its own history and political culture.

State political systems, however, are not immune from national political forces, and changes in the politics of a state cannot be understood without a knowledge of national trends. Shifts in the power of national political parties directly affect the fortunes of state political parties. The regeneration of the national Democratic party during the New Deal years gradually transformed the politics of northern states, fostering the development of competitive two-party systems throughout the region.

The successful presidential candidacies of Dwight Eisenhower, Richard Nixon, and Ronald Reagan reshaped the political system of southern and border states, bringing about the demise of the Solid Democratic South. In these states the Republican party became competitive in presidential, congressional, and most statewide races, though it lagged behind in legislative and local contests. Kentucky is a border state, and since the 1950s it has been significantly affected by these national trends.

Most of the research done by students of state political parties and elections has been centered on the questions raised and the hypotheses advanced by V.O. Key, Jr., in his classic work entitled *Southern Politics* (1949) and his pioneering study, *American State Politics: An Introduction* (1956). In more recent years there have been several valuable studies of southern states (Bass and DeVries, 1977; Lamis, 1984; Black and Black, 1987). More detailed studies of individual states are needed to develop generalizations about state politics as well as to identify the factors that cause variations in state political systems. Contemporary studies that fill this need are in short supply (one good example is Bryan, 1974).

This book is a study of politics and elections in the commonwealth of Kentucky, a state whose politics is in many ways typical of that in southern and border states where traditional Democratic control has been undermined by national political forces. This is a study of the changes in Kentucky politics over the last two decades and more particularly a study of the characteristics of parties and elections in the last decade. The emphasis is on state, rather than on national, elections because these are central to an understanding of the Kentucky political system. Much of our attention is devoted to the most important election in any state, the choice of a governor.

Primary Election Campaigns

In most Kentucky gubernatorial elections, the Democratic primary is more significant than the general election: there are more serious candidates and there is closer competition, the campaigns are longer and more expensive, and there is more public interest in the campaigns. In at least four out of five cases, the winner of the Democratic primary is elected governor. For these reasons the main focus of this book is the Democratic gubernatorial primary.

State primary elections have been neglected by the political scientists who specialize in state politics. One recent study (Jewell, 1984) analyzes gubernatorial primaries in northern states, giving particular attention to those political parties that attempt to influence the outcome of primary elections by endorsing candidates at preprimary conventions. The major purpose of such endorsements is to select the strongest possible candidate and to avoid or minimize the divisive effects of primary contests. Most southern Democratic party organizations have made no efforts to influence the outcome of primaries, partly because these organizations have been relatively weak and partly because, until recently, Republican gubernatorial candidates have not constituted a serious threat. The Republican party in Louisiana, however, has informally made preprimary endorsements, and both parties in Virginia have recently used state conventions instead of primaries in an effort to gain greater unity and prospects for victory in the general election.

The definitive study of Democratic primaries in southern states from the late 1920s through the 1940s was V.O. Key's *Southern Politics* (1949). The focus of that study was on various patterns of factionalism in primary elections. Some state Democratic parties were dominated by a single faction; some were split between two factions over a prolonged period; others were splintered among a variety of short-term factions, each associated with a particular candidate. Key paid particular attention to bifactionalism in the Democratic party because it offered an imperfect substitute for competitive two-party politics. The best detailed study of a bifactional system was Allan Sindler's (1956) analysis of Louisiana.

Political scientists have continued to analyze southern primaries using Key's model of factionalism. The most systematic work, by Earl and Merle Black (1982a), measuring changing patterns of southern primaries, has drawn the conclusion that traditional factionalism has declined. Now that governors in most southern states can succeed themselves, the incumbent is usually able to maintain his personal organization to be used in a bid for renomination. But there are few examples of factional continuity from one administration to the next. The Blacks have also measured the slow growth of competition in Republican primaries (1982b).

What is lacking from the study of southern primaries is in-depth examinations of the primary system over a period of years in individual states. If primary competition is no longer organized along factional lines, we know very little about what has replaced factions, how campaigns are organized, and how voters make choices in primary elections. Yet Democratic primaries remain important in most southern and border states. They are often more competitive than general elections for statewide office. Turnout in Democratic primaries is much higher than in Republican primaries and sometimes higher than in the general election. In most southern and border states, as in Kentucky, the winner of the Democratic primary is usually elected governor.

The last comprehensive study of Kentucky politics (Jewell and Cunningham, 1968) analyzed the factionalism that pervaded Democratic primaries for state offices. This factional system was based not on regional, economic, or ideological differences but on personal loyalties. The leaders of the two factions, Earle Clements and A.B. "Happy" Chandler, formed alliances with other state political leaders and with the leaders of rival factions at the county level. The two factions often ran slates of candidates for the major statewide offices. Many active political workers at the local level apparently remained loyal to one faction over an extended period of time. In the absence of survey data, it was impossible to determine whether substantial numbers of voters had similar loyalties to a faction.

That book was hardly in print before the bifactional system began to fade away. No longer did state political leaders play the role of kingmaker. At the county level there was a gradual decline of political leaders who were able to dominate local politics and control votes and similarly a decline in local factionalism.

In our research on Kentucky politics, we have tried to determine what has replaced the bifactional system. What determines the outcome of Democratic gubernatorial primaries? To answer that question, we begin by examining the role of political activists, the persons who staff the organizations of candidates in Democratic gubernatorial primaries. Hundreds of Democrats who played significant campaign roles in one or more of the last three gubernatorial primaries (1979, 1983, and 1987) have been surveyed, using an extensive mail questionnaire.

In recent years political scientists have rediscovered local political activists as a valuable source of information about party organizations. Specifically, they have surveyed local party leaders and also delegates to state party conventions in a number of states (though there are not comparable studies of persons active in gubernatorial primaries). These studies in other states provide a base of comparison to determine whether the characteristics and attitudes of Kentucky political activists are typical of those in other states (Conway and Feigert, 1968; Hofstetter, 1973; Costantini and King, 1984; Rapoport, Abramowitz, and McGlennon, 1986).

In Kentucky we find that, though new political workers are recruited in each campaign, a large proportion of the active workers in primaries are veterans who work consistently from one election to the next. It is important to determine what kinds of persons these are, what are their attitudes and motivations, and—most importantly—how they choose a candidate for whom to work. We believe that the best way to understand modern political organizations in Kentucky is to understand the men and women within them.

Traditionally in Kentucky, candidates for statewide office have spent months touring the state, meeting with local political leaders, and, as the campaign progresses, speaking at rallies and meeting the voters. This is still a major component of the primary campaign. But in Kentucky, as in the rest of the country, the campaign on television has assumed greater importance because candidates can reach a much larger proportion of the voters more often. The Democratic gubernatorial primary attracts considerable attention on television, and the debate on Kentucky Educational Television has an impact comparable to the impact of presidential debates on the national campaign. The success of candidates for governor depends heavily on their ability to package their message effectively in "sound bites" for the evening news and their skill in answering questions in debates.

It is also essential that a winning candidate use campaign advertising effectively. He or she needs skilled professionals to create the advertising campaign that will present a positive image of the candidate and will package the candidate's message well. This requires, of course, that the candidate have a message or a theme that will appeal to the voters. The candidate may also have to take the risk of using negative advertising to undermine a front-running opponent.

A large-scale television advertising campaign is expensive, and a serious candidate for governor has no choice but to raise the necessary funds. The candidate who falls far behind in the money-raising marathon must either drop out of the race or be relegated to the role of a minor player in the campaign. This means that much of the candidate's time in the early phases of the campaign must be devoted to raising money and that the most important component of the candidate's organization is the fund-raising apparatus. It means that in the early stages of a campaign the credibility of a candidate is judged largely by his or her ability to raise funds.

To understand the dynamics of these primary campaigns for major office, we will examine in some detail the campaigns for governor and lieutenant governor in 1987. To demonstrate the role that money had come to play in Kentucky politics, we have collected facts and figures on campaign financing, particularly in the Democratic primary.

Ideally, we should use this study of primary elections in Kentucky to test hypotheses developed in other studies of state primary elections, particularly in the southern and border states where the primary still surpasses or equals the general election in importance. Unfortunately, these hypotheses have not been developed, and these studies have not been made.

The traditional system of Kentucky primary elections was typical of those in many southern states, though not all of them had such strong factionalism and most of them had the runoff election that Kentucky lacked. We suspect that trends in Kentucky primaries are similar to some of those occurring (but not adequately studied) in most southern states. The changes in primary campaigns—the growing costs and the increasing importance of television—reflect a national trend, one that has been more publicized in presidential races but is occurring in the states as well (Jewell, 1984). We hope that our study will be replicated and our findings tested in other border and southern states so that it will be possible to draw some generalizations about modern primary campaigns.

Two-Party Competition

The trend toward the Republican party that has swept through most southern and border states has been felt in Kentucky elections, except at the gubernatorial level. Republican presidential candidates have been increasingly successful in appealing to Kentucky voters. Kentucky voters are not as conservative as those in some southern states (at least as measured by the voting record of their congressmen), nor were they as critical of desegregation policies and civil rights legislation when these issues dominated southern politics. But Kentucky voters have been suspicious of northern liberal candidates running on national Democratic tickets. Dwight Eisenhower almost carried Kentucky in his first race and carried it in his second. Kentucky voted for Richard Nixon in all three of his presidential races. The only two Democratic presidential candidates it has supported since 1952 have been southerners: Lyndon Johnson in 1964 and Jimmy Carter in 1976. Kentucky voted twice for Ronald Reagan and supported George Bush in 1988. Kentucky has also frequently elected Republicans to the Senate in the last forty years, starting with John Sherman Cooper in 1946. In House races, in addition to the traditionally Republican Fifth District, Kentucky has consistently elected Republicans in two other districts since 1978.

In most southern and border states, the national Republican trend has extended to state politics, enabling the state Republican party not only to elect members to Congress but to win a larger number of gubernatorial elections and to make gradual gains in the state legislature and local offices. The Kentucky Republican party has not made comparable progress in state elections, despite the fact that throughout the twentieth century the party has been a significant force in Kentucky politics. It has rarely failed to win at least 40 percent of the vote in races for governor and senator, and it has usually held at least 20 to 25 percent of the seats in the legislature. By contrast, in most southern states until the 1960s, the Republican party did not consistently run candidates, or at least serious candidates, for statewide office, and legislatures in the deep South had few if any Republican members.

In the last thirty years, the Republican party in most southern and border states has made significant gains in state as well as national elections, while the Kentucky Republican party has stood still or slipped backward. There has been only one Republican governor elected in the last forty years. The Republican party had more difficulty recruiting a credible candidate for governor in 1983 and in 1987 than it did in the 1950s and 1960s. The Republican contingent in the legislature has been smaller during the 1980s than it was in the 1960s.

We will examine the Kentucky Republican party, its leadership and organization, in some detail in an effort to determine what has gone wrong and why it is so difficult for the party to capitalize on the successes that national Republican candidates have had in Kentucky. We will also describe the 1987 Republican primary and general election campaigns for governor as a case study that illustrates the party's difficulty.

While Republican electoral successes in southern states have been described and analyzed by political scientists (Lamis, 1984), little attention has been paid to the development of Republican party organization in these states or the successes and failures of the party in gubernatorial and legislative races (but see Kemple, 1980; Theodoulou, 1986). Thus, we are not able to draw many comparisons between the Republican experience in Kentucky and in other border and southern states.

There has been considerable scholarly attention to voting patterns in the South, much of it based on voting survey data. We know that over the last two decades the proportion of southerners splitting their votes in national and state elections has increased dramatically. The proportion of southern voters identifying with the Democratic party has declined, while the proportion of independents has increased and the proportion of Republicans has increased more gradually (Beck, 1977; Campbell, 1977; Hadley and Howell, 1980; Stanley and Castle, 1988). Survey data are not available in every state to measure trends in party identification. The state-level data that are available show that the proportion of Democratic identifiers has been declining and there is considerable variation among states in the relative gains in Republicans and in independents (Swansbrough and Brodsky, 1988).

When we examine Kentucky voters, we find that there has been a large increase in split ticket voting, that large proportions of voters have voted often for Republicans for national office while continuing to support most state Democratic candidates. Data on party identification in Kentucky (reported in chapter 12), however, fails to show evidence of the party realignment that has been occurring to various degrees throughout the southern and border states. Kentuckians have remained relatively stable in their professed party identification as well as in their party registration at the same time that they have grown much more independent in their voting behavior. In recent years students of voting behavior have raised a number of substantive and methodological questions about the meaning of party identification and the conventional ways in which it is measured (for a summary, see Shively, 1980). These questions are pertinent to Kentucky where the traditional concept of party identification fails to adequately explain the current behavior of Kentucky voters.

Kentucky is more rural than the average state, and in the last half century it has had weaker two-party competition than the average state. Both of these differences help to explain why politics in Kentucky is not typical of politics across the country. Kentucky also differs from the typical southern state; it is more rural, it has fewer black citizens, and it has a larger bloc of voters with a long tradition of voting Republican. The trend toward greater two-party competition is weaker in Kentucky than in most southern and border states. But many of the changes in campaign styles that are occurring across the country can be found in both the primary and general elections in Kentucky.

2

DEMOCRATIC PARTY ORGANIZATION

The Role of the Governor

Tradition and Change

In Kentucky the governor is usually recognized as the most important leader in the Democratic party. The governor has traditionally been strong in Kentucky—as a legislative leader and as a politician—even though the constitution prevents his or her serving two consecutive terms. Democratic control of the governorship has been so common in the last sixty years that party leadership has not gravitated to other elected officials or to the party chairman. There is very little precedent for determining who will exercise party leadership in periods of Republican gubernatorial control (Jewell and Cunningham, 1968: 39). During the only Republican gubernatorial administration in recent years, that of Louie B. Nunn, 1967-71, Lt. Gov. Wendell Ford, a Democrat, laid claim to party leadership.

The factions that dominated Kentucky politics from the mid-1930s to the late 1960s, which were identified with A.B. Chandler and Earle Clements, are described in some detail in chapter 3. They had their origin in Chandler's victory over Thomas Rhea in the 1935 gubernatorial primary. Chandler and Clements were strong party leaders who built statewide networks of followers among local officials and party activists. When he became governor, Bert Combs succeeded Clements as leader of one faction. After their terms as governor, all tried to pick their successors and continued to make endorsements in Democratic primaries.

The dominant role of the governor in factional politics of the 1950s and 1960s has been described as follows:

> The governorship is the major prize sought by the rival factions in the party, and the outcome of the gubernatorial primary and general election determines which

faction will dominate the party for the next four years. When a governor takes office, he is both a factional and a party leader, and he inherits the support of three groups of Democrats. First are those who have a sense of loyalty to the faction that the governor represents and who have supported its candidates over a period of years. . . . A second group of voters consists of those who identify themselves more strongly with the party than with a faction and who tend to support any Democratic governor. A third group, consisting mainly of local politicians and office-seekers, are those who support the governor—whatever their prior allegiance—because they respect his political power and his ability to dispense various kinds of favors. [Jewell and Cunningham, 1968: 39]

The disappearance of factions in the 1970s coincided with the trends that weakened the close relationship between the Democratic party and state government. Changes in state and federal laws and practices, purchasing and accounting procedures, and public records all made it difficult for the party to operate directly in state government. Operating under the new rules of the game, Governors Wendell Ford and Julian Carroll (1971-79) continued to maintain a strong interest in and influence over the state party organization but transferred to that organization day-to-day responsibility for various forms of patronage. In each case they selected a party chairman, J.R. Miller and Sonny Hunt respectively, to whom they delegated extensive authority.

The next two governors, John Y. Brown and Martha Layne Collins, did not fully utilize the political resources available to a governor nor did they employ many of the tactics perfected by their predecessors. Brown, elected on an antipatronage platform, was totally unconcerned with party affairs; at times he even thwarted party efforts. Governor Brown failed to see how the party organization could help him, and he was defeated on the gubernatorial succession issue partly because party leaders failed to help him out. Unlike her predecessor, Collins, a grass-roots organizer and campaigner, had ambitious goals about rebuilding the state party apparatus. She was much more active in party affairs than Brown had been, but her impact on the party organization appears to have been limited.

Wallace Wilkinson, Collins's successor, has taken a strong interest in the party organization, making a vigorous effort to establish his control of the party machinery. He brought in a contingent of loyal supporters who worked diligently to assure that the county organizations were controlled by persons loyal to the governor.

The governor can exercise several major functions as party leader: selecting chairmen and thus controlling organization and restructuring the party apparatus; controlling patronage; recruiting and campaigning for candidates, with possible involvement in legislative primaries; and party-building efforts, such as raising money, speaking, staying in touch with the counties.

Controlling the State and Local Party Organization

A Democratic gubernatorial nominee's first important task is the naming of a state party chairman—usually his or her primary campaign chairman—and gaining control of the state party organization. In the Kentucky Democratic party, as in most state parties, it is assumed that a governor is entitled to select the state party chairman. The priority that a governor gives to that selection is often a good indication of the importance the governor attaches to his or her role as party leader. Wendell Ford selected J.R. Miller, widely regarded as one of the most skillful and experienced party leaders in the state. John Y. Brown had a series of four chairmen during his term, most of whom were close friends and supporters of Brown but who had little experience or interest in party affairs.

On paper the Democrats have a large and elaborate party structure. The state convention meets during presidential election years, its members chosen at county mass meetings. As of late 1988, the Democratic State Central Committee (DSCC) contained fifty-five voting members and eight ex officio members. The DSCC selects its members in a variety of ways, with some members elected at the state convention, some elected at congressional district meetings, and some appointed by virtue of holding other party or elected offices. The DSCC includes the president of the Kentucky Democratic Women, plus four members of the state legislature.

The governor's control of the party depends on his ability to organize the forces loyal to him to dominate the state convention and select delegates to the national presidential convention and members of the central executive committee. The reorganization of local/state party organizations occurs every four years in a presidential year. In 1956, when factional divisions were deepest, Governor Chandler had to battle with Senator Clements to win control of the state convention, but normally there is little or no opposition to gubernatorial control over the party machinery. The state convention meets about six months after the governor takes office, when his or her prestige and power are usually high. The constitutional ban on a second successive term for the governor tends to erode his or her political influence as the term progresses (Jewell and Cunningham, 1968: 39-41).

A state party convention under Governor Carroll illustrates the power of a governor to restructure the state party apparatus. When the convention met in 1976, he had been in office for a year and a half (having succeeded Ford when he moved to the Senate). The governor filled every position in the party, top to bottom. For example, one of Carroll's key county contact persons was designated chair of the nomination committee for the state convention. The state party chairman, Sonny Hunt, gave the governor's appointee a list of the nominees for all positions. The chair selected by the governor convened the meeting and announced whom the governor wanted chosen. The meeting lasted less than a minute. The designated chair then put the names in nomination as nominees of the committee, and each election was without opposition. In county and precinct elections, occasionally some group would offer a challenge, but it rarely had the strength to win. Any serious threat would be isolated, and its members usually soon co-opted.

One of Governor Wilkinson's priorities was to establish control of the Democratic party machinery. According to a seasoned party loyalist, "There is a party organization, and parallel to that there is an organization very loyal to the governor—the two are often separate at the local level. You have that today, with Wilkinson having a strong following among activists, separate from the party organization; that is one of the weaknesses of the party."

The governor's efforts began on April 23, 1988, when precinct elections were held. The following Saturday there were elections of the county party executive committees and delegates to the state convention. The Wilkinson forces worked very hard to take over the local party organizations, to take charge of the Democratic party. They began at the precinct level, recruiting Wilkinson campaign activists to be elected precinct leaders. To find these persons, the Wilkinson state organization worked with its former county campaign chairmen across the state. The organization held workshops for Wilkinson gubernatorial supporters to educate them as to how to capture their respective precinct elections—how to get enough Wilkinson people out in each precinct.

On June 4, 1988, two thousand delegates attended the state convention, which was orchestrated by the Wilkinson leadership. On the morning of the state convention, seven congressional district conventions were held, and the delegates in each district elected five people (two men, two women, one youth) to serve on the state central committee. The Wilkinson forces had to make sure that a majority of these people elected from each district would be Wilkinson supporters. Each district convention also elected a presidential elector and an elector alternate. In the afternoon the delegates met as the state convention and elected seven at-large members to the state central committee. Also, three National Democratic Committee members and two at-large presidential electors (and two alternates) were chosen. A highlight of the convention was the routine selection of Wilkinson's candidates for party chairman and vice-chairman: state representative Jerry Lundergan and Sue Carroll Perry, the county clerk from

Shelby County, where she had chaired Wilkinson's primary and general election campaigns.

In order to find people to run for the local party offices, the state Wilkinson forces had to work within the constraints and politics of the individual counties. The goal was to capture the party organizations in all 120 counties. In the local reorganization the Wilkinson forces had good control over all the congressional districts except the Third. In every district, the five elected people were Wilkinson supporters, except in the Third District, where the governor won only two out of the five.

Occasionally, the Wilkinson forces were not able to wrest control of a county organization. Such clashes occurred across the state; and they were of central importance, since they would determine the leadership of the local party for four years. One such conflict occurred in Clark County (a rural county in central Kentucky) where Wilkinson supporters challenged supporters of Senate president pro tem John "Eck" Rose (a frequent critic of the governor) for control of the county executive committee and lost. Rose intended to use the local organization in his 1990 reelection bid. Furthermore, Rose's credibility in opposing Wilkinson's legislative proposals, particularly his opposition to the governor's succession amendment, was at stake. The Rose forces' victory—by a margin of 33 to 28—reflected the intensity of the battle. "In terms of registered Democrats represented, tallies showed that delegates for 18,375 voters voted for the pro-Rose slate, and delegates for 12,646 favored the Wilkinson slate." In the aftermath of the election, a new executive committee was formed in Clark County which in turn selected James Coleman as its chairman. It is not without importance that Coleman had served as county chairman for Brereton Jones's 1987 lieutenant gubernatorial race, suggesting that the impact of an election for executive committee membership will carry forward into yet another gubernatorial race. The impact was not lost on the Wilkinson faction, which challenged the election before the state Democratic party. "Eck" Rose won again, as presumably did Brereton Jones (*Courier-Journal* (*C-J*), May 1, 1988, pp. B1, B6).

Controlling Patronage

Patronage can be a major tool of gubernatorial leadership, and thus it is essential that the governor control patronage, directly or indirectly. Under Governor Ford, most questions of patronage were left to his party chairman, J.R. Miller, and party executive director, H.K. Taylor, at state party headquarters. But Ford made certain decisions in his office, such as those regarding regulatory matters. The moving of most state patronage to the party headquarters coincided with J.R. Miller taking over the party for Governor Ford—and Miller, who made the Kentucky Democratic party into a nationally recognized institution, probably insisted on having these functions.

Governor Carroll participated in certain patronage decisions within the governor's office—especially involving appointments to various boards and commissions. Carroll left local job patronage primarily to the Democratic party headquarters, where Mike Templeton and Sonny Hunt handled it. Much of the business patronage was handled by Sonny Hunt at state party offices.

In contrast to Carroll, Governor Brown, a party outsider, passed decisions on jobs, personal service contracts, and regulatory matters to his cabinet secretaries and their executive departments. Some persons accused Brown of substituting cronyism for patronage. Lists of potential appointees to commissions and boards were coordinated by a young administrator in the governor's office, and then decisions were made by a tight, intimate circle including the governor.

Governor Collins, a seasoned party supporter, came into office intending to restore total control of patronage to the governor's office but was not completely successful in doing so. During the Brown administration, the executive agencies had been given so much control over appointments that it was difficult for the governor's office to regain full control. Moreover, concerning local patronage, Governor Collins did not devote as much personal attention to the local parties as she had said she would. According to one political expert, "Maybe she should not—she had a lot of things to do, and too much involvement in patronage might have been a problem." Under Collins, however, the governor's office did take over much of the responsibility that had previously been handled by the state party headquarters. Her staffers worked directly with the contact people in each county on matters involving employment or state business. State party chair Coleman was involved in the extent he was able to make appointments for contributors to see Collins about patronage matters.

Governor Wilkinson has taken control of patronage as much as possible, centralizing matters in his office and state party headquarters. Wilkinson wants qualified people who are loyal to him. Though much of the detailed patronage work is done in party headquarters, the final decision is made by Wilkinson and his inner circle in the governor's office. Wilkinson has insisted on being heavily involved in these decisions; it is clearly his style of governing. Within the governor's office, the director of the Office of Constituent Services works closely with the executive director of the party on details of the county patronage process.

Influencing Elections

During Ford's administration J.R. Miller and H.K. Taylor at party headquarters were involved in targeted local, state, and national races. Although Governor Ford had little direct involvement in state legislative races, his party leaders had his blessing to help legislative candidates who strongly supported the administration.

During Governor Carroll's term his office and state party headquarters were involved in a number of elections. But, according to Carroll, he rarely participated in recruiting candidates and rarely intervened in a legislative primary. The former governor does not recall much personal involvement—such as that carried out by Chandler, Combs, and Breathitt. Of course, local supporters would use the governor's name. A person who agreed to provide support (including contributions) to a candidate endorsed by Carroll's local leaders understood that he or she was doing a favor for the governor. It was usually clear who were the local Carroll leaders, and they often supported candidates. But the local Carroll organizations did not target legislators opposed to the governor, presumably because there were few, if any.

For example, Carroll allowed the influence of his office to be used to enlist support from Democratic sources for James Amato's mayoral race. Carroll's political friends in Lexington would say, "The governor would like you to be for Jim." No promises were made or asked for, and there was never a quid pro quo. Carroll was not personally involved in this effort.

In keeping with his "nonpolitical" stance, Governor Brown did not directly engage in influencing local, state, and national races. If his county party chairs and loyal supporters became active in elections, they were working entirely on their own.

Governor Collins did not become actively involved in candidate recruitment, but she endorsed Edward Coleman's efforts with the state legislative Campaign Coordinator Program (described below). Collins dealt with organization matters only upon Coleman's infrequent requests. She dealt with local party leaders when Coleman needed her input or the governor's personal contact with them.

In the 1988 state legislative primary, Governor Wilkinson did make some financial contributions to incumbents. Wilkinson's county contacts did assist with candidates who were friends of the governor and the governor's loyal coterie. Obviously, there are risks to being involved in campaigns, as Wilkinson has been doing, but if one raises money more quietly, it may be possible to have some impact with less risk.

The governor can be very important in helping the election of a congressman, senator, or president in the state. Ford was instrumental in Huddleston's first successful U.S. Senate campaign; the governor traveled the state on behalf of Huddleston's candidacy. Carroll was very active in carrying Kentucky for Jimmy Carter—and this helped Kentucky. Governor Collins was a staunch supporter of Walter Mondale in 1984; she was chosen one of the cochairmen of the national presidential convention. In late 1987 Wilkinson at first leaned toward supporting Governor Dukakis, but he discovered that some of his major supporters were for Sen. Al Gore, Jr. In January 1988 Wilkinson invited all the local party chairmen to the mansion, and they said they wanted to be for Gore in the Democratic presidential primary contest; so newly appointed party executive director Kim Kearns became involved in Gore's campaign—she helped orchestrate and coordinate it in Kentucky. After the primary Wilkinson was asked to become Dukakis's Kentucky state party chairman, and he campaigned for the Massachusetts governor.

Party-Building Activities

Governor Ford was a preeminent party supporter; he helped strengthen the party apparatus around the state, building on the framework of his own organization. According to one longtime party activist, "Ford wouldn't have missed a party function." The governor attended party fund-raisers, organization meetings, local county rallies, and other campaign affairs. Ford was in daily communication with his party leaders about the party organizational matters.

Carroll did a lot of work for candidates and local parties by going around the state attending functions and making speeches; he gave more than 800 speeches in his term. He helped local as well as state and legislative candidates by going to campaign affairs. The state headquarters' finances were a major concern; the building would have been foreclosed without the contributions that Carroll helped raise. Carroll took a strong interest in assisting and promoting the state Democratic party and its 120 county party organizations.

Governor Brown had disassociated himself from the party. He was not interested in any party-building activities. He was an antiparty, antipatronage chief executive. Governor Collins came into office with party experience, promising to play a more active role in party affairs, to deal with party leaders, in a way that Brown had not. Depending on her time constraints, Collins took a lot of day-to-day or week-to-week interest in party affairs. Her two state party chairs had as much contact with Collins as they needed to run successfully the state party apparatus.

According to Edward Coleman, Collins was the best political governor he has ever seen. "She did not forget where she came from. She is a great grass roots person—rain or shine." Large fund-raising events had to revolve around her demanding schedule. She attended all the Century Club affairs and held parties at the mansion and Churchill Downs. She attended all the Jefferson-Jackson dinners and the populist Grass Roots Club's picnics. Coleman had excellent access to Collins when he needed to talk to her, and he was able to arrange meetings for those county politicians who felt it necessary to talk to her. Coleman usually contacted her about two times a week and communicated with her office much more frequently than that.

Collins assisted Coleman in money raising in various ways. She attended the important fund-raisers, including various functions she hosted at the mansion. She gave her advice on naming individuals who could help Coleman in fund-raising in the different counties and statewide; and she knew a lot of the right people to contact and gave Coleman the leverage to use her resources. She encouraged her staff to assist Coleman in any matters pertinent to fund-raising.

Wilkinson came into office with a commitment to rebuild the party, precinct by precinct, and he has constructed an organization whose members will demonstrate a fierce personal commitment to him. Many of these are persons who had never been active in politics before Wilkinson's gubernatorial candidacy. The Wilkinson organization has sought to promote a high level of grass-roots party involvement. Wilkinson has been a very visible, enthusiastic governor who has taken a hands-on approach to party leadership.

Veteran party leaders often argue that once the political party lost a major portion of its patronage because of the increase in merit jobs and campaign reforms, interest in the party faded considerably. The Democratic party also suffers when there is a governor in office who pays little attention to the organization and fails to attend party functions. That has been lacking, definitely under Brown and even under Collins. Although Collins intended to follow the example set by Ford and Carroll, and attended many party functions, she did not have time to become heavily involved in local party-building activities. Wilkinson has been actively involved in party-building activities, with a vision of the party as a personalistic, loyal following.

State Party Chairman

Huckshorn (1976) delineates three different types of party chairs: the chair who has been selected by the governor and performs those tasks assigned by the governor; the chair of the administration party who gains that position independent of—or in opposition to—the governor and thus has considerable freedom of action; and the chair of the opposition party. As we have made clear, the Democratic chairman in Kentucky falls into the first category.

In Kentucky a single four-year gubernatorial term undermines state party organizational continuity; a new chair is selected right after the primary election by the winning gubernatorial candidate. During several recent administrations there has been considerable turnover in the chairmanship; over a nine-year period from mid-1979 to mid-1988, nine different persons held the position. This lack of continuity obviously makes it difficult for any single chairman to accomplish very much or have any lasting impact on the state party.

When Ford was elected governor, he chose a skillful, powerful political leader and party builder to run the Democratic party—J.R. Miller from Owensboro. Miller was recognized widely for his grass-roots organizational, fund-raising, campaign, and mobilizing skills. It was during his term, and that of party executive director H.K. Taylor from Morehead, that most of the responsibility for patronage decisions was moved from the governor's office to state Democratic party headquarters. Miller was well enough known in national Democratic circles that he succeeded in making the Kentucky Democratic party into a nationally recognized institution. Nearly halfway through Ford's administration, Miller and the governor parted ways; supposedly, Miller wanted to succeed Ford as governor, but Ford would not give him his early support. Also, Miller was upset with the governor's strong involvement in Huddleston's Senate race and then with Ford's decision to run for the other Senate seat himself. After Miller relinquished the party chairmanship, William Sullivan was selected to chair the party apparatus.

Howard P. "Sonny" Hunt, Carroll's handpicked chair from Danville, worked hard with the counties to take care of patronage from state party headquarters. Hunt was a very forceful party chair who kept in regular communication with the governor's county contact people, but he was not as concerned as some chairmen with party-building activities. Hunt was also concerned with helping deserving Democrats to do business with the state, and his handling of insurance premiums eventually led to his conviction and a jail sentence.

Governor Brown was responsible for selecting four party chairmen during his tenure—Larry Townsend, Robert Cobb, Tracy Farmer, and Paul Patton. The first three were men who had worked very closely with Brown, and each was selected because of his organizational and fund-raising abilities. But because Brown had very little interest in party affairs and refused to follow traditional patronage practices, most of his party chairmen were unable to be effective in maintaining the effectiveness of the party organization. One experienced Democratic politician described party headquarters under Brown as "a toothless tiger" because of the governor's lack of interest in party organization. If the Kentucky Democratic organization had had a tradition of chairmen who won office on their own and acted independently of the governor, the party organization might have remained strong despite Brown's inattention. But he followed the Kentucky tradition of appointing the chairmen and then largely ignored them and the organization.

Townsend, a Louisville business executive, ran Brown's last-minute media-blitz primary campaign and the general election campaign. Townsend recognized the need for the party to have operating funds, and he established the Century Club as a funding mechanism for the party. Early in Brown's administration, Townsend had much influence and took charge of certain patronage matters. But Townsend, a strong individual, soon became discredited because he often lost objectivity in dealing with party and administration matters. Brown's second party chair, Louisville businessman Robert Cobb, was subjected to tremendous abuse because the party faithful expected patronage and could not believe that Brown really was not going to dispense it—except to his cronies. Even after he vacated the party chair's office, Cobb was often besieged by people to help them in gaining favors from the administration. Brown's third party chair, Lexington banker Tracy Farmer, tried to exert influence on Brown's behalf but was handicapped by Brown's lack of interest in party affairs.

Paul Patton, an eastern Kentucky coal executive and judge executive of Pike County, was the only one of the four who had held elective office. By the time he took the chairmanship, local political leaders had recognized that the Brown administration was not going to follow traditional patronage practices, and Patton was subjected to less pressure from local leaders than his predecessors had been.

Patton, while recognizing his lack of power, believes he had a good reputation "as best chairman since J.R. Miller." On the average he spent two days a week on the job. He spent much of his time developing contacts and trying to provide assistance to people, without having many resources. Patton had the least authority of all Brown's party chairs because, unlike the others, he seldom had contact with Brown. In fact, in the eighteen-month period of his chairmanship, Patton talked to Governor Brown about the Democratic party only twice and once about Pike County. Patton believed that he had two main responsibilities: to try to elect Democrats and to help Democratic leaders. He was sometimes able to help deserving Democrats get state jobs because of his personal contacts in state government, not because he had authority to speak on behalf of the governor.

As state party chair, Patton assisted Democratic congressional candidates who were in competitive races; the party headquarters gave priority to the campaigns of incumbent Rep. Ron Mazzoli and challengers Don Mills and Terry Mann. The Mann race was given particular attention because Mann was perceived as having a chance to win. Patton helped some state legislative candidates to carry out media campaigns and direct mail operations. He also tried to involve the state party central committee, the governor's handpicked group, more than his predecessors had done.

Governor Collins's first party chair was state senator Joe Prather, president pro tem of the Senate, who had served as her primary campaign's cochairman and who served as party chair for only a year, beginning with Collins's primary victory (May 1983–May 1984). Prather found it difficult to do both his Senate and his party job at the same time. During the 1984 legislative session, Prather spent nearly all of his time on the Senate job; at other times he divided his time roughly in half. For assistance with both jobs, he relied heavily on one aide, John Cooper. Ex-chairman Paul Patton proved to be very helpful with the complex business of implementing a national convention delegate selection process that would meet the standards of the national Democratic party. He had developed the plan and followed through on it, even handling the hearings around the state.

As party chair, Prather had as much contact with Collins as he needed on party matters. She would be available and accessible to his requests. Prather did not get involved much with local contact men who handled patronage. The county patronage was mostly handled in the governor's office. After Prather left, the state party headquarters was involved somewhat in contracts; in isolated cases Prather would become involved.

Edward Coleman was party chairman for much of the Collins administration—approximately from May 1984 to May 1987. Collins chose Coleman because of their close association during her campaign; he not only was in charge of organizing and running Collins's campaign in Franklin County but also assisted in directing some other Collins campaign county organizations. When Coleman, a resident of Franklin County, was chairman, 100 percent of his time was devoted to the task. During any spare hours he attended to his horses and other farm responsibilities. He had to give up his real estate and appraisal businesses in order to devote full time to party activities. Officially, he had no executive directors, but Brenda Frank assumed that title in order for her to attend certain national party functions (e.g., seminars given by the national party that were strictly for state executive directors and state chairmen).

Coleman was involved in patronage more than Prather, but basically patronage was handled through the governor's office. At the Century Club functions (the horse races, cocktail parties, gatherings at the mansion), Coleman would always invite the top heads of all the state departments, the individuals who make the state's decisions, to socialize and mingle with the contributors. For example, contributing engineers could socialize and become friendly with the cabinet secretary and other representatives of the Highway Department or Finance Department. Insurance company contributors could mingle with representatives of the Insurance Department.

Coleman has described his term as a time of growth, in which headquarters adopted new political techniques, installed computers, and, through the surplus from Collins's 1983 campaign, paid off the nearly quarter-million dollar debt on the headquarters building. One of Coleman's innovations, the Campaign Coordinator Program for state legislative candidates, will be discussed in more detail later in the chapter.

In May 1987 Danny Briscoe, a former state insurance commissioner under Governor Brown, was named to head the Democratic party. It was Wilkinson's first official appointment after winning the party's gubernatorial nomination. It is traditional for the state party chief to step aside so the Democratic nominee can put his own person in the job. Briscoe, a lawyer, served in the administrations of Louisville mayors Frank Burke and Harvey Sloane and had worked in several state and local campaigns. In the late summer of 1984, Briscoe became one of the first people to go to work for Wilkinson, coordinating media and polling. After organization chairman J.R. Miller (state party chairman under Governor Ford) left the campaign early in spring 1987, Briscoe took over the campaign.

Briscoe was Wilkinson's closest and most influential adviser, and he had orchestrated the successful primary and general election campaigns. These qualifications could have made him a strong state chairman. But he was not particularly involved in party-building activities; his efforts were largely focused on helping to set up the new administration. He maintained only a skeletal crew at state party headquarters.

Danny Briscoe resigned as party chairman in February 1988, but he was not replaced until the state party convention in June 1988. He wanted to spend more time on his law practice and his activities as a lobbyist. In the interim Wilkinson asked Kim Kearns of Lexington, his director of constituent services in the governor's office, to assume the full-time position as executive director of the state party apparatus; Kearns did not want to be designated party chairman. During Wilkinson's primary campaign, she had worked with her mentor, J.R. Miller, in running the statewide county organization campaigns and had stayed on after he departed, becoming the district coordinator of four of the seven congressional districts.

At first Kearns assisted with party operations from her constituent services' desk in the governor's office; her constituent directorship included participating in the dispersal of the governor's patronage and projects in selected congressional districts—helping favored constituents with roads, nonmerit jobs, and contracts. She also helped to plan the presidential delegate selection process.

Upon becoming full-time state party executive director in March 1988, Kearns set out to accomplish two important tasks: selecting the national convention delegates and reorganizing the local/state party organization. The presidential delegate process consumed a lot of Kearns's time; in the end a total of sixty-five delegates and eighteen alternates were selected, along with ten super delegates. Kearns was responsible for overseeing details of the Kentucky delegation's participation in the Atlanta presidential convention.

Rep. Jerry Lundergan, one of Wilkinson's chief allies in the General Assembly, was chosen his second state party chairman. Lundergan represented the Seventy-sixth District in Fayette County, the district in which Wilkinson lives. He had been in the legislature since 1980, except for one two-year term. His election surprised no one; he was Wilkinson's chosen candidate before the state Democratic convention opened on June 4, 1988. As chair, Lundergan said he would not draw a salary but would reimburse himself for his expenses. Usually, the chairmanship is a full-time job with a salary; but in March 1988 the party had hired Kearns as executive director to run the day-to-day activities of the party.

During his very brief tenure, Lundergan established the political department of headquarters, and he hired a fund-raiser. He was the main spokesman for the party and official overseer of the party machinery. He had regular contact with the governor's office. Although Lundergan lacked extensive contacts in the counties, he was interested in strengthening the local county party organizations. Lundergan was state party chair for only three months. He stepped down because of a controversy that had arisen concerning his catering company, which allegedly had done business with the state in violation of a state law that prohibits legislators from receiving state contracts without competitive bidding.

At the urging of Governor Wilkinson, state Democratic leaders unanimously chose former Powell County judge executive Bill Patrick to be Wilkinson's third party chairman on August 29, 1988. Patrick had been Wilkinson's commissioner of local government since January 1988. Wilkinson decided on Patrick for the job because of his longtime involvement with the party (as former head of the Young Democrats), his willingness to make it a full-time job, and his popularity with state legislators and other public figures (such as Sen. Wendell Ford). Wilkinson appeared before the party's fifty-five-member central executive committee to recommend Patrick.

Functions and Activities of the Democratic State Party

The responsibility for developing organizational strength, supporting local parties, raising funds, recruiting and assisting candidates, and registering and mobilizing voters rests in the state party organization. When a party has controlled the governorship for the last two decades, the resources for carrying out these duties and rewarding party workers are plentiful. Are there some functions that individual party chairmen consider particularly important or that they give greater priority than in the past? We can draw some conclusions by focusing on the party organization during the administrations of Collins and Wilkinson.

Staff and Budget

During Edward Coleman's term the permanent state headquarters' staff included six individuals; in addition to Coleman these included a quasi-executive director, an accountant, a computer specialist, Coleman's secretary, and a telephone receptionist/typist. The average monthly basic budget of approximately $30,000 covered not only salaries but building maintenance, computer costs, and miscellaneous expenses.

During Wilkinson's administration the average monthly basic budget of party headquarters has remained at about $30,000. The money is used for staff salaries, consulting fees, building maintenance, computer expenses, and travel in the state for the deputy political directors. Early in the administration the staff at headquarters included ten persons: the executive director, an accountant, three members of the political department, four support receptionists/secretaries, and a fund-raiser. After the 1988 general election, the political department was disbanded in order to save money.

Money Raising

Kentucky has a tax check-off system for political parties. For each taxpayer who designates funds for a party, $1.50 is paid to that state party and 50 cents is given to the local party. The amount received by the state Democratic party from these funds fell from about $130,000 in 1983 to $93,000 in 1987. Legally the state party may use the funds for salaries and upkeep of state headquarters; they cannot be paid out to candidates. The proportion of taxpayers participating in the tax check-off has been dwindling (from 16 percent in 1977 to barely 5 percent in recent years), a decline that implies fading public interest in political parties (Goldstein, 1989). The Democratic party has made an extensive, but apparently unsuccessful, effort to persuade more party activists to use the tax check-off. Every year Coleman contacted CPAs and other tax preparers, and the state party sent selected news articles about the check-off for every county newspaper and county party newsletters.

A major responsibility of the state chairman, perhaps his biggest job, is to raise funds for the party. It is a never-ending task. Historically, Democratic candidates and elected officials have been poor contributors to the state party. A state chair has to raise money for the party and also for selected candidates (e.g., Terry Mann for Congress and targeted state legislative candidates in 1986). In addition to funds from the state tax check-off system, the state Democratic party has recently been getting about $50,000 to $60,000 yearly from the national party's Dollars for Democrats mass-mailing fund-raiser. The chairman must raise funds through personal direct contact with numerous potential and current contributors across the state. In doing so, the chairman must compete with Democratic candidates who are raising funds for both the primary and the general election.

Governor Brown started the Century Club with annual membership dues of $1,000. The funds, which go to the state party, come from a couple of hundred members, mostly vendors with the state. There are two to three functions annually for Century Club members—usually a black tie party at the governor's mansion and an outing at Churchill Downs. Another annual fund-raiser is the Jefferson–Jackson Day Dinner. Usually around $150,000 is raised from the occasion.

The party is somewhat successful in maintaining a base of regular contributors. There is a master list maintained on the state party's computer. These lists are shared generally with statewide general election party candidates. The lists are not shared with statewide candidates in the primary.

Coleman also established another group of small contributors—the Grass Roots Club. Coleman's goal was not so much to obtain funds for the state party as to create an organization of ardent party-oriented workers who wanted to make some small financial contribution to their party. The Grass Roots Club is made up of party faithful who cannot afford to give large sums of money. Many of the members hold county executive committee positions or precinct jobs. Membership in the Grass Roots Club is $15 for an individual or $25 for a family. The state party holds pot luck picnics, by congressional districts, for the members, which Governor Collins attended faithfully during her term. During Coleman's term the Grass Roots Club had about four thousand to five thousand members.

During the Wilkinson administration the state party headquarters has continued to use these fund-raising mechanisms. During his brief term as chairman, Lundergan hired Dale Emmons as a full-time fund-raiser; but Patrick, who succeeded him, has assumed most of the party fund-raising responsibilities.

Relations with the National Party

The state Democratic party has benefited from the increased assistance given by the national party to state party organizations, helping them to professionalize their operations and providing services to Democratic party hopefuls at all levels. Because some state party organizations were unable to finance their own operations, the national party undertook national fund-raisers for states. These included Dollars for Democrats, a national mailing program, and a national phone bank to raise funds; the national party returned to the state parties almost 90 percent of the funds raised. The national party also holds seminars for state administrators, field workers, and candidates on organizational and campaign techniques. For its part, state party headquarters assists national candidates when they come to Kentucky, particularly during presidential campaign years.

Services to Candidates and Local Parties

Because of her experience in party organization and campaigns at the grass-roots level, Governor Collins supported Coleman's efforts to provide a broader range of services to party organizations and candidates at the county level. During Coleman's term the party invested $150,000 in a sophisticated Honeywell computer. Using the computer resources, Coleman sought to upgrade and update the party's lists pertaining to registration, voting, and campaign contributions and to make these available to candidates. Since most counties did not have headquarters or any computer resources, Coleman supplied lists or labels to the county party groups. A few counties had computer modems permitting direct access to the state party computer. The headquarters' budget was increased substantially because of his efforts to computerize the operation and assist a greater number of Democratic local, statewide, and national candidates. Of course, Coleman had to raise considerably more funds than his predecessors in order to pay for this expanded operation.

During the Wilkinson administration the party continued to maintain sophisticated computer files: lists of contributors, county leaders, registered voters, political activists, and frequent voters. However, the state party headquarters sold the large-scale computer purchased by Coleman during Collins's administration. The new party leadership felt that it had become too expensive to maintain and required a skilled person to operate it. The state organization began to rely on professional political vendors to provide the lists, labels, and phone numbers that it needed.

Although the Democratic party held registration drives, particularly in presidential election years, this was not one of the higher priorities of the party headquarters during either the Collins or Wilkinson administration. Coleman was more interested in making maximum use of the computerized registration records available from the secretary of state's office, records that include the frequency of voting over a five-year period. Coleman purchased lists of telephone numbers for all voters from a Texas phone bank company. Coleman wanted to identify the frequent voters and compile as much information as possible on this group.

Public opinion polling has not normally been a function carried out by state party headquarters. Under Coleman's direction the party began conducting polls as part of the plan to aid legislative candidates in 1986 and also in support of Terry Mann's unsuccessful congressional race that year. In 1987 the state headquarters conducted polls every two weeks a few months before the primary on the popularity of various statewide candidates running in the primary. After the results leaked out, Coleman received a lot of criticism for this policy, particularly from candidates who ranked low in the polls. Coleman believed that the party headquarters should gain experience in polling and that the information would be useful to primary candidates, particularly those who could not afford to conduct their own polls. The party supplied all the Democratic candidates with information on their specific contests. During the Wilkinson administration the state party has not run its own polls but has hired professional pollsters, who obviously have much more polling experience than the state party headquarters.

During the Wilkinson administration the state party headquarters has tried to rebuild and revitalize local party organizations. Governor Wilkinson was committed to rebuilding the party, starting at the precinct level. Kim Kearns, who had been trained in local organization by the legendary J.R. Miller, was particularly interested in party-building efforts at the local level. Early in Wilkinson's term his supporters, many of whom had never before been active in party politics, moved into positions of power in the county organizations. Some of them became very involved in the 1988 legislative races, supporting candidates who were committed to Wilkinson. Not all the people in the local organizations are Wilkinson people; in some counties there are combinations of Wilkinson supporters and others. In those eastern Kentucky counties where the parties are often fragmented, the Wilkinson forces represent one of the factions and control state patronage. In most of the counties, however, the Wilkinson forces are firmly in control of the party organization.

The state party headquarters has worked closely with the governor's office in implementing his Capital to the Counties Program, under which Wilkinson makes two- or three-day trips to the different congressional districts with his entire cabinet. On the first night of each of these trips, there is a Democratic party function—Martha's Picnic—somewhere in the district. The picnic is for the benefit of both the governor and the party. The remaining part of the two-day program is spent meeting with interested citizens, who attend office hours with the governor and his cabinet officials.

Legislative Races

Edward Coleman developed and implemented a plan to help legislative candidates in some marginal seats—providing interns, polling help, and assistance in targeting key precincts in the district. Coleman gave priority to this program despite the rather large Democratic margin in the legislature and the fact that a large proportion of seats are safe for one party or the other. Coleman created the Campaign Coordinator Program, with Collins's wholehearted support, to ensure the party's continued domination in the legislature with good, party-oriented legislators and to make legislators more responsive to the needs of the state party.

In 1986 Coleman employed for the summer twenty-two political science student interns to assist in the state legislative races and also in Terry Mann's congressional race. Coleman met with the House and Senate leadership, and together they targeted incumbents who might be in trouble. They selected about eighteen races that they felt were critical. In half of these races, Democrats were challengers against incumbent Republicans or open seat contests. Coleman worked with other legislators and local county Democratic executive leaders to recruit the strongest candidates. The student interns were given an intensive instructional training program under the auspices of a political scientist/professional consultant who had been holding yearly training seminars for candidates at all levels under Coleman. Along with the student interns, some of the legislative candidates and their staffers also attended the two-week briefings. The consultant tried to teach them how to run a successful campaign, how to use computer analyses about frequent voters and public opinion polls in their areas. In order to get assistance from the program, targeted candidates had to promise that they would conduct a door-to-door campaign. The targeted candidates were given assistance with whatever they needed, such as designs for brochures, radio spots, and mass mailings.

Using the state party computer and other hired student pollsters, they polled in the targeted legislative district areas in order to provide the candidates with valuable information for their races. Using targeting techniques, they were able to provide the candidates with past statistics (looking at frequent voters) on the most important precincts in their districts. Besides paying for the student interns, the state party was able to channel limited funds to some of the targeted legislative races. The Democrats won about 60 percent of the targeted races; some others they recognized were not winnable because incumbent Republicans were strong.

A somewhat similar effort was made by Democratic headquarters in the 1988 legislative races, but it was focused on candidates who were strong supporters of Governor Wilkinson. The headquarters' staff sought to provide assistants to advise targeted electable candidates, helping them with advertising, pamphlet making, yard signs, speech writing, door-to-door skills, fund-raising, and use of direct mail. They also provided these candidates with statistical information about voters and public opinion in their districts. A special event was held to raise funds for these activities. In the 1988 legislative primary, Wilkinson did make some financial contributions to incumbents. Wilkinson's county supporters did assist with candidates who were friends of the governor and the governor's loyal coterie.

Patronage

"Patronage is the currency of politics in Kentucky, and to be effective as a political leader the governor must spend it wisely" (Jewell and Cunningham, 1968: 43). One of the few certainties in a campaign for governor is that nobody wins without making commitments. Some are made on issues, but many involve some form of patronage. In Kentucky the basic types of patronage include traditional jobs, appointments to boards and commissions, and opportunities to do business with the state, or to avoid or influence regulation. Once a candidate wins the office of governor, he or she must respond to campaign contributors, and it is expected that the new governor will allot his or her patronage to friends and to those who helped get him or her elected. It is a traditional practice for a gubernatorial candidate to promise a prospective supporter a position or a contract in exchange for a campaign contribution, with greater or lesser specificity.

The description by Jewell and Cunningham (1968) of the structure of patronage more than two decades ago is still accurate:

> In each county the governor chooses a contact person (in some cases the county party chairman) for the administration. He or she is usually someone who supported the governor actively during the primary, often as his/her campaign manager. He or she is selected carefully and, once chosen, is rarely replaced during the administration except in the case of death or illness. Although county leaders may make suggestions, the choice is the governor's. The administration communicates with the contact person on patronage matters, and he or she is its major source of information about developments in the county. There are others in each county who have access to the governor's office and state party headquarters, including the county chairmen, some county officeholders, and other individuals who have provided valuable support to the governor's organization. [pp. 42-43]

The role that the governor can play in patronage remains essentially the same as what was described in the previous study (Jewell and Cunningham, 1968):

Although there are many kinds of patronage available to the governor, his or her freedom in dispensing it has been steadily declining as a result of the merit system and state and national legislation restricting the use of governmental funds. As these resources have declined in sheer volume, however, the governor's effectiveness as a political leader has not declined. Even though the governor has less to offer, the favors that he can dispense continue to be valued by local politicians. A promise to conduct a feasibility study concerning a park may be worth as much as a promise to build a park a few years ago. The fact that these patronage resources are declining, however, makes it all the more important that they be expended with great care and skill. [pp. 44-45]

Governor Ford began the practice of leaving most patronage decisions to the state party headquarters. Ford felt very strongly about moving most patronage from the governor's office, especially decisions involving local patronage. Ford remembered, with horror, the long patronage lines inside and outside the governor's office during the administrations of Combs, Breathitt, and others. Maintaining liaison with the leaders of 120 counties requires a vast amount of information about the personalities, rivalries, and recent political history of these counties. In contrast to earlier Democratic administrations, under Ford the state party headquarters became the major channel of communications between the state and county party organizations. County political leaders would bring their problems and their requests to J.R. Miller, and subsequently William Sullivan and executive director H.K. Taylor, who would confer with the governor's office.

Personal service contracts were handled by the secretary of finance in coordination with Miller and Taylor at state party headquarters. The final decisions generally lay with the finance executive; the party leaders had much input but not veto powers. Insurance patronage—the division of insurance premium income among insurance companies whose owners were supporters of the administration—was generally handled by the commissioner of insurance and state party headquarters. The governor's office was kept informed through the insurance commissioner, who also served during Carroll's administration.

Appointments to commissions and boards were usually coordinated by Miller and Taylor at party headquarters, William Wester in the governor's office, and the secretary of finance. Ford kept certain patronage functions primarily in the governor's office; for example, his political adviser, William Wester, handled most regulatory matters.

As governor, Carroll maintained the Ford practice of leaving most questions of patronage to state party headquarters and chairman Sonny Hunt. Carroll persuaded the legislature to change the law to give the administration greater discretion in filling civil service jobs; it could choose among the persons with the top five test scores (instead of the top three) in hiring. In practice it is cumbersome for a governor to hire someone because bureaucrats want to make their own choices; they will not publicize a job opening until a person has been found to fill it, giving that person a chance to take the exam before other potential replacements or the governor can react. To deal with this problem, Governor Carroll's office adopted a rule that vacancies had to remain open for thirty days, a change that opened up those jobs to patronage. The bureaucratic system is not always easy for even a governor to master, particularly because of the limiting four-year gubernatorial term. Appointments were handled by Carroll's staff, which maintained "blue jackets" on each board or commission, showing vacancies and including letters recommending persons and a checklist of who was supporting whom. Carroll would go through this information himself and make the appointments.

Much of the business patronage was handled in Democratic headquarters by Sonny Hunt. Carroll made it a rule not to engage in this area at all; he thought it was risky because of potential investigations. During the Carroll administration the *Courier-Journal* (and particularly its top investigative reporter, Livingston Taylor) was watching very closely for cases of abusing patronage and contracts in state government. Carroll was sensitive to this problem and tried to avoid talking to anyone who wanted to discuss doing business with the state, but he made exceptions for a few close friends who insisted on seeing him and tried to explain the limits of what he could do. Regulatory requests were often handled through the governor's office. Examples of regulatory requests included a certificate of need for a hospital or an entrance way to be approved by the Highway Department.

Fayette County provides a good illustration of how county patronage operated during Carroll's administration. The two Fayette County contact men dealt with fewer daily problems and requests than contact people in other counties. Requests involving roads, sewers, and traffic lights were passed to the mayor's public works administrator. The contact men told the natural resource officials in Frankfort, for example, that when Lexington's commissioner of public works asked for something it was as if they were making the request. Since small jobs were not of major importance in thriving Fayette County and since most Frankfort politicians considered themselves experts on Fayette County, the local contacts had little to do with jobs. From time to time, they would receive calls from Frankfort to find out if a potential appointee was loyal to the governor. The contact men advised Frankfort on some personal service contracts, for example, for young lawyers, many of whom had walked precincts and made small contributions and the rest of whom, it was assumed, would help later.

Occasionally, the contact men would get a direct call about a job or project such as a traffic light and would pass it along with more or less enthusiasm, depending on the role a suitor had played in campaign work or in the local power structure. On government issues they would call the governor's office; on job patronage and contracts they would contact party headquarters.

The large contributors in Fayette County were usually interested not in jobs but rather in legislation, regulation, contracts, permits, or public improvements. But on occasion the relatives of contributors wanted to be janitors at the horse park or assistant director of an agency. The contact men would give Sonny Hunt a list of job requests and an indication of priorities because there were always more applicants than openings. The county contact people did not participate in the process after sending the list to the party chairman.

Lexington's acquisition of Triangle Park is a good example of a contact person's involvement in receiving a type of patronage for a metropolitan community. The contact man received a call from a member of the Civic Center Board; the board member ran a company for a powerful community gatekeeper. The board member told the contact person what the board wanted—a lot for parking to be purchased from the L & N Railroad to satisfy the Civic Center's bond requirements, so that the board could change a central triangle of land from paved parking to an open, planted park. The Civic Center Board had learned that the contact man would play some role in the decision of the governor about providing the more than $4 million that was needed. The contact man met with the governor, before Carroll's meeting with a committee of the Civic Center Board, to discuss the members of the board and the economic strength they represented. The committee representing the board made its presentation and answered some questions about needs and costs of the project. After a brief discussion the governor turned to the contact man and said, "Should we do it, Bobby?" The contact man said yes. The governor said, "Okay, let's do it," and the commitment to the project had been made.

During Carroll's administration the insurance contracts were an open and important part of patronage. The rapid escalation of the cost of insurance policies, especially the workers' compensation coverage of state employees, turned a small-scale patronage practice into a major scandal. For many years insurance agents who backed the winning candidate for governor got small shares of the state's insurance business. When court decisions, black-lung awards, and the burgeoning state payroll sent workers' compensation costs skyrocketing in the 1970s, the Ford and Carroll administrations created one big policy and issued it to one agency for dispersal.

"Suddenly, there was a huge pool of commission money to distribute to political allies." Since insurance licenses could be owned by companies not controlled by insurance experts, commissions could be paid to companies owned by friends and relatives who were not truly in the insurance business and who did not perform any real services. "During Carroll's 1974-79 tenure, more than $85,000 in such commissions were distributed." After a prolonged federal investigation of the Ford and Carroll administrations, it was the insurance scheme that was targeted in the prosecution of Sonny Hunt and two other persons: Charles J. McNally, a longtime friend of Hunt, and James E. Gray, cabinet secretary in the Carroll administration (*C-J,* July 5, 1987, p. D1).

Sonny Hunt pleaded guilty and went to prison for nearly two years because of his involvement with the insurance commission distributions. The convictions of McNally and Gray were eventually overturned by the U.S. Supreme Court in *McNally v. United States,* which "rebuked federal prosecutors across the country for stretching the federal mail-fraud statute to the breaking point in trying to put allegedly crooked politicians and their pals behind bars" without a clear mandate spelled out in the statute. The federal investigation did have impact on state policy: "There are now laws requiring that most state insurance policies be subject to competitive bidding" (*C-J,* July 5, 1987, p. D1).

Governor Brown's brand of patronage, "cronyism"—rewarding your friends—brought about stark changes in the dispersal of jobs, personal service contracts, and appointments to commissions and boards. The governor's cabinet secretaries and their departments were given wide discretion in regulatory matters and in the awarding of jobs and personal service contracts. There were county contact people, former local campaign chairs, but they were not generally used in making patronage decisions. Some cabinet secretaries were more involved than others in patronage matters. For example, Secretary of Transportation Frank Metz, Secretary of Human Resources Grady Stumbo, and Secretary of Finance George Atkins were powerful handlers of their respective departments' patronage.

The governor's office was directly involved in appointments to commissions and boards. Brown and his inner circle of friends would consider lists (from department secretaries, state party headquarters, and others) of potential appointees that were coordinated by an assistant in the governor's office. Usually friends of the governor would be the recipients of the appointments. Sometimes appointments were made at the whim of the governor, such as a college acquaintance whom he recalled but who had no personal or political ties to the governor who was appointed to the Workman Compensation Board.

During the Collins administration much of the patronage was handled by a group of four: Bill Collins, the governor's husband; Secretary of Public Protection Earl Wilson; Secretary of Finance Mac Thompson; and Secretary of Transportation Floyd Poore. These men met on a regular basis at the mansion to make strategic patronage decisions. Toward the end of her administration, due to adverse publicity and attacks in the press, Collins reduced the influence of this group, and Larry Hayes became more important in the dispersal of patronage.

In chapter 8 we focus on the role of individual contributors in gubernatorial campaigns and provide several illustrations of how patronage in the form of jobs, personal service contracts, and appointments to boards and commissions was distributed to campaign contributors during the administration of Governor Collins. The act of giving as a prerequisite for getting is traditionally and particularly prevalent in the case of architects, engineers, accountants, attorneys, and others who do business with the state under personal service contracts.

During the Wilkinson administration much of the jobs patronage has been handled by a small coterie within the administration. Rogers Wells, the secretary of finance, and Dr. Floyd Poore, the public liaison for Wilkinson, direct the patronage operation, aided by the governor's nephew Bruce Wilkinson, the appointments secretary; David McNally, the chief of staff; and Carol Angel, the director of constituent services. State party chair Bill Patrick and executive director Kim Kearns participate in some county jobs and summer placement decisions. Of course, the final decision on all forms of patronage remains with Governor Wilkinson. The rule of thumb that governs any dispersal of patronage is "only take care of those people who supported Wilkinson in the gubernatorial primary." The patronage stipulation of 1987 primary support severely limited the potential applicant pool and, according to many observers, lowered the quality of gubernatorial appointees.

The dispersal of personal service contracts has primarily been guided by Poore, Wells, John Kelly (assistant to Wells), and Milo Bryant, the secretary of transportation. Wells and Poore are the chief participants in dealing with regulatory matters. Bruce Wilkinson has major responsibility for appointments to commissions and boards, but these recommendations also are channeled through Wells and Poore. Since the governor is deeply involved in patronage appointments, decisions have been made slowly, and positions have often remained vacant for long periods of time.

Local Party Organization

During the late 1980s there has been a reasonably well-organized Democratic party organization in at least two-thirds of the counties. There are some noticeable gaps in the heavily Republican Fifth Congressional District. The real strength in each county is the executive party committee, and three to four members are the prominent leaders. Usually, the precinct committee people are an inactive group except for party reorganization purposes. A key figure in each county is the contact person, designated by the governor to handle patronage. We will focus on the local party organizations in Jefferson County and Fayette County and summarize some of the characteristics of rural organizations.

Louisville

According to Jewell and Cunningham (1968):

> At one time the "regular organization" in Jefferson County had achieved a degree of political control that was unmatched in the urban parties of Kentucky. The Jefferson County organization was built by Michael J. Brennan, who nurtured the party while it was out of power during the 1920s and developed it into an effective machine from 1933, when the Democrats captured office in Louisville, until his death in 1938. . . . After Brennan's death, the organization was dominated by the mayor of Louisville for several years. . . . From 1947 until the early 1960s the Jefferson organization was run by the triumvirate of McKay Reed, Mrs. Lennie McLaughlin, and John Crimmins. Mrs. McLaughlin (known as "Miss Lennie") was in charge of a highly efficient organization of loyal precinct workers. [pp. 71-72]

For many years the county executive committee endorsed candidates in state, legislative, county, and city races, a process in which Reed and McLaughlin played a very important part. Democratic precinct workers spread the word about endorsements to voters, frequently handing out sample ballots in the precincts and at the polls. The organization had a nucleus of more than two thousand patronage employees who could be counted on to work on election day (Jewell and Cunningham, 1968: 73-74).

In 1963 the party organization abandoned the practice of endorsing candidates in gubernatorial primaries; while the purpose was to maintain harmony in the party, the consequence was greater disunity, as precinct leaders worked for different candidates. After Breathitt's nomination and election, those local leaders who had supported him challenged the county leadership for control of the party. After Breathitt intervened, both sides agreed on a new chairman, Thomas Carroll, who was not tied to any local faction. In 1967 the Jefferson County organization united behind Henry Ward, Breathitt's candidate for governor. Despite Breathitt's efforts, the Jefferson County Democratic organization remained fragmented into at least five groups: old-line precinct workers, the new generation of political amateurs, remnants of the Chandler-Waterfield faction, labor unions, and black political leaders (Jewell and Cunningham, 1968: 74-76).

The Jefferson County Democratic party of the 1980s has operated somewhat differently than in the past. There is the marked influence of the cooperative relationship between the mayor and county judge. There has been a proliferation of personal organizations—those of county officials and legislators; the elected county officeholders, in particular, are able to develop independent fiefdoms.

Since 1969 the Democrats in Jefferson County have had an open primary, that is the party organization has not made endorsements in the primaries. This practice, which occurred at the time when the Democrats regained control of the city and the county, has opened up the party and weakened organizational control. Although incumbents would prefer the endorsement system, the open system is here to stay and has allowed a strong group of political amateurs to gain entry into the party.

Today there is a fairly strong and vigorous organization at the precinct and legislative district levels. It is still important to have the personal support of the organization people. If these people are against a candidate in a primary contest, they can make it very difficult—particularly in the working-class areas. Although the importance of the media in metropolitan campaigns has grown dramatically in the last two decades, the organization is still a significant factor in Jefferson County in getting out the vote. A lot of organizational work is necessary in the Third District to generate large turnouts.

The Democratic party has been able to engender a high level of unity among its major elected officials. When Harvey Sloane was elected mayor in 1973, he was able to pull in only three aldermen with him, but in 1975, in midterm, he endorsed a whole slate that won. When Sloane became county judge executive in 1985, he was able to develop a close working relationship with the new Democratic mayor, Jerry Abramson, that contributed to greater unification in the county party.

Candidates in Jefferson County, particularly the elected county officials and some legislators, usually build their own campaign organization. In his first campaign for mayor, Sloane found that he had better success in those legislative districts where he had created his own organization of loyal workers than in those where he relied heavily on ward and precinct leaders. Gradually, he has integrated his own followers with the party organization. He picked up additional local supporters in his two unsuccessful runs for governor in 1979 and 1983.

Patronage is less important to Democratic politics in Louisville and Jefferson County than it used to be. Neither the office of mayor nor that of the county judge executive controls large patronage resources. Much of the county patronage is controlled by other elected county officials. Today there are many limitations on exercising patronage, partly because of the merit system and influence of unions. Party leaders find they cannot get much political work out of their employees. To some extent this shortage of patronage workers does weaken the party. Patronage workers are said to be more committed in elections for city and county offices than for contests at other levels because they see that their jobs are at stake. But, according to Sloane, "I am not convinced that patronage workers are that effective." Enthusiastic, committed political workers are needed for successful campaigns.

In recent years there has been more unity in the local Democratic party than was true when a rivalry existed between Mayor Sloane and county judge executive Todd Hollenbach. All of the major party officials and elected leaders, for example, have played a role in selecting the county party chairman. The local organization worked effectively in recruiting legislative candidates in 1988, and they succeeded in having a strong group of candidates.

Candidates for statewide office frequently seemed to be puzzled about how to campaign in Jefferson County because it is so large with its forty two legislative districts and because the party structure is strong and diverse. Individual officeholders in Jefferson County often act quite independently of each other in political matters. Statewide candidates do seek the support of the mayor and the county judge; it gives them some visibility, but the public leaders have been trying to minimize endorsing candidates.

One political expert notes that Mayor Abramson's involvement in county party politics seems more subtle than that of the other officeholders; yet he is the most popular figure in Jefferson County. In 1988 the Louisville mayor became quite involved in the general election of several state legislative candidates and the presidential nominee Dukakis; he energetically walked the area neighborhoods on behalf of Democratic candidates.

Lexington

Jewell and Cunningham (1968) described the Fayette County Democratic organization of the 1960s in the following terms:

> From the turn of the century until his death in 1937, Fayette County and Lexington had a political boss, William "Billy" Klair. . . . Within a few years after Klair's death, R.P. "Dick" Moloney became the dominant figure in Fayette County, while he served the Clements, Wetherby, and Combs administrations as a highly effective legislative leader until his death in 1963. Today there is neither a

> dominant Democratic leader nor a strong party organization in the county. The lower income precincts in the center of the city, which were the base of the Klair and Moloney organizations, have become heavily outnumbered by the suburban precincts. State patronage has been handled by the administration's contact man, and county patronage is controlled by individual officeholders in the courthouse; a system of nonpartisan elections isolates the urban county from the Democratic party. The county executive committee lacks finances and patronage; it makes no endorsements in primary elections; and as a result, control of the committee is not hotly contested [except by the ruling state administration]. [pp. 76-77]

The Fayette County organization was even more fractionalized than the organization in Jefferson County. While the Chandler-Waterfield forces were strong enough to carry Fayette County in the gubernatorial primaries from 1955 through 1967, most of the party leaders and the formal party organization were allied with the Combs-Breathitt faction during the period from 1960 to 1967, and several leaders served in those administrations (Jewell and Cunningham, 1968: 77).

Although factionalism has faded away, the Fayette County Democratic party in the 1970s and 1980s has been more of a holding company for individual politicians than a powerful or cohesive organization; the organization has lacked a real function. Party loyalties are not of major importance to voters; many Democrats vote Republican, especially in congressional and presidential elections. The formal party structure is much less important than in Jefferson County. The precinct leaders and those who chair the legislative districts do not wield power by endorsing candidates in primaries. Job patronage is a less important factor in the Fayette County organization than in most counties, because the local economy is strong and incomes are relatively high.

The local officeholders all control some patronage from their own centers of power—the sheriff, circuit clerk, and county clerk; but they are not a strong part of the Democratic party organization, as they are in the smaller rural counties. Democratic members of the state legislature build their own personal organizations of workers. The long-term practice of nonpartisan city elections decentralized political power; and the merger of Lexington and Fayette County, with nonpartisan elections, eliminated the partisan elections to the fiscal court and stripped the county judge of his power. As a consequence of these factors, many local public officials in Fayette County who are Democrats play no active role in the county Democratic party. For example, according to some local party members, Mayor Scotty Baesler (a longtime Democrat) often appears quite distant and disengaged from the local party apparatus.

School board politics has not been associated with the Fayette Democratic party organization in recent years, contrary to the pattern in many other counties where the school superintendent is a key Democratic politician. For example, most people do not even know to what party either former superintendent Guy Potts or present superintendent Ronald Walton belongs.

The local organization has tended to be manned by people who are really interested in Democratic party politics; of course, they relish the fruits of patronage too. For the most part, many of the active Fayette County party leaders under Ford, Carroll, and Collins were longtime committed Democrats. The Fayette chairmanship has traditionally been controlled by the governor. Under Governor Ford, Don Webb, a young lawyer from an eastern Kentucky political family, was selected county chairman; Webb later became a millionaire business leader. During Carroll's administration cattle farmer Mike Molloy ran the party apparatus as an avocation. Political activist Ree Caribou, who was originally brought into the organization by Molloy, joined because of Democratic loyalties; she was later chosen to run the Fayette organization by Governor Brown, a close family friend. During Brown's administration Caribou's husband, Lou, served as commissioner of parks, and she was employed by state party headquarters in Frankfort. Under Collins the county chair was Don Wallace, an architect and real estate developer, who believed in limited levels of party organization. When he took office, Wallace had already been involved in Fayette politics for some time. He had been one of the loyal troops—organizing precincts and contributing and raising funds.

When Wallace Wilkinson took office, he selected a new county chairman: George Ewen, who had been an ardent Wilkinson supporter in the primary and also a member of county attorney Norrie Wake's team. The Fayette County organization was reorganized with members loyal to Wilkinson. Members of the party committee who had supported Lexingtonian Steve Beshear in the primary were not reelected. The party has a headquarters in property owned by Wilkinson and has a part-time secretary. The meager budget to maintain a party headquarters is financed with an annual dinner honoring deserving party workers.

An Assessment of Democratic Party Organization

The Kentucky Democratic party organization is no longer divided into factions, but it is still dominated by the governor. The nomination of a new governor results almost instantly in the reorganization of state Democratic headquarters. Because governors serve only one term and because they frequently change chairmen one or more times during a term, there is very little continuity in leadership of the state Democratic organization. Few of the chairmen in recent years have been major political leaders, and few of them have stayed in office long enough to have any significant impact on the party organization.

Recent governors have differed in the interest they have shown in party affairs. Governors like Ford, Carroll, and Collins have devoted some time and attention to party-building activities, including raising funds and providing assistance to the party's candidates and to county organizations. In contrast, Governor Brown had no interest in strengthening the party organization or making use of its resources.

When the Democratic party was divided into factions, a major task facing any new governor was to gain control of the state organization and to help his supporters control local party organizations, a task that was occasionally difficult, as Chandler discovered in 1956. Most recent governors have been able to assume control without any difficulty. Governor Wilkinson, who had been an outsider in Democratic politics, has followed a strategy reminiscent of factional governors, trying with considerable success to place his supporters in complete control of state and county organizations and to eliminate those Democrats who had supported other candidates in the primary.

When John Y. Brown took office in 1979, there was some reason to believe that the governor's role in patronage would decline in importance. Brown's immediate predecessor, Julian Carroll, had been severely damaged by mistakes made by his administration and his party chairman in the handling of patronage. Brown was committed to "running government like a business," a policy that seemed incompatible with patronage. But, after a four-year hiatus, Governor Collins restored most of the traditional patronage practices. And Wallace Wilkinson, despite his business background, has continued these practices. Some governors, such as Ford and Carroll, have preferred to have patronage matters (particularly jobs) handled primarily at state party headquarters while others, such as Wilkinson, have assigned these chores largely to state officials. It does not seem to matter much where the work is done. The significant variable is the governor's attitude toward, and direct interest in, patronage.

Though the party organization may play a role in administering patronage, the system is not designed to strengthen the organization itself but to reward those who have supported the Democratic gubernatorial nominee. Increasingly, that support is measured more by financial contributions than by organizational work. Those who are rewarded are less often the loyal political activists and more often the major contributors of campaign funds, because modern campaigns are more dependent on expensive media advertising than on local organization. The nature of patronage has changed. Low-paying state jobs (highway crews and summer jobs in parks) are less important because they are limited in number and because they are, of course, unattractive to major financial contributors. Of greater importance are appointments to major positions in the executive branch and various boards and commissions (such as university boards of trustees) because these do interest major contributors. Despite the restrictions in state and federal laws (such as requirements for open bidding on state jobs), many of those making campaign contributions do so in an effort to gain an advantage, or at least to ensure they will be considered, when their firms seek to do business with the state. We will examine the link between this form of patronage and financial contributions in greater detail in chapter 8.

The various changes in the Democratic party have loosened the linkages between the state organization and the organization in major urban counties such as Jefferson and Fayette. With the demise of factionalism, there is less reason for a governor to take an interest in the party organization of those counties, although this continues to be the pattern in Fayette County. The nature of patronage has also affected these counties. Residents of Jefferson and Fayette seeking rewards in Frankfort are not so much the party activists as the wealthy business and professional persons, who may not play any role in the local party organization.

3

DEMOCRATIC GUBERNATORIAL PRIMARIES, PAST AND PRESENT

OVER A forty-year period, from 1947 through 1987, with only one exception, the winner of the Democratic primary has been elected governor. For that reason the most interesting and important state political battles have been fought in the Democratic party. From the mid-1930s to the late 1960s, Kentucky politics was dominated by two factions, named after their dominant leaders, Earle C. Clements and A.B. "Happy" Chandler. Since 1971, however, these factions have faded away, to be replaced by a shifting pattern of personal alliances. At the same time, strategy for winning a primary election has changed, with local organizations declining in importance and the mass media—particularly television advertising—becoming central to the campaigns.

Traditional Democratic Factionalism

The term *factionalism* has often been used to describe Democratic politics in southern and border states, since V.O. Key, Jr., called attention to its importance in his study of *Southern Politics* (1949). Key classified southern Democratic parties and primaries into three groups: multifactional, bifactional, and unifactional. Because the term is often used loosely, we will define exactly what we mean by a bifactional system.

The bifactional system in the Kentucky Democratic party from 1935 through 1967, as it applied to the gubernatorial primary, had the following characteristics: (1) There were usually only two serious candidates in the primary, and the winner seldom had much more than half of the vote. (This was a prerequisite established by Key in defining a bifactional system.) (2) The winner of the primary was always a candidate identified with either the Clements or Chandler faction, though there was not always a direct conflict between these two factions in the primary. (3) The governor (who could not succeed himself) usually tried to dictate the

Table 1. Outcome of Democratic Gubernatorial Primaries

	Number of Candidates		Percentage of Vote Received	
Year	Total	With 5% or more of vote	Winning candidate	Top two candidates
1935	5	3	45.1	87.2
1935*	2	2	52.7	100.0
1939	4	2	52.5	98.3
1943	4	3	53.6	85.6
1947	3	2	54.9	98.3
1951	3	2	75.1	97.1
1955	3	2	51.4	99.2
1959	4	2	52.3	98.6
1963	4	2	53.8	97.0
1967	10	3	52.2	80.4

*Runoff election

choice of his successor. (4) There were alliances between the leaders of statewide factions and local factions that existed in many of the county Democratic organizations. (5) There is limited and inconsistent evidence about whether significant numbers of voters had a continuity loyalty to one or another of the factions and its leaders. In the absence of survey data on voters, this possibility must be measured by county-level aggregate voting data.

If we examine the nine gubernatorial primaries from 1935 through 1967 (table 1), we find that nearly all of them meet the criteria for bifactionalism defined by V.O. Key, Jr. In 1935 (but not thereafter) the law provided for a runoff election, and this helps to explain the larger number of candidates in that election. In 1951 Lawrence Wetherby was running as the incumbent (having succeeded Clements when he became senator), and this helps to explain why he had no serious challenger. The 1967 primary was an aberration because it had so many candidates, at least three of whom were major and two of whom (Chandler and Waterfield) were associated with the same faction.

The modern Democratic factions had their origin in the administration of Gov. Ruby Laffoon (1931-35) (table 2). Laffoon, of Madisonville, and Tom Rhea, of Russellville, had built a factional organization, primarily in western Kentucky, that was strong enough to get Laffoon elected in 1931; and Laffoon supported Rhea for the gubernatorial nomination in 1935. But Rhea was challenged by the lieutenant governor, A.B. Chandler, who criticized the Laffoon administration for its efforts to adopt a sales tax. Earle Clements served in the Laffoon administration and was Rhea's campaign manager in the 1935 race against Chandler.

Table 2. The Pattern of Factionalism in Democratic Gubernatorial Primaries

Year	Clements-Combs faction	Chandler faction	Other major candidates
1935	Tom Rhea	A.B. CHANDLER	
1939	John Y. Brown, Sr.	KEEN JOHNSON	
1943		LYTER DONALDSON (lost election)	Ben Kilgore
1947	EARLE CLEMENTS		Harry Lee Waterfield
1951	LAWRENCE WETHERBY		
1955	Bert Combs	A.B. CHANDLER	
1959	BERT COMBS	Harry Lee Waterfield	
1963	NED BREATHITT	A.B. Chandler	
1967	HENRY WARD (lost election)	A.B. Chandler	Harry Lee Waterfield
1971	WENDELL FORD Bert Combs		

Note: Winners are capitalized.

Before 1935 the direct primary was optional under state law, and the administration's plan was to win the nomination for Rhea in a state convention, which it expected to be able to control. But a number of Democratic leaders favored a primary, and Lieutenant Governor Chandler found a way to bring it about. When Governor Laffoon left on a trip to Washington, Chandler waited for word that the train had actually left the state and then called a special legislative session to adopt a compulsory primary law. Laffoon hurried back and tried to cancel the call but was overruled by the courts. The legislature adopted the compulsory primary, and it took effect in the 1935 election. The Laffoon forces were able to amend the primary bill to require a runoff if no candidate won a majority, but the strategy backfired. Chandler was a close second in the primary and won the runoff; subsequently, he persuaded the legislature to end the runoff feature.

In 1938 Chandler lost a highly publicized primary campaign to unseat Sen. Alben Barkley; but when the other senator (Marvin Logan) died the next year, Chandler resigned and was appointed to the Senate by Keen Johnson, who succeeded him as governor. In the 1939 primary Keen Johnson had the advantage of incumbency and the support of the Chandler faction; these enabled him to defeat John Y. Brown, Sr., who had the support of both Earle Clements and the Rhea organization. Johnson's choice as his successor, Lyter Donaldson, had little difficulty being nominated in 1943 but was defeated by a Republican in the general election. Chandler had been elected to the Senate in 1940 and to a full term in 1942, but in 1945 he resigned to become baseball commissioner.

Donaldson's defeat and Chandler's shift from politics to baseball appeared to spell an end to the Chandler faction and created a vacuum in Kentucky politics. Earle Clements emerged to fill that vacuum. He had been elected to the state Senate in 1941 and to the U.S. House in 1944 and had built a strong organization in western Kentucky that had some of its roots in the Rhea-Laffoon organization. In 1947 he forged an alliance with the Jefferson County organization and won the gubernatorial nomination, defeating Harry Lee Waterfield, another western candidate who at that point was not directly linked to either of the factions.

In 1950 Clements won election to the U.S. Senate and was succeeded by Lt. Gov. Lawrence Wetherby, whose political base was in Jefferson County. In 1951 Wetherby was nominated to a full term by a lopsided majority. Clements continued to play a vigorous and skillful role in Kentucky politics from Washington, and it appeared that the Clements-Wetherby faction was in command.

But Happy Chandler reappeared on the scene. When his term as baseball commissioner ended in 1951, he returned to Kentucky and began to rebuild his political career. He remained strong in central Kentucky, and he forged an alliance with Harry Lee Waterfield, who remained popular in the western counties. In 1955 Clements selected a relatively obscure state judge, Bert Combs, to run for governor. Chandler, with Waterfield as his running mate, waged a vigorous personal campaign and narrowly defeated Combs.

The Clements-Chandler conflict rose to new heights of intensity in 1956, when Clements and Wetherby refused to turn over control of the Democratic party organization to Governor Chandler. Clements won renomination to the Senate over a candidate supported by Chandler. The Democratic state central executive committee nominated Wetherby as the candidate to run for the Senate seat of Alben Barkley, who had died suddenly. In the summer of 1956, thousands of voters met in county conventions all over the state to choose delegates to a state convention, where (after much dispute and battles over credentials) Chandler forces won control of the party. When both Clements and Wetherby were defeated by Republicans in November, they blamed Chandler for failing to support them.

Four years later, in 1959, Chandler threw his support to Harry Lee Waterfield as the gubernatorial nominee. There were two potentially strong challengers to Waterfield: Bert Combs and former Louisville mayor Wilson Wyatt. After prolonged negotiations, Earle Clements persuaded Combs and Wyatt to run as a team: Combs for governor and Wyatt for lieutenant governor. Combs and Wyatt were nominated and elected, and Clements appeared to be in control once again. Clements was appointed highway commissioner in the Combs administration, but a serious split developed between the two men, Clements resigned, and Bert Combs became the de facto leader of the faction.

In 1963 Combs selected Ned Breathitt, a former legislator and member of his cabinet, as his choice for governor. He was challenged by Happy Chandler, who once again had Waterfield as his running mate. Although Breathitt was widely perceived as the underdog, he defeated Chandler. Combs was highly popular in eastern Kentucky, had firm support from the Jefferson County organization, and was able to win broad support from younger, liberal voters without factional loyalties; Breathitt, in turn, had strength in western Kentucky. Despite Chandler's defeat, Waterfield was elected lieutenant governor and fought unsuccessfully to win control of the Senate.

In 1967 Breathitt picked Henry Ward as his choice to run for governor. Ward was a highly respected administrator, who had been highway commissioner during much of the Combs and Breathitt administrations, though he was not a particularly effective campaigner. Both Chandler and Waterfield sought the gubernatorial nomination, along with two other serious candidates and five minor ones. The primary appeared to be an enormous victory for the Combs-Breathitt-Ward forces; Ward gained an absolute majority, Chandler had only 28 percent, and Waterfield less than 11 percent. But in the fall election Ward was defeated by Republican Louie Nunn, who had the open support of Happy Chandler.

The 1971 primary marked the end of the traditional Democratic factions. Bert Combs, who had been serving as a federal judge, resigned and returned to the campaign trail as a candidate for governor. He hoped to rebuild the old organization that had been so successful for him and for Breathitt. But Wendell Ford, elected lieutenant governor in 1967, had taken control of the party machinery and was building his own political organization, utilizing many of the skills that he had learned in the Clements-Combs organization. Ford had been a top aide to Governor Combs and had been elected to the senate in 1965 with the endorsement of Governor Breathitt. In short, the battle for the 1971 gubernatorial nomination took place within the Clements-Combs faction, and it was won by Wendell Ford. There was no Chandler-faction candidate in the primary, although Chandler ran a highly unsuccessful campaign (winning 4 percent of the vote) as an independent in the general election.

This capsule history of Democratic factional politics over a third of a century simplifies what was actually a complex pattern of shifting alliances among political leaders. While we have concentrated on gubernatorial politics, other battles were fought out over congressional and other offices. Clements and Chandler were the most prominent and enduring politicians of their generation, and gradually their names became attached to the two major factions in the Democratic party. But it would be a mistake to assume that most state politicians remained attached to a single faction throughout their political careers.

A few examples will illustrate the fluidity of factional Democratic politics. Keen Johnson had been elected lieutenant governor in 1935 on the Tom Rhea slate but ran for a full gubernatorial term with the support of Chandler forces. His opponent in 1939, John Y. Brown, had the support of Rhea and Clements but at other times ran for high office as an independent. Lyter Donaldson, picked by Keen Johnson to succeed him in 1943, had been associated with Rhea and had Clements's support when he ran for governor. Clements and Waterfield had been allies for some time before they ran against each other in 1947, long before Waterfield became associated with Chandler. Chandler supported Clements in his bid for governor in 1947. Although the Clements-Chandler rivalry reached its most intensive level from 1955 through 1959, Clements broke with Combs and actually supported Chandler in the 1967 race.

Kentucky politics from the 1930s to the mid-1960s was not only bifactional but also highly personal. There were a relatively small number of politicians who operated at the state level and who remained prominent in politics for remarkably long periods of time. Chandler's last run for governor in 1971, for example, occurred forty years after he was elected lieutenant governor; and he was still endorsing gubernatorial candidates in the 1987 primary. Clements was a major figure in state politics for about forty years. Waterfield's first and last campaigns for governor were twenty years apart.

These and the other major political leaders developed their political strength first at the county level and then became significant players in the state Democratic game. They became experts in the art of political maneuvering, in cutting deals in the traditional "smoke-filled rooms." When an ambitious politician undertook a run for the gubernatorial nomination, he did not begin by barnstorming across the state or hiring a media expert to develop sophisticated advertisements. He started out by trying to mobilize support from state and local political leaders. There were usually only two major candidates running in the gubernatorial primary, partly because of the strength of bifactional loyalties, but also partly because candidates seemed reluctant to stay in the race unless they would win commitments from a significant proportion of the state's political brokers.

Chandler's strength as a factional leader was his personal style as a campaigner, his lively oratory, his folksy manner, his legendary memory for names and faces, and his skill in grabbing onto issues—such as the sales tax—that would have popular appeal. His political strength in the primaries from 1955 through 1963 was also based heavily on his alliance with Harry Lee Waterfield.

Clements's political strength was based very heavily on his skill as an organizer. He was never a skillful orator and would hardly be described by anyone as folksy, but he was a man of great determination and loved to build organizations and exercise power. From 1947 to 1960 he had maintained more control over the Democratic primary game than anyone else. After eight years of the Clements and Wetherby administrations, it was Clements alone who determined that Combs would inherit the mantle. For the first few months of the Chandler administration, he actually prevented Chandler from gaining control of the party machinery, and he almost succeeded in renewing his power at the 1956 state convention. In 1959 it was Clements who mediated the Combs-Wyatt rivalry and decided that Combs would head the ticket and Wyatt would take second place.

The Combs and Breathitt administrations (1959-67) served as a transition from the traditional factional system to a newer style of politics. Combs was initially elected with the support of the Clements administration and during his term demonstrated mastery in negotiations with local political leaders, particularly in the eastern counties. But Clements resigned as highway commissioner during the first year, leaving Combs fully in command of the administration and ushering in a new Combs faction. Combs was able to enlist supporters on the basis of his programs: educators, union members, liberals and reformers, and many residents of the larger metropolitan areas—activists who did not have strong loyalties to the traditional factions. Breathitt relied less on the traditional factions than on modern media techniques to win the nomination over Chandler and then won a narrow victory in the November election. The Breathitt administration continued the programmatic thrust of the Combs administration, while developing new programs for civil rights and the regulation of strip mining (Pearce, 1987).

Tip O'Neill, the former Speaker of the U.S. House, was fond of saying, "All politics is local." Though he was speaking from a lifetime of experience in a very different state, his conclusion is applicable to Kentucky. As we have said, politicians who operated at the state level got their start and maintained a base of support in the county. Moreover, for factional leaders and candidates to win gubernatorial primaries, they had to have local organizational support. They often gained that support by developing alliances with local politicians, particularly in those counties where local factions prevailed.

A study of county Democratic organizations (Jewell and Cunningham, 1968) carried out in the mid-1960s concluded that "most county organizations are characterized by factions clearly recognizable by those familiar with politics in the county" (p. 47). A sample of forty counties was examined in some detail. In almost half of the counties, there were local factions that were oriented toward state rather than courthouse politics. Some of these were counties where Democratic officeholders stayed out of state factional conflicts, and others had only Republican officeholders. In about one-third of the counties (primarily Democratic and marginal ones), there were two distinct factions that played a part in both state-level and courthouse politics. There were a small number of counties having courthouse factions with few if any ties to state factions, and there were a few counties dominated by a single faction that might be allied with one of the other state factions. It should be noted that in some eastern counties, characterized by large extended families, factions were often based in part on family ties.

The variety of local factional politics and the sheer numbers of local political leaders made it difficult for state factional leaders to maintain strong links with local organizations; and over a period of time there were often shifting alliances between the state and local level. But the linkages between state and local factions helped to maintain factionalism at both levels. Because the state Democratic party was divided into two factions, local politicians competing for patronage or other benefits from state leaders were likely to be rivals at the local level. The existence of local factions forced candidates for statewide office to choose sides in recruiting local supporters. They were dependent on local leaders to provide organizational help, manpower, and voting cues to voters in state primaries.

In those counties where the leading faction had a stable alliance with a state faction, the organization was often able to provide consistent majorities for the candidates endorsed by the state faction. This, of course, enhanced the bargaining power of local leaders in dealing with state leaders. It also created the impression of stability in state factional alignments. In reality, the linkages between state and local factional leaders were not highly stable over a period of several elections in many counties.

The linkages of state and local factions also affected slating for statewide office. During the period when the traditional factions were strongest, the gubernatorial candidates often endorsed a slate of candidates for some or all of the other statewide offices. The slate of candidates sometimes campaigned together, and the slate was identified in some newspaper stories and advertising; but it is not evident that many voters were familiar with the makeup of slates except for the pairing of candidates for governor and lieutenant governor. The effectiveness of statewide slating depended almost entirely on the willingness of county leaders allied with the state faction to endorse the same slate of candidates and work for it in the campaign. Frequently, the county leaders made changes in the slate, particularly if they believed that other candidates were more popular in the county (Jewell and Cunningham, 1968: chap. 4).

It is impossible to measure accurately how much effect slating had on the voters. Rarely did an entire slate of candidates win nomination, and there were several cases of candidates for governor and lieutenant governor from opposing slates being nominated, including Breathitt-Waterfield in 1963 and Ford-Carroll in 1971. At the county level, if a candidate who was dropped from the slate ran poorly, that could not be attributed to nonslating because the local popularity of another candidate was usually the reason for nonslating.

The most interesting question about the traditional Democratic factions, and the most difficult to answer, is whether significant numbers of voters during this period had long-term loyalties to factions or factional leaders, comparable to the loyalties that many voters have toward political parties. To answer this question with any precision, we would need survey data on the voters' perceptions of, and attitude toward, the factions and also panel survey data to determine whether voters actually voted for candidates of the same faction over a period of several elections. In reality, we have absolutely no survey data on voting behavior in Democratic gubernatorial primaries during the period when the factions were strong.

By examining county-level aggregate voting returns for a series of elections, we can determine whether a majority of voters in some counties consistently voted for candidates of the same faction. If this proved to be true, it would suggest that the local organizations allied to the faction were consistent and effective in delivering votes. It would not prove what percentage of voters were consistent in voting for the same faction over time. Even if the majorities for one faction were so strong as to suggest that many voters were voting consistently, we could not tell what their reasons were. Some voters might simply be following the advice of the local organizations, some might be voting regularly for a candidate—such as Chandler—without being conscious of factionalism, while some others might be deliberately supporting those candidates they identified with a faction.

A previous study (Jewell and Cunningham, 1968: 138-47) measured the voting patterns in counties for the three gubernatorial elections (1955-63) in which there was a clear choice between candidates of the two factions, as well as the 1967 race, in which Ward, representing one faction, and Chandler and Waterfield, representing the other, all ran for governor. (For the purpose of this analysis, we combined the Chandler and Waterfield votes in 1967.) Out of a total of 120 counties, there were 25 won by the Clements-Combs candidate in all four elections; there were 28 counties won by the Chandler candidate in three races, and in 12 of these the combined Chandler-Waterfield vote had a plurality in 1967. In other words, there were 53 relatively consistent counties out of 120. Most of the consistent Clements-Combs counties were found in eastern Kentucky, but there were a few in Western Kentucky, and Jefferson was in this category. The counties won by the Chandler-Waterfield coalition in at least the first three elections were mostly in the Bluegrass and southcentral areas.

A closer examination of county voting patterns (including some non-gubernatorial contests), however, suggests that there was more consistency of voting for individual candidates than for factions. Most of the counties where Chandler won the most consistent support were in or near the Bluegrass area. Waterfield was strongest in the far west (his home base) and in some southcentral counties. The counties carried by the Chandler and Waterfield faction in the 1955-63 primaries were largely a combination of the ones where each was strong. There was suprisingly little continuity between the counties where Clements ran strong for governor or senator and those where Combs and Breathitt were strongest. There was even very little overlap between Combs's race for governor in 1955 and Clements's race for the Senate the next year. Clements ran best in parts of western Kentucky, and Combs ran best in eastern Kentucky.

V.O. Key, Jr. (1949), in his examination of southern primaries, contrasted bifactional patterns with what he called "friends and neighbors" voting: the tendency of voters to support the candidates who came from their own or nearby counties. The county-level voting patterns in Kentucky Democratic primaries appear to reflect a combination of friends-and-neighbors and factional voting. Candidates were likely to get the largest share of votes in counties close to home; they often won a plurality of the vote in which their factional partners were strong; and they picked up additional strength in counties that had a strong local organization with which they had been able to establish an alliance.

Democratic Registration and Turnout in Primary Elections

To understand patterns of turnout in Democratic primaries, we must first examine patterns of partisan registration. In recent years approximately two-thirds of registered voters have been Democrats. In the last four gubernatorial years, 1975-87, the proportion of Democratic registration was remarkably stable: 67.3, 68.8, 68.8, and 68.3.

But there is great disparity in party registration from one part of Kentucky to another. In 1987 there were 34 counties, mostly in western Kentucky, in which the Democratic proportion of registration was 90 percent or higher (ranging as high as 98 percent in Elliott County) (table 3).

Table 3. Democratic Patterns of Registration and Turnout in 1987 Gubernatorial Primary

Counties (N)	Total Dem. regis. (000s)	Total Dem. regis. (%)	Total Dem. prim. vote (000s)	Total Dem. prim. vote (%)	Dem. gen. elect. vote (000s)	Dem. gen. elect. vote (%)	Dem. prim. vote as % of Dem. regis.	Dem. prim. vote as % of Dem. gen. elect. vote
Jefferson 69% Dem. regis.	230	17.6	108	17.1	77	15.0	47.0	141.7
Fayette 67% Dem. regis.	52	4.0	34	5.3	22	4.3	64.5	155.1
Campbell & Kenton 68% Dem. regis.	64	4.9	23	3.7	32	6.3	36.6	73.5
Major metro 69% Dem. regis.	347	26.4	167	26.3	130	25.6	48.0	128.0
Dem. regis. over 90% (34)	250	19.0	137	21.6	85	16.7	57.7	161.0
Dem. regis. 80-89% (24)	299	22.7	146	23.0	106	20.7	48.8	138.2
Dem. regis. 50-79% (29)	326	24.8	146	23.0	123	24.1	44.7	118.7
Dem. regis. under 50% (29)	94	7.1	39	6.2	66	12.9	42.1	60.1

Source: Calculated from data compiled by the State Board of Elections.

There were 24 others with Democratic registration in the 80 to 89 percent range. At the other extreme, there were 29 counties with less than 50 percent Democratic registration (dropping as low as 14 percent in Jackson County). In the middle are 29 counties in the 50 to 79 percent Democratic range, in addition to the four major metropolitan counties (Jefferson, Fayette, Campbell, and Kenton), which range from 65 to 70 percent Democratic.

Over 40 percent of the total Democratic registration is found in the overwhelmingly Democratic counties (80 to 98 percent); half is in the moderately Democratic counties (50 to 79 percent); and only 7 percent is in the counties with a majority of Republican registrants (table 3).

In 1987 the distribution of the primary vote approximated the distribution of registration, but there were some significant differences. Democratic voters were most likely to vote in the primary in those counties with the heaviest Democratic registration. In the state as a whole, 48 percent of registered Democrats voted in the gubernatorial primary. That figure was almost 58 percent in the counties registered over 90 percent Democratic but only 42 percent in the counties less than 50 percent Democratic. Among the major metropolitan counties, the proportion was highest (65 percent) in Fayette and lowest in Kenton and Campbell.

What this means is that statewide Democratic candidates must concentrate much of their effort in these overwhelmingly Democratic counties. Relatively small counties can obviously have a disproportionate influence on the Democratic primary if they are registered heavily Democratic and have a heavy turnout in the primary.

There are two pragmatic reasons for a voter to register as a Democrat: to vote in statewide primaries or to vote in local primaries. It is clear that the huge disparities in the proportion of voters registered as Democrats result from variations in local politics. In those counties where local politics is dominated by the Democratic party, an overwhelming proportion of voters is registered as Democrats. There is little reason for persons inclined to the Republican party to register that way because the Republicans have few statewide primary contests. In counties that are more closely competitive (including the four major metropolitan counties), the Democrats have a more modest majority of registrants. The Republicans have a majority of registrants generally in counties where they have local control. The Republican advantage in registration in such counties is less overwhelming because persons who are inclined to vote Democratic have some incentive to register Democratic in order to take part in statewide primaries.

One way of illustrating the importance of local primaries is to examine registration and primary turnout in a year when only local elections were held, such as 1985 (table 4). In that year, in the strongly Democratic counties, the turnout in local Democratic primaries, as a percentage of registration, was about ten percentage points higher than in the 1987 gubernatorial primary. By contrast, it was more than ten percentage points lower than in 1987 in the major metropolitan counties where there was less Democratic primary competition than in the more rural Democratic counties.

The number of persons voting in the Democratic gubernatorial primary is frequently greater than the number who vote for the winning Democrat in the November election. In the 1979 Democratic primary, turnout was slightly higher (102 percent) than in the general election; and in 1983 and 1987 it was considerably higher (117 percent in 1983 and 126 percent in 1987). There are several reasons for this difference. When the general election is perceived to be lopsided, public interest may fade and

Table 4. Democratic Patterns of Registration and Primary Turnout in Local Races, 1985

Counties (N)	Total Dem. regis. (000s)	Total Dem. regis. (%)	Total Dem. prim. vote (000s)	Total Dem. prim. vote (%)	Dem. prim. vote as % of Dem. regis.
Jefferson 64% Dem. regis.	246	17.3	90	12.3	36.7
Fayette 64% Dem. regis.	65	4.6	25	3.4	38.4
Campbell & Kenton 65% Dem. regis.	69	4.9	24	3.3	35.1
Major metro 64% Dem. regis.	381	26.8	139	19.0	36.6
Dem. regis. over 90% (33)	245	17.2	166	22.7	67.8
Dem. regis. 80-89% (25)	348	24.5	201	27.4	57.8
Dem. regis. 50-79% (29)	351	24.7	185	25.3	52.9
Dem. regis. under 50% (29)	98	6.9	42	5.6	42.5

Source: Calculated from data compiled by the State Board of Elections.

turnout may drop. This seems to have been the case in 1987 when only 48 percent of registered Democrats voted in the general election. In some cases, the supporters of Democrats who lose in the primary may stay home or vote Republican in November. This may have happened in some metropolitan counties in 1987.

There is a more important reason for the disparity between Democratic primary turnout and Democratic votes cast in the general election. Substantial numbers of voters who are "closet Republicans" and who expect to support the Republican candidate in the fall are registered Democrats and frequently vote in the Democratic primary.

In the 1987 gubernatorial election, this disparity was greatest in the counties with over 90 percent Democratic registration; the ratio of Democratic primary to general election votes was 161 percent. The ratio was also relatively high in Fayette (155 percent) and Jefferson (142 percent). On the other hand, in counties with less than 50 percent Democratic registration (where Republicans usually register Republican), the comparable ratio was only 60 percent.

Patterns of Competition in Recent Gubernatorial Primaries

The modern, postfactional gubernatorial primaries have been characterized by close competition and, increasingly, by large numbers of candidates (table 5). The only lopsided primary victory occurred in 1975, when Julian Carroll was the incumbent, having succeeded Ford as governor

Table 5. Results of Democratic Gubernatorial Primaries, 1971-87

Year	Candidates	Vote	Percentage	Plurality
1971	Wendell Ford	237,815	53.0	42,137
	Bert T. Combs	195,678	43.6	
	6 others	15,174	3.4	
	Total	448,667		
1975	Julian Carroll	263,965	66.3	150,680
	Todd Hollenbach	113,285	28.5	
	2 others	20,739	5.2	
	Total	397,989		
1979	John Y. Brown, Jr.	165,158	29.1	25,445
	Harvey Sloane	139,713	24.7	
	Terry McBrayer	131,530	23.2	
	Carroll Hubbard, Jr.	68,577	12.1	
	Thelma Stovall	47,633	8.4	
	4 others	14,175	2.5	
	Total	566,786		
1983	Martha Layne Collins	223,692	34.0	4,532
	Harvey Sloane	219,160	33.3	
	Grady Stumbo	199,795	30.3	
	3 others	15,807	2.4	
	Total	658,454		
1987	Wallace Wilkinson	221,138	34.9	57,934
	John Y. Brown, Jr.	163,204	25.8	
	Steve Beshear	114,439	18.1	
	Grady Stumbo	84,613	13.4	
	Julian Carroll	42,137	6.6	
	3 others	8,187	1.3	
	Total	633,718		

when the latter was elected to the Senate in 1974. Although the Ford-Combs race in 1971 was not a continuation of the bifactional contests, it resembled earlier races in being a close, two-man race.

Collins's victory in 1983 was by far the closest gubernatorial primary in many years, providing a margin of only 4,500 votes, less than one percentage point. The 1979 and 1987 races had much in common. Each had a much larger number of serious candidates than had been common in gubernatorial primaries. Each was a very close race, won by much less than a majority. And each resulted in an upset victory for a newcomer in electoral politics. Although Wilkinson's eventual margin, 58,000 votes and nine percentage points, was substantial, no one anticipated such a large margin until the votes had been counted.

The one characteristic of bifactional politics still found in some primary contests has been the attempt of the incumbent governor to choose his successor. In 1971 there was no Democratic incumbent, and in 1975 Julian Carroll was seeking election to a full term. But in 1979 Carroll used the full political resources of his office in an unsuccessful effort to get McBrayer nominated. Four years later, Governor Brown's preference for Grady Stumbo was well recognized, but it was not until the closing days of the race that Brown publicly endorsed Stumbo and actively campaigned for him—an effort that was too little and too late. In 1983 Governor Collins made no effort to select the nominee, though many of her political allies were working for Beshear.

What are the stepping-stones to a gubernatorial nomination? What are the most common backgrounds of serious candidates for governor? In the five primaries from 1971 through 1987, there were eighteen serious candidates (including George Atkins who dropped out and endorsed Brown late in the 1979 campaign). Three of these—Combs in 1971 and Brown and Carroll in 1987—were former governors, and they were all unsuccessful.

The most common pattern followed by candidates has been to run for one or more statewide offices. Carroll was elected lieutenant governor (after serving as Speaker of the House) and succeeded to the governorship. Ford, Stovall, Collins, and Beshear were all serving as lieutenant governor when they ran for governor, and all except Ford had been elected to another statewide office previously. George Atkins made his abortive run for governor while serving as auditor. Four candidates ran after winning local or congressional office. Sloane had been mayor of Louisville, Hollenbach had been county judge of Jefferson County, and Carroll Hubbard was serving in Congress. McBrayer and Stumbo had both held appointive positions in the administration of the governor who endorsed them; McBrayer had earlier served in the legislature. Stumbo, like Sloane, was considered a serious candidate in his second race largely because of his strong showing in the first primary.

John Y. Brown (in 1979) and Wallace Wilkinson were the only major candidates who ran for governor without having previously run for elected office or having held an appointed office; and they were both elected. Both men were successful business persons, with some practical experience in working on statewide campaigns of other candidates. This may be the beginning of a trend, with a larger proportion of gubernatorial candidates being political amateurs who are wealthy enough to finance a large share of their campaigns.

The Ford-Combs Contest in 1971

The two leading candidates in the 1971 primary had much in common and disagreed about little except who would make the better governor. Ford had served as Combs's chief administrative assistant during much of his administration, had been elected to the state senate in 1965 with the strong support of Governor Breathitt, and was completing a term as lieutenant governor, the highest Democrat in the state administration.

The two men were political moderates, skillful political organizers, and capable administrators. The campaign was relatively dull, because there was little serious disagreement on issues and because both candidates were moderate in their oratory. The sharpest area of disagreement concerned support for education and higher taxes. Combs had the strong support of the Kentucky Education Association (KEA); Ford charged that Combs was therefore committed to the tax increases supported by KEA. Ford may have benefited from public resentment at the teachers, who had staged an abortive strike for higher pay the previous year.

Perhaps the most important difference between the two candidates was their organizational bases of support. Combs relied heavily on the traditional county organizations, particularly in rural areas, that he had been so successful in recruiting and nurturing during his administration. Ford was familiar with these organizations and their leaders because of his role in the Combs administration. But he recognized that most of these local leaders were still loyal to Combs and that some local organizations were becoming less powerful. For these reasons Ford built his own organization, made up largely of younger leaders. He started early and established an organization in every county. Some of his contacts had been made in the insurance business and the Kentucky Junior Chamber of Commerce, which he had headed. Many leaders had worked in his campaign for lieutenant governor.

Ford recognized that a population shift was occurring from rural to the larger urban counties; without neglecting rural Kentucky, he made a particular effort to win votes in the larger urban areas. He apparently gave priority to northern Kentucky and to Jefferson County, which had been a Combs stronghold but which Combs neglected in the 1971 campaign.

Ford's strategy paid off. He won more than 60 percent of the votes in Jefferson County, and he had an even larger margin in northern Kentucky. Ford, from Owensboro, had a strong appeal in both urban and rural sections of western Kentucky, winning more than 60 percent in the First and Second districts. Combs was strongest in the eastern counties. He had almost a 2 to 1 lead in the Seventh District and a majority in the Republican Fifth District.

Carroll's Triumph in 1975

In 1975 Julian Carroll was nominated with two-thirds of the vote and a majority of 150,000, the most lopsided victory since 1951, the last time that there had been an incumbent running who had succeeded from the lieutenant governorship. After serving four years as Speaker of the House during the Nunn administration, Carroll had run for lieutenant governor on a slate with Combs in 1975, winning while Combs lost to Ford. During his three years as lieutenant governor, Carroll had had an uneasy relationship with Ford. At one point during this period, Ford appeared to be urging Carroll to run for the Senate in 1974 against Republican Marlow Cook, who was perceived (correctly) by many Democrats as vulnerable. If successful, this maneuver might have enabled Ford to play a role in the choice of his successor. Ultimately, however, Ford ran for the Senate and won; Carroll became governor with a huge head start on the 1975 nomination race.

Carroll's only significant opponent was Todd Hollenbach, the Jefferson county judge. While Carroll had been planning his campaign ever since becoming lieutenant governor, Hollenbach entered the race only four months before the primary. He had little name recognition outside of Jefferson County and little ability to raise campaign funds. Hollenbach was outspent by Carroll by more than a 2 to 1 margin.

There were few issues in the campaign. Hollenbach proposed a tax cut, a position that Carroll described as irresponsible. Carroll said little about specific issues but promised to continue the kind of administration that he had run for the first year.

There was never much doubt about the outcome of or interest in the race; consequently, the turnout was very light, about 38 percent of the Democratic registered vote. Carroll carried his home county of McCracken by a margin of 15 to 1 (over 11,000 votes); Hollenbach carried Jefferson County by 54 percent (about 4,500 votes); and Carroll won 117 of the remaining 118 counties.

Brown's Upset Victory in 1979

In the 1979 gubernatorial primary, Democratic voters were offered a wider range of serious candidates than at any time since the beginning of bifactional politics. (The 1967 race had had more candidates, but only three had gained more than 5 percent of the vote.)

The Carroll administration strongly supported Terry McBrayer, forty-one, a former legislator (1965-75) and majority floor leader, who had served as commissioner of commerce during part of Carroll's term. Carroll had built a strong organization at the local level, and this was fully mobilized on McBrayer's behalf. The administration's backing helped McBrayer to finance the most expensive race in the campaign, almost $1.9 million. Moreover, Governor Carroll, one of the best stump speakers in modern Kentucky history, campaigned tirelessly for McBrayer across the state. There were some disadvantages to the endorsement, however. McBrayer, who was not well known across the state, was sometimes seen as simply a tool or "puppet" of the Carroll administration, and he was handicapped by charges of scandal and corruption leveled at the Carroll administration and rumors of federal investigations that were repeated by most of the other gubernatorial candidates.

Harvey Sloane, forty-three, was a physician who had served a very successful term as mayor of Louisville. He was generally perceived as a liberal and reform candidate who had some support from labor unions as well as from the well-organized teachers of the state. He had been the first candidate to enter the race, and his campaign was also well financed. Late in the race he collected endorsements from major urban newspapers. One of Sloane's handicaps was not being well known outside of Jefferson County. McBrayer and Sloane appeared to be the front-runners for much of the campaign.

Carroll Hubbard, Jr., forty-one, of Mayfield, was serving his third term as congressman from the First District. He was well known in the district as a specialist in constituent services and communication, but beyond western Kentucky he was not a particularly familiar figure. He had a conservative record that was better suited to the First District than to a statewide electorate. A major theme of his campaign was a series of charges against alleged waste and corruption in the Carroll administration.

Thelma Stovall, sixty, was serving as lieutenant governor after twenty years of practicing "musical chairs," winning election alternately as secretary of state and treasurer. Her strongest base of support was in the labor union movement in Louisville, where she had first become active in politics. A few months before the primary she had attracted public attention by calling a special session of the legislature to make some tax reductions. She had won the primary for lieutenant governor in 1975 against ten opponents (beating the closest one by 36,000 votes), although four of them were better financed. Once again, in 1979, she had much less financial support than most of her opponents, spending only $217,000 of the $5.8 million that was spent in the campaign.

George Atkins, elected state auditor in 1975, had been able to use his office quite effectively to spotlight examples of waste and political favoritism in the Carroll administration, and this was naturally a major theme of his campaign. Twelve days before the primary he dropped out of the race and threw his support to Brown.

Two months before the primary election, barely in time for the filing deadline, John Y. Brown, Jr., forty-five, entered the race. He was a familiar figure in Kentucky, but he had never before run for political office. His father, John Y. Brown, Sr., had run repeatedly for statewide office over a period of many years; he rarely won, but he was always a serious candidate, and he did serve for some time in the state legislature. John Y. Brown, Jr., made his fortune when he bought out Colonel Sanders and built Kentucky Fried Chicken into a highly successful fast food chain. He had been a sports entrepreneur, owning the Louisville Colonels in the American Basketball Association. He had dabbled in politics, working in political campaigns and learning how they were run. And, shortly before entering the primary, he had married Phyllis George, the former Miss America and television personality.

All of the gubernatorial candidates except Brown used traditional organizational techniques in building their campaigns. They began by developing a network of local organizations in as many counties as possible, utilizing the individuals who had worked with them in previous campaigns. McBrayer had the obvious advantage of inheriting the organization that Julian Carroll had built and nurtured during his two statewide campaigns and during his five years as governor. This organization was presumed to be particularly strong in rural counties and through western Kentucky. In addition, McBrayer, an experienced politician—though never before a statewide candidate—had considerable organizational success in parts of eastern Kentucky. Harvey Sloane began with a strong, loyal organization that he had created in Louisville while running for and serving as mayor. He had considerable success in attracting liberal political activists in the other large urban areas.

Carroll Hubbard's strongest base of organizational support was obviously in western Kentucky, in the First District where he had served as congressman after several terms in the state legislature. He had to compete with Julian Carroll, however, for organizational support in the west; and the geographical base of his support was obviously much narrower than those of McBrayer and Sloane. While she had to compete in Louisville with Sloane, Thelma Stovall had considerable organizational help there in working-class districts and in the labor movement. Across the state she had a personal organization developed from a quarter-century of campaigns for statewide office as well as considerable union support. George Atkins's organizational strength was relatively thin, although he had run one successful statewide race.

Having started their organizations, most candidates devoted months to touring the state, meeting voters, giving speeches, raising money, and expanding their organizations. Kentucky voters, it was assumed, wanted to meet their candidates firsthand and not merely read about them in the press or see their television commercials. This was particularly important for those candidates who lacked high name recognition. Harvey Sloane, for example, tried to get attention and improve his image outside Jefferson County by conducting 1,200 miles of "walks" across the state.

John Y. Brown largely ignored the traditional techniques of campaign organization and made no effort to win the support of courthouse politicians. Not only did he lack the time to follow this traditional path, but he also considered it a waste of time and effort. He did not enjoy the prospect of wooing the courthouse politicians, and he chose not to do it. Neither did he look forward to the prospect of shaking tens of thousands of hands and making stump speeches all over the state; but he recognized that personal contact with the voters was necessary. Brown solved this problem by traveling around the state in a helicopter, usually accompanied by Phyllis George Brown and sometimes by other celebrities. He would emerge from the helicopter long enough to greet local supporters, shake a few hands, make a brief speech, and then take off. This unorthodox technique seemed to work. He was able to cover a lot of ground, and he created excitement wherever he went.

Television also played an important part in the 1979 primary campaign. The three candidates who made the most use of television advertising were the three who could afford it: McBrayer, Sloane, and Brown. In retrospect, it is Brown's television campaign that is remembered and often credited with winning him the election. He had several advantages over Sloane and McBrayer in the use of television. Because Brown was largely financing his own campaign and had almost unlimited resources, he could plan the advertising campaign well in advance and could afford the best television specialists. But Brown's advantages in using television were not entirely financial. He proved to be a more skillful performer than either McBrayer or Sloane. One of his more effective techniques was to film thirty-minute commercials, in which he answered questions from a small audience, aided by his wife who moved through the group with a microphone. Brown's skill as a television performer was evident not only in commercials but in debates with the other candidates. As is usually the case, the debates were more important for what viewers learned about the candidates' styles than what they learned about issues.

Throughout the campaign voters were treated to a heavy dose of charges and countercharges, many of them focusing on the Carroll administration. Hubbard and Atkins were most outspoken in their allegations of wrongdoing by members of the Carroll administration. Atkins's position as auditor gave both visibility and credibility to his charges. Carroll not only defended his administration but launched counterattacks on the other candidates. He criticized Sloane, for example, for the abortion policies of Louisville General Hospital and for Sloane's handling of school busing in the city. Hubbard was criticized by a number of candidates for his practice of deluging constituents with congratulatory notes for such accomplishments as graduating from high school.

Late in the campaign, as other candidates began to realize that Brown was gaining strength, more of their attacks focused on him. There were criticisms of his life-style, particularly his penchant for high-stakes gambling. When Atkins pulled out of the race and endorsed Brown, there were inevitable charges that Brown had paid Atkins's campaign debts. But criticisms of Brown's life-style did not appear to stick or do him much damage.

Most of the time, Brown appeared to be above the political fray. The voters were evidently tired of negative advertising and appreciated the positive tone of Brown's campaign. The insults and charges being exchanged by other candidates supported Brown's theme that it was time to abandon old-style politics in Kentucky. While others led the attack on the Carroll administration, Brown profited from these charges because he was the candidate promising to avoid favoritism and cronyism and "run Kentucky like a business." While McBrayer had the support of the old factional leaders (including both Combs and Chandler), Brown was promising a new style of politics that was not dominated by factions. While candidates such as McBrayer, Stovall, and Hubbard were perceived as old-style politicians, Brown was a fresh face on the political scene, with an unorthodox style, a fresh approach, and a glamorous wife.

Brown won only 29 percent of the vote, but he finished 25,000 votes ahead of Sloane and more than 33,000 votes ahead of the administration's candidate, Terry McBrayer. At the end of the primary campaign, he clearly was the candidate with the greatest momentum.

In geographical terms Brown won the election by finishing first or second in every congressional district. He won the Second and Sixth, finished behind Sloane in the Fourth and far behind him in the Third, finished behind McBrayer in the Fifth and Seventh, and finished behind Hubbard in the First District. Brown was a statewide candidate; he had no particular regional base, although he was strongest in Fayette county and the Sixth District. He won at least one-fourth of the vote in every district except the Third (which contains most of Jefferson County), and even there he had twice as many votes as any candidate except Sloane. Sloane got at least one-fourth of the vote in four districts; McBrayer did so only in the Fifth and Seventh districts in the east, which he won by at least 40 percent; Hubbard did so only in the First District; and Stovall got no more than 13 percent in any district. Brown was a statewide, rather than a regional, candidate because his television campaign reached most of the state, and he did not rely on local organizations concentrated in only parts of the state.

The lesson of the 1979 campaign seemed to be that you can win a gubernatorial primary election without an organization but you cannot win it without television. To be more precise, traditional techniques of organization appeared to be declining in importance, but a candidate must have the financial resources to buy extensive television advertising and the personal skill to make good use of it. Carroll Hubbard, Thelma Stovall, and George Atkins never had a serious chance at the nomination in large part because they could not afford to buy much television time. The low-budget, high-name-recognition campaign that had worked for Stovall in the 1975 lieutenant governor's race was totally inadequate in the 1979 governor's race.

There were also other factors explaining the outcome. None of the other candidates had strength throughout the state. Terry McBrayer and Harvey Sloane were the only two candidates with enough financing to be competitive, but each of them had significant liabilities. Neither of them generated much excitement as campaigners, either in person or on television. While Sloane dominated Louisville, Stovall drained some support from him in this city; a more serious problem was his lack of support in rural counties. McBrayer was strong in eastern Kentucky but was dependent on Carroll's organization for support in the west, but Hubbard competed with the Carroll organization in that area. McBrayer's biggest asset—the support of the Carroll administration—was his biggest liability.

In the last analysis, however, Brown won because of his own strategy, skills, and resources. When he joined the race, none of the candidates who had been campaigning for so long had captured the public's imagination, but all of them had enough support so that the race could be won by gaining a third of the vote or less. Brown used television to bring his image and his message to public attention quickly and forcefully across the state. His style and issues appealed to an electorate that was tired of old politics and jaded with negative campaigning. He was the right candidate at the right time with enough resources.

Martha Layne Collins: A Photo-Finish in 1983

One lesson learned from the 1983 gubernatorial race was that all primary elections are different; in other words, one election does not constitute a trend. The 1983 election proved that organization politics was still important, but it also confirmed the growing importance of television advertising and of large-scale financing to pay for it.

There were three significant candidates in 1983: Harvey Sloane, Grady Stumbo, and Martha Layne Collins. Harvey Sloane was the only loser who emerged from the 1979 race without serious damage to his career. He had finished that race a strong second, and many observers believed he would have won if Atkins had stayed in the race or been willing to support Sloane. In 1981 he won reelection as mayor of Louisville, maintaining his power base. He was able to begin the 1983 race with much greater name recognition than he had enjoyed at the start of the 1979 campaign. He entered the 1983 race as the front-runner.

Grady Stumbo was a doctor, running a rural clinic in eastern Kentucky when Governor Brown selected him to run the human resources cabinet. It was a difficult job because resources were scarce and programs had to be cut, but he handled it with skill and received favorable attention in the press. Despite his lack of political experience, Stumbo decided to enter the governor's race. He expected to run well in the eastern counties, and he hoped to have labor union support for his populist campaign. He also counted on support from the Brown administration, though a public endorsement did not come until very late in the campaign. Throughout the campaign Stumbo was viewed as the underdog, particularly as it became obvious that he was falling behind in the effort to raise campaign funds.

Martha Layne Collins of Versailles, a public schoolteacher and the wife of a dentist, started out in politics working in Wendell Ford's campaign. Gradually, she developed skill and experience in organizational politics, and in 1975 she decided to run for statewide office. The job she sought, clerk of the court of appeals, was relatively obscure and was abolished as an elective position a few years later. She won with one-third of the vote, against four opponents. Four years later she ran for lieutenant governor, against six male opponents. At least three of her opponents were better known or more experienced. William Cox, a former legislator and a key aide to Governor Carroll, had the full support of the Carroll administration. Todd Hollenbach, the Jefferson County judge, had run for governor in 1975. Joe Prather was a veteran legislator and a leader in the Senate. But Cox, perceived as the front-runner, was damaged by some of the accusations against the Carroll administration. Collins won the primary, gaining 23 percent of the vote and beating Cox by some 3,300 votes. She entered the 1983 primary with years of experience in organizational politics, the advantage of two successful statewide races, and the visibility enjoyed by the lieutenant governor. She also had the advantage—or disadvantage—of being a woman candidate.

There were three keys to the success of Collins's campaign: fund-raising, local organization, and effective use of television. The Collins campaign spent nearly $2.5 million to win the primary election. The Collins fund-raising effort, in which her husband played a major role, had produced over $1 million by early January, more than either of the other candidates. The fact that her campaign was able to raise so much money so quickly had two consequences: it made possible the planning of an extensive television advertising campaign, and it established her credibility as a candidate at a time when many observers assumed that Sloane was the front-runner.

The Collins organization made the decision early in the race to run a statewide race, to make an effort in every county. Local organizations were established throughout the state, building on the individuals and groups who had worked in Collins' previous campaigns. She campaigned in every county, even those with relatively few Democratic votes, and repeatedly emphasized that she had visited and understood the needs in all 120 counties. A particular effort was made to organize the counties surrounding Jefferson, rather than conceding them to Sloane. Collins was also very successful in attracting support from local officeholders and activists who were frustrated by Governor Brown's policy of benign neglect of the party organization and local leaders. Collins concentrated as much as possible on personal campaigning at the local level and sometimes passed up forums and opportunities to debate the other candidates.

The Collins media campaign was extensive and skillfully prepared. Although Collins was not a strong debater in forums, she was an effective performer in televised advertisements. These stressed her experience in government, her familiarity with the state (all 120 counties), her use of the lieutenant governor's office as a kind of ombudsman to deal with problems, and her concern—as a former teacher—with education. She clearly was not running on a feminist platform, but a major purpose of her advertising was to convince voters that a woman could be a strong and effective governor. In the closing weeks of the campaign, her organization ran some negative advertising targeting Harvey Sloane, an attack that her advisers felt had some impact.

Her television campaign was not heavily issue oriented, and she did not develop bold new programs to deal with state problems. While she emphasized the need for improving education and raising standards of teaching and learning, she avoided commitments for expensive education programs. She consistently emphasized that she would avoid raising taxes.

Harvey Sloane started the campaign with the same organizational base in Jefferson County that he had had in 1979. He also succeeded in picking up considerable support from established political leaders around the state, at least in part because he was perceived as the front-runner. He made an effort to appeal more to business persons, stressing his efforts to attract and keep business in Louisville. Sloane had the necessary resources to run a large-scale television campaign, and he did so. However, Sloane is not a very dynamic campaigner, and his low-keyed speaking style may have damaged him in personal appearances, debates, and television commercials.

With regard to issues, Sloane tried to broaden his base of support and moderate his liberal image. But he made two strategic decisions on issues that alienated some of his natural constituencies and probably cost him the nomination. The question of a right-to-work bill became an issue in the campaign because of recent efforts by some groups to enact it in the legislature. Sloane refused to take a stand against the bill (without actually advocating it), and this neutral position cost him much of his support from labor unions, who shifted to Grady Stumbo. He also chose to fully endorse the right-to-life position on abortion, a position that damaged his standing among more liberal women.

Grady Stumbo had considerable strength in eastern Kentucky, but he did not develop a real statewide organization at the county level. Stumbo explained one reason for his difficulty in attracting organization support. The practical politicians he met with told him, "I'd be for you if you could win." Throughout the campaign Stumbo was hurt by his difficulties in raising money. This handicapped his advertising campaign and also undermined his credibility. Eventually (with help from Brown's supporters and some personal loans), he was able to spend almost $1.2 million. But his television campaign was less extensive and effective than those of his opponents. Stumbo is an effective stump speaker, and he made the most of that skill and of his image as a fresh face in state politics. His campaign themes were heavily populist.

Eight days before the primary election, Governor Brown publicly announced his endorsement of Stumbo and said, "I could no longer stand by and watch my state not have the very best." He started a whirlwind campaign across the state. Phyllis George Brown taped television shows with Stumbo, patterned after the successful ones she had done with Brown in 1979. At the time when Brown made his endorsement, Stumbo was believed to be eight to ten percentage points behind the two leaders; he finished the campaign less than four points behind Collins.

It appears that Brown's endorsement and campaign provided Stumbo with important momentum and made the campaign closer. But political observers wondered why Brown had not joined the campaign earlier, helping Stumbo to raise money and mobilizing support for him. Brown was unpopular with many persons, including local officeholders and politicians, and his endorsement was not an unmixed blessing for Stumbo. But the endorsement may have been an unintended blessing for Collins. Because Stumbo and Sloane were competing for the labor and liberal vote, the last-minute gains made by Stumbo were probably largely at Sloane's expense. Brown's late decision to enter the race in 1979 destroyed the possibility of a Sloane victory that year. Brown's last-minute decision to actively endorse Stumbo in 1983 probably cost Sloane his second chance for the nomination.

Martha Layne Collins won the primary by about 4,500 votes over Harvey Sloane. It was the smallest margin of victory in a Democratic gubernatorial primary victory in at least sixty years, though Collins's percentage of the vote was higher than Brown's in 1979.

Collins ran strongest in the central part of the state. She won the Bluegrass Sixth District with 46 percent. She won the northern Fourth District by 43 percent, including about 45 percent of the vote in Kenton and Campbell counties. She carried the Republican Fifth District by 46 percent. She led the Second District by a narrow margin over Sloane. Sloane finished behind Collins in every district except the Third, which he carried with 55 percent and a 32,000 vote margin over the third-place Collins. Stumbo won the Seventh District with an impressive 52 percent and surprisingly won the First District by a narrow margin over Collins.

Techniques of Modern Primary Campaigns

Modern Democratic primary campaigns for governor are very different from those of thirty years ago. Factionalism is dead, and the day of the kingmaker is over. No longer can a handful of leaders decide which candidates can run for office and which should step aside and wait their turn. Most of the political leaders who dominated their counties have faded away. At one time, it was essential for candidates seeking statewide office to meet and bargain with these local leaders, many of whom were believed to control substantial numbers of votes.

Despite the example of John Y. Brown's campaign in 1979, most of the successful candidates for major state offices have given a high priority to building local organizations. One of Sen. Wendell Ford's sources of long-term political strength in Kentucky is his organization of local supporters. Local organization was a major asset for Martha Layne Collins in her 1979 and 1983 campaigns and an asset for Wallace Wilkinson in 1987. Stumbo's ineffectiveness in organization building was a significant liability.

But organization has taken on a new meaning. While it is still important for gubernatorial candidates to visit officeholders in the courthouses, it is more important to enlist the support of larger numbers of experienced political activists across the state. Their role is described in more detail in the next chapter. Candidates who have a limited base of support among the more experienced political activists have learned how to recruit talented persons who are political amateurs but have developed organizational skills in businesses and organizations. In his 1971 campaign for governor, Wendell Ford relied heavily on contacts he had made during years of activity in the Kentucky Junior Chamber of Commerce. In their 1987 campaigns both Wallace Wilkinson and Brereton Jones relied heavily on business persons and other political amateurs to fill the ranks of their organizations.

Organization is still important in a political campaign, but candidates today have a wide range of options in constructing an organization. The range of organizational work to be done has also changed, with much greater attention being paid to fund-raising, because the costs of campaigning have escalated.

The most important change in primary campaigns, of course, is the new importance of television advertising. Contrary to popular myth, John Y. Brown, in 1979, was not the first politician to discover the potential of television advertising. Television advertising and coverage were important ingredients in Edward Breathitt's successful campaign against Happy Chandler in 1963. But the victories of Brown in 1979 and Collins in 1983 resulted in large part from the fact that their television appearances and advertisements were more effective than those of their opponents.

In the 1987 gubernatorial campaign (described in detail in chapter 4), television assumed even greater importance. In the closing weeks of the campaign, the debate among the top three candidates—Brown, Beshear, and Wilkinson—was largely carried on through commercials. The inability of Stumbo and Carroll to raise enough funds for frequent advertising practically excluded them from this debate. And the late surge of the electorate to Wilkinson is largely explained by the effectiveness of the message delivered in his commercials. In Kentucky, as in the rest of the country, television has become the central forum of political campaigns. Candidates must not only learn how to gain favorable coverage of their campaigns but be able to purchase television time and media experts to shape and package their message most effectively.

4

THE 1987 DEMOCRATIC GUBERNATORIAL PRIMARY

ON MAY 26, 1987, Wallace Wilkinson won the Democratic gubernatorial primary with 35 percent of the vote; he finished nine percentage points and 58,000 votes ahead of his nearest competitor, John Y. Brown. Two weeks earlier Wilkinson's own poll had shown him trailing Brown by fourteen points; a *Courier-Journal* poll in early March had shown Wilkinson running fifth, with only 7 percent of the vote.

How did Wilkinson come from so far behind to win the race? How did the campaigns of the front-runners, Brown and Steve Beshear, collapse? What made the race so volatile and the voters so unpredictable? In an effort to answer these and other questions, we will examine the 1987 campaign in some detail: the candidates, their campaign strategies and resources, the development of issues, and the use of television.

The 1987 campaign deserves attention because it was one of the most interesting in recent years and because Wilkinson's victory was a major upset. But it also deserves attention because in many ways it was typical of recent gubernatorial campaigns. In 1987 there was a large field of major candidates, as in 1979. There were major shifts in voter sentiment during the campaign, as in both 1979 and 1983. Television debates and advertising had a significant effect on the outcome, as in both previous primary elections. Finally, in both 1979 and 1987 the election was won by a wealthy political amateur who could afford extensive television advertising and made effective use of it.

The Candidates

Each of the five candidates brought significant political strength to the campaign. John Y. Brown had been elected governor in 1979 and could claim a number of achievements during his administration. Steve Beshear was completing eight years in high office, as attorney general and then as lieutenant governor. Grady Stumbo, a cabinet member in the Brown administration, had finished a close third in the 1983 gubernatorial primary. Julian Carroll had served a previous five-year term as governor from 1975 through 1979. Wallace Wilkinson had never held or even sought political office, but he was a wealthy businessman with considerable experience in raising campaign funds.

John Y. Brown, Jr., first became known in Kentucky as the owner of Kentucky Fired Chicken and the Louisville basketball team, but he established his reputation as a politician during his whirlwind campaign in the 1979 Democratic gubernatorial primary. While he won the primary with only 29 percent of the vote, he defeated former governor Louie Nunn in the general election by a more comfortable margin.

In many respects, Governor Brown's administration was a success. As promised, he did run government like a business. He streamlined state government, reducing full-time positions by about 20 percent and dismissing several thousand workers. He sharply curtailed the patronage system and the use of personal service contracts for political purposes, and he reformed state investment practices. In the face of economic recession and severe revenue shortfalls, he avoided a tax increase by curtailing programs. But his repeated assertions that he had made the cuts without reducing essential services were widely criticized by those concerned about cutbacks in education and social services. Many state workers who were dismissed sued successfully to get their jobs back. His personal efforts to attract new business to Kentucky failed to prevent a net loss of jobs and a growth in unemployment.

Some of Brown's most serious problems were personal rather than governmental. During his last year in office, serious questions were raised about his personal finances and his gambling debts, and one of his prominent friends pleaded guilty to a drug charge. Moreover, Brown was critically ill for some time because of complications following by-pass heart surgery. A few months after his term ended, Brown's political reputation was damaged when he entered the senatorial primary against Senator Huddleston and then dropped out for health reasons after polls showed him far behind.

As the 1987 primary campaign grew closer, political observers began to believe that Brown would run again and that he would be the front-runner. Brown was only fifty-three years old; he had lost weight and regained his health; and he seemed to be bored with dabbling in business. It was generally believed that his record of clean government and no new taxes had been popular. After dropping numerous hints about running and testing the political waters, he filed for office on February 20, shortly before the deadline.

Lt. Gov. *Steve Beshear* had enjoyed the role of front-runner until Brown entered the race. Though only forty-two years old, he had extensive experience in politics and government. After three terms in the legislature, representing Fayette County, he was elected attorney general. Four years later he was elected lieutenant governor. He entered both races as an underdog, but in both he demonstrated his skill and experience in building a statewide political organization, though he was not at his best as a personal campaigner. Beshear also benefited from his clean image and reputation for integrity.

As attorney general he succeeded in building a reputation as a protector of consumer interests and an opponent of utility rate increases, but he alienated more conservative Kentuckians by some of his actions on social and religious issues, notably his ruling that the Ten Commandments must be removed from classroom walls to comply with a U.S. Supreme Court decision. As lieutenant governor he worked hard to strengthen his political position and gained some media attention by establishing a Kentucky Tomorrow Commission to survey the state's needs and recommend broad policies for the years ahead.

Grady Stumbo ran third in the 1983 gubernatorial primary, but his ability to win 30 percent of the vote, despite his lack of financing and his status as an underdog, had impressed many politicians. Some felt he could have won if Governor Brown had supported him more effectively and earlier in the campaign. Stumbo entered the 1987 primary with greater name recognition and more political experience than in 1983. But he faced one major drawback. Instead of having the support of the incumbent administration and benefiting from some of Brown's popularity, he faced John Y. Brown as one of his opponents. Moreover, as a candidate without much personal wealth, he faced two millionaires among his opponents in 1987.

Julian Carroll brought to the campaign both assets and liabilities that were unique. He had a record of public service and political success unmatched by any other candidate. First elected to the Kentucky House from Paducah in 1961, he served four years as speaker and three years as lieutenant governor, before succeeding to the governorship (after Governor Ford's election to the Senate) in 1974 and being elected to a full term in 1975. During his five years as governor, he had an extensive record of accomplishments, particularly in education; and the state enjoyed a level of economic growth that made possible expanded budgets without tax increases. He was unusually successful in leading the legislature from the governor's office.

But the Carroll administration was plagued by scandals, particularly insurance-fee kickbacks. Questions were raised about some of Carroll's financial transactions, and he was subjected to a grand jury questioning during a prolonged federal investigation.

Carroll's decision to enter the 1987 gubernatorial race surprised and puzzled most political observers. They were sure that he could not win and did not understand why he did not share that political judgment. Carroll brought to the campaign a wealth of experience and knowledge and unmatched skill as a traditional political orator. At age fifty-six, he was vigorous and energetic. But he entered the campaign perceived by nearly everyone as a certain loser, a perception that would make it very difficult to attract funds and recruit campaign workers.

Wallace Wilkinson grew up in Casey County, one of the poorest and most Republican counties in Kentucky. He got his start in business in the mid-1960s by opening a college bookstore in Lexington and then developing a highly successful national business buying and reselling used college textbooks. During the 1970s he started buying and selling farms. In the 1980s he became a developer of office buildings, a hotel, and subdivisions; a bank owner; a coal mine operator; and a multimillionaire. The range and diversity of his business enterprises and the boldness of his business deals attracted attention throughout the state. When he ran for governor, the major newspapers examined his financial dealings and holdings in great detail.

When Wilkinson entered the gubernatorial primary, it was his first effort to gain public office, though he had been finance chairman of Harvey Sloane's gubernatorial campaign in 1983 and had chaired John Y. Brown's abortive race for the Senate in 1984. He ran for governor on his record of achievement in business, and he brought to the campaign a reputation for hard work and determination. When Wilkinson announced for governor in September 1986, at age forty-five, he had already been building his organization and campaigning across the state for many months.

The Brown Campaign

John Y. Brown entered the campaign as the acknowledged front-runner, and this was an important asset. He had little difficulty raising large sums of money. Although he had been distrusted in the past by many party activists, in 1987 he was able to enlist the support of many Democratic activists who believed he could win. Polls showed substantial approval of his record as governor, his fiscal conservatism, and his honesty—though there was some concern about his life-style and gambling.

There were some liabilities, though the Brown campaign did not seem to recognize them. Some voters wondered about Brown's motivation for running again; did he have goals he wanted to achieve, or was he simply bored? There was a substantial bloc of voters, apparently, who were strongly anti-Brown and who were prepared to support whatever candidate seemed most likely to defeat Brown. While Brown's 1979 primary victory had been remarkable in many respects, it was based on only 29 percent of the vote. Finally, there was the inherent disadvantage of the front-runner status—the fact that it can lead to complacency.

In 1979 Brown had won the nomination by using television, a helicopter, and centralized phone banks, but without relying on traditional local organization. In 1987, however, the Brown campaign set up an organization in every county. These organizations included a number of local and legislative officeholders and other activists who expected him to be a winner; they also included a number of business and professional persons, perhaps attracted by his governing style. Despite this organizational base, the Brown campaign appeared to attach less importance to organization than to the media campaign and the personal campaigning of the candidate.

The Brown campaign spent almost $3.5 million during the primary, second only to the Wilkinson campaign. These financial resources were entirely adequate, enabling Brown to buy all of the television advertising time that he needed. The remarkable thing about the Brown campaign fund was that it came almost entirely from outside sources rather than from Brown himself. While John Y. Brown could have afforded to make a large investment in his campaign, as he had done eight years earlier, he found it to be unnecessary. In the first two months after he filed, from February 20 to April 21, the Brown campaign raised $2 million, setting a new record in Kentucky politics for concentrated fund-raising. When the *Courier-Journal* analyzed the sources of the first $2 million, it found that the average contribution was nearly $1,200 and that large proportions came from business and professional persons. The explanation for Brown's remarkable success in raising funds seems clear: most everyone expected him to win, and there are many people who want to support a probable winner.

The basic strategy of the Brown campaign was that of a front-runner. It was important to foster the widely held belief that Brown was going to win. It was unnecessary to take risks, to attack other candidates, to make expensive policy commitments. Brown's own strategy seemed to be to run like an incumbent, to tell the voters: "If you liked my first administration, you'll like this one even better." The implicit motto of the campaign seemed to be: "Four More Years!" In debates he often ducked specific questions about public policy by promising to govern as well as he had done in the past. One of the weaknesses of his strategy was a failure to make clear to the voters why he was running for governor.

Until the last few weeks, it seems fair to say that Brown dominated the campaign, at least as a celebrity and the front-runner. He campaigned harder than he had in 1979 but less intensively than most of the other candidates. He reached about 100 counties, traveling more often by automobile and less by helicopter. He attracted good crowds, but those who came to see him often seemed more curious than committed. One reporter who covered Brown extensively said that his campaign visits followed a set routine. He would usually arrive in a van and move through the crowd trying to shake every hand but paying no attention to what people said. He would often give a ten-minute speech, talking about what a good governor he had been in tough economic conditions and how he would do even better in more prosperous times.

In late May, under the headline "Brown's campaign style frustrates his opponents," the *Courier-Journal* (May 21, 1988, p.1) reported on Brown's visit to a picnic in Warren County. Brown arrived late with his wife Phyllis, shook hands for a few minutes, gave a short interview to a local television crew, passed up the chance to make a speech, and drove away. Steve Beshear's wife Jane had been working the crowd for two hours before the Browns arrived. But, despite the brevity of their appearance, "the people in the line and at the tables talked of the Browns, the Browns, the Browns. And little else."

The Beshear Campaign

Steve Beshear started the campaign as the front-runner, but he lost that status quickly when Brown entered the race. He had the support of some leading figures in the Collins administration, though Collins herself took no stand and there was no concerted effort by her administration to support him. He had the support of a number of officeholders and activists around the state, though this was not an unmixed blessing. One reporter commented that the crowds attending Beshear rallies were often small and were made up largely of "political hacks," persons who had a stake in a Beshear victory.

Beshear had the support of the state AFL-CIO, though some unions were supporting Grady Stumbo. Terry Turner, who managed the AFL-CIO campaign, told *Courier-Journal* political columnist Bob Johnson that labor organized its largest campaign ever to mobilize labor voters, "and the result was the efforts were just literally meaningless. Our efforts just pale in comparison to what can be done on television today if you've got the money" (*C-J*, June 14, 1988, p. D1). Beshear also had the endorsement of the Kentucky Education Association (KEA), which provided about $90,000 worth of cash and political services at all levels. The political director of KEA shared Turner's belief that the messages of his organization were drowned out by the much more extensive political messages on television. Beshear agrees with the viewpoint that television advertising has undermined the influence of organizations on their members. Beshear was also the target of some organized groups, notably antiabortion and fundamentalist groups, but it is difficult to judge their effectiveness.

Beshear has always had a reputation as a strong organizer, and he believes that he had the best county organization in the race, with nearly all of the counties organized. He attempted to keep the support of those who had worked for him in the first two statewide races, many of whom had been inexperienced in politics when they first supported him. Some observers felt that Beshear had not worked effectively enough to maintain the organization that he had created in the first two races. In some counties he relied heavily on local officeholders; in Jefferson County, for example, the county sheriff provided the core of the organization. In putting together his county organizations, he tried to combine these established Beshear supporters with some of the traditional courthouse workers who were now joining his camp, as well as other activists who were primarily interested in issues. There were some doubts about whether this blend of supporters produced effective county organizations.

The Beshear campaign spent about $2.9 million, more than a million behind Wilkinson and some $600,000 behind Brown, but a substantial sum for a Kentucy political campaign. Beshear, who lacks the personal wealth of Brown and Wilkinson, ultimately loaned his campaign $130,000. Beshear's ability to raise that much money was impressive. He got a head start in the fund-raising race; he had raised $1 million by the end of 1986. During most of that time Beshear was perceived as the front-runner, and there was uncertainty about whether Brown would enter the race. In the last month of the campaign, as Beshear began to lose ground in the polls, he raised only half a million, compared to $1.4 million raised by Brown. Beshear believed that he was significantly handicapped in the television advertising campaign because Brown and Wilkinson had more resources. But the Beshear campaign ran a great deal of television advertising, and it is unlikely that the discrepancy in funding was crucial to the outcome of the campaign.

It is difficult to define the underlying strategy of the Beshear campaign, and this may have been one of Beshear's fundamental problems. The Beshear campaign never defined a clear theme or gave the voters a reason to vote for him. As lieutenant governor, Beshear had organized the Kentucky Tomorrow Commission to develop long-range plans but made little use of its findings. He prepared a number of position papers on issues, but they had little impact on the voters. Once Brown had entered the race, the Beshear campaign became obsessed with the necessity of knocking Brown off his pedestal, and it eventually decided that this could only be accomplished through negative advertising. We will examine the consequences of that decision later in the chapter when we look at the media campaign.

Steve Beshear was not a natural born campaigner. He campaigned tirelessly because it had to be done, but he never seemed to be enjoying it. Beshear told us that, while he enjoys meeting people, a statewide campaign is too long, too frantic, and too tiring. Beshear can be an effective public speaker, but in this political campaign he was too often on the offensive, making snide comments about his opponents. Perhaps because of this, he succeeded in personally antagonizing a number of others in the race.

The Stumbo Campaign

Grady Stumbo began the 1987 gubernatorial campaign with a number of assets. He had gained name recognition, political experience, and wide respect from his strong showing in the 1983 campaign. He was the only candidate from eastern Kentucky. He had a chance to capture labor's endorsement. He had some well-defined issues as part of the populist theme in his campaign. But he no longer had the support of John Y. Brown or the incumbent administration. He was running against two millionaires, and he had neither personal resources nor skill in money raising.

Stumbo had not had an extensive county organization in 1983 but had relied on help from the Brown administration and the United Mine Workers. Four years later he still lacked an effective local organization, though he received some help from organized labor. He did not have staff members at the state level who had the skill and experience to build a county-level campaign. Most local Democratic officeholders and activists were seeking a candidate who seemed to have a better chance of winning.

Stumbo's campaign was severely limited by the shortage of financial resources, a problem that had plagued him in the 1983 campaign. Then he had been criticized for borrowing money in order to make personal loans to his campaign. In 1987 he was more cautious. Stumbo spent a little more than $750,000 in the campaign, with $150,000 coming from a personal loan. His campaign fund was $2 million less than Beshear's and over $3.5 million less than Wilkinson's. As a result he was able to use television commercials only sparingly. On several occasions during the campaign, he ran thirty-minute commercials on local channels in less expensive time periods, gearing these to his fund-raising efforts. Apparently, he raised enough from these commercials to pay for them, but they seemed to have little impact on the campaign. What he lacked in 1987, of course, were the fund-raising efforts of John Y. Brown and his friends, who had helped in 1983.

The Stumbo campaign strategy was apparently designed to broaden Stumbo's base of support. His speeches continued to be populist in tone: attacking the vested interests and the high cost of campaigning, speaking up for the working man, urging greater attention to health care and the needs of eastern Kentucky. But he made a conscious effort to appeal more to urban areas and to business and professional people. His campaign style was more conservative, and he dressed more conservatively as he campaigned across the state. As one observer put it, "Stumbo's campaign never found a groove and never got moving." He failed to generate the enthusiasm among many voters that he had enjoyed four years earlier as a fresh face in politics.

He spent less time on the campaign trail in 1987 than he had four years earlier. He was not particularly effective in working the crowds and making small talk. One feature of his campaign that worked well was working briefly at various jobs, such as a waiter in a diner or a grocery store clerk. His campaign was chronically underfinanced and understaffed, and it was often poorly organized. One example of poor organization was a speech on a flatbed truck in a Bowling Green parking lot late on a Monday afternoon. There had been no advance work for the speech. He had a small band to help attract a crowd, but no one could find an electrical outlet to plug in the instruments and speakers. And so Stumbo spoke to the band members, his driver, the local campaign chairman, and a "crowd" of sixteen. One Saturday afternoon a five-county Stumbo rally in West Liberty, complete with free food, attracted only about seventy people. Whatever message Stumbo was preaching, it could not have much impact if he could not reach the voters in person and could not afford much television advertising.

The Carroll Campaign

When Julian Carroll began to drop hints that he was considering another run for the governorship, most observers were puzzled and surprised. They did not know why he would want to undertake such an effort; and they did not understand why Carroll, a skilled and experienced politician, thought he had a chance of winning. Despite his knowledge of state politics and government, his skill as an orator and debater, and his heavy commitment of time and energy, Carroll faced one overwhelming obstacle. Because almost no one believed he could win, there were few who were willing to commit their time and resources to his campaign.

Carroll's geographic base of support was in western Kentucky. A native of Paducah, he was the only true western Kentuckian in the race. He also sought to build a political base on the Christian vote, located primarily in the western counties. For years Carroll had been a lay preacher and had cultivated ties with church organizations. He had been strengthening these ties for several years before the 1987 primary, and he hoped that he could mobilize this bloc of church people to work actively in his campaign. Carroll was disappointed in the campaign and electoral support that he actually got from these groups. He was surprised to find that Christian groups were particularly unforgiving of the scandals that had plagued his administration. He also found that some of the church groups were strongly anti-Beshear, because of Beshear's position on abortion and on the Ten Commandments in the schools. They wanted to support whichever candidate had the best chance of beating Beshear and did not perceive Carroll to be that candidate.

When he ran successfully for statewide office in 1971 and 1975, Julian Carroll had a strong county-level organization, consisting of local officeholders and active Democratic workers. But twelve years later, most of that organization had faded away. In the intervening elections the Carroll loyalists had transferred their loyalties to the other candidates for whom they had worked. Like all pragmatic political workers, they wanted to support a winner in 1987, and few of them saw Carroll as a potential winner. Carroll recruited a few of his old supporters and some of his Christian allies to organize counties for him in 1987, but the results were disappointing. There were a relatively small number of counties—mostly western and southern—in which he had a modest organization. Carroll told someone that the person running his campaign in Louisville was "the only one left" of his supporters. In a few counties in western Kentucky, he was apparently able to trade support with one or another candidate for statewide office, to supplement the efforts of his own organization.

The Carroll campaign had a major problem: the shortage of resources. His campaign spent a little less than Stumbo's, just under $750,000. In April Carroll borrowed $250,000 to loan to his campaign, but he eventually raised enough money to repay the loan. He resisted the temptation to loan more to the campaign late in the race when it was obvious that he was not going to win. Carroll had difficulty raising money for the obvious reason that few expected him to win. The consequence was that he did not run any advertising statewide and was limited to some advertising on television stations covering western Kentucky. Whether he would have won a significantly larger number of votes if more television viewers had been able to see and hear his message we will never know.

It is difficult to define a consistent, coherent strategy that guided the Carroll campaign. Before launching the campaign, Carroll held a lengthy press conference in which he tried to deal with the issue of scandals in his administration, admitting some mistakes and denying other charges. Perhaps as a consequence of this, and perhaps because he was not perceived as a serious challenger, other candidates did not discuss these problems during the campaign. It might be said that Carroll's basic strategy was to use whatever resources he had. He built county organizations where he could. In his speeches he tried out a variety of issues—moral, economic, educational—looking for something that might work. Aside from his criticism of Beshear on moral issues, he rarely attacked the other candidates. He reminded voters of what had been accomplished in his administration and tried to present an image as the most knowledgeable, experienced candidate in the race.

Carroll campaigned personally in about half of the counties, the most limited of all the gubernatorial campaigns. He campaigned the old-fashioned way, shaking hands, greeting old friends, reminding those he met of what he had done for them during his administration. And he gave old-fashioned stump speeches in his unique manner, combining the styles of preacher and politician.

At the Fancy Farm picnic in August 1986, his emphasis on moral and family issues suggested that these would become the main focus of his campaign. But in succeeding months he largely ignored these issues, talking instead about his proposals for economic development, educational reform, and curbing drug abuse. When he was campaigning in Frankfort, he claimed to be the state workers' best friend. Because he only ran a few television commercials, on western stations, he had little opportunity to test the effectiveness of these various themes in advertising.

The Wilkinson Campaign

When Wallace Wilkinson began traveling around the state to enlist support, he was a well-known businessman, at least in the Lexington area, but he was totally unknown as a political candidate. In December 1986, after many months of campaigning, only 44 percent of voters polled by the *Courier-Journal* had heard of Wilkinson (while other candidates ranged from 72 to 91 percent), and only 4 percent supported him for governor. Wilkinson's major asset was his wealth, which he was willing to spend generously in the campaign. Another asset was his own personality—his unflagging energy and determination.

It was in 1984, after the collapse of John Y. Brown's campaign for the Senate, that Wilkinson began to build a statewide organization. He began developing the contacts that he had made in the Sloane campaign. He started hiring a few staff members to help with organizational work. One of these was Donna Moloney, who had extensive experience in state and national campaigns; she joined his firm as a public relations expert in August 1984 and was quickly put to work coordinating contacts with supporters and planning meetings and events, including a series of political dinners. Later in the campaign she took on the job as office manager and shared much of the responsibility for scheduling.

Over a period of three years, the Wilkinsons held dinners at their home about once a week, to which they invited ten to twenty people. They would have a chance to listen to Wilkinson, ask him questions, and discuss the governorship. Staff members took notes of issues and questions raised at these dinners. Most of those invited on a particular evening came from a single county, and about eighty counties were covered over the three years. At first, most of those invited were persons he had met in the course of business, but the lists grew to include more of the prominent leaders and political figures in the counties. Wilkinson also utilized the contacts of key staff people who had been more active in politics. The staff would follow up these dinners, contacting those who had attended and collecting more names of potential supporters from them. This method of operating enabled Wilkinson to build a county-level organization that was more broadly based than the traditional Democratic party workers at the courthouse level. Reporters covering the campaign were surprised by Wilkinson's ability to build such a strong local organization in a nontraditional mold.

Wallace Wilkinson spent almost $4.3 million in the primary campaign. When the postprimary financial report was filed, it showed that Wilkinson had loaned his campaign more than $2.3 million; but by the beginning of October, enough money had been raised to repay the entire loan from Wilkinson. Obviously, the Wilkinson campaign had enough resources to maintain a large state organization and to buy all the television time that it wanted. He outspent Brown by some $800,000, but the battle of the millionaires was not decided by the difference in spending levels. Wilkinson and Brown each had all of the resources needed, and each could have provided more money if necessary from personal funds. Wilkinson's advantage over Beshear was greater, some $1.4 million. But Wilkinson's major financial advantage over Beshear was his personal wealth. This enabled Wilkinson to plan an expensive organizational and media campaign from the beginning, secure in the knowledge that he could spend whatever was necessary. Beshear had to plan his media spending more cautiously because funds were not unlimited.

His extensive financial resources enabled Wallace Wilkinson to start building an organization early and to create a large campaign staff. Early in the campaign he utilized several persons already working in his business enterprises; later on more of his campaign staff were working full time. By the time the campaign reached its climax in May 1987, the staff totaled thirty persons.

One of the key figures who served on the staff for more than a year was

Danny Briscoe, who had particular responsibility for media, issues, and polling. He had run Harvey Sloane's campaign for mayor and John Y. Brown's brief campaign for the Senate, as well as serving in state government. Bruce Wilkinson, the candidate's nephew who had worked in his business enterprises for twenty years, was another who started working on the campaign early. Doug Alexander was hired as the campaign press secretary early in 1986. He was a public relations consultant, with no previous experience in political campaigns. In the summer of 1986, two field representatives were hired, one for the eastern part of the state and one for western Kentucky. John Kelly, a young investment banker with political experience in Louisville, worked throughout the campaign as the advance man.

Although Wilkinson initially financed most of the campaign himself, as the campaign progressed fund-raising became an increasingly important part of the enterprise. Wilkinson picked as his chief fund-raiser Roger Wells, a longtime friend from Glasgow. A number of other persons played major roles in campaign funding, including Floyd Poore, who was responsible for raising funds in northern Kentucky. He had been a fund-raiser for Martha Layne Collins and had served for a time as transportation secretary in the Collins administration.

One other staff member played a key role in the campaign for a time, starting in September 1986. J.R. Miller was a veteran political leader in his mid-seventies from Owensboro, with decades of experience in organizing political campaigns, particularly at the local level. He had played a key role in Wendell Ford's campaigns and had served as state Democratic chairman when Ford was governor. Miller's major responsibility was organization at the county level. He had more extensive contacts, particularly in western Kentucky, with local officeholders and activists than did anyone else on the staff. Because of his personality and experience, Miller also wanted to play a major role as a strategist in the campaign. Eventually, this led to conflicts with Danny Briscoe; at stake were questions of strategy and the more basic question of who was running the campaign. Early in 1987 Miller left the campaign.

The Wilkinson campaign had ample financial resources, a large staff, an extensive county organization, and an energetic candidate; but four months before the May primary the campaign was making little headway and could accurately be described as "dead in the water." Polls showed Wilkinson getting only 4 or 5 percent of the vote and not gaining. Of course, there was reason to hope that Wilkinson would gain strength when the television advertising campaign was in full swing, but that would be possible only if the campaign was able to develop themes and strategies that appealed to the voters.

The major problem facing the Wilkinson campaign early in 1987 was lack of agreement on basic strategy for the media campaign. In some respects the campaign had a clear strategy. It began with the assumption that the major asset of the campaign was the candidate: Wallace Wilkinson. He was willing to invest unlimited time and energy in personal campaigning, and he was very effective in dealing with people one-on-one. There was also consensus that a successful campaign required both a strong county-level organization and a large-scale media campaign. In that sense, the Wilkinson strategy resembled Collins's successful game plan in 1983 more than Brown's winning strategy in 1979, which relied primarily on television. But the campaign did not yet have a central theme that could be developed in television ads. Wilkinson needed a theme that would distinguish him from the other candidates; he needed to explain why he was running for governor. As one staff member said at the time, "I'm not sure they know what our message is out there." The voters did not know what the Wilkinson message was because the campaign leadership was still searching for a message.

In January 1987 Danny Briscoe called Peter Hart, the veteran campaign consultant in Washington, for the name of someone who might be hired to rescue the campaign and, more specifically, to serve as a strategist and to develop the major themes for the media campaign. Peter Hart recommended James Carville, and on February 1 he arrived in Frankfort to begin the rescue operation.

Carville, a native of Louisiana now working out of Austin, Texas, is a relative newcomer in the consulting field. In 1984 he ran Lloyd Doggett's successful Texas primary and unsuccessful general election campaign for the Senate and in 1986 managed the upset victory of Bob Casey for governor in Pennsylvania. He is a colorful character, who calls himself a "cowboy" and dresses appropriately. One journalist described him as "a political Clint Eastwood. He rides in alone, blows away the bad guys, then rides out of town again—for a fee." Carville is also a thoughtful and articulate professional who can make a convincing case for his theories about how to win media campaigns. Carville had managed the previous campaigns in which he had participated. His role in the Wilkinson campaign was more specialized. After diagnosing the problems afflicting the campaign, he was to develop strategies and major themes. In practice, he dealt with every aspect of communications, writing speeches, composing questions for polls, designing the television ads. His responsibilities overlapped those of Danny Briscoe. In theory that should have led to conflict; in practice they worked closely together. We will discuss Carville's contributions to the campaign in more detail when we examine the role of issues and media in the gubernatorial campaign.

Reporters who covered Wallace Wilkinson on the campaign trail were amazed by his performance, particularly his effectiveness in meeting voters one by one. Ferrell Wellman, the television journalist who has been covering campaigns for twenty years, told us, "I have never seen a candidate so single-minded, so determined, so aggressive, and with such an ability to campaign long hours." At any gathering where he appeared, he shook every hand in sight; someone said, "You can't just walk by him when he is campaigning."

Wilkinson once described his campaign style as "hand-to-hand combat." He was a very physical campaigner, grabbing, hugging, and even slapping voters. One observer said that Wilkinson "has this great touchy-feely thing on the campaign trail." One reporter described him as "a great grabber, like Wendell Ford." Someone else claimed that Wilkinson has "a very meaningful handshake." (This was the campaign in which Beshear was criticized publicly for having a "weak handshake.") One veteran observer compared Wilkinson's one-on-one style to that of Chandler in his prime. He was particularly effective campaigning in the rural areas, where his personal style of campaigning may be most appreciated. Wallace Wilkinson's wife Martha campaigned much of the time on her own and matched him in vigor and enthusiasm if not in grabbing and hugging.

The Wilkinson campaign style was more than just a physical phenomenon. He created the impression that he genuinely enjoyed campaigning and meeting people, even when he had been doing it for hours on end. He was egalitarian in his approach, spending as much time with someone who was unemployed as with a banker. He is a great salesman, and one of his major accomplishments in one-on-one conversations was convincing people that he had a chance to be elected and that he would make a great governor.

Wilkinson was less effective as a stump speaker than he was as a handshaker. The substantive content of his speeches was not memorable, but he delivered the message well. He talked about his personal background, growing up in rural Casey County, his experience as a businessman, and some of the themes of his campaign: the charge that state government was ignoring many rural counties, the need to end "business as usual in Kentucky politics," and the need for new ideas in Frankfort.

The Media Campaigns

The conventional wisdom among politicians and reporters is that the 1987 gubernatorial primary was decided by the media campaign and particularly by the television ads of the major candidates, and there is no reason to doubt this thesis.

All of the gubernatorial candidates had a full array of professional campaign consultants, particularly media advisers and pollsters. Brown's media consultant was Robert Squire, one of the best known and most successful in the country. There was some criticism by other members of the campaign staff that Squire had too much control over the campaign but did not devote enough personal attention to the race and was slow to recognize that Brown was in deep trouble. Beshear's media consultant was the Doak-Shrum firm; his pollster was Hickman-Maslin; and Tommy Preston, a veteran political consultant from Lexington, handled local aspects such as relations with the press. There were reports of friction between the Preston organization and the national consultants; and after Beshear's defeat both his state and national consultants, perhaps inevitably, came under criticism. Wallace Wilkinson hired Sawyer-Miller as media consultant and Mark Mellman as his pollster but relied very heavily for strategic planning on James Carville, who worked in headquarters for the last four months of the campaign. Wilkinson also hired a Lexington governmental firm, State Research Associates, to carry out research and help him develop positions on a variety of issues.

Most voters learn about the candidates and issues in a statewide campaign, not by personal contact with candidates or campaign workers, but by the newspaper, radio, and television coverage of what the candidates say and by paid political advertising, primarily on television. We will examine each of these in turn.

Free Media Coverage

During the campaign the media reported occasionally on what candidates were saying in their speeches, particularly those delivered to organized groups (labor, business, education), and on what they said in televised debates. There were two debates televised live on Kentucky Educational Television (KET), the first on April 13 sponsored by the Prichard Committee and devoted to education issues and the second on May 13 following the normal KET format and covering all issues.

The first KET debate gave the candidates a chance to demonstrate that each was committed to improving education in the state, including the continuation of the educational reforms adopted by the legislature in 1985 and 1986. Clearly, the Prichard Committee, which sponsored the debates, was hoping for such commitments from the candidates. For the most part, they complied. Wallace Wilkinson, however, made it clear that he was dissatisfied with these approaches and that he wanted to try new methods of improving education, including benchmark schools and incentive pay to teachers in schools that had outstanding records.

The reporters inevitably raised questions about educational reforms, such as how smaller classes and higher teachers' pay could be funded; and the answers to these questions had a significant effect on the campaign. As might be expected, the candidates were most reluctant to promise higher taxes. John Y. Brown indicated that local units of government should pay more of the cost of education, and he favored repealing House Bill 44, which places severe limits on the levels of local property taxes. His opponents, particularly Beshear and Wilkinson, were to use this statement in weeks to come as proof that Brown would be a "high tax" governor. (Beshear ducked the issue of H.B. 44 by saying the legislature would never repeal it.) Wilkinson made clear his opposition to a tax increase and announced that he would raise revenue instead through a state lottery—the issue that was later to become the keystone of his campaign.

Taxes and revenue, not surprisingly, played a major role in the May 13 debate on KET, though by that point in the campaign each of the candidates was repeating positions that had been emphasized both in speeches and in advertising. Wilkinson repeated his proposal for a lottery and insisted that it could be implemented by the end of 1988 if approved by the voters in November of that year. Stumbo pledged to find the necessary resources to pay for educational reform, increasing taxes on corporations and the wealthy if necessary. Brown, Beshear, and Carroll each indicated that changing the state income tax system to conform to the new federal law might be a reasonable way to raise revenue if that proved necessary, while Wilkinson flatly opposed such a step. Under questioning from Beshear, Brown changed his position and opposed the repeal of H.B. 44.

The debate was enlivened by some interchanges between candidates. Several of the candidates made personal attacks on Beshear. Beshear predicted that Stumbo would drop out of the race in return for a promise of a job by Brown. Brown refused to disclose more about his personal finances. Beshear repeated his standard line about the importance of integrity. Carroll criticized *Courier-Journal* reporter Bob Johnson for asking him why he entered the race since no one expected him to win.

The debate revealed once again the casual approach that John Y. Brown was taking to the campaign and his apparent failure to prepare for the debates. Brown continued to avoid specific commitments about what he would do as governor, saying at one point about his first administration, "It'd be more of the same, but better." At one point he said that he favored limiting state employees to 30,000 and seemed surprised to be told the present total was 34,000. When asked why he had not been actively involved in promoting educational reform since his first administration, he said, "I've been waiting for this job to turn up." When given a good opportunity to explain what motivations had led him to run again, he said (probably very accurately), "I dabbled around some in business but really didn't find that that interested me. I really miss being governor."

The two televised debates were important not only because of the coverage given to them by the media but also because the positions taken by the candidates—particularly on taxes—became the themes of televised commercials. The debates were particularly important to Wilkinson, as an underdog, because they attracted attention to his position on the issues and provided him with a platform to launch his campaign for a lottery. Candidates for office are always competing for coverage in the media, and some do this more successfully than others. Perhaps the best example of this is the tactics used in the last ten days or so by the Wilkinson campaign. Wilkinson, using a helicopter, moved from one part of the state to another, making speeches and attending rallies. By repeated visits to various counties, he was able to get continuing attention in the local media. Because his extensive travels coincided with polls showing he was gaining, the media gave particular attention to his campaign.

In the last week before the election, the Wilkinson organization launched a twenty-five-hour marathon. While obviously an atypical example, it illustrates the intensity and enthusiasm of the Wilkinson campaign. Wilkinson flew from one stop to the next. The trip started in Casey County in the morning, moved on to Elizabethtown for a visit to a senior citizens' center, then to a restaurant in Fulton, and to Louisville for a press conference. There was a visit to Maysville, a trip into Ohio to talk about the lottery used there, and a return to Maysville for an evening rally. Back in Louisville late in the evening, Wilkinson visited a bowling alley, a restaurant, a grocery store, and the United Parcel Service headquarters that operates all night. Then he went to a shop to buy T-shirts with the slogan "25 hour day" for everyone in the entourage. Early in the morning Wilkinson was in Lexington to meet with the early shift of Lextran bus workers and ended the marathon with a press conference in Frankfort.

Television Advertising

The television advertising campaign was fought out largely among Brown, Beshear, and Wilkinson. Because of his limited budget, Stumbo ran a smaller number of ads that attracted less attention. His advertising did not have enough impact either to help his campaign or to damage any of the others. For these reasons we will concentrate on the advertising battles of Brown, Beshear, and Wilkinson.

During the early weeks of the television campaign, in March and early April, each of the major campaigns ran "feel-good" ads to try to develop a positive image about its candidate. Wilkinson was the first entry into the television commercial derby. One of his ads attacked old-style politics and urged a fresh approach to state problems; another summarized his background and his rise from poverty. They had no appreciable impact. The early Brown ads focused on the candidate's personality and his return to politics. One critic described their theme: "I was a great governor. Now I'm back. Aren't you lucky!" There was no effort by Brown to articulate his reasons for running again or to establish any theme to the campaign. The Beshear ads were also focused on the candidate and were rather bland. Some emphasized his record of office. Another commercial showed him at home with his kids, talking about the importance of education, and ended with him shooting a basket (successfully, of course).

Wilkinson and Beshear each ran an ad that stirred up some controversy without having much immediate impact. Late in March Wilkinson held a press conference to attack the deal made by the "Collins-Beshear" administration to bring the Toyota plant to Kentucky. He charged that the administration had paid too high a price and repeated his criticisms in a commercial. While most observers considered the attack on Toyota a mistake, the Wilkinson campaign believed it had been successful in making voters pay attention to Wilkinson for the first time.

In an effort to dramatize the importance of keeping industry in the state, the Beshear campaign ran an ad showing the candidate swinging a bat in an empty lot in front of an abandoned factory; in the background was a sign with the name of the company that makes the "Louisville Slugger" bat, a sign partly covered by a "CLOSED" sign. The campaign had failed to get permission from the company, which filed suit against Beshear, pointing out that it had not closed but just moved across the river into Indiana. Onlookers debated whether the Beshear campaign had been hurt by its mistakes or helped by the attention being given to its ad.

Early in April Brown appeared to have a comfortable lead in the race. His own polls showed that he had about 40 percent of the vote and a 15 percent margin over Beshear. There seemed to be no reason to change the advertising tactics of the Brown campaign. Beshear's situation was entirely different. The polls showed that he had a favorable image with voters, but he seemed to be locked into second place. In early April Beshear's advisers suggested that the only way to overtake Brown was to launch a negative campaign against him. They recognized that it was a gamble, because a negative campaign might seem to be out of character for Beshear and might hurt his image and his standing in the polls. But they believed it was the only way that Brown's strength could be undermined.

Based on polling data, the Beshear advisers believed that Brown's lifestyle was his greatest vulnerability. If this was true, a negative campaign that was personal in nature would be the most effective; it would also carry the greatest risk of hurting Beshear. By mid-April it became clear that Brown might also be vulnerable on policy questions, particularly taxation. The decision was made to run a series of negative ads, attacking Brown's life-style and his policies, and the campaign was launched at the beginning of May. One typical commercial, which was run frequently, included a series of news reports and headlines: "Governor Brown called today for deep cuts for the poor, the sick, and public schools. . . . Abandoning the state budget debate, Governor Brown left for Florida. . . . In a breaking scandal, Governor Brown admitted losing more than $1 million in one bad night at Vegas. . . . Brown admits gambling, denies use of cocaine. . . . Governor Brown was closely linked to the principal target in the yearlong gambling and narcotics investigation. . . . This was the sixth tax increase of Governor Brown's four years in office."

The Beshear campaign also ran a commercial poking fun at the Brown life-style, using the format of the well-known television program "Lifestyles of the Rich and Famous" and a Robin Leach clone as narrator. A couple of excerpts will capture the flavor of the ad: "Living in grand style in New York, Florida, California, Las Vegas, and occasionally, even Kentucky. . . . But, out of office, the fab couple isn't on the A-list anymore. So they're running for governor a second time. . . . From fried-chicken franchise to one of the world's most high-rolling life-styles. Financed not simply with his money, but with yours." The humorous approach, even if a little heavy-handed, might have been the most effective and perhaps least risky for Beshear. The tactic had worked in the 1984 "hound-dog" commercials that Mitch McConnell used against Senator Huddleston. But the "life-styles" commercial was a sixty-second spot, and it is difficult to buy sixty seconds of political advertising on many stations. One consequence was that the commercial ran infrequently and was seen less often than the other negative ads.

The Beshear advertising campaign seems to have had several effects. It damaged Brown, it hurt Beshear's positive image, and it forced Brown—however slowly and reluctantly—to launch a counterattack. Brown and Beshear launched a series of television commercials attacking each other but focusing primarily on policy questions and particularly taxes. Each was trying to pin the "high-tax" label on the other. Brown's commercials claimed that Beshear was an irresponsible politician whose many promises to special interests would inevitably lead to higher taxes. Beshear focused on the property tax issue. In one commercial, Beshear sat in front of a television set on which Brown was shown in the April 13 debate urging repeal of the cap on property tax; Beshear punched the button on his remote control and ran the clip again.

Inevitably, this debate played into Wallace Wilkinson's hands. A Wilkinson adviser saw a Brown and a Beshear commercial run back-to-back one day and was inspired to capitalize on them. One Wilkinson commercial used the Brown and Beshear ads on taxes and said: "Aren't you fed up? Then speak up. Vote for Wallace Wilkinson." Another commercial ran a graphic saying, "Steve Beshear says John Y. Brown will raise taxes," and then reversed the names on the screen, while the announcer said, "They're both right, and that's wrong. Brown and Beshear would fund their programs by raising your taxes." The ad concluded with Wilkinson saying, "We have a choice: higher taxes or a lottery."

The choice between higher taxes and a lottery became the main theme of the Wilkinson campaign, but it did not emerge until the last few weeks before the primary. When James Carville joined the campaign as chief strategist in February, he emphasized the importance of developing a single, consistent theme for the campaign, one that would distinguish Wilkinson from the other candidates. In his speeches and commercials, Wilkinson stressed the sense of optimism in the state, the need for fundamental change, the belief that Wilkinson could make a difference. A paragraph in a Wilkinson brochure summarized this often repeated theme: "Kentuckians are proud. They're winners. The people here can do anything but their leadership has failed them. We can't continue to watch our kids leave Kentucky for better opportunities. They do not go because they want to, but because they think they have to. We owe them more than that. We're better than that. On our worst day, we're better than that."

A more specific theme of Wilkinson speeches and ads was the need for jobs and economic growth: "We need jobs in Kentucky, and I know how to build them. I know how to attract business development. I've been doing it my whole life. We need new ideas. That's how I built my success here. We need to jump-start this state's economy! We can't be competitive following leaders who've never known how to compete."

While these themes appeared to strike a responsive cord among many voters, particularly in rural areas, they were not powerful enough to put Wilkinson in front. By mid-April, the polls suggested he had no more than 10 percent of the vote, and by early May he was in the 13 to 15 percent range. All the experts agree: The issue that turned the election around was the proposal of a lottery instead of taxes.

The lottery made Wilkinson's stand against higher taxes credible. Most candidates running for governor in Kentucky promise no new taxes, and those who are elected often find it necessary to ignore these promises. Voters are familiar with this pattern, and they have learned to be suspicious of these promises. But Wilkinson offered the lottery as an alternative, one that seemed both realistic and attractive to many voters. When his opponents charged that a lottery could not raise enough money to fill the revenue gap, Wilkinson simply claimed that they were wrong; and the voters had no reason to doubt his assertions. The lottery also provided Wilkinson with an effective vehicle for attacking his opponents. As we have seen, Wilkinson capitalized on the Beshear and Brown commercials that accused each other of favoring higher taxes. He ran ads saying that both accusations were correct and that he offered a choice between higher taxes and a lottery.

The Wilkinson themes are illustrated by one ad that ran late in the campaign: "John Y. Brown and Steve Beshear call for higher taxes and oppose a state lottery. But that means you pay for the same old programs the same old way. Well, Kentucky's got a choice. New Leadership Wallace Wilkinson says no to new taxes. He proposes a state lottery, new ideas to get Kentucky moving again."

The other advantage of the lottery issue is that it appealed to large numbers of Kentuckians who wanted an opportunity to play the lottery. After Wilkinson began stressing the lottery, one reporter traveling with Beshear heard lots of factory workers asking Beshear if he was for a lottery, and he waffled on the issue. One voter was asked why he had switched allegiance from Brown to Wilkinson. He said that he and four of his friends had been driving to Cincinnati every Friday night to buy lottery tickets, and they were tired of making the drive. There were examples of persons who paid little attention to the campaign but who told friends they were going to vote for "that guy who wants a lottery."

The lottery issue was a valuable one for Wilkinson because it appealed to his natural constituency. Wilkinson was at his best among rural voters, and he also did well among working class voters in the cities. Neither Beshear nor Brown had a personal style that appealed to these groups, and some of them obviously resented Brown's wealth and celebrity status. But they liked Wilkinson's style, they disliked the idea of tax increases, and many of them welcomed the chance to play the lottery. The lottery also fit Wilkinson's theme of being antiestablishment. As Carville explained it, all of the "right people" said that we didn't need a lottery, that it would be bad for people; but the people knew what they wanted.

The lottery was not, of course, a new issue. It had been around for a long time, and there had been unsuccessful efforts in the legislature to adopt a constitutional amendment to permit a lottery. The conventional wisdom was that a lottery could not be passed because of opposition by religious groups in the Bible Belt. Julian Carroll told us that the church-oriented voters in western Kentucky, whom he knew best, were strongly opposed to both a lottery and higher taxes; but forced to make a choice, many of them decided that the lottery was the lesser of the two evils.

The Wilkinson campaign staff did not recognize the potency of the lottery issue early in the campaign. In the first KET debate on April 13, Wilkinson proposed that the state raise revenue for education through a lottery instead of higher taxes. The next day Martha Wilkinson and two other women spent the day campaigning in rural sections of Clark County. They were surprised to find voters much more enthusiastic about Wilkinson, primarily because of the lottery. Martha Wilkinson described a typical voter's comment about Wallace Wilkinson: "I watched that forum last night on TV, and he was the only one that made sense, and I love the lottery." Back in Lexington, the women reported their findings to Wilkinson, Danny Briscoe, and James Carville. The result was a decision to produce a commercial that contrasted the other candidates' support for taxes with Wilkinson's "new idea," a lottery instead of higher taxes. The commercial, which aired on April 21, launched the new phase of the advertising campaign. As the television advertising campaign progressed, it became clear to the Wilkinson staff that the commercials offering a lottery instead of higher taxes, in contrast to the "high-tax" stands of other candidates, were working, and this became the dominant theme of the campaign—both in commercials and in Wilkinson's speeches.

In the closing days of the campaign, Beshear and Brown began to attack Wilkinson's plan for a lottery. They argued that it would not raise enough revenue and would raise it too slowly to meet the state's immediate needs. Brown vacillated on the issue. He criticized it on the same grounds that Beshear used, said that he was not opposed to its being put on the ballot, and proposed a sweepstakes on the Kentucky Derby as an alternative. It was not a clear alternative to the simple theme of the Wilkinson campaign.

The Brown campaign had been very slow to react to the Wilkinson initiatives, but a few days before the election, Brown began running commercials directly attacking Wilkinson. Their theme was that no one really knew anything about Wilkinson and that he was promising expensive new programs that would inevitably lead to higher taxes. The commercials were not only too ineffective and too late to have any impact but, by directing an attack on Wilkinson, they may have reinforced the impression that Wilkinson was the only candidate who might beat Brown.

In the closing days of the campaign, Wilkinson ran a commercial described by one of Brown's staffers as the best commercial he had ever seen. It was simple and direct. Wilkinson stands on a flatbed speaking to a crowd. He asks, "Do you want higher taxes?" and the crowd shouts, "No." "Are you for a lottery?" and the crowd shouts, "Yes."

Polling the Volatile Voters

The 1987 gubernatorial primary was unusual because the preferences of voters changed dramatically in the closing weeks of the campaign. At least one-fifth of the voters remained undecided a week or two before the primary. John Y. Brown lost about ten percentage points in the last month of the campaign. And Wallace Wilkinson's support rose from less than 10 percent in late April to about 25 percent in the last week of the campaign to 35 percent on primary election day.

Public opinion polls played a more important role in this election than in any previous Kentucky election. For the first time, the *Courier-Journal* carried out three statewide polls on the governor's race, from mid-November to late April. More polls were carried out by the major candidates, including several one-day polls late in the race; and several of these polls were released to the media. The release of media and candidate polls late in the campaign appears to have had a significant impact on the race. By demonstrating that Wilkinson was gaining ground and had apparently overtaken Beshear, the polls convinced a number of anti-Brown voters that Wilkinson had the best chance of beating Brown. This led to late shifts of support from other candidates to Wilkinson.

A number of the candidates and campaign staff members whom we interviewed criticized the *Courier-Journal* for conducting and publishing polls and also criticized the media for paying so much attention to polls released by candidates. Obviously, polls showing a candidate far behind can have a devastating effect on his campaign and his ability to raise money and mobilize workers. In reality, of course, most major newspapers in most states publish the results of their own and other polls; and this situation is not likely to change.

The *Courier-Journal* released the results of three statewide Bluegrass polls, on December 7, March 15, and May 3 (table 6). All of the polls showed Brown comfortably ahead and Beshear in second. The poll released on May 3 was perhaps the most important because it suggested there had been little change over a six-week period. Brown still held more than one-third of the votes, Beshear was making little progress toward catching him, and Wilkinson was still back in the back with Stumbo and Carroll.

The Bluegrass polls can be criticized in one important respect. Each was conducted over a ten- to-twelve-day period and was released six days or more after it was completed. This leisurely approach to polling resulted in the release of results that were out of date by the time they were published. The *Courier-Journal* did not conduct a survey during the last four weeks of the campaign, and therefore it was unable to report the large shifts of opinion that took place. This is probably fortunate, because if a survey had been conducted as slowly as the earlier Bluegrass polls, the *Courier-Journal* would have been reporting a few days before the primary voting predictions that were seriously out of date.

On May 14 the press reported the results of polls released by Wilkin-

Table 6. Polling Results in 1987 Gubernatorial Primary (in Percentages)

Source	Bluegrass Polls			Beshear Poll	Wilkinson Poll	Brown Poll	Wilkinson Poll	Primary Outcome
Date of polling	Nov. 13-22	Feb. 26 -Mar. 9	Apr. 17-28	May 6-7	May 9-11	May 22	May 21	May 26
Date of release	Dec. 7	Mar. 15	May 3	May 14	May 14	—	—	—
Candidates:								
Wilkinson	4	7	9	13	15	21	25	35
Brown	20	35	36	31	29	31	27	26
Beshear	11	17	20	24	14	16		18
Stumbo	10	11	8	9	7	6	**	13
Carroll	11	10	9	7	7	6		7
Other	12*	—	—	—	—	—		1
Undecided	31	20	18	16	28	20		—
Total	99	100	100	100	100	100	100	100

Source: The Bluegrass polls were published in the *Courier-Journal*; the candidate polls were reported in the same newspaper.

*Harvey Sloane was listed in the first Bluegrass poll and got 12 percent.

**Data unavailable.

son and Beshear (table 6). Both showed that Brown was losing ground; Beshear's poll showed him gaining on Brown with Wilkinson far behind; Wilkinson's poll showed that Beshear was losing ground and that Wilkinson had overtaken him and was now in second place. The difference between the polls was largely a question of timing. In the closing days of the campaign, Wilkinson's pollster was conducting surveys almost continuously; his data showed that Wilkinson was still running behind Beshear on May 6 and 7 (the dates of the Beshear poll) but had moved ahead of him by May 9-11.

A major reason why the poll results shifted so drastically in the closing days of the campaign was that a large proportion of voters, one-fifth to one-fourth, remained undecided. Wilkinson's data (and to some extent Brown's) showed that the proportion of undecided was growing as late as the last week of the campaign. The Wilkinson staff argued that their candidate was likely to be the beneficiary of the large undecided vote; if these voters were going to support Brown or Beshear (the better-known candidates), they would have done so by that time.

The Brown organization continued to do polling in the last week of the campaign, and on Friday the 22d the results showed Brown leading Wilkinson by a 31 to 21 margin. The Brown staff members were confident that the lead would hold up, despite the fact that their survey showed 20 percent still undecided.

The Wilkinson pollster completed a final poll on Thursday the 21st, showing that Brown's lead over Wilkinson had narrowed to 27 to 25. When we asked Wilkinson staff members when they were convinced that they had the primary won, they pinpointed the time as 3:00 A.M. on Friday before the primary, when they examined these results. Although they were still behind, they clearly had the momentum and fully expected to win. (The next day Wilkinson publicized these results, but the credibility of his claim was damaged when he made a mistake and claimed a lead of 27 to 25 percent.)

Though there are variations in the details of the various polls, they all describe losses by Brown and by Beshear and large gains by Wilkinson in the last three to four weeks of the campaign. Wilkinson's gain is well documented and dramatic: he polled 10 percent or less in late April; 15 percent by May 9-11; 25 percent by May 21; and 35 percent on May 26 at the polls.

Explaining the Outcome of the Primary

How do we explain the rapid shifts in voter support during the closing weeks of the campaign? Why did Brown lose his comfortable lead late in the campaign? What went wrong with Beshear's campaign? Most important, how did Wilkinson succeed in more than doubling his strength during the last two weeks of the campaign?

It is important to remember that at least 15 to 20 percent of the potential electorate remained undecided until the last few days of the campaign. For some reason, substantial numbers of voters were unwilling to make a commitment to any of the candidates. There are some observers who claim that voters never pay much attention to a primary campaign until after Derby Day (the first Saturday in May). If many voters had been inattentive, this could explain both the undecided vote and the softness of the support that did exist.

Failure of the Brown Campaign

There are several explanations for Brown's loss of support from about 36 to 26 percent. Brown was undoubtedly hurt by the attacks in the commercials run by both Beshear and Wilkinson in late April and May. The attacks on his life-style may have been damaging, and the charges that he was a "high-tax" governor were clearly damaging. The Brown campaign was not well prepared for these attacks. It was unable to cope with the "high-tax" charges. The belated Brown commercials attacking Wilkinson may have backfired by identifying him as Brown's most serious challenger. Brown could never decide how to handle the proposal for a lottery or even what stand to take on it, and his staff lacked polling data on the lottery issue. Also, Brown was never able to answer the questions about why he was running for governor.

Brown was further handicapped by the fact that there appeared to be an upper limit on his potential support, a limit that was perhaps as low as 36 percent; and at the same time there appeared to be a large bloc of voters who were strongly anti-Brown, many of whom were willing to support whatever candidate seemed to have the best chance of beating Brown. If Brown was unlikely to get more than 30 to 33 percent of the vote and if Wilkinson was gaining strength, Brown's best chance of winning would occur if Beshear and Wilkinson ran about even, perhaps each getting about 25 percent of the vote.

The attacks on Beshear by the Brown commercials (along with Wilkinson's attacks) were very damaging to Beshear. A collapse of the Beshear campaign was not in Brown's interest, and the Brown staff fully understood this; but they were unable to prevent it. The Brown campaign staff (along with everyone else) underestimated the Wilkinson surge. Until the last few days, they did not believe that Wilkinson posed a serious threat. And they had no plan to deal with this threat, no campaign theme that Brown could use in the closing days.

At the end, Brown remained confident and insisted on demonstrating his confidence in public. Over the Memorial Day weekend preceding the election, Brown played golf in a celebrity tournament in Louisville and went to a Reds game in Cincinnati. While Wilkinson was still touring the state, shaking hands and seeking votes, Brown was on the golf course and at the ball game. It is impossible to tell whether this display of confidence cost him votes, but it at least symbolized an air of unreality in the Brown camp at the end of the primary.

Collapse of the Beshear Campaign

Steve Beshear, on the other hand, for the last two weeks of the campaign knew he was beaten. He continued to run commercials and to campaign, but those who covered his campaign perceived the atmosphere of defeat that pervaded it. Beshear had been damaged by the advertising attacks of both Brown and Wilkinson, and his own image had been damaged by the anti-Brown campaigns he had run. Polls showed that voters blamed him more than others for running a negative campaign.

Beshear was also seriously damaged by the polls and the stories in the media demonstrating that Wilkinson was making rapid gains in popularity and had apparently taken over second place and thus become the only serious challenger to Brown. Bob Johnson, the respected political correspondent of the *Courier-Journal,* wrote a story on the Friday before the election saying that the campaign had become a two-man race between Wilkinson and Brown and describing Brown's last-minute advertising campaign against Wilkinson.

One important consequence was that a number of local officials and activists who had been working for Beshear shifted their support to Wilkinson because they wanted to defeat Brown and support a winner. Some of them had originally told Beshear that they would support him as long as he was the strongest alternative to Brown. It also appears that some of Carroll's active political supporters made the same shift.

Ordinary voters who were anti-Brown and who read the newspapers followed the same course, defecting from Beshear, or in some cases Carroll, to support Wilkinson. One important group of voters who apparently made a late shift to Wilkinson was state workers who were determined to prevent Brown's renomination.

If there had been few polls or little attention in the press to the polls, it seems unlikely that such a major shift in voting support would have occurred. In any primary election with a substantial number of candidates, voters do not want to waste their vote but to support someone who has a chance of winning. In states with a runoff primary, this is a less important consideration, because voters get a second chance even if the first vote is wasted. The opinion polls in Kentucky almost served as the first step in a two-stage primary; they demonstrated who the two top leaders would be, giving the voters a chance to choose between them.

Reasons for the Wilkinson Surge

Wallace Wilkinson won for the same reasons that the other candidates lost; he succeeded in doing what they failed to do. By late April, when Wilkinson's advertising campaign began to capture attention, there was a large proportion of voters who were either not satisfied or at least not enthusiastic about any of the other candidates. There was, in other words, a large number of potential Wilkinson voters.

Wilkinson's campaign had a clear message, and in the last few weeks the central focus of that message—a lottery instead of higher taxes—was one that appealed to a large majority of voters. Wilkinson had the resources necessary to deliver that message, in a series of well-executed television commercials, again and again in the closing weeks of the campaign.

In the last two weeks before the primary, Wilkinson made a concerted effort to capture as much free media attention as possible. He was constantly on the move, visiting important cities every few days to get more local media coverage, staging a twenty-five-hour day of campaigning to attract attention. (As an example, he visited Owensboro four times in the last nine days.) While Wilkinson intensified his personal campaign efforts,

Brown continued to work at a leisurely pace before his weekend of golf and baseball; and the steam was going out of the losing Beshear campaign. Consequently, Wilkinson dominated the "free media" in the closing days of the campaign.

The release of media and private polls late in the campaign helped Wilkinson just as they hurt Beshear. They demonstrated that Wilkinson had a chance and that a vote for him was not a wasted vote. Anti-Brown workers and voters defected from Beshear and Carroll to support Wilkinson. Moreover, the undecided voters who liked Wilkinson's televised messages or who liked him when they met him on the campaign trail now knew that he was a serious candidate, the only one with a chance of catching Brown.

Wilkinson won because he had all the resources that were needed; because he campaigned longer, harder, and better than anyone else; because he found a campaign theme that appealed to many of the voters; because he had four serious opponents and needed only about one-third of the voters for a victory; because his major opponents damaged each other with negative advertising; and because he alone had momentum in the closing days of the campaign, and every voter who was following the campaign knew it.

The 1987 gubernatorial primary demonstrated once again the importance of television advertising in elections and the advantage enjoyed by a candidate who can afford lots of ads and can package a message with appeal to voters. It showed how important television can be to a candidate who is not well known to voters before the campaign. It proved how rapidly public opinion can change when large numbers of voters are uncommitted and when they gain much of their information about issues and candidates from television. And it showed how much attention voters pay to publicized polls in primary elections when they are trying not to waste their votes.

5

THE 1987 DEMOCRATIC PRIMARY FOR STATEWIDE OFFICES

WHILE PUBLIC attention is focused on the gubernatorial primary, candidates are running for seven other statewide races. Most of these candidates start the race with low visibility and limited resources, but they must gain the attention of the same set of voters who participate in the gubernatorial race.

In the past many of these campaigns have been relatively low-keyed, low-cost affairs, using traditional organizational techniques. But these campaigns have begun to acquire some of the characteristics of a gubernatorial campaign, with greater expense and greater use of television. In this chapter we describe in some detail the best example of this new style of campaigning, the 1987 primary for lieutenant governor, and we describe more briefly some of the other contests for statewide office in that year.

The 1987 campaign for lieutenant governor deserves special attention because it was Kentucky's first high-powered and most well-financed lieutenant gubernatorial race and because Jones's victory surprised so many observers. But it also deserves attention because in many ways it was typical of recent gubernatorial campaigns. In the 1987 lieutenant gubernatorial race, there was a large field of candidates, as there were in the 1987 and 1979 gubernatorial races. There were major shifts in voter sentiment during the campaign, as in the 1987, 1983, and 1979 gubernatorial primaries. Television advertising had a significant effect on the outcome, as in the last three gubernatorial primary races. Finally, in the 1987 lieutenant gubernatorial race (as in both the 1987 and 1979 gubernatorial races), the election was won by a wealthy political amateur who could afford extensive television advertising and who used it effectively.

On May 26, 1987, Brereton Jones won the Democratic lieutenant gubernatorial primary with 33 percent of the vote; he finished seven percentage points and 40,000 votes ahead of his nearest competitor, David Armstrong. Three weeks earlier the Bluegrass state poll had shown him trailing the front-runner Armstrong by nine points, with 39 percent of the likely voters still undecided. Another *Courier-Journal* poll in early March had shown Jones running last, with only 3 percent of the vote. How did Jones come from so far behind to win the race? Why did the campaign of the front-runner, Armstrong, never gain momentum? What made the race so volatile and the voters so unpredictable?

Each of the five candidates brought significant political strengths to the campaign. David Armstrong, Alice McDonald, and David Boswell were all completing four years in high office—as attorney general, superintendent of public instruction, and commissioner of agriculture, respectively. Paul Patton, a former state chairman of the Democratic party under Gov. John Y. Brown, was completing a second term as Pike County (Kentucky's richest coal county) judge executive. Brereton Jones had served in state Republican legislative politics in West Virginia almost twenty years earlier, but he had never held or sought political office in Kentucky. Jones was a wealthy Kentucky thoroughbred horse farmer with considerable experience in raising charitable and political campaign funds.

The Armstrong Campaign

David Armstrong began his political career as a southern Louisville precinct worker and used those connections to receive low-level political appointments, including assistant police court prosecutor and juvenile court judge. Only fours years after completing law school, Armstrong nearly upset incumbent Jefferson County Attorney J. Bruce Miller in the Democratic primary. In 1975 he successfully turned back Republican Commonwealth Attorney Ed Schroering's bid for reelection.

In 1983 Armstrong easily captured the nomination for state attorney general. Armstrong supporters frequently noted his office's aggressive, though unsuccessful, prosecution of state treasurer Frances Jones Mills on campaign-abuse charges. It generated headlines and controversy and reinforced a "tough on crime," faintly populist image, but it did not win points with Democratic politicians. Armstrong, age forty-five, brought to the lieutenant gubernatorial campaign a clean image, a reputation for integrity and hard work, and a record of action on child abuse, victims' rights and protection of the elderly.

David Armstrong's acknowledged status as the front-runner was both an asset and a liability. As attorney general with a commendable record, he had statewide name recognition. But his status appeared to lead to complacency. The Louisville resident counted on a strong grass-roots effort to get more than half the vote in Jefferson County. He had been endorsed by U.S. representative Ron Mazzoli, Louisville mayor Jerry Abramson, and some other Louisville-area officials. His friends and supporters also included lawyers, judges, local public officials, some labor groups, teachers, and consumer groups from around the state. In fact, Armstrong had hoped to receive significant endorsements from both the AFL-CIO and the Kentucky Education Association.

Armstrong was also able to capitalize on the advantages of incumbency during the campaign. For example, his office had a booth at the state fair in the summer of 1986 (his campaign paid for another "political" booth). There were also frequent public service announcements on radio, "informational" state-paid brochures that mentioned his "distinguished career," and press conferences to unveil programs. There was an increasing number of press releases issued by his office during the campaign (*C-J,* May 22, 1987, p. A12).

Although the Armstrong campaign professed to believe in the value of organization, the campaign was not extensively organized outside of Jefferson County. Because of miscalculations and limited financial resources, the campaign did not hire field representatives and other staffers to work the diverse counties in eastern, western, and northern Kentucky.

Armstrong, who lacked personal wealth, had difficulty raising funds. By September 30, 1986, he had only solicited $77,000; and in the last three months of the year, he collected another $114,000. Late in the campaign, he loaned his campaign almost $63,000. His total spending in the primary was $582,000, compared to the $2.2 million and $1.6 million spent by Jones and Patton, respectively.

The campaign primarily relied on billboards and limited mailings to maintain Armstrong's name recognition and support throughout the state. The campaign not only lacked the resources for an extensive television advertising campaign but underestimated the impact that it could have. Armstrong's personal campaign was less extensive than any of the other candidates. He is not a natural born campaigner; he does not inspire his supporters; and he lacks charisma and excitement, though he projects sincerity and engages people easily.

The McDonald Campaign

Alice McDonald spent her childhood in Chalmette, Louisiana, a small farming community just outside New Orleans. After several years as a teacher in her hometown, in 1967 she moved to Louisville after marrying Glenn McDonald, a Kentucky lawyer and now a Jefferson County district judge. McDonald's entry into state politics started in 1975 with Julian Carroll's gubernatorial campaign and in 1976 she cochaired Jimmy Carter's state campaign. Subsequently, she held appointive positions in local government.

After one term in Frankfort as deputy superintendent of public instruction, in 1983 she was elected superintendent of public instruction. During her term in that office, she was accused by her critics of politicizing the Department of Education by hiring and giving contracts to people with political connections and by efforts to get campaign contributions from department employees and local school superintendents. She also developed a reputation as a tenacious promoter of primary, secondary, and adult education programs.

Although Alice McDonald had a smaller campaign budget than most of the others, she had the advantage of holding statewide office. McDonald expected to get the votes of many teachers and women, as well as her neighbors in Jefferson County. She had a statewide network of political connections, both from the earlier Carroll administration and from her successful campaign for superintendent of public instruction, on which she hoped to capitalize.

She had the highest name recognition of any candidate, but much of it was negative—apparently because of political controversies in the Department of Education. Alice McDonald was constantly under attack for using her office for political purposes. Her accusers pointed to numerous examples of self-promotion. She sent out huge numbers of certificates of recognition, bearing her name, to students with records of high attendance. For many years she had followed the practice of having herself photographed with individual teachers at statewide meetings and making the pictures available to each teacher's hometown press. Her photograph was also prominent in several Department of Education publications, including a booklet that featured a list of recent educational reforms (*C-J,* May 22, 1987, p. A12).

McDonald's organizational efforts were limited. She was counting on support from women and teachers, powerful county school superintendents, her past political friends, and a broad base of support statewide. She did not have a large paid staff or an ardent volunteer apparatus to establish formal county organizations throughout the state. McDonald, whose advertising did not start until the week of May 11, emphasized direct mail. She targeted voters with her materials, tailoring her message to the interests she had identified. Besides "general voters," McDonald's targets included women, minorities, teachers, and Catholic educators. She often included photographs of herself with powerful Democrats, including former lieutenant governor Thelma Stovall and Sen. Wendell Ford (*Lexington Herald-Leader* (*H-L*), May 18, 1987, p. B1).

In the 1983 race, she was assailed for seeking contributions from state education workers. As she raised money for the lieutenant gubernatorial race, the same complaints surfaced again. In fund-raising efforts, Mc-

Donald, like her fellow state officeholders, trailed the millionaires Patton and Jones throughout the race. By the end of 1986, she had raised a total of $68,168; and by the end of the campaign, McDonald had spent $341,517, which included a $90,000 personal loan.

McDonald is a friendly and energetic personal campaigner. She knows how to work a crowd and has her picture taken with everyone. Throughout her travels, she courted women and teachers. By mid-May, McDonald had visited all 120 counties.

The Boswell Campaign

David Boswell grew up in western Kentucky, principally in Sorgho, a small farming community west of Owensboro. He traces his interest in politics to his grandfather, Erle A. Mulligan, who was a political power broker in Daviess County for four decades, most of that time sitting on the local school board. Boswell won his first campaign as an underdog, running against an incumbent state legislator in 1977, when he was only twenty-seven and was an assistant planner for Owensboro's Metropolitan Planning Board. He won a reputation in the legislature as competent but not outstanding. His legislative initiatives include measures to help farmers and antiabortion measures.

In 1983 Boswell won a competitive race for agriculture commissioner, defeating two better-known opponents, a more experienced legislator and a previous agriculture commissioner. During the campaign Boswell sought more than the farm vote. "Our strategy was to appeal to the voter as a whole, rather than target people with a particular interest in agriculture," according to his campaign manager, Gay Dwyer (*C-J,* April 13, 1987, p. B6). Boswell claimed as his successes as agriculture commissioner the battle against the horse disease equine viral arteritis, his spirited defense of the tobacco production-quota program, and his efforts to promote farm produce cooperatives.

As the youngest lieutenant gubernatorial competitor, at age thirty-seven, Boswell entered the campaign without personal wealth and with limited name recognition but with a record in legislative and statewide office and with a reputation as a hard worker who was accustomed to being the underdog in elections. Although he had the smallest campaign budget, he did have the advantage of being commissioner of agriculture. Boswell was hoping for help from farmers, labor, and his fellow legislators, led by House Speaker Don Blandford, especially in his native western Kentucky. Boswell picked up one key endorsement from the United Mine Workers. Although the AFL-CIO did not endorse a candidate, state representative

Ron Cyrus, the executive secretary of the state AFL-CIO, said Boswell "came very close."

Boswell's campaign was chronically underfinanced and understaffed. His organizational efforts were very ineffectual. There was no statewide organizational apparatus; labor and legislative friends were able to provide little assistance in establishing county organizations manned by hardworking volunteers. Boswell's own poll, taken in February 1987, showed that he trailed Armstrong and McDonald in name recognition. On the campaign trail, Boswell is personable and pleasant but lacks charisma and is not an inspiring speaker.

Media criticism of Boswell for his political use of his office was not as feverish as in the case of McDonald. But he did draw criticism in 1986 for printing and distributing $35,000 worth of yardsticks bearing his name. One month before the primary election, 39,000 copies of his department's quarterly publication were mailed out, containing twelve pages which mentioned him forty times and included four photographs of him (*C-J,* May 22, 1987, p. A1). During the month of the primary election, Boswell appeared on $39,000 worth of broadcast advertising to promote a Department of Agriculture program—a new marketing service for farmers. Several stations refused to broadcast the thirty-second radio and television announcements, however, and other stations added a disclaimer (*C-J,* May 1, 1987, p. B1, B5).

Boswell was severely limited by a shortage of campaign funds and was the most poorly funded candidate in the race. He had solicited $131,081 through September 30, 1986, and by the end of the year had raised a total of $162,070. At the close of the race, Boswell's total spending amounted to $315,434, including a $10,100 personal loan.

Boswell's strategy was to build on support from labor groups and state house members and his friends and neighbors in western Kentucky. He targeted farmers by using the advantages of his statewide office. However, the strategy proved ineffective; his base of support was too narrow, and he lacked the resources to broaden it with a television campaign.

The Patton Campaign

Paul Patton grew up in eastern Kentucky, weaned on factional politics. A graduate of the University of Kentucky, he became a well-respected, wealthy coal operator and a seasoned Pike County politician. Patton worked his way up the political ladder and earned a reputation as an astute, fair, but tough political leader. As the last of the four state Democratic party chairmen in the early 1980s (1982-83) during Governor Brown's administration, Patton became one of Kentucky's most able professional political administrators. He developed his own contacts, tried aggressively to help Democratic leaders and their constituents, and especially (and not typically) brought the state party's machinery into the effort to elect local Democrats.

In 1981 Patton was elected Pike County judge executive, after an expensive and competitive factional battle. As county judge, Patton utilized his political, administrative, and business skills to enhance the quality of life of his constituents, whose income by any standard is well below the poverty level. He won high marks from his fellow county judge executives and some local politicians, if not from his factional enemies. Among his accomplishments were better roads and other public services.

When Patton announced for lieutenant governor in November 1986 at age forty-nine, he brought to the campaign extensive experience in politics and government and a strong base in eastern Kentucky. Patton's victory formula was based on two foundations: a strong organization built from the political resources of his fellow judge executives to supplement his own contacts made as state party chairman, together with a solid, unwavering, large vote from his native mountains. The Pike County judge executive was the only true eastern Kentuckian in the race for lieutenant governor.

The Patton campaign concentrated very hard on building a statewide organization. Out of a budget of about $1.6 million, at least $600,000 was geared toward what he called the "political" vote. Patton had a big staff, eleven full-time people, most of them working to maintain contact with local leaders. The campaign had chairmen in about sixty-five counties but no more than twenty or twenty-five counties with a really effective organization, and these were spread out all over the state.

Patton hoped to run best in rural Kentucky. His campaign sent out a high volume of direct mail, concentrating on about 125,000 voters, based on geography and how often they voted. Most of the mailing went to about eighty counties. The staff ignored some eastern Kentucky counties where it seemed unnecessary to send mailings and for the most part ignored Daviess County and most of Jefferson, along with Fayette. The campaign sent out nearly a million pieces of direct mail in all. Patton ran television spots the last six weeks of the campaign and concentrated on radio in the last two weeks.

Patton's campaign style is very folksy; his political rhetoric is tinged with a mountain accent, and he projects a very sincere, caring image. He is a tenacious, hardworking campaigner. He crisscrossed Kentucky's 120 counties several times during the race.

The former coal operator had ample financial and political resources with which to conduct a very expensive, ambitious campaign. By the end of December 1986, floating on a wave of money from eastern Kentucky, a good bit of it his own, Patton had taken the fund-raising lead among candidates for lieutenant governor with a total of $760,661. An accounting of spending following his defeat showed that Patton had spent $1,586,581, including a $556,000 loan and a $220,000 candidate contribution. Patton's premise going into the campaign was that about 20 to 25 percent of people would vote based on geographic loyalties, 20 to 25 percent would vote based on politics (the advice of local officials), and 50 to 60 percent would vote based on the information they got through the media. The geographic factor was important; Patton and Armstrong both carried their areas, with Boswell third. In retrospect, Patton probably overestimated the effectiveness of support by local leaders. He believed that his experience as party chairman and contact through the county judges would give him a large advantage in winning local officeholders and that voters, lacking interest in the lieutenant governor's race, would be inclined to follow political leaders. In reality, it appears that many local leaders who endorsed Patton did not work effectively for his nomination.

The Jones Campaign

Brereton Chandler Jones grew up on a dairy farm in West Virginia, the son of a state senator who for decades was the most powerful politician and businessman in the county. At age twenty-five Jones won a West Virginia House seat as a Republican, the political party of his parents. In his second term he unseated the House minority leader. But Jones soon lost his taste for politics, was uncomfortable with the direction of his party, and decided against becoming a professional politician. He quit politics in 1968 to concentrate on his Huntington real estate development business, which was making him wealthy (*C-J,* April 6, 1987, pp. B1, B3).

Jones began another career in 1972, when he came to Kentucky with his wife, Elizabeth Lloyd, to her childhood home, Airdrie Farm in Woodford County. Jones leased a portion of the farm from his father-in-law and began to work with horses. Airdrie Stud, now a large and successful thoroughbred operation, has grown to 2,700 acres and almost 300 horses, including the winners of European and American classic races (*H-L,* March 2, 1987, pp. C1, C3).

On December 31, 1975, Jones registered as a Democrat. In response to criticisms during the campaign that he was a former Republican and not a native Kentuckian, Jones had a light but controlled reply: "I was and am very fond of my mama, and when I was born she happened to be in West Virginia. I got to Kentucky as quickly as I could" (*H-L,* March 2, 1987, p. C12).

Before initiating his political career in Kentucky, Jones worked as fund-raising chairman for the McDowell Cancer Research Foundation, chaired Governor Collins's task force on the state Medicaid program, and served on the University of Kentucky Hospital Board and the U.K. Board of Trustees. His highest profile of public activity was as head of the Kentucky Health Care Access Foundation. Overcoming pervasive disbelief from the medical community at its outset, the foundation has enlisted 2,300 doctors to provide free health care for more than 25,000 Kentuckians below the poverty level who are not poor enough to qualify for Medicaid.

Jones entered politics with the race for lieutenant governor, making his decision almost exactly ten years after his change of party affiliation. He made his decision on a Florida vacation, in some part because of a chance meeting with William H. May of Frankfort, one of Kentucky's classic power brokers. Until May died the next year, he was an acknowledged expert on the politics of highway and political finance. May was so impressed with Jones's incredible success in getting Kentucky doctors to give free medical care that he urged Jones to run for governor—but first for lieutenant governor. Jones's other godfather in Kentucky politics, the late Edward Prichard, Jr., also encouraged him to run for office.

When Jones announced for lieutenant governor in October 1986 at age forty-seven, he had already been building his organization, raising funds, and campaigning across the state for many months. Jones ran for lieutenant governor on his record of achievement in business and his leadership skills from his diverse charitable endeavors and had large personal financial resources. Jones was the only major candidate who had not served in Kentucky statewide elective, appointive, or party office.

All of Brereton Jones's opponents were elected officials, with the name recognition and political networks that are usually essential in winning a race. Jones's counterstrategy was simple: Spend a lot of money—much of it his own—on television and direct mail to get name recognition and support and build a political network from those who knew him from his work in health care and education.

The voting public of Kentucky perceived Brereton Jones as the classic amateur candidate, a considerable feat of conscious production on Jones's part and unconscious cooperation on the part of the press, since he was, in fact, an experienced veteran of two terms as a West Virginia Republican legislator. Both the designed advertising and the first several paragraphs of each newspaper and television story portrayed one piece of reality: Jones had come to Kentucky from West Virginia, made himself into a millionaire in the prestigious thoroughbred horse business, and used his hard-won wealth and influence to develop a program of free health care for indigent Kentuckians that did not rely on government support.

Jones started with a limited geographic base—the central Kentucky Bluegrass region. As a "private citizen running against politicians," he had no name recognition among voters. He won the endorsement of former governors Breathitt, Chandler, and Wetherby and by the end of the race practically swept newspaper endorsements in the Bluegrass region and northern Kentucky. The three governors played a very useful role. All three of them appeared at a news conference on October 24, 1986, and they were featured in an effective television ad that provided early respectability to Jones's candidacy. Breathitt was also very useful in working the phone at state headquarters, in calling people and asking them to work for Jones, and in setting up contacts.

Although unable to gain organized group support, such as AFL-CIO and KEA, the Jones campaign was able to neutralize these groups so they would not support anyone else, especially the front-runner Armstrong. Jones was willing to talk issues with them; he was perfectly willing to tell KEA he is against collective bargaining for teachers and thinks teachers make a big mistake emphasizing that issue.

Jones picked a famous Kentucky sports figure to be his state campaign chairman—his key media actor. Dan Issel, the highest male scorer in Kentucky basketball history, was used to deliver Jones's central message. Sports figures are always credible in Kentucky politics, and Jones picked the best of all. In his first political role Issel, also a former Republican, promoted an absolutely clean, noncontroversial image; he extolled Jones as the successful horseman and well-respected businessman who wanted to serve his fellow Kentuckians. This celebrity state chairman was excellent on the campaign trail—a good introduction to people. Issel broke down barriers because he is warm, articulate, and popular with crowds.

This "political amateur" had very able and experienced people running his state organization. His campaign manager, Steve Miller, was effective in organizational planning and in developing campaign strategy. He worked closely with Jones's Washington pollsters and media consultants.

Jerry Anglin, who was appointed state organization director, had experience and skill in building county organizations. When Anglin started working for Jones in August 1986, Jones and Miller had already visited about half of the counties and developed contacts in about one-fourth of them. In addition to Anglin, who handled two districts, the Jones staff included four field representatives who would serve as the advance persons, coordinating activities when Jones was in the district. A separate office was also maintained in Jefferson County under Miller's supervision, and an experienced Fayette County politician handled that county.

Faith Miller, who had handled public relations for various government agencies and political campaigns, worked on media primarily in the first half of the campaign. As press agent, she had to stay in contact with reporters, for whom she prepared detailed press kits. She targeted reporters and media in general in counties of opponents' strength, particularly in eastern Kentucky, where she had worked for a coal group. She also contacted experts to prepare various position papers on issues.

Jones's broad strategy was to begin by building a strong organizational base and then to develop a media campaign later in the race. While the conventional political wisdom was that organization was only worth 5 percent in a campaign, he believed the figure was closer to 20 percent; he also considered it a prerequisite to successful fund-raising.

Steve Miller started traveling with Jones in January 1986. They averaged about three days a week of traveling during that first year. This included short trips in central Kentucky and two- or three-day trips to eastern or western Kentucky. The travel priorities were based on Miller's theory as to where the election had to be won. Initially, they focused their travel on those counties that vote 3,000 or more in a Democratic primary for governor and tried to develop an organization or contact in each one of those counties. At first they focused primarily on western Kentucky, and then they turned to eastern Kentucky. These were areas that they thought would be responsive to Jones's message about the need to make sure that every Kentuckian gets his "fair share."

In their first visit to a county, they were careful to make contact with the local officials. Although most local courthouse officials provide little campaign help to candidates, they talk a great deal with many others in the county about politics and candidates. It was important at the start that these officials perceived Brereton Jones as a viable candidate and that they believed he would finish the race and spend as much as he needed in order to win the nomination. Although Jones had to pay his respects to the courthouse group, he did not want to depend on them and largely found that he could not.

For the first six months of travels, Jones concentrated on meeting individuals. They often asked local officials, business leaders, and other contacts for names of persons who were not necessarily established politicians but who might help the campaign. When they came through the counties the second time, they would contact these people, and only then did they try to find specific county chairmen.

In making their local contacts, they drew on a variety of sources. Steve Miller had been active in the Junior Chamber of Commerce, had worked in Harvey Sloane's campaigns, and had made many contacts with sheriffs while working for the constitutional amendment on sheriffs' succession. Some of the volunteers came from the health care network with which Jones had been working; some came from Jones's contacts with the State

Agriculture Board; others resulted from Jones's contacts on the U.K. Board of Trustees and with U.K. alumni.

Jones preferred to build an organization of amateurs, though some had worked in politics before. He wanted people who were not only enthusiastic and hardworking but well respected in the community. This was important to the image he was trying to build. The political amateurs were not scarred by previous political battles. But members of county Democratic executive committees were often valuable because of their experience and their demonstrated interest in politics.

The campaign used these activists for all of the traditional local activities: door-to-door organizing, contacts with local media, running phone banks, and putting up yard signs. The campaign, for example, distributed about 30,000 yard signs around the state, in addition to 500 large signs placed along highways. The campaign worked hard to stay in touch with activists. They sent out regular newsletters. In mid-February they held about 150 "I Love Kentucky" Valentine's Day parties across the state, where those attending were shown a videotaped message from Jones along with all of his commercials that had been completed.

One feature of the Jones campaign was a series of barbecues at the family farm in Woodford County, held once or twice a week during the fall of 1986, with perhaps thirty to forty supporters or potential supporters at each. More than two thousand attended a Fourth of July picnic at the Jones farm.

Jones had ample funds with which to conduct his successful campaign. By the end of December 1986, Jones had raised about $350,000 from outside sources and loaned about $225,000 to his campaign, for a total of $575,000. The final figures for the primary election, reported in July 1987, showed that Jones spent just over $2,200,000; almost three-quarters of this— $1,631,000—came from a personal loan. He had spent about $600,000 more than Patton, and his personal funds loaned to the campaign were twice as much as Patton's.

The Jones campaign did not schedule a single major fund-raising event. Jones raised a lot from his friends and fellow horse breeders early in the campaign. Later in the campaign the pace of fund-raising declined. At a time when the candidates for governor were raising an unprecedented amount of money, it was difficult for a relatively unknown candidate for lieutenant governor who was given little chance of winning to raise funds. After the primary campaign was over, Jones made some progress in raising money to pay off his debt, but he had trouble competing with Wilkinson, who was raising a huge amount of money to pay off all of his debt. A major source of funding in Kentucky is business and professional persons who want to do business with the state; and from their viewpoint, a contribution to a candidate for lieutenant governor, even one perceived as a possible winner, is not a wise investment.

The Jones campaign gave high priority to county organizations, primarily focusing on fifty-three counties where about 70 percent of the Democratic primary vote is cast. But they had at least a minimum organization, with an active chairman and chairwoman, in more than 100 counties. Organization in Jefferson County was a particular problem, because of Armstrong's strength; and it was one of the responsibilities of Steve Miller, the campaign chairman. Miller's goal was for Jones to run second in the county and trail Armstrong by not more than thirty percentage points, and this was accomplished. The campaign targeted two mailings in Jefferson County and had an extensive advertising campaign on television.

The other candidates had conceded eastern Kentucky to Patton; because Jones and Miller thought Armstrong was their leading opponent, they went into easten Kentucky counties trying to appeal to those local politicians who were not factional allies of the Patton supporters. Factional politics still prevails in a number of the eastern counties. Some political leaders in these counties requested election-day funding from the Jones headquarters, and they were flatly rejected. Providing election funds that might be used to buy votes could obviously damage the clean image Jones was trying to build.

The Media Campaigns

Most voters learn about the candidates and issues in a statewide campaign, not by personal contact with candidates or campaign workers, but by the newspaper, radio, and television coverage of what the candidates say and by paid political advertising, primarily on television.

Free Media Coverage

During the campaign the media reported occasionally on what candidates were saying in their speeches, particularly those delivered to organized groups (labor, business, education), and on what they said in an hour-long debate televised live on Kentucky Educational Television (KET) on May 6, 1987.

At the KET debate the five candidates were asked about the possibility of calling a special session because, under Kentcky's constitution, the lieutenant governor becomes acting governor when the governor is out of the state. Both McDonald and Jones said that they would be willing, as acting governor, to call a special session of the General Assembly against the governor's wishes but that the circumstances would have to be unusual. When asked what type of relationship they would have with the new governor— a relationship that sometimes in the past has been fraught with discord—both said they would work as team players. But Jones and McDonald said they would pursue their own agendas if they disagreed with the governor.

Jones was the only candidate who acknowledged that he sought the office of lieutenant governor as a springboard for governor. Jones said he "absolutely" wanted to be governor but that as lieuteant governor he could learn about the state bureaucracy, focus on important issues, and learn "which of the political leaders you can trust and which ones you can't." Jones's opponents—Armstrong, McDonald, Boswell, and Patton (who changed his stand later in the race)—sidestepped questions about their political aspirations. All said they had set their sights for now only on the office of lieutenant governor. The lieutenant governor has few official duties other than presiding over the Senate and acting as governor when the governor is outside the state. But the office comes with an annual budget of $1.2 million and ample time and means for its occupant to gain statewide name recognition (*C-J,* May 6, 1987, pp. A1, A12.)

While all of the candidates tried to make good use of the free media, Jones was particularly effective in doing so. Jones always answered every question and gave the impression of being painfully honest. Candor was a trademark of his campaign. An example is the fact that he readily acknowledged from the start that he was running for lieutenant governor so he could become governor. Jones made his amateur, frank image work for him. He gave carefully thought out answers to questions about his switch in party loyalty to the Democratic party. Against aides' advice, he allowed reporters to watch him film the carefully produced television commercials that propelled him past better-known rivals in his first race for public office in Kentucky. But Jones's candor often stopped at the gates of Airdrie Stud; he refused to let a television reporter photograph him at Airdrie late in the campaign, fearing that an image of wealth would turn off voters. Brereton Jones was endorsed by a total of ten daily newspapers and ten weeklies, compared to a total of three newspapers endorsing anyone else in the lieutenant governor's race. These endorsements were the result of extensive efforts by Jones and his staff to develop contacts with the press as well as specific attempts to generate endorsements. Faith Miller, in charge of media relations, contacted practically all newspapers in the state to ask if they would be making endorsements in the campaign. While many politicians believed that endorsements were not important in such a race, the Jones staff believed that they were. In fact, one of the Jones television commercials late in the campaign featured the press endorsements.

Polling and Television Advertising

The conventional wisdom among politicians and reporters is that the 1987 lieutenant governor's primary was decided by the media campaign and particularly by the television ads of the major candidates; and there is no reason to doubt this thesis. The television advertising campaign was fought out largely between the two millionaire candidates—Jones and Patton. Because of their limited budgets, Armstrong, McDonald, and Boswell ran a smaller number of ads that attracted less attention.

Two of the candidates, Jones and Patton, had an array of professional campaign consultants, particularly media advisers and pollsters. Jones used Peter Hart, one of the most respected national pollsters, to carry out polls for him. At the end of 1986, Jones replaced his original media consultant because of disagreements over campaign strategy and replaced him with Frank Greer, who was recommended by Hart. Patton's consultant for most of the campaign was Lexingtonian William Wester. In early May Patton hired his own Washington consultant, Gary Nordlinger, to produce a supplemental media campaign.

It is interesting to trace the successful utilization of polls by the Jones campaign. Jones spent a lot of money on polls conducted by national pollsters Peter Hart and Jeff Guerin. They did a benchmark poll in March 1986, a benchmark poll in February 1987, and three polls after that; all had issues in them, but these got narrower as they got closer to the election. In the first benchmark poll, they were concerned with name recognition, issues, and attitudes toward Brereton Jones. The polls showed that being a West Virginian and a rich horse farm owner were not serious liabilities. The polls did show that the voters liked a nonpolitician, someone from the private sector. Also, the polls showed a strong pride in Kentucky; people liked living there and wanted to believe there was some hope for improvement.

Jones discovered that his first polls did not include questions on all the issues that he considered important; the polls showed education and jobs/economic development were the leading issues, but there was no mention of agricultural concerns. Thus, in the second benchmark poll, Jones had the pollsters add "saving the family farm," and this issue ranked high even in Jefferson County, probably because of all the local, state, and national media coverage about the plight of farmers and the displacement of small farms.

Jones's pollster carried out a series of polls late in the campaign to provide guidance about places where they needed to do media buys. For example, in northern Kentucky the Jones campaign was leading with 17 percent, with Armstrong having 13 percent, and 45 percent being undecided. Therefore, they increased their television advertising in northern Kentucky to appeal to the undecideds. Louisville consistently had the lowest number of undecided votes, so it did not pay to expand the planned advertising coverage. The campaign returned to western and eastern

Kentucky with more media buys because the polls showed that both areas had many undecided voters.

Beginning in January 1987, when he arrived in Kentucky, Frank Greer maintained daily contact with the Jones campaign staff and had a hand in every aspect of the operation. He watched the Jones campaign and got a feel for the entire organization. studying its strengths and weaknesses. Greer sent an organizational person to Kentucky to help them set up their phone banks, and he hired a Washington company to do the direct mailing operation. However, Brereton Jones wrote most of the commercials himself.

When the polls showed how important the farm issue was, Jones insisted that the media consultant, Greer, produce commercials promoting various farm themes—"save the family farm," "send farm products abroad instead of other forms of aid," "use made in Kentucky products," and so on. It was clear to Jones (from polling and campaigning around the state) that people in eastern and western Kentucky felt left out—the Golden Triangle issue. And Jones's theme was designed to overcome this, to suggest working together—the team approach.

Jones's use of paid media was superb. His television ads were judged by some observers to be the most professional and most skillfully executed of any in the 1987 campaign (including the gubernatorial). He obviously studied his polls and emphasized in television advertising what the undecided voters wanted to hear: "save the family farm," "promote made-in-Kentucky products," "get tough on crime," "provide vocational education and not rely on welfare," and so on.

In April Jones aired mostly the same ads that he had used in March, which stressed his leadership on health care and education issues and pushed his plan for "Made in Kentucky" labels on the state's food products. The ad in which the three former governors—Chandler, Breathitt, and Wetherby—endorsed Jones was particularly effective. A vocational education spot was added, and new ads were recorded the week of April 20. At the close of the race, the campaign added a spot that promoted the twenty newspaper endorsements received by Jones.

Not only were Jones's ads well produced, but Jones was good at delivering his message: Jones would "bring people together to solve problems" in the same way that he did to help build a cancer center in Lexington and set up a system for free health care for poor people. The script of his "vocational education" ad is typical of the tone of his commercials: "Growing up on a small farm in Kentucky, I learned the value of hard work. As I've traveled to every county in Kentucky, I've seen the tremendous pride, the tremendous spirit of our people—people who want to work. As your lieutenant governor, I want to work to break the cycle of poverty, to get people the vocational education and training they need to get off welfare and on their feet. Together we can make the right things happen; we can build a brighter future for all of Kentucky."

Another of Jones's commercials developed his theme about promoting Kentucky agriculture: "When we walk in a store, most of us don't know where the food comes from. That's why we should proudly put the Kentucky label on all products. It makes sense to say made in America, and it makes twice as much sense to say made in Kentucky. And when you buy a pound of hamburger, you should know if it came from Argentina or if it's good Kentucky beef. With the Kentucky label, we can help our own farmers and provide jobs for our own people. Together we can make the right things happen for Kentucky."

Paul Patton, who also wrote his own ads, started his television effort in February, with two name-recognition spots that ran mostly on Lexington stations and those serving western Kentucky. Patton's new round of nine spots in March and April was more issue oriented and ran on more stations, including those in Louisville for the first time. A biographical ad traced Patton's life from a straight-A report card in grade school to success in the coal business and politics. Two other spots focused on his work as judge executive of Pike County, the state's largest in area. One showed an illegal garbage dump cleaned up by Patton's solid-waste-control program. Patton said solid waste was a statewide problem but could be solved. "We did it here and we can do it for all of Kentucky" (*C-J,* April 20, 1987, pp. B1, B14). Another ad said Patton increased the county's rural water supplies five fold, doubled meal programs for the elderly, increased recreation facilities 50 percent, nearly doubled the miles of blacktopped roads, and more than doubled fire-protection facilities, while cutting administrative costs 47 percent.

Patton's television commercials struck many observers as traditional, old-fashioned, and dull. When Patton brought in a national media consultant with less than one month to go in the campaign, there was some change in the advertising style. In the last two weeks of the campaign Patton also ran a great many spots on radio. These simply told who Patton was and what he had done, that he had made a real difference as Pike County's judge executive.

The race for lieutenant governor, the most expensive in Kentucky history, escalated over the weekend of April 18 as the two millionaires resumed television advertising that continued until the May 26 election. While Jones and Patton were escalating the television campaign, late in April, Armstrong started advertising on television and radio in an effort to pick up a proportionate share of the approximately 40 percent of the vote that was still undecided. Armstrong's ads touted his record as attorney general for crime victims, child safety, senior citizens, and consumers. McDonald did not run any paid television commercials until May 11. In the ads McDonald argued that "her experience in education made her the best candidate because education consumes half the state budget and is the avowed priority of all the gubernatorial candidates." In an apparent effort to deflect criticism of her political activities as superintendent, McDonald said on the ads: "Change is controversial. I had to shake up the system to shape up the system." Similarly, Boswell did not start until May 11 with paid television commercials. For Boswell, "the most poorly funded candidate in the race, the medium, and the money, was the message. 'Boswell stops the buck,' one TV spot said as an animated deer—with dollar signs for antlers and eyes—comes to a screeching halt" (*C-J,* May 10, 1987, p. B5).

Jones's highly effective television commercials were critical to the success of his campaign and thus to the outcome of the election. The media campaign in this race differed from that in the governor's race, however, in two important respects. There was no negative advertising by any of the candidates for lieutenant governor, and there was no interaction among their commercials. None of the candidates produced and aired new commercials to counter the arguments being made by their opponents' ads. One of the important consequences was that Jones's clean image was not damaged by any of his advertising or by that of his opponents.

Polling the Volatile Voters

The 1987 lieutenant gubernatorial primary was unusual because the preference of voters changed dramatically in the closing weeks of the campaign. At least one-third of the voters remained undecided ten days before the primary. As the proportion of undecided voters dropped, David Armstrong failed to get many of them. And Brereton Jones's support rose from 9 percent in late April to about 23 percent in the last week of the campaign to 33 percent on primary election day.

Public opinion polls played a more important role in this lieutenant gubernatorial election than in any previous one. For the first time, the *Courier-Journal* carried out two Bluegrass state polls on the lieutenant governor's race, from mid-February to late April. More polls were carried out by the major candidates, and several of these polls were released to the media. The release of media and candidate polls late in the campaign appears to have had a significant impact on the race.

According to the results of the Bluegrass state poll, which was conducted from February 26 to March 9, Armstrong led his four rivals for the Democratic nomination for lieutenant governor. But the poll found that

Table 7. Polling Results in 1987 Lieutenant Gubernatorial Primary (in Percentages)

Source	Bluegrass Polls		Jones Poll	Jones Poll	Jones Poll	Primary Outcome
Date of polling	Feb. 26- Mar. 9	Apr. 17-28	May 4-5	May 17-18	May 20-21	May 26
Candidates:						
Jones	3	9	12	20	23	33
Armstrong	21	18	18	18	19	26
Patton	9	14	13	13	20	23
Boswell	10	8	7	5	6	10
McDonald	10	11	8	6	8	7
Other	—	—	—	—	—	1
Undecided	47	39	42	38	24	—
Total	100	99	100	100	100	100

Source: The Bluegrass polls were reported in the *Courier-Journal*; information on the Jones polls was provided by the candidate's staff.

the race was still wide open—almost half the voters were undecided. The poll, taken after the February 25 filing deadline, showed that Armstrong was the choice of 21 percent of the 518 registered Democrats who said they were likely to vote in the May 26 primary election. McDonald and Boswell polled 10 percent, Patton 9 percent, and Jones trailed with only 3 percent, (table 7).

The Bluegrass state poll found that Armstrong held a commanding lead in Jefferson County, where he served as commonwealth's attorney. He also did well in the Bluegrass area around Lexington. But his margin over the other candidates was insignificant outside of the state's largest urban areas. Boswell, an Owensboro native, led in western Kentucky, and Patton led in eastern Kentucky. McDonald's support was spread about evenly throughout the state, and she did especially well among women. Much of Jones's limited support was in the Bluegrass region (*C-J,* March 22, 1987, pp. A1, A14).

In a Bluegrass state poll conducted seven weeks later—April 17-28, Armstrong's lead had shrunk in the race for lieutenant governor (table 7). Entering the final three weeks of the campaign, 39 percent of the likely voters were still undecided, all five candidates were relatively close, and no one was out of contention. Armstrong was the choice of 18 percent of the 528 likely Democratic voters polled. He led Patton by four percentage points, a difference that was not significant given the poll's margin of error of four percentage points. McDonald got 11 percent, Jones 9 percent, and

Boswell 8 percent. The support for McDonald and Boswell had not changed significantly since the earlier Bluegrass state poll. In contrast, Patton picked up five points since the earlier poll and Jones six points—a surge that moved him from behind the pack into the thick of the race.

This second Bluegrass state poll found that none of the candidates had been able to generate significant support from all regions of the state. Armstrong drew half of his support from Jefferson County, where he was the choice of 51 percent of the likely voters. Patton's eastern Kentucky base gave him about half of his support, and more than half of Boswell's strength was from western Kentucky. Jones's main strength was in the Lexington-Bluegrass and Louisville regions. About one-third of McDonald's support came from Jefferson and nearby counties.

The headline on the *Courier-Journal* story reporting the poll read "Jones, Patton gaining on Armstrong in race for lieutenant governor—Jones, Patton gain momentum." By emphasizing the gains by Jones and Patton, rather than Armstrong's lead, the story on the poll provided an important boost to both the Jones and Patton campaigns (*C-J,* May 4, 1987, pp. A1, A20).

However, Armstrong's first television advertisements did not appear until the day after the polling was completed; until then, his advertising was limited to billboards in Jefferson County. The smaller campaign budgets of Boswell and McDonald had kept them off television to that point. Boswell began his advertising the last week in April, airing thirty-second radio spots.

The Jones campaign carried out three tracking polls during May (table 7). These show that a large proportion of the voters made up their minds very late; almost 40 percent were undecided in mid-May, and one-fourth were undecided a few days before the election. From late April to mid-May, while the proportion of undecided remained approximately unchanged, Jones's support grew at the the expense of Boswell and McDonald, while support for Armstrong and Patton remained level. In the last ten days or so, Jones and Patton each gained a disproportionate share of the undecided vote, but Jones's share was larger.

Early in the campaign, when the polls showed Jones with only 3 or 4 or 5 percent, his staff did all that they could to manipulate the responses to the polls in the media and among potential supporters, emphasizing that the number of undecideds in the race was about 50 percent. Late in the campaign, when the Jones staff had much more encouraging data from its own polls, as well as from data released to them by gubernatorial candidates, it became very important to release such survey findings to the media. Staff members hand-carried to the television stations and the press some of these poll results and tried to get interviews about the polls. Peter

Hart's reputation enhanced the prospects that the media would report these encouraging poll results. The Jones campaign kept its supporters informed weekly with an insider's newsletter on how the campaign was progressing and constant reporting of the polls.

Explaining the Outcome of the Primary

Nearly every successful candidate for lieutenant governor in the last forty years had followed the same career path. They had built a strong base of political support in one part of the state (Wetherby, Wyatt, and Stovall in Jefferson County; Beauchamp, Waterfield, and Carroll in western Kentucky). They had been elected to statewide office one or more times (Stovall, Collins, Beshear) or else had played a prominent role in the legislature (Ford, Carroll).

David Armstrong, David Boswell, and Alice McDonald were each trying to follow that route. Each had a definable regional base (and Armstrong was particularly strong in Jefferson County), and each held statewide office. In addition, each had an important specialized constituency in the state: Armstrong appealed to lawyers, judges, and prosecutors; Boswell worked hard to mobilize farm support; and McDonald claimed the support of the education establishment. In the past these credentials would have been enough.

Each of these traditional candidates had some weaknesses, of course. Neither Armstrong nor Boswell were dynamic campaigners or particularly effective speakers. McDonald was hurt by continuing charges that she had politicized the Department of Education. Boswell was not well known except in western Kentucky and among farm groups. Armstrong did not have either the staff or the statewide organization that one would expect a front-runner to have.

But the fundamental reason why these candidates lost was that the other two candidates, Jones and Patton, who lacked some or all of the traditional attributes, raised the stakes in the lieutenant governor's race. In 1983 the top spender spent $361,000, and $1,225,000 was spent on the lieutenant governor's race. In 1979 one candidate spent $624,000, the total was almost $1,400,000, but the winner (Martha Layne Collins) spent only $111,000. But the total cost of the 1987 campaign was over $5 million. Jones spent $2.2 million, and Patton spent almost $1.6 million; and they spent much of this money on television advertising. For the first time a lieutenant governor's race was fought out largely on television, and the victory went to the candidate with the personality, the media advisers, and the resources to win that battle.

In addition to buying the necessary television time, a large bankroll can make it possible to create and staff an adequate state headquarters, complete with field representatives, press agents, and newsletters. Both Patton and Jones understood the importance of organization and were able and willing to invest resources in it. They had the two strongest statewide organizations in the campaign, and this was a significant asset to each of them.

Patton's organization was a traditional one. It was built on the local officeholders and county party leaders across the state whom Patton had come to know during his tenure as state party chairman; and this base of support was particularly strong in eastern Kentucky. One reason why Patton lost was that this organization support was much less solid than he had anticipated, because many of the local leaders outside eastern Kentucky gave only lip service to his campaign.

The Jones organization, created with much greater difficulty, relied on a wide variety of community leaders, some but not all of whom had been active in politics. It proved to be more reliable because its members had a stronger personal commitment to Jones. It typifies modern techniques of political organization and demonstrates that a newcomer to state politics who has good staff assistance can organize the state as well as or better than someone relying on traditional approaches.

Jones was able to buy more time on television than his opponents and used that time most effectively. He hired a top professional as his media adviser but was actively involved in planning the themes of the ads and even in writing them. He is a superb campaigner, not only in person but on the screen; and this was the most important reason why his advertising campaign was successful.

For months Jones campaigned around the state, meeting individuals and speaking to small groups; but there was no evidence in the polls that he was making an impact on the electorate. None of the other candidates, however, had attracted strong, solid support; and the proportion of undecided voters remained very high. When the commercials began to run on television, Jones began to climb in the polls; and when polls showed that Jones was gaining momentum, voters who perceived him favorably began to take him seriously as a candidate. While it is impossible to measure the importance of newspaper endorsements, this must also have strengthened his campaign in the closing days.

In a campaign dominated by personalities rather than issues, Jones had a great personal advantage over his opponents. His campaign demonstrated once again that television can shape public attitudes and perceptions rapidly during election races. It also demonstrated how late in the campaign voters may make choices in a second-level race and how rapidly they may change their minds in a campaign dominated by television.

Democratic Primaries for Other Statewide Offices

Every four years Democratic voters choose candidates for six other statewide races, in addition to governor and lieutenant governor: secretary of state, attorney general, auditor, treasurer, superintendent of public instruction, and commissioner of agriculture. (The clerk of the court of appeals was also elected through 1975.) All of these officials are barred by the constitution from serving a second consecutive term, and thus they often seek to stay in Frankfort by winning another statewide office.

Of the twenty-six persons elected to one of these lesser statewide offices in four elections, 1971-83, eight ran in the succeeding election for lieutenant governor (three successfully), and two lost a race for governor. Nine others ran for a different lesser office, six successfully. From 1971 through 1983, Frances Jones Mills and Drexell Davis, Sr., held statewide office, usually trading the offices of secretary of state and treasurer. In 1987, however, Mills lost her race for treasurer, and Davis retired (though his son sought office). James B. Graham was elected superintendent of public instruction in 1975 and auditor in 1979, but he lost a second campaign for superintendent of public instruction in 1983 and for treasurer in 1987.

Running for statewide office for the first time is a difficult undertaking. Most candidates have previously held local or legislative office, and some have worked in statewide campaigns for other candidate. Traditionally, new candidates have started with a political base in their own county and have tried to put together a network of supporters among officeholders and political activists in as many of the 120 counties as possible. During the period when factionalism was stronger, some statewide candidates were able to win a place on a slate headed by a gubernatorial candidate.

Generally, these are low-visibility races, and name recognition is the key to success for most candidates. In the past most of these have also been low-cost races, precluding much reliance on expensive campaign managers and television advertising. In recent years, however, there has been an escalation in the amount of funds spent and the amount of television advertising bought in these campaigns. Table 20 in chapter 8 documents the growth in campaign spending for lesser offices from 1975 through 1987. It lists the amount spent by the winner and also by the highest spender.

To shed some light on primary campaigns for a range of state offices, we present analyses of the 1987 campaigns for attorney general, auditor, and superintendent of public instruction. All were highly competitive, relatively expensive races, and all represented defeats for the candidate who was the front-runner early (and sometimes quite late) in the campaign. What efforts did they make to build an organization across the state? How extensive were their financial resources? How extensively did they use media advertising? What issues did they raise? How can we explain the outcome of these races?

The Candidates

On May 26, 1987, state representative Fred Cowan, Jr., of Louisville won the Democratic attorney general primary with surprising ease, taking just over 50 percent of the vote and recording a margin of 45,808 votes over the front-runner, Jefferson County Commonwealth's Attorney Todd Hollenbach. A third candidate, Raymond Kirk of Lexington, an attorney who described himself as volunteer counsel for the state Railroad Commission, garnered less than 40,000 votes (less than 10 percent of the total vote).

Fred Cowan, Jr., an attorney, won his first electoral office by upsetting ten-term Republican state representative Bruce Blythe from Jefferson County's Thirty-second District. In the legislature he kept a relatively low profile but won a reputation as a liberal. Cowan began campaigning for attorney general in early 1986, and he seemed assured of an easy primary victory until Hollenbach entered the race. Todd Hollenbach had appeared to have a bright political future in 1969 when he was elected Jefferson County judge at only twenty-nine years of age. But, beginning in 1975, he lost four straight elections, including three statewide campaigns: a huge loss to the sitting governor, Julian Carroll, in the Democratic primary and successive losses for lieutenant governor in 1979 and 1983. In 1984, however, Hollenbach was elected Jefferson County commonwealth's attorney.

On May 26, 1987, Robert Babbage of Lexington won the Democratic state auditor primary with 62 percent of the vote; he finished more than 100,000 votes ahead of his competitor, Drexell Davis, Jr., of Frankfort. The two-man race for the Democratic nomination for auditor of public accounts pitted two political heirs in their first quest for statewide office. Bob Babbage, thirty-five, whose grandfather, Keen Johnson, was lieutenant governor from 1935 to 1939 and governor from 1939 to 1943, had been planning a statewide race for some office for years. Many who know him believe his ultimate political goal is to become governor. Babbage had been a financial consultant and had held several positions in public agencies. When he ran for auditor, he was in his sixth year as an at-large member of the Lexington Urban County Council. Drexell Davis, Jr., thirty-five, was a merit system employee in the state-local finance office of the Department of Local Government until he resigned in the fall of 1986 to run for office. "Drex" Jr. was best known as the son of Drexell "Drex" Davis, Sr., sixty-five, who had been elected to statewide office for the previous twenty years as secretary of state twice, state treasurer twice, and clerk of the state court of appeals once.

On May 26, 1987, John Brock, superintendent of Rowan County schools, won the Democratic superintendent of public instruction primary, taking just 26.9 percent of the vote and recording a margin of slightly more than 4,000 votes over state representative Roger Noe of Harlan (25.9 percent). The other contestants were former state superintendent Raymond Barber of Lexington (19.3 percent); Harry "Gippy" Graham of Frankfort, former administrator in the state Department of Education (11.2 percent); Louisville high school teacher Sherleen Sisney (10.9 percent); and Evelyn Travis, a retired Louisville schoolteacher who dropped out of the race and threw her support to Noe too late to have her name removed from the ballot (5.8 percent).

John Brock of Morehead, forty-nine, a former teacher and principal, for the past eleven years had been superintendent of Rowan County schools, where he had made some impressive improvements in the school system. Roger Noe of Harlan, thirty-seven, has taught at Southeast Community College since 1974 and was first elected to the legislature in 1977. He had been serving for several years as chairman of the House Education Committee and had played a key role in the education bills passed in recent sessions.

Building an Organizational Base

Any candidate trying to build an organizational base for a statewide campaign must start with the assets he or she has and the contacts that have been developed during previous political efforts. The nucleus of a candidate's political base is normally the home county. The race for attorney general was unusual because both Hollenbach and Cowan were political leaders in Jefferson County, though Hollenbach had been far better known for a longer period in the county. Bob Babbage had an advantage in the auditor's race because he held countywide office in Fayette, the second largest county.

None of the candidates made any serious effort to build a political organization in all or even most of the counties. They lacked the time, resources, and contacts to accomplish this. Most of the candidates tried to set up organizations in the counties with the largest populations and, more specifically, the largest numbers of voters in Democratic primaries. In addition, they concentrated on counties in their part of the state, as well as on ones where they had political contacts. For more than a year Cowan made trips to various counties around the state trying to raise money and establish local organizations. Babbage was also aggressive in developing county-level organizations. Each of them succeeded in creating working organizations in forty to fifty counties. The candidates for school superintendent relied more on the educational organizations supporting them to establish the county bases. Hollenbach and Davis appear to have made the weakest organizational efforts, apparently relying on their presumed advantage in name recognition. Within Jefferson County, both Hollenbach and Cowan utilized those members of the Democratic organization whose loyalty they could command. Statewide candidates from outside Louisville seemed to find that Jefferson was an unusually difficult county to organize.

Several of the candidates had enough resources to hire professional campaign staffs. Babbage, for example, hired two full-time workers, in addition to employing an advertising agency. Cowan also employed media consultants. Roger Noe had a full-time scheduler and an office manager and hired an experienced campaign consultant from New York. Brock did not hire any outside campaign staff.

Group Endorsements

Sometimes organized interests are central to a political campaign. Roger Noe got support from the Kentucky Education Association (KEA), and John Brock enlisted school superintendents on his side. Both Cowan and Hollenbach needed support from attorneys across the state. Both Cowan and Noe sought the support of fellow legislators, and they played a particularly important part in Noe's campaign.

Roger Noe's campaign illustrates the advantages and risks of group endorsements. When Noe began to think seriously about running for superintendent of public instruction, his first step was to seek and obtain the endorsement of the 30,600-member Kentucky Education Association, without which he probably would not have entered the race. As chairman of the House Education Committee, Noe had worked closely with the KEA on many pieces of legislation. The KEA endorsement was expected to bring him needed campaign money and the backing of teachers.

Some observers believed the KEA endorsement was less of an asset than a liability for Noe. KEA was very helpful in financial assistance and in establishing contacts for Noe in various parts of the state. But KEA's organizational efforts were woefully inadequate, and it fell far short of its original plan to have a coordinator for Noe in each school building. Noe was disappointed in the campaign efforts by the teachers, who often seemed cautious, reluctant, or uninterested in active involvement in politics. The superintendents appeared to be better organized and more united in their political activities on behalf of Brock, at least in the 1987 campaign.

Noe's opponents were critical of his relationship with KEA, saying that

Noe was partial to teacher interests and unable to unify education groups. Education reform groups tended to be a little suspicious of Noe because of the KEA link, though Noe was identified with reform. A Kentucky superintendents' group honored Noe a month before the KEA endorsement but then would not return Noe's calls during the campaign. Throughout the campaign Noe declined to say whether he favored mandatory collective bargaining for teachers, an issue KEA has pursued for years. "My position on professional negotiations is that it's been a terribly divisive, destructive issue for as long as I've been in the General Assembly, and I'm not making [it] an issue in my campaign," Noe said.

Campaign Techniques

The nature and scope of the campaigns, particularly the use of television, was largely dictated by financial resources. In the race for attorney general, Fred Cowan spent just over $450,000, five times as much as Todd Hollenbach. Bob Babbage outspent Drexel Davis by almost a 10 to 1 margin in the race for auditor; the figures were $294,000 to $32,000. Roger Noe outspent John Brock by more than 2 to 1, $181,000 to $86,000, in the race for superintendent of public instruction. Noe was the leading spender in that contest, and Brock was third.

Polling can be a valuable asset to a candidate who uses it well, but it is also an expensive asset. Bob Babbage did not conduct any polls but made some use of the polls conducted by the Democratic party and by gubernatorial candidates that were made available to him. Fred Cowan had enough resources to conduct two polls, one in January 1987 and one in early May. Both polls showed that Cowan was running far behind Hollenbach, though he had gained some ground in the second poll. The poll also suggested that Hollenbach's support was soft and that he was not well known to viewers. They suggested that if voters had more information on Cowan he could win the race.

The polls used by Cowan were important because they had a major impact on his campaign strategy. The polls convinced Cowan that Hollenbach was vulnerable and could only be beaten by an aggressive campaign that would call attention to Hollenbach's vulnerabilities but that would risk being labeled as "negative." Hollenbach had been the subject of several grand jury investigations, had been criticized for some of his actions as commonwealth attorney, and had come under attack for business activities and a traffic accident.

Several of the candidates made extensive use of mass media techniques. Babbage spent $80,000 on television, the focal point being a commercial in which viewers watched money being burned and heard the message, "We're running out of money to burn, Kentucky. Erase waste."

Cowan launched an aggressive campaign of television ads charging his opponent with misconduct in office and questioning his integrity. His opponent, Hollenbach, lacked the resources for a statewide television campaign. Neither Brock nor Noe made significant use of television commercials.

Because television advertising is so expensive and because it is difficult for those running for the lesser statewide offices to attract much public attention, the debates televised on KET assumed particular importance in the campaign. In the race for attorney general, the KET forum on May 5 changed the whole dynamic of the campaign. Like a prosecuting attorney in a capital case, Cowan ticked off a list of charges, ranging from past grand jury investigations to claims of favoritism in return for campaign contributions to an allegation that Hollenbach had left the scene of an accident he caused. "The issue is integrity," Cowan said, adding that the charges cast doubt on Hollenbach's fitness to serve. Hollenbach responded angrily, calling Cowan's tactics "wild and reckless charges," but he did not answer the charges directly. Following the debate, the press began to pay attention to Cowan's charges and he reiterated his attacks in televised commercials.

The May 6 KET debate on the auditor's race gave Bob Babbage a vehicle to publicize his plans for streamlining state government and his criticism of the "musical chairs" practice that his opponent's father (Drexel Davis, Sr.) had used for years in running for statewide office. Pressed by Babbage to detail the benefits of the "musical chairs" system, Davis listed several of his father's accomplishments and said, "He may have played musical chairs, but each time they stopped the music, he had a seat."

As a minimum, statewide candidates who cannot afford more expensive media might be expected to mail out leaflets or letters to all the voters, but even this may be too costly for some candidates. The computerized registration system, however, makes it possible to target those persons who have voted in the primary most consistently in the past and are therefore most likely to vote again. For candidates who can afford little or no television advertising, a targeted direct mail plan assumes particular importance. Roger Noe, for example, spent a substantial part of his budget, $71,000, on targeted direct mail.

Candidates for statewide office travel from county to county making speeches, contacting groups, and enlisting support—usually concentrating on the counties where they have tried to build local organizations. One purpose of those organizations, of course, is to arrange meetings and events for the candidate when he comes to the county.

How does a candidate make good use of the day or half day that he or she will spend in a medium-sized county? How can you gain some attention and have some impact when you are not well known and there is little interest in your campaign? Fred Cowan described the typical pattern that he would follow: "I went to the courthouse, perhaps spoke to the Kiwanis Club, perhaps a press conference, went to some radio stations, maybe met with a few key people." In many places the campaign would not spend a full day, and some time would be spent in fund-raising: a number of individual appointments to seek money. Most candidates find it useful to touch base with the local courthouse officials, hoping to gain some support or at least make their presence in the county known to local politicians. In Cowan's race for attorney general, he found that often the commonwealth and county attorneys were most helpful to him.

In reality, of course, it is difficult for those running for most statewide offices to meet large numbers of voters or to draw a crowd for a speech. Candidates for these offices, in search of a crowd, often showed up at rallies being held by candidates for governor or lieutenant governor, to work the crowd as much as possible. In his campaign for auditor, Bob Babbage, for example, estimated that he went to five or six rallies of each candidate for the more important offices.

The trend toward more expensive races and greater use of television in campaigns may continue for the offices that are most visible and are perceived as stepping-stones to the governorship, such as lieutenant governor. The costs of races for other offices may rise more gradually, simply because it is difficult to find financial contributors willing to invest in candidates for auditor or secretary of state. Because it is so costly to buy enough advertising to gain name recognition, those candidates who hold statewide office and thus already have some name recognition will continue to have a major advantage over newcomers.

6

PARTY ACTIVISTS

IN RECENT years an extensive literature has developed on the attitudes, motivations, and activities of party activists—on differences between "amateurs" (see Carney, 1958; Wilson, 1962; Hirschfield, Swanson, and Blank, 1962) and "professionals" (see Kent, 1923; Salter, 1935; Forthal, 1946) and on the reasons why convention delegates support certain presidential candidates (Abramowitz, McGlennon, and Rapoport, 1986a, 1986b). But very little attention has been paid to activists who work in statewide primary campaigns. This is unfortunate, since volunteer activists continue to play a crucial role in statewide primary elections, even in an era of professional campaign managers and media-oriented campaigns. Volunteer staffers are still key actors in the nominating and campaign decision-making processes. This chapter focuses on Kentucky Democratic gubernatorial activists because they are the heart and core of the state's political nominating process. In contrast, in some other states it is the precinct workers who are the most vital actors.

An examination of gubernatorial activists in Kentucky can provide valuable insight into the activities and motivations of statewide elite workers in general. These are the most active and vital political volunteers who contribute to the overall political process in innumerable ways—recruitment of candidates, management of campaigns, fund-raising, and so on.

This chapter addresses several important questions: Who are the Kentucky Democratic primary gubernatorial activists? How do they compare—demographically and politically—to those in other states? Are Kentucky activists fairly typical of elite political workers in general?

There is a vast literature on the demographic and political characteristics of party activists—local precinct chairmen (e.g., Conway and Feigert, 1968), local ward leaders (e.g., Hofstetter, 1973), delegates to presidential nominating conventions (e.g., Roback, 1980), delegates to state party presidential nominating conventions (e.g., Abramowitz, McGlennon, and Rapoport, 1986a), state central party committee members (e.g., Bell,1985), congressional primary activists (e.g., Johnson and

Gibson, 1974), party leaders and activists (e.g., Costantini and King, 1984), campaign contributors (e.g., Hedges, 1984), and so on.

Previous research has demonstrated that certain social and demographic characteristics distinguish voters from nonvoters (e.g., Campbell, Converse, Miller, and Stokes, 1960; Verba and Nie, 1972; Wolfinger and Rosenstone, 1980). Likewise, the political activist is distinguishable from the nonactivist on the basis of similar characteristics (Patterson, 1963; Milbrath, 1965; Pomper, 1965; Wiggins and Turk, 1970; Verba and Nie, 1972; Roback, 1974; Abramowitz et al., 1986a). Voluminous research on partisan leaders has indicated that party activists are an elite social and political group (see Crotty, 1967; Patterson and Boynton, 1969; Boynton, Hedlund, and Patterson, 1969; Marvick, 1968; Johnson and Gibson, 1974; Abramowitz et al., 1986a; Bell, 1985). Generally, party activists tend to have income, occupation, and education levels that are substantially higher than the average for their states.

It is important to examine the demographic and political characteristics of gubernatorial activists in order to gain insight into what leads them to make their individual political choices. We shall analyze two distinct types of personal characteristics—general personal background (e.g., education, age, religion, etc.) and political experiences or activities (e.g., years of active political involvement, etc.). Previous research suggests that party activists tend to be higher status individuals than the average Kentuckians, and we would expect that difference to be even greater because we are dealing with an elite group of political activists.

We would like to compare the personal and political characteristics of Kentucky activists with those of persons active in state primaries in other states, to find out whether the Kentucky group is typical or has some unique characteristics. Unfortunately, no such data set is available. Consequently, for our comparison we will use Abramowitz et al.'s (1986a) sample of 17,628 delegates to twenty-two state party conventions in eleven states that in 1980 chose delegates to national nominating conventions. We would expect each of the groups to include many of the most active workers in political campaigns, and in that sense each is an elite group of activists. But there may be some differences between the Kentucky group and the national sample that do not reflect differences between Kentucky activists and those in other states but rather differences between persons active in gubernatorial primaries and those who are elected to state conventions.

We examine the political characteristics of the gubernatorial activists for several important theoretical reasons. The motivations of long-term professional party activists may be different from those of short-term workers who are attracted or mobilized by a particuar campaign. If we know to what extent these gubernatorial activists have a long-term political commitment, it will help us understand motivations for general political activity and activity in a particular campaign. A detailed political profile of these elite workers will provide valuable clues to the kinds of motivations that might be important to them. Information about previous party activity, political positions held, types of electoral campaign participation, and years of active involvement in politics can enhance our understanding of the motives of these gubernatorial primary activists.

We have survey data from individuals heavily involved in Democratic gubernatorial primaries in Kentucky for 1979, 1983, and 1987. Each candidate or a high-ranking staffer in his or her campaign provided a list of county, district, and state chairmen and treasurers, and these lists constituted the sampling frame of activists. Questionnaires were mailed to those active in the 1979 and 1983 primaries following the November 1983 general election. In all, 2,000 people were contacted, and responses were received from 734 (37 percent) of those surveyed, a return rate deemed acceptable in view of the length (16 pages) of the questionnaire. After the May 1987 primary, 1,500 questionnaires were mailed to those identified as active in the 1987 campaign, as well as those who had responded to the surveys sent out in 1983. Responses were received from 596 (316 nonpanelists and 280 panelists—40 percent) of those surveyed.

Comparison of Kentucky Primary Activists with Those in Other States

A comparison of the demographic and political characteristics of Kentucky elite gubernatorial workers with those of Democratic state presidential convention delegates in eleven other states may help us gain not only some clues about whether gubernatorial activists differ in some substantial ways from presidential activists (e.g., more "professionals" and fewer newcomers to politics in gubernatorial contests) but also some understanding about political activists in general. Abramowitz et al.'s (1986a) large national sample permits us to make comparisons with southern and border states (which would be most similar to Kentucky), as well as to make a national comparative analysis. The Kentucky gubernatorial activists and the state presidential convention delegates are a fairly comparable group of workers—drawn from a similar echelon and from essentially the same layers of political workers.

Table 8 presents a comparative demographic and political profile of the Kentucky Democratic gubernatorial activists with Democratic state presidential convention delegates in five southern and border states (Missouri, Texas, Virginia, South Carolina, and Oklahoma) and with those

Table 8. Demographic and Political Characteristics of Activists in Kentucky and in Other States

Characteristic	K (1979/83 & 1987) (%)	SD (1980) (%)	ND (1980) (%)
Years lived in state			
Less than 5 years	3.5	4.9	6.9
5 to 10 years	2.3	8.0	9.4
10 to 20 years	5.5	14.8	14.6
More than 20 years	88.7	72.3	69.1
	100.0	100.0	100.0
Income			
to $14,999	5.8	15.9	19.7
$15,000 to $24,999	14.1	28.1	30.9
$25,000 to $34,999	18.7	23.6	23.6
$35,000 or more	61.3	32.4	25.8
	99.9	100.0	100.0
Education			
Grade school only	2.2	1.2	1.5
Some high school	5.7	3.6	3.0
Graduated high school	18.5	13.1	14.9
Some college	25.3	26.9	27.3
Graduated college	17.2	18.5	19.8
Postcollege	31.1	36.7	33.5
	100.0	100.0	100.0
Occupation			
Lawyers	10.4	N/A	N/A
Technical professionals	5.4	N/A	N/A
Other professionals	2.2	N/A	N/A
Teachers & counselors	8.0	N/A	N/A
Students	1.0	N/A	N/A
Elected & appointed public officials	14.9	N/A	N/A
Insurance & real estate	6.6	N/A	N/A
Other businessmen	15.8	N/A	N/A
Private administrators	4.2	N/A	N/A
Farmers	6.4	N/A	N/A
White-collar workers	3.5	N/A	N/A
Blue-collar workers	4.8	N/A	N/A
Homemakers	5.4	N/A	N/A
Retired	11.4	N/A	N/A
	100.0		
Type of county residence			
Metropolitan	21.1	N/A	N/A
Nonmetropolitan	78.9	N/A	N/A
	100.0		

Table 8 (cont.)

Characteristic	K (1979/83 & 1987) (%)	SD (1980) (%)	ND (1980) (%)
Sex			
Female	28.7	51.0	49.8
Male	71.3	49.0	50.2
	100.0	100.0	100.0
Evangelical or "born again"			
Yes	41.9	32.5	21.6
No	58.1	67.5	78.4
	100.0	100.0	100.0
Age			
18-29	4.3	18.5	20.2
30-39	23.5	26.4	28.7
40-49	26.3	20.6	18.4
50-59	22.4	19.0	18.1
60-69	17.0	12.1	11.3
Over 69	6.5	3.4	3.2
	100.0	100.0	99.9
Race			
White	98.9	80.8	89.2
Black	1.1	16.6	7.6
Hispanic	—	1.4	2.0
Oriental	—	0.2	0.3
Indian	—	1.0	0.9
	100.0	100.0	100.0
Political activity of parents			
Not active	13.3	N/A	N/A
Voted regularly	45.6	N/A	N/A
Ran for office	1.8	N/A	N/A
Worked campaigns	3.7	N/A	N/A
Ran & voted regularly	8.3	N/A	N/A
Worked campaigns & voted regularly	20.6	N/A	N/A
Ran, worked, & voted regularly	6.7	N/A	N/A
	100.0		
Political ideology			
Very liberal	6.0	17.8	18.8
Somewhat liberal	30.5	36.4	40.4
Middle of the road	26.0	22.6	21.9
Somewhat conservative	32.3	19.7	16.3
Very conservative	5.2	3.4	2.6
	100.0	99.9	100.0

Table 8 (cont.)

Characteristic	K (1979/83 & 1987) (%)	SD (1980) (%)	ND (1980) (%)
Party identification			
Strong Democrat	75.3	81.4	75.6
Democrat, but not too strong	17.3	11.6	14.7
Independent, closer to Democrats	4.7	5.5	8.0
Completely independent	1.5	1.3	1.5
Independent, closer to Republicans	0.5	0.2	0.3
Republican, but not too strong	0.2	—	—
Strong Republican	0.5	—	—
	100.0	100.0	100.1
Years active in politics			
Less than 5 years	16.0	31.6	38.1
Between 5 & 10 years	18.1	22.3	22.1
Between 10 & 20 years	28.3	22.5	20.1
More than 20 years	37.6	23.6	19.6
	100.0	100.0	100.0
Frequency of involvement in political campaigns in last 5 years			
Active in all	40.2	38.4	29.8
Active in most	32.3	27.9	26.4
Active in few	26.4	24.6	29.4
Active in none	1.1	9.0	14.4
	100.0	99.9	100.0
Kinds of campaigns active in (can check as many as apply)			
Local	83.9	83.4	73.4
State legislative	62.5	68.8	59.9
Congressional	57.7	63.6	55.7
Gubernatorial	97.5	60.0	48.3
Other statewide	57.9	N/A	N/A
Presidential	47.8	67.6	59.4
Political positions held now (can check as many as apply)			
Member local party committee	35.7	54.7	52.7
Chairman local party committee	14.5	15.0	16.9
Elected to state or legislative office	4.5	3.4	2.5
Elected to local office	17.4	15.5	9.9
Appointed to government office	5.0	10.4	8.9

Table 8 (cont.)

Characteristic	K (1979/83 & 1987) (%)	SD (1980) (%)	ND (1980) (%)
Kinds of groups active in (can check as many as apply)			
Labor unions	9.6	14.4	16.5
Civil rights groups	4.2	24.2	19.0
Educational or teachers groups	16.0	29.0	26.0
Other professional groups	33.8	24.5	20.8
Businesses	33.3	17.8	13.7
Church-related organizations	31.8	30.9	26.8
Women's rights groups	6.3	18.5	18.1
Public interest groups	24.4	25.7	22.4
Farm groups	17.6	10.2	12.0
Conservation/ecology groups	6.5	12.3	14.4
Antiabortion groups	3.9	3.6	5.5
Other issue-oriented groups	8.3	17.8	17.1

Note: Totals in all tables may not equal 100.0 percent because of rounding or multiple responses.
K = Kentucky Democratic Gubernatorial Activists in 1979/83 and 1987
SD = Democratic Southern/Border State Presidential Activists from 5 states in 1980
ND = Democratic National State Presidential Activists from 11 states in 1980

in a national sample of eleven states (Arizona, North Dakota, Maine, Colorado, Utah, Iowa, and the earlier named southern/border states). The Kentucky data include those who worked in 1983 and/or 1979 (N = 682) and those elite workers in 1987 who were not part of our earlier sample (N = 316).

Demographic Profile

An examination of some demographic characteristics of the 998 gubernatorial activists reveals that most have lived in Kentucky for a long time: more than 88 percent for over twenty years, under 4 percent for less than five years. (Some of the data in these profiles are not included in table 8.) Almost two-thirds earn over $35,000 a year and less than 6 percent under $15,000. Almost one-third have postgraduate education; over half of these are in professions requiring a postbaccalaureate degree, including the predictable 10 percent attorneys. Nearly another one-fifth graduated from college, and one-fourth more attended college. Only about 6 percent did not complete high school.

The Kentucky activists have a higher level of income than the national sample, a contrast that is surprising, given the relatively low income levels of the population in Kentucky. This may be because a number of those recruited to work actively in Kentucky gubernatorial campaigns are expected to play some role in fund-raising. Kentucky activists have an education level nearly as high as the national and southern samples, although general education levels in Kentucky are well below average. Another difference is the tendency for the gubernatorial activists to be longer-time Kentucky residents, compared to state-residency patterns of activists in other states.

About one-fourth of the Kentucky activists are lawyers, teachers, or other professionals. Almost one-fourth are business persons. And about 15 percent are elected and appointed public officials. There are relatively few farmers and white-collar or blue-collar workers. There are only a few homemakers, though more than one-fourth of the sample are women.

The overwhelming majority of the activists are Protestants, including two-fifths who are evangelical (or "born again"), with only 13.3 percent Catholics, less than 2 percent Jews, and less than 5 percent who identify themselves as agnostic, atheist, or having no religious identification. The proportion of "born again" persons in the Kentucky sample is slightly higher than among southern activists and nearly twice as high as in the national sample. Clearly, this is a regional phenomenon.

The Kentucky sample is almost evenly divided among age groups: the thirties, the forties, the fifties, and those sixty and older. There are significantly fewer young people in the Kentucky sample—perhaps because the Kentucky sample is an elite group of party activists. Almost 99 percent of the Kentucky group are white, a much larger percentage than in the national and particularly the southern sample.

Most of these gubernatorial elites in Kentucky were raised in politically active families; one-fifth of their parents worked in campaigns and voted regularly, and more than two-ffths voted in most elections.

Political Profile

A study of the political characteristics of the Kentucky gubernatorial activists shows a wide range of political experiences, but the majority are seasoned politicos. Almost three-fourths report that they participated in all or most political campaigns in the last five years. Over one-third have been active in Kentucky politics over twenty years, and only 16 percent for less than five years. It is obvious that these are people whose involvement in politics is substantial and consistent, year in and year out. This is significant because these individuals have been identified as the most active workers in the campaigns of particular candidates. In addition, more than one-third of the Kentucky activists have been actively participating in gubernatorial politics for more than twenty-five years.

Kentucky activists have been slightly more active in recent political campaigns than their national counterparts and have also been active in politics over a longer period of time. Clearly, the Kentucky activists are a more stable, long-term "professional" group than we find in the national sample. The Kentucky political elites are closer to the southern Democratic pattern but include more long-term workers. The national presidential delegate sample includes more newcomers to the political arena and is therefore made up of political workers who have been neither consistently as active nor as active over such a long period of time as the gubernatorial elite workers.

Many of the Kentucky political elites hold party and other political positions. Over one-third are members of their local party committees, and almost half that number hold local party chairmanships. More than one-sixth hold public elective offices, mostly at the local level. The 1987 gubernatorial activists were asked about prior electoral activity; 45 percent had run for public office at least once, 31 percent had been elected at some time in local elections, and 5 percent had won state legislative office.

By comparison with their counterparts in other states, the Kentucky activists hold significantly fewer local party positions. One possible explanation is that party committee positions mean less at the local level in Kentucky because local politics is less competitive. There may also be a division of labor in Kentucky between those who hold high-level positions in primary campaigns and those who work in the local party. Persons active in party organizations in other states may be particularly likely to attend state conventions.

In examining levels of participation in various kinds of political campaigns, we are interested in discovering whether most activists work in almost every level of politics, national, state, and local, year in and year out, or whether many of them specialize in only one level of elections perhaps because of a commitment to specific candidates. Ideally, both our Kentucky and our national samples would include both gubernatorial and presidential campaign activists. Instead, we must compare a sample of Kentucky gubernatorial primary activists and a national sample of delegates attendng state conventions to support presidential candidates. By definition, each sample is active in a different level of politics.

There are some significant differences between the two groups. Those in the national sample of presidential activists were heavily involved in local politics, and 50 to 60 percent of them were active in each of the other levels of campaigns. The southern presidential sample was consistently more active in each level of politics than the national sample, though the differences were not large. Since fewer than two-thirds of the national sample of presidential activists described themselves as being active in presidential campaigns, presumably about one-third of them were new to presidential politics, though some had worked at other levels.

An overwhelming proportion (almost 84 percent) of Kentuckians who are heavily involved in gubernatorial primaries have been active in local campaigns, and 50 to 60 percent have worked in most of the campaigns in other levels of elections, although the average falls below 50 percent for presidential races. A cross tabulation of the Kentucky data allows us to generalize about how many types of campaigns the gubernatorial activists participated in. About one-third of them were active in almost all kinds of campaigns at the national, state, and local levels. About 13 percent were active in presidential, gubernatorial, and local races at least. Some 15 percent worked in all levels except the presidential. About one-fourth were regularly active only at the gubernatorial and local levels. And about 15 percent participated only in gubernatorial politics or had not been consistently active at any level.

Party Identification

Contemporary political scholars suggest that people living in southern and border states may possess dual party predispositions—Democratic for local and state elections and Republican for national elections. They have even found such differences, at least in the strength of party identification, among party activists (Hadley, 1985; Niemi, Wright, and Powell, 1987). Therefore, in our 1987 survey, we questioned the activists about both their national and their state party identifications. There are a larger proportion (78 percent) who identify strongly with the state Democratic party than those (61 percent) who identify strongly with the national Democratic party.

We find that the strongest national and state party identifiers participate more at the various levels of electoral contests. Also, party identification has a greater impact on activity in presidential races than on other types of political contests. Activists with strong to moderate state party identifications but weaker national party identifications are only half as likely to be involved in presidential campaigns. This difference is much smaller when we look at involvement in other levels of campaigns.

In the 1983 survey, we used the same general party identification question that was asked the presidential delegates. Over 73 percent of the Kentucky activists consider themselves strong Democrats, and another 20 percent identify as "Democrats, but not too strong." The proportion of strong Democratic identifiers in Kentucky is slightly lower than the national sample and (surprisingly) is eight percentage points lower than is found in the southern sample.

Interest Group Involvement

We want to know how involved political activists are in interest groups—for several reasons. They may be recruited into political activity because of their commitment to groups that are politically oriented. Their concern about issues or commitment to an ideological position may be explained, at least in part, by their loyalties to a group. Similarly, the preference of an interest group may influence their choice of a candidate to support. To put the question more broadly, do political activists have divided group loyalties, or are they primarily interested in Democratic party politics?

Perhaps the most thoroughly documented aspect of the interplay between interest groups and activists is the phenomena of sponsored membership. In some states it is common for interest group leaders actively to recruit their members to be delegates to state and national nominating conventions. Sponsored membership may vary from state to state and from election to election. For example, Thomas Marshall (1981) reports that in Minnesota "the issue activists have demonstrated a continuing interest in taking their issues to political parties. Feminists; pro- and anti-abortion advocates; educators; farmers; organized labor; racial, sexual preference, and ethnic minorities; and others have all organized into issue caucuses within one or both parties and have sought to elect their spokespersons to party posts and influence party policy-making" (p. 153).

The Minnesota Democratic-Farmer-Labor (DFL) and Independent Republican (IR) parties are the best examples of this model of party activists, and it is manifest in the loyalties of delegates to the parties' preprimary endorsing conventions for statewide office. This does not mean that all the delegates to such conventions are motivated by the concerns of interest groups. But an unusually large proportion of delegates to the Minnesota party conventions, including those with long records of party activity, have strong commitments to issues and organized interests. These political parties are coalitions of organized interests.

Jewell (1984) asked delegates to both the 1982 DFL and IR conventions if, in seeking election as a delegate, they were primarily interested in a candidate, a platform issue, or both. The results are as follows:

	DFL delegates	IR delegates
Both	43%	23%
Issue only	37	25
Candidate only	11	14
Neither	9	38

In the Abramowitz et al.'s (1986a) study of delegates to eleven state party conventions in 1980, Francis and Benedict (1986) report that over 60 percent of all delegates surveyed reported being active in groups outside the party (either single or multiple group memberships). After analysis of the motivations, issue positions, and ideology of these delegates, the authors concluded that "in spite of the activities of interest groups, the political parties are still decidedly identifiable bodies possessing a high degree of loyalty and varying degrees of ideological unity" (p. 123). In addition, as part of this same study, Hauss and Maisel (1986) reported that the belief that the parties have been overtaken by extremists or "ideologues" is but a myth. At the state convention level, they found that "both parties seem dominated by well-informed activists who are committed to traditional electoral strategies and mainstream electable candidates" (p. 224).

Past research suggests that Kentucky political actors consider themselves political activists first and interest group members second (Jewell and Cunningham, 1968), as contrasted with political elites in more ideologically and issue-oriented states such as Minnesota. Both the gubernatorial workers in Kentucky and the 1980 national sample of state presidential convention delegates were asked to identify the groups in which they had been politically active. In terms of interest group involvement among the different Democratic samples, we see that the Kentucky elite workers are less active than the national sample in the kinds of groups we usually associate with national Democratic politics: labor unions, civil rights groups, educational organizations, women's rights groups, and conservation/ecology groups.

We conclude that Kentucky political activists are less likely than Democratic activists in other states to be active in those interest groups that are most politically oriented and identified with the Democratic party. (We do not think this is a result of the different composition of the two samples.) As a consequence, the Kentucky political workers are likely to be more independent of such influences. They come closer to having undivided loyalty to the Democratic party; and a smaller proportion of them are likely to judge candidates in terms of their agreement with positions taken by these interest groups.

Political Ideology

The Kentucky elite volunteers are almost evenly balanced in their political ideology: 36.5 percent of them say they are liberal, 37.5 percent are conservative, and 26 percent cling to the middle of the road. Most liberals and conservatives use the adjective *somewhat* rather than *very* to describe their position. This balanced position makes the Kentucky activists considerably less liberal than either the southern or the national sample of presidential party activists. One reason for this difference, particularly in the South, may be that presidential politics attracts activists who are more in tune with the liberal position of the national Democratic party. The fact that Kentucky activists are less likely to be active in interest groups oriented to the national Democratic party helps to explain their weaker commitment to liberal positions. It is also worth recalling that 8 percent of the national sample and 17 percent of the southern sample are blacks who are more liberal in their preferences, and this contributes to the more liberal profile of these groups.

Conclusion

The Kentucky Democratic primary gubernatorial activists are the elites of party activists. Although they are longtime Kentucky residents, they are not typical Kentuckians in profession, education, or wealth. Their involvement in various types of political contests is intense, and year in and year out they apparently try to find candidates for whom they can campaign. They might be classified as "professional" long-term workers, in contrast to "amateurs" who are drawn into politics by a particular candidate, goal, or issue.

We have noted many similarities, socially and politically, between Kentucky gubernatorial supporters and the state presidential convention delegates in Abramowitz et al.'s (1986a) eleven-state study. Most of the differences between the two groups reflect the greater stability of activity, membership, and involvement of Kentucky gubernatorial activists compared to that found in presidential delegates in other states. Kentucky gubernatorial activists appear fairly typical of political activists in general, with a few noteworthy exceptions: their long-term stability of participation, their lower level of involvement in interest groups, and their greater conservatism.

Motivations of Political Activists in Gubernatorial Primaries

In recent years, political scientists have focused considerable attention on the motives, goals, and purposes of political leaders and activists, but they have paid little or no attention to state primary activists. Our purpose in this section is to identify the reasons why such persons become actively involved in gubernatorial primaries.

The motivations of gubernatorial primary activists can be analyzed from the perspective of the incentive literature (Clark and Wilson, 1961; Wilson, 1973; Olson, 1965; Moe, 1980). Research on political leaders' and activists' motivations has often been guided by Clark and Wilson's distinction among three types of incentives that organizations may offer participants in return for their contributions: "material," "solidary," or "purposive." "Material" incentives are tangible rewards that have monetary value or can be translated into monetary terms. "Solidary" incentives are intangible rewards that result mainly from the act of associating and include socializing, group identification, member status, and fun seeking.

"Purposive" incentives are also intangible but pertain to the stated ends of association rather than to association per se; they involve suprapersonal ends—"the demand for the enactment of certain laws or the adoption of certain practices" (p. 135).

Over the last two decades, numerous researchers have adopted or adapted Clark and Wilson's categories in analyses of political activists of various types—party leaders and activists (e.g., Costantini and King, 1984), campaign contributors (e.g., Hedges, 1984), delegates to presidential nominating conventions (e.g., Roback, 1980), local ward leaders (e.g., Hofstetter, 1973), and so on. The dominant concern of these analyses has been to determine why people are active in politics, not why they become involved in particular candidates' campaigns. Whatever the focus of these studies, the Clark and Wilson typology is clearly the prevailing conceptual framework in the analysis of political motivations. There is, however, considerable divergence among these studies in operationalizations of the Clark-Wilson motivational categories.

While the Clark-Wilson categories and adaptations and extensions thereof continue to hold sway in the literature, studies of local party organization have suggested other models. Kent (1923), Salter (1935), Gosnell (1937), and Forthal (1946) presented a "professional" model, in which the party organization was seen as attracting and disciplining workers through material incentives, making nonideological appeals and orienting itself toward obtaining votes. Carney (1958), Wilson (1962), and Hirschfield et al. (1962), on the other hand, presented an "amateur" model, in which the party activist is seen as more ideologically oriented, seeking reforms or improved services. A "candidate-oriented" model was summarized by Schlesinger (1965), who argued that the basic unit of party organization is focused on a collective effort to capture a single public office. Neither material nor ideological, the organization seeks control at some time, however far in the future.

We will explore sources of activists' motivations for participating in gubernatorial primaries in terms of material incentives, solidary incentives, purposive incentives, and attraction to or linkage with a candidate. The first three of these models have their theoretical foundations in the incentive theory literature, while the underpinnings of the fourth are in Schlesinger's (1965) "candidate-oriented" model of party organization.

Predictors of Incentives

If, as there is strong reason to assume, different persons have different motives for becoming active in political campaigns, then an important question arises: Is there any discernible patterning to the distribution of motivations? That is, are certain types of people more likely to be motivated by certain kinds of incentives? There has been some attention to this question in the literature, but no body of theory is available to help us find answers. The literature provides only scattered hints about the factors that might shape motivations.

Are younger, better-educated persons, or those most active in certain groups, or ideologues likely to have stronger issue motivations? Are those who have been most active in politics or who have held more party positions less affected by issues? These possibilities relate to the distinction between the more professional and experienced party leader who is driven by career or job goals or social or friendship factors and the younger, enthusiastic amateur who is motivated by issues. This distinction between professional and amateur is almost certainly overdrawn, but it nonetheless provides a good starting point.

Reasons for Involvement in Gubernatorial Campaigns

Respondents to our questionnaire were asked about their activities and motivations for participation in the 1979, 1983, and/or 1987 primaries. For each primary in which they indicated that they had actively supported a gubernatorial candidate, they were then asked to consider a set of items pertaining to their motivations for involvement. Consequently, many respondents gave reasons for their involvement in all three primaries, while others explained their involvement in either 1979 or 1983 or 1987. Reasons for becoming involved in the 1979, 1983, and/or 1987 primary campaigns were probed in a series of thirteen Likert-type items, similar to those used in several previous studies.

Table 9 summarizes the respondents' stated motivations for active involvement in the 1979, 1983, and 1987 gubernatorial primaries. The most conspicuous features of these responses for all three primaries are the emphasis placed upon supporting particular candidates, the widespread endorsement of "good citizen" motivations, and the lack of emphasis on material incentives. Over 80 percent of the respondents said that "supporting a particular candidate I believe in" was a very important reason for their involvement. Similarly, more than three-quarters asserted that "fulfilling civic responsibilities," "influencing policies of government," and "working for issues" were very or somewhat important motivations. By contrast, more than 70 percent indicated that business and personal political gains were not very important factors in their involvement.

These findings bear out conclusions reached in several prior studies. For example, both Kirkpatrick (1976), in her study of delegates to the 1972 presidential nominating conventions, and Hedges (1984), in his study of campaign contributors, reported that those activists downplayed business reasons and other material incentives to roughly the same extent as did the

Table 9. Activists' Motivations for Involvement, 1979, 1983, 1987

Motive	Number	Very important	Somewhat important	Not very important	Not at all important	Total percent
To work with a certain group of people with whom I have political ties	546	31.0	40.8	15.0	13.2	100.0
	861	26.9	38.2	19.6	15.2	99.9
	549	20.2	33.7	25.5	20.6	100.0
To develop social contacts with people with similar interests	536	20.5	31.7	21.6	26.1	99.9
	854	16.7	36.4	23.0	23.9	100.0
	549	13.1	33.2	26.8	27.0	100.1
To enjoy the excitement of the campaign	544	28.3	32.9	22.4	16.4	100.0
	865	26.5	37.0	18.6	17.9	100.0
	549	21.7	37.3	20.0	20.9	99.9
To work with friends and relatives who support a particular candidate	531	26.7	33.0	20.3	20.0	100.0
	816	24.0	34.6	21.0	20.5	100.1
	549	20.4	34.2	23.9	21.5	100.0
To work for a candidate because of personal friendship with him or her	551	42.1	24.1	17.6	16.2	100.0
	823	36.7	32.4	14.7	16.2	100.0
	549	37.5	31.3	18.0	13.1	99.9
To help my own political career	536	9.3	21.1	20.9	48.7	100.0
	814	6.9	19.9	21.7	51.5	100.0
	549	5.8	15.5	21.5	57.2	100.0
To obtain a local or state government job	534	4.7	12.0	12.2	71.2	100.1
	806	2.1	5.6	13.8	78.5	100.0
	549	2.4	5.6	12.9	79.1	100.0
To make business contacts	513	5.7	18.5	20.5	55.4	100.1
	846	5.3	18.8	26.5	49.4	100.0
	549	6.6	18.9	24.0	50.5	100.0
To work for issues I feel strongly about	508	51.0	36.8	8.5	3.7	100.0
	858	61.0	27.3	7.6	4.2	100.1
	549	72.5	23.5	2.6	1.5	100.1
To influence policies of government	540	38.1	39.3	12.4	10.2	100.0
	864	40.6	41.2	9.8	8.3	99.9
	549	39.5	38.1	12.8	9.7	100.1
To fulfill my civic responsibilities	517	45.1	34.4	11.6	8.9	100.0
	864	44.7	37.6	10.1	7.6	100.0
	549	38.8	39.0	13.3	8.9	100.0
To support a candidate who advocates the goals of an interest group of which I am a member	538	23.6	29.2	11.3	35.9	100.0
	799	22.8	24.5	16.3	36.4	100.0
	549	23.3	25.0	14.2	37.5	100.0

Table 9 (cont.)

Motive	Number	Very important	Somewhat important	Not very important	Not at all important	Total percent
To support a	563	82.4	14.9	2.3	0.4	100.0
particular candidate I	866	87.5	10.5	1.6	0.5	100.1
believe in	549	85.6	12.6	1.6	0.3	100.1

Note: The first entry in each cell is for 1979, the second for 1983, and the third for 1987. Totals may not equal 100.0 percent because of rounding.

Kentucky activists. Also, more than 75 percent of the contributors in Hedges's study and the Republican convention delegates in Roback's (1980) cited "good citizen" reasons as underlying their political involvement; that percentage is similar to the "good citizen" responses of the Kentucky gubernatorial activists. The new element, distinctive to table 9 and not emphasized in prior research, is of course the candidate motivation of the Kentucky volunteers. Attraction to a specific candidate was clearly the predominant motivator in the gubernatorial primary campaigns analyzed here. This motivation may or may not be equally strong in other political settings, but at the very least typologies of activists' motivations should be expanded to take it into account.

In comparing the results for 1979 with those for 1983 and for 1987, it is apparent that the percentages on individual items are similar for all motivational items. The 1983 activists did stress "civic responsibilities" and "influencing policies of government" somewhat more, whereas the 1979 activists rated more positively "working with a particular group," "obtaining a local or state job," and "interest group goals." In contrast, the 1987 elite volunteers stressed "working for issues" somewhat more than either the 1979 or 1983 activists. But these differences were relatively minor and should not be permitted to obscure the overriding similarity of responses in the three primaries.

In order to explore the structure of the activists' motivations, factor analysis was used to reduce the thirteen items to a smaller number of underlying dimensions. Table 10 presents the pattern matrices, using an oblique rotation. The item on "support of a particular candidate I believe in" had to be excluded from the factor analyses since most activists strongly emphasized this reason, thus creating very little variation.

The remaining twelve items formed three dimensions, accounting for 51.1 percent of the total variance in 1979, 48.8 percent in 1983, and 49.8 percent in 1987. The first dimension, on which the highest-loading items included "to work with a certain group with whom I have political ties," "to develop social contacts with people with similar interests," "to enjoy

Table 10. Motivations for Involvement in 1979, 1983, 1987 Primaries: Oblique Rotated Factor Matrices*

	Solidary			Material			Purposive		
Motive	1979	1983	1987	1979	1983	1987	1979	1983	1987
To work with a certain group of people with whom I have political ties	.724	.507	.602	.046	.198	.109	−.085	.096	.095
To develop social contacts with people with similar interests	.624	.370	.737	.163	.249	.089	.088	.248	.068
To enjoy the excitement of the campaign	.533	.326	.725	.053	.273	−.008	.048	.083	.042
To work with friends and relatives who support a particular candidate	.685	.899	.629	−.049	−.130	−.088	−.030	−.020	−.020
To work for a candidate because of personal friendship with him or her	.446	.427	.198	−.070	.013	.176	.017	−.036	−.163
To help my own political career	−.009	−.035	−.031	.809	.724	.742	−.036	−.048	−.007

the excitement of the campaign," and "to work with friends and relatives who support a particular candidate," quite clearly tapped solidary motivations. Similarly, the high loadings of "to help my own political career," "to make business contacts," and "to obtain a local or state government job" indicate that the second factor tapped material motivations. Four other items ("to work for issues I feel strongly about," "to influence policies of government," "to fulfill my civic responsibilities," and "to support a candidate who advocates the goals of an interest group of which I am a member") formed a third dimension that fit very nicely with the concept of purposive incentives (although the loadings on the interest group item were lower than for most other items in 1979 and 1987). The very same motivational items loaded on the same factors in each of the three primary campaigns. These dimensions are, of course, what would be anticipated on the basis of the Clark and Wilson typology of incentives, and the results

Table 10 (cont.)

Motive	Solidary			Material			Purposive		
	1979	1983	1987	1979	1983	1987	1979	1983	1987
To obtain a local or state government job	−.034	.030	.044	.701	.507	.531	−.080	.051	−.019
To make business contacts	.114	.047	.035	.535	.653	.609	.114	−.029	.047
To work for issues I feel strongly about	−.004	−.008	.018	−.154	−.165	−.060	.589	.648	.413
To influence policies of government	−116	−.160	−.067	.134	.149	.245	.581	.464	.539
To fulfill my civic responsibilities	.112	.030	.102	−.079	.027	−.074	.392	.290	.501
To support a candidate who advocates the goals of an interest group of which I am a member	.118	.114	.106	.125	−.004	.116	.275	.448	.148
Eigenvalue for unrotated solution	2.95	3.12	3.28	1.81	1.45	1.44	1.38	1.29	1.25
Percent of total variance	24.50	26.00	27.40	15.00	12.10	12.00	11.50	10.80	10.40

*Direct Oblimin Rotation using the SPSSX factor analysis procedure. The total variance explained in 1979 is 51.1 percent; for 1983, 48.8 percent; for 1987, 49.8 percent.

presented in table 10 thus bear out earlier indications that the Clark-Wilson typology is empirically fruitful (see e.g., Hofstetter, 1973; Hedges, 1984).

On the basis of these factor analyses, sets of items were combined additively to form a summary score for each respondent on each dimension in a given year. Thus, a respondent's scores on the 1979 "to work with a certain group with whom I have political ties," "to develop social contacts with people with similar interests," "to enjoy the excitement of the campaign," and "to work with friends and relatives who support a particular candidate" items were summed to create an index of solidary incentives for that year. The same was done for 1983 and 1987; and parallel procedures were followed for the remaining dimensions. Since, as table 10 indicates, the "to work for a candidate because of personal friendship with him or her" item did not load highly on any of these factors (though in both 1979 and 1983 it did load moderately on the "solidary" factor), it was used by itself as an indicator of the fourth type of motivation to which we referred above—attraction to or linkage with a candidate.

In each year none of these motivational dimensions proved to be highly related to any other. Accordingly, we are dealing with motivations that are, by and large, independent of one another. On the other hand, scores on a given motivational dimension in 1979 were strongly correlated with scores on the same dimension in 1983 and 1987. Still, there was enough slippage among the 1979, 1983, and 1987 motivations that these activists were obviously not identically motivated in the three primary campaigns. This was especially true on the candidate-linkage dimension, which is not at all surprising in light of the candidate turnover from 1979 to 1983 to 1987.

Explaining Activists' Motivations

In previous research (1984), drawing on our survey of 734 activists who played substantial volunteer roles in the 1979 and/or 1983 gubernatorial primary campaigns, Miller studied whether certain types of people are more likely to be motivated by certain kinds of incentives. The dependent variables for the 1979 and 1983 incentive models include the three motivational indices—solidary, material, and purposive—plus the candidate-linkage motivational item discussed above. The independent variables include demographic characteristics (sex, age, education, place of residence, income, years of residence in Kentucky, and occupation) and personal political variables (political positions held, frequency of political involvement, years of active involvement in Kentucky politics, and political philosophy).

Let us briefly summarize the findings of multiple regression analyses. In the solidary model for 1979, age, residence, frequency of activity, and candidate preference are all related to solidary motivations, with younger, rural, and more intensely involved activists being more solidary oriented. Elite workers from nonmetropolitan counties have fewer available alternatives for satisfying the need for association. It is a natural tendency among younger people to look for personal social connections via politics and civic organizations. The significance of frequent involvement substantiates earlier findings that a solidary reason is one that keeps people in politics and brings them back again and again even though it may not be the original reason for involvement (see Conway and Feigert, 1968). The 1983 results for the solidary model are highly consistent with those for 1979. Again, those who lived outside urban areas, who were younger, and who were more intensely involved were significantly more solidary in motivational tendencies.

For the material model for 1979, the significant findings are that the more materialistically motivated activists were younger, males, and those who held or had held more political and/or party positions. The significance of young, male materialism fits societal norms: career advancement is anticipated. In 1983 younger activists were again more materialistic, as were lawyers, public officials, and businessmen. In Kentucky (as elsewhere), the practice of law has always been associated with the exercise of political influence.

The 1979 findings for the purposive model reveal a very different set of influences. The only significant findings are that those with more education tended to be more issue oriented and civic-minded, while lawyers were far less purposively oriented than any other occupational group. More educated people might be expected to be more issue oriented and civic minded, for education involves, to some extent, formulating thoughts about public concerns. As for lawyers, the findings concerning purposive motivations reinforce the image that was suggested by the findings for material motivations: lawyers tend to be oriented toward personal gain rather than the advancement of political causes. In 1983 lawyers were again significantly less purposive than every other occupational group. Those who had been intensely involved in political campaigns over the past five years were also significantly more purposive, as were those who had lived longer in Kentucky.

In explaining the candidate-oriented motivation, we find that activists with higher incomes were significantly more motivated by personal friendship with a candidate. This makes considerable sense: wealthier people are more likely to move in elite circles, wherein they come to know prominent politicians. Moreover, wealthier people are more likely to be sought out by candidates for contributions of money and expertise. Workers (including farmers and blue- and white-collar workers) were significantly less candidate oriented than members of any other occupational group—hardly surprising in a state lacking a strong labor movement or a tradition of mass participation in party affairs. In Kentucky gubernatorial candidates are not drawn from the ranks of the lower classes, and the bonds of personal friendship tend to be restricted to the members of one's own social class.

In both 1979 and 1983 we also found some evidence that different motivations were emphasized by supporters of particular candidates. The supporters of candidates who were more closely identified with the traditional organization were more likely to stress solidary and materialistic motivations than those backing candidates who were "outsiders." Supporters of some candidates were significantly more candidate oriented than others. There were few differences among the candidate groups in the emphasis put on purposive motivations.

Overall, we found considerable comparability in findings for the motivation models in both primary campaigns. The differences between the two campaigns are suggestive of changes in the political environment between the two periods and the type of candidates running in both primary contests.

By identifying motivations for working in specific gubernatorial campaigns, we shed new light on why people become actively involved in politics. The motivations of Kentucky gubernatorial primary activists are, as we have seen, reasonably similar to those uncovered in studies of other groups of political workers (see e.g., Kirkpatrick, 1976; Roback, 1980; Hedges, 1984). When we examined the motivational responses of these activists in detail, we saw that differences in motivation were largely reducible to three underlying dimensions—the same three motivations outlined by Clark and Wilson: solidary, material, and purposive. This is true despite the fact that Clark and Wilson sought to explain the nature of political organizations and we have been examining gubernatorial activists who are not in a formal organizational setting.

We have gone on to examine the sources of variation in activists' motivations for participating in gubernatorial primaries. Since no well-articulated theory exists, this has primarily been an exploratory analysis. Activists' motivations for involvement are, in part at least, understandable in terms of their personal and political characteristics, experiences, and preferences. These activists differed from one another in terms of their motivations for involvement in some fairly predictable ways (lawyers, for example, being more motivated by material considerations).

On the other hand, these variables have only very limited predictive power, for several reasons. The activists are quite homogeneous in many characteristics, and many of them emphasized more than one of the broad categories of motivations—making distinctions between those holding these motivations less clear. There is also a methodological problem, because we were forced to correlate demographic and political characteristics existing in 1983 with motivations for involvement in both 1979 and 1983 campaigns. Also, to some extent, differences in motivation are apt to be idiosyncratic—subject to a matrix of personal and situational factors far too complex to be fully understood by the participants themselves or reliably and validly measured via the tools of survey research.

Perhaps the primary lesson to be learned from this analysis is that it is perilous to study motivations for high-level political activity apart from the context provided by the specific political campaign. Not only are some activists drawn to political involvement by their attraction for or linkage with a particular candidate (a point too often ignored in prior studies of activists' motivations), but different candidates, to judge from our Kentucky data, tend to attract rather differently motivated campaign workers. At one level, political observers have long known this, the enduring image of the 1968 campaign for the Democratic presidential nomination serving as a superb case in point of differences in political motivations among active supporters of different primary candidates (e.g., the purposive supporters of Eugene McCarthy and George Wallace, as opposed to the solidary and material motivations of many Humphrey activists). But this insight has not sufficiently informed systematic research on activists' motivations. Our findings in Kentucky about the role of particular candidates in attracting activists with different motivations represent a step toward redressing this oversight.

Future Political Activity

Some studies of political party workers have focused on why activists remain involved in politics and what they would miss most if they gave up politics. Conway and Feigert (1968) showed that ideological or purposive rewards were the principal attraction for Democratic and Republican precinct chairmen, but when asked what they would miss most if they gave up their posts, they cited personal or social rewards most often. Eldersveld (1964), in a study of local Detroit political party members, and Grupp (1971), in a study of members of the John Birch Society, found, in at least 50 percent of the relevant cases, that individuals who initiated their membership for purposive reasons replaced those reasons with either material or solidary incentives. Bowman, Ippolito, and Donaldson (1969), in their study of the maintenance of activism among local party officials in two Massachusetts and three North Carolina communities, found that factors that apparently distinguished those who planned to continue from those who planned to quit were the relative importance attached to party loyalty and to the importance of the party office.

In another study, Bell (1985) found that among California state central committee members, members of both parties were primarily motivated by purposive concerns, but ties to the community and the party followed right behind. Purposive motivations appeared to sustain these activists, and feelings of allegiance increased over time. When these political workers were asked what they would miss most if they were to end their political activity, over 43 percent of the activists mentioned that they would miss most what can generally be categorized as the "feeling of contributing to a cause or issue I believe in." Bell's findings suggest that the future political party will be dominated by purposive activists. In contrast to Bell's findings, in their study of Democratic and Republican Pittsburgh committeepersons, Margolis and Owen (1985) found that the most important sustaining motivations for political involvement included "less obligation or commitment toward the party as an organization, more concern for personal interest, and less concern for party and community interest" (p. 320).

When questioned whether they would be willing to remain active in politics, three-fifths of the Kentucky gubernatorial activists in 1983 and 1987 said that they would definitely be willing to remain politically active, and another one-fourth stated that they would probably be willing. Less than 1 percent of the elite volunteers responded that they definitely would be unwilling to remain active in politics.

In order to have a better understanding about why Kentucky activists are so willing to remain involved in electoral battles, we develop a model of willingness to remain active in politics. We posit that those who are long-term, frequently mobilized, and more strongly identified with the Democratic party would be more likely to want to remain politically involved. Also, we suggest that activists who are more solidary oriented or material oriented would indicate a greater willingness to remain in politics. A solidary reason is one that keeps people in politics and brings them back again and again (Conway and Feigert, 1968). Those activists who are highly motivated by material concerns would want to keep reaping the monetary and other tangible patronage rewards of political involvement. Furthermore, workers who identify strongly and positively with the primary and their specific campaign group (i.e., "good feelings" about the primary) and who do not experience a devastating primary loss should tend to desire future political involvement.

The sample for this model includes the supporters of all the Democratic gubernatorial candidates in 1983. The dependent variable for the regression analysis involves the willingness to remain active in politics in the future; it is measured by a five-point Likert scale. The independent variables include activists' broad motivations for involvement, attitudes about their political involvement, previous level of political activity, personal political characteristics, and candidate preference indicators.

The regression results summarized in table 11 indicate that the independent variables explain almost one-third of the variation in 1983 gubernatorial primary workers' willingness to remain active in the future. Personal political variables, motivations for involvement, and attitudinal views about the 1983 primary are all related to future political involvement. Activists who are more long-term, intensely involved, and more strongly identified with the Democratic party appear to be more willing to remain active in politics.

Table 11. Activists' Willingness to Remain Active in Politics in the Future

Independent variables	B	BETA
Personal political variables		
Frequency of activity	.198***	.199***
Years of activity	.010**	.140**
Party identification	.252***	.255***
Motivations for 1983 primary involvement		
Solidary incentives	−.024	−.090
Material incentives	.070***	.178***
Purposive incentives	.040**	.116**
Candidate-centered incentives	−.021	−.029
Attitudinal views about 1983 primary	.047***	.244***
Participation in 1983 primary		
Hours worked	−.0002	−.005
Money contributed	.0005	.061
Candidate preference		
Sloane '83	−.008	−.005
Stumbo '83	.032	.016
(Collins '83 reference category)		

R^2 = .323
** = Significant at .01 level; *** = significant at .001 level
B = unstandardized coefficients
BETA = standardized coefficients

As for the differences based on motivations for involvement, supporters who expressed a greater willingness to remain actively involved in politics tended to be significantly more material oriented and purposive oriented in their incentives for primary participation. It is apparent that some supporters are more desirous of tangible political rewards as a result of their involvement, while others are more issue oriented and civic-minded and concerned with achieving "good government." One would expect the purposive motivations to be more transitory (as are candidate-oriented incentives); it is surprising that political volunteers who enter a campaign for a particular cause or purpose indicate a greater willingness to remain active in politics. In contrast, we would anticipate that solidary incentives would be associated with future political involvement, but this expectation is not substantiated in the regression results (in fact, the opposite tendency is noted).

As shown in table 11, attitudinal views about the 1983 primary are also related to activists' willingness to participate in future electoral contests. Workers who "cared most about what the campaign organization said or did," "were most interested in sticking with politics because of their primary involvement," "experienced good relationships with their primary coworkers," and so on were significantly more willing to remain

Table 12. What Activists Would Miss Most about Political Involvement

	1979/83 (N = 481)		1987 (N = 425)	
Responses	No.	%	No.	%
Excitement of campaign	170	35.3	216	50.8
Meeting people/social contacts	82	17.0	184	43.3
Working with friends and relatives	88	18.3	62	14.6
Working with group which shares political ties	122	25.4	57	13.4
Civic service	37	7.7	21	4.9
Influencing government policies	276	57.4	146	34.4
Working for issues	90	18.7	80	18.8
Personal ends	7	1.5	1	0.2
Candidate-oriented factors	42	8.7	38	8.9

Note: Activists could give two different answers.

actively involved in politics. This bears out our expectation that activists who "identify" strongly and positively with the primary and their particular campaign group and who do not experience a demoralizing primary loss would tend to desire future political participation.

An examination of activists' responses in 1983 and 1987 to an additional question—"What would you miss most if you gave up political activities?"—provides further insight into elite volunteers' willingness to remain in politics (table 12). More than one-half in 1983 and one-third in 1987 responded that they would miss "influencing government policies." This result substantiates Bell's (1985) earlier findings that purposive incentives were very important for state central committee members' sustained political involvement. More than one-third in 1983 and one-half in 1987 also stressed that they would miss the "excitement of campaigns"; and another one-fourth in 1983 and less than 14 percent in 1987 mentioned "working with a group with whom they have political ties." More than two-fifths in 1987 stressed "meeting people and making social contacts"; in contrast, less than 17 percent of the 1983 sample stressed this reason. All of these types of solidary motivations for continuing political participation were also frequently mentioned in Conway and Feigert's (1968) study of local precinct chairmen.

There is obviously no simple explanation for the willingness of many political activists to remain active in politics. They do not seem to get "burned out" often, despite the obvious frustrations associated with losing campaigns. The more active a person has been for a longer period of time, the greater his or her willingness to remain active in politics. Those who emphasize material and purposive incentives seem more committed to long-term activity, yet when asked what they would miss most, activists are most likely to mention solidary motivations as well as their influence on public policy. We should recognize that, in responding to a question about staying in politics, political workers may often be responding to short-term enthusiasms and frustrations, such as their attitude toward the most recent campaign; six months later their answer might be different. Our surest prediction is that the more involved and committed a person is to campaign politics, the longer he or she is likely to remain an active participant.

7

CANDIDATE CHOICE AMONG GUBERNATORIAL PRIMARY ACTIVISTS

VERY LITTLE is known about what brings state party activists into a particular candidate's primary campaign. Since volunteer staffers are still key actors in the nominating and campaign decision-making processes, a better understanding of what leads them into particular candidates' camps is long overdue.

Activists might be drawn to a particular candidate for many different reasons. The *amateur* model assumes that active campaign workers are recruited from outside the party system to campaign for certain causes or candidates (Carney, 1958; Wilson, 1962). This model may be appropriate in certain settings, but it can be rejected out of hand for Kentucky, where most primary workers have extensive political experience. The *factional* model posits that most primary workers have an enduring loyalty to a certain party faction, which dictates their choice of a candidate. This model is obviously applicable in highly factionalized party systems, but as we saw earlier, the factional structure of the Kentucky Democratic party has become extremely fluid over the last two decades; consequently, the factional model does not seem applicable to the problem at hand. Under the *professional* model, which we test in this chapter, the members of a large and relatively stable pool of active party workers choose up sides in each intramural contest, selecting candidates on the basis of a combination of long-standing political predispositions and situation-specific influences.

Our research (as reported in chapter 3) has shown that in any gubernatorial primary a relatively small proportion of the most active political workers are amateurs, who are playing an active campaign role for the first time. Instead, a large proportion are long-term participants in the process—persons with extensive experience in gubernatorial politics who expect to remain active in politics and who enter each gubernatorial primary season with the expectation that they will play a role in one of the campaigns.

The factional model differs from the professional model because it assumes that most political activists have long-term loyalties to one of the factions and start each gubernatorial primary season with a predisposition to support the candidates of that faction. As we have shown in chapter 4, however, the traditional factional system has disappeared from Kentucky politics, and therefore we would not expect to find party activists choosing sides in a gubernatorial race on the basis of factional loyalties.

Factionalism as a Motivation for Support by Activists

Most prior research on factionalism has studied external factional behavior over time, without examining the individual behavior of factional members. Contemporary knowledge about factionalism is fixed within the framework of Key's (1949) two themes: the disorganized and consequently personalistic politics of factions and the impact of economic and social influences on a dominant party's factional system. Scholars have typically followed Key's lead in studying only the forms of factions, and the causes and effects of those forms, differentiating unifactionalism, bifactionalism, and multifactionalism (see Black and Black, 1982a).

Most studies of factions in southern and border states, patterned after Key's seminal work, measure factional support quantitatively by mapping the geographic areas of continued, durable support for particular factions. Aggregate statistical analyses of voting data are utilized rather than any broad-scale analysis of the role of party activists in factions. The unit of analysis in such studies is the faction rather than the individual party activist, and the issue of continuity of support accordingly often does not arise. Thus, we do not have any data from the earlier time period (beginning with the 1920s and 1930s) that would document the importance of factional loyalties, even though political activists must have played a major role in building the factions in the southern and border states. Sindler's study (1956) of Louisiana's factions is one of few research endeavors that pays attention to the role of activists; Sindler notes the importance of local workers in strong factional county organizations and their ties to the state factions.

There are no studies of factional activists—especially no interview data—for any southern or border state. No one has asked political workers or voters anything about factional reasons for their support for candidates in the southern and border states. We assume that there were voter loyalties, but we have more reason to believe that political elites had longer-term loyalties to the traditional factions than the average voters.

The Erosion of Traditional Factionalism in Kentucky

As we noted in chapter 4, there has been a long history of factional gubernatorial politics among Kentucky's Democrats, and the two dominant Kentucky factions were based primarily on personalities—"Happy" Chandler and Earle Clements. But there has not been a Democratic gubernatorial primary that clearly aligned one of the traditional factions against the other since 1967.

Since the Kentucky factions were based primarily on personalities, they endured only as long as a few strong politicians dominated the Democratic party. The motivations, for the most part, that underlay Kentucky's traditional factions were more personal loyalties than geo graphic, ideological, socioeconomic, or ethnic interests (see Sindler's analysis of Louisiana's factions, 1956). Consequently, the traditional factions began to fall apart about the time that Chandler and Clements each became relatively inactive in Kentucky politics. Also, splits occurred in the dominant Combs-Breathitt faction when Combs ran against Ford for governor in 1971.

What was the role of political activists in these traditional Kentucky factions? What factors gave factions their continuity? It is commonly assumed that old-time local elite activists were the "glue" that held together the factions; these ardent supporters played a key role in the electoral activities of the factions (see Jewell and Cunningham, 1968). But Kentucky political activists were not studied, and were never systematically surveyed, during the period when Democratic primaries were dominated by factionalism. Consequently, we have no data on the strength or persistence of activists' loyalty to specific factions.

We do know that the local county factions had strong links to the state factions. These local organizations had lasting power because the local activists were motivated to continue to work for particular factions, especially because of the rewards of the former patronage system. If the powerful local factions had not existed, often based around particular families, the statewide factions probably would not have had the same importance.

Now the personalities who symbolized the traditional factions have left the scene, and a whole new generation of activists have become involved in Democratic politics. These younger activists have no reason for loyalty to the old factions. It remains to be seen whether new factions will develop that are capable of persisting from one election to the next. Political analysts would generally agree that the 1979, 1983, and 1987 Kentucky gubernatorial primary election campaigns involved no durable factional divisions.

Perceptions of Factionalism

If traditional factional loyalties have disappeared from Kentucky politics, what has taken their place? Is there evidence of continuity of support in the choices among candidates made by the activists who work in gubernatorial primaries?

We assume that certain patterns of continuity should be found in recent Democratic primaries. We would expect that the active supporters of Collins and Sloane in their 1979 electoral races would be part of their 1983 primary campaign organizations. Also, we would anticipate that the basic Atkins-Brown alliance would be an important part of Stumbo's 1983 primary campaign group. Moreover, we would expect that the elite volunteers for Brown in 1979 and for Beshear and Stumbo in 1983 would jump on these election bandwagons in 1987.

Factionalism among activists requires not only continuity of support for particular candidates but also evidence that activists perceive factions to exist and have some sense of loyalty to them. If activists believe that factions still exist in Kentucky politics, we want to know how they define this term.

We included questions about "factions" in our 1983 survey. Almost 70 percent of the activists felt that their coworkers in the 1983 primary campaign made up a political group or "faction" (cohesive, durable group). And more than 62 percent felt that the supporters of one or more of the other candidates made up factions in 1983. The corresponding figures for 1979 were somewhat lower. Almost 58 percent felt that their coworkers made up a faction, and more than 53 percent felt that the supporters of one or more of the other candidates made up factions in 1979.

In terms of perceptions of different candidates' activists in 1983, more than 79 percent of Stumbo supporters perceived that they belonged to a faction; this is compared to 71 percent of Collins activists and 67 percent of Sloane activists. In 1979 more McBrayer supporters (66 percent) believed that their coworkers made up a faction than the supporters of the other candidates (65 percent of Sloane's, 63 percent of Brown's, 60 percent of Hubbard's, and less than 56 percent of both Atkins's and Stovall's supporters).

Although many activists define political groups as *factions*, some of them use this term very loosely and not the way political scientists would define factions; others describe factions in terms of specific political leaders or courthouse groups. Respondents were asked to define the main special or defining characteristic of their primary campaign group and of the opponents' in 1979 and/or 1983. Most frequently, activists simply named candidates or characterized groups in terms of meaningless bland terms, i.e., "sincere, determined, hardworking group." We found that activists were more likely to place a factional label on the "other group" rather than on their own. The only significant references to labor factions occur in 1983 when the other faction is described that way. The term *administration faction* (or *antiadministration faction*) comes up most frequently in 1979 as a description of the other faction (i.e., almost 25 percent). We note that these political workers are just as likely to refer to local factions as they are to state administration factions.

Activists' Choice of Gubernatorial Candidates

If political activists play an important role in gubernatorial campaigns, we want to determine how they make their choices among the gubernatorial candidates. What criteria are important in selecting a candidate? Are there important differences between the types of political activists who support one candidate or another? In order to win the support of activists, must candidates make commitments to particular interest groups or on particular issues? Are the political activists attracted primarily to candidates with particular ideological positions? Or do activists select a candidate to support largely on the basis of personal friendship and previous contacts?

To answer these questions, we will look at a number of variables that might be expected to distinguish one group of supporters from another or to affect the choices made by activists. We will carry out a multivariate analysis to weigh the relative importance of the variables that appear to be important. We may find that some of these individual variables are important in explaining the support for one candidate in one election even though they do not subsequently turn out to have broader importance in explaining the choices made by activists.

Variables Affecting Activists' Choice of a Candidate

In studies of vote choice in general elections, party identification is often treated as a "standing commitment" on the voter's part; it may provide a framework within which voting decisions are made. By the same token, we might anticipate considerable continuity of candidate choice from one primary to the next, as supporters of Candidate X in one primary join the organization of Candidate X in the next primary or (in the absence of Candidate X) perhaps support Candidate Y, whom they perceive as allied or associated with Candidate X. We might aso expect to find that some candidates closely identified with the political establishment draw their support largely from political *professionals*, while political newcomers recruit their workers largely from *amateurs*.

Another factor that might shape candidate choice concerns broad *motivations for political activity*. As discussed earlier in chapter 3, Clark-Wilson's motivation typology (solidary, material, and purposive incentives) has informed analyses of various types of political activists, including party leaders and volunteers, campaign contributors, convention delegates, and local ward leaders. These studies, however, have been concerned with determining why people become politically active in the first place, not why they become involved in a particular candidate's campaign. But such motivations still underlie the choice of a particular candidate. For example, an "establishment" candidate would presumably attract a greater share of volunteers whose motivation was solidary than would a candidate from outside the party mainstream, more of whose supporters might be purposively motivated; similarly, an odds-on favorite should attract more workers who are materially motivated than a candidate whose chances appear dim.

There is no theoretical reason for expecting differences in the *demographic* characteristics of activists supporting particular characteristcs. But we will explore some of the more obvious personal differences among political activists supporting different candidates.

In some states primary election campaigns are focused heavily on conflicts between *interest groups* and debates over *programmatic issues.* Political activists might be recruited to candidate campaigns because of their commitment to particular interests and issues. In American politics there has been an increasing entry into political campaigns of individuals who are strongly committed to a particular interest—women's issues, labor, education, business, pro or antiabortion, civil rights, and so on. In the past interest groups have played a relatively small role in Kentucky primaries. Is there any evidence from recent Kentucky primaries that significant numbers of activists are becoming committed to a candidate out of loyalty to groups that advocate particular interests?

Prior researchers have argued that candidate choice in conventions and primaries often involves a trade-off between a candidate's ideological or issue position and his or her electability (Abramowitz, McGlennon, and Rapoport, 1986; Jewell, 1984; Stone and Abramowitz, 1986b). However, in Kentucky Democratic politics, this trade-off is usually not critical because any nominated Democratic gubernatorial candidate should be electable. This should make it possible for Democratic activists to select candidates based on programmatic rather than purely strategic considerations, just as analyses of mass voting behavior indicate that the perceived ideological similarity between voter and candidate underlies electoral choice. However, it should also be noted that Kentucky Democratic politics has consistently been more personalistic than ideological, concerned "more with style than substance" (Peirce and Hagstrom, 1983: 384). In such a climate, candidates' programmatic appeals tend to be muted. That being the case, activists-candidate similarity on the issues seems likely to play a less decisive role in Kentucky than it would in most other states.

Continuity of Support

The factional alignments of the past were largely irrelevant to the elections of 1979, 1983, and 1987. In 1979 long-standing rivals Chander and Combs joined forces behind the same losing gubernatorial candidate (Terry McBrayer). In 1983 Chandler supported a candidate (Martha Layne Collins) with apparent roots in the other faction, while Combs supported a candidate (Harvey Sloane) with no apparent factional roots at all.

In 1979 a self-proclaimed outsider, John Y. Brown, Jr. entered the primary at the last minute and upset Gov. Julian Carroll's attempt to pass the governorship on to his designated successor, Terry McBrayer. In 1983 Governor Brown also failed in his attempt to anoint another factional outsider, Human Resources Secretary Grady Stumbo. In 1987, although there was no overt action by Governor Collins on behalf of any candidate, it was well known that her top political lieutenants and her state party chairman were working hard for Lt. Gov. Steve Beshear. The surprise victor, Wallace Wilkinson, was a political newcomer with strong roots in the 1979 and 1983 Sloane campaigns; but Louisville mayor Harvey Sloane threw his support to Beshear. "Happy" Chandler supported the outsider Wilkinson, and Combs supported Stumbo, his eastern Kentucky favorite son. Former governor Carroll was unable to attract his former factional allies.

Is there any substitute for traditional factionalism in Kentucky? Is there any sign of continuity of supporters from one candidate to another? In order to discover whether there was much continuity of support for a specific clustering of candidates, we asked explicit questions about support for particular candidates in the 1979, 1983, and 1987 primaries.

Table 13 provides a cross tabulation of candidates supported by activists in 1979 and 1983. We note that 52 percent of McBrayer supporters worked for Collins, in contrast to 34 percent for Sloane and 10 percent for Stumbo. We would expect McBrayer activists to favor a more seasoned politician like Collins. As anticipated, more than 77 percent of Sloane's 1979 supporters reported their active involvement in his 1983 second gubernatorial race. Despite Brown's support for Stumbo in 1983, only one-fourth of Brown supporters and only a few Atkins supporters worked for Stumbo in that year.

As another measure of continuity of support, more than 56 percent of the elite workers who supported Collins in 1983 stated that they worked actively in her 1979 lieutenant governor's electoral contest. Of those who worked for Sloane in both primaries, 54 percent made up their minds to work again for him in 1983 very early in the campaign. As for Atkins supporters, less than 28 percent of those who worked for Atkins in 1979 supported him actively in his 1983 lieutenant governor's primary campaign.

Table 14 provides a cross tabulation of 1979/83 candidates' supporters by those of 1987. (The sample consists of members of our earlier study.) As

Table 13. Continuity of Activists' Support, 1979 and 1983

	1983 Candidates			
	Collins	Sloane	Stumbo	None
1979 Candidates				
Atkins	21	5	5	6
	56.8	13.5	13.5	16.2
	6.9	2.1	4.2	8.7
Brown	53	36	31	5
	42.4	28.8	24.8	4.0
	17.4	15.1	26.1	7.2
Hubbard	14	7	7	2
	46.7	23.3	23.3	6.6
	4.6	2.9	5.9	2.9
McBrayer	131	85	26	10
	52.0	33.7	10.3	4.0
	43.0	35.6	21.8	14.5
Sloane	13	76	6	3
	13.3	77.6	6.1	3.0
	4.3	31.8	5.0	4.3
Stovall	27	17	22	2
	39.7	25.0	32.4	3.0
	8.9	7.1	18.5	2.9
None	46	13	22	41
	37.7	10.7	18.0	33.6
	15.1	5.4	18.5	59.4

Note: The first entry in each cell is the number of activists; the second entry is the percentage of the 1979 candidate's supporters who worked for the 1983 candidates; and the third entry is the percentage of the 1983 candidate's supporters who worked for the 1979 candidates.

582 activists worked in both primary campaigns; 28 activists worked in 1979 only; 81 activists worked in 1983 only.

we would anticipate, a large percentage (42 percent) of Collins "professional" volunteers worked for the insider, Beshear; but 26 percent of them supported the outsider, Wilkinson. Along with Sloane's personal endorsement, Beshear also received assistance from more than 39 percent of Sloane's supporters. But Wilkinson, Sloane's 1983 state campaign fundraiser, did attract more than 27 percent of Sloane's former workers. Stumbo, whose 1987 campaign never ignited widespread public support, had the active support of almost one-half of his 1983 elite volunteers. Brown, the front-runner until the last week of the campaign, had the support of more than 28 percent of Stumbo's 1983 activists and more than one-fifth of Collins's workers.

Table 14. Continuity of Activists' Support, 1983 and 1987
(1979/83 Panel Members)

	1987 Candidates				
	Beshear (N=76)	Brown (N=45)	Carroll (N=14)	Stumbo (N=31)	Wilkinson (N=49)
1983 Candidates					
Collins	38	20	5	4	24
	41.8	22.0	5.5	4.4	26.4
	50.0	44.4	35.7	12.9	49.0
Sloane	31	12	9	5	22
	39.2	15.2	11.4	6.3	27.8
	40.8	26.7	64.3	16.1	44.9
Stumbo	7	13	—	22	3
	15.6	28.9	—	48.9	6.7
	9.2	28.9	—	71.0	6.1

Note: The first entry in each cell is the number of activists; the second entry is the percentage of the 1979/83 candidate's supporters who worked for the 1987 candidates; and the third entry is the percentage of the 1987 candidate's supporters who worked for the 1979/83 candidates.

215 panel members worked in the 1983 and 1987 gubernatorial primaries; 11 panel members worked in the 1979 and 1987 gubernatorial primaries; 22 panel members worked only in another 1987 statewide primary; 24 panel members did not participate at all in a 1987 primary.

Table 15 is based on data from the new participants in our 1987 study. It shows that Beshear supporters had come primarily from the Collins and Sloane campaigns, as did the majority of Wilkinson and Brown activists. Stumbo, of course, drew almost 58 percent of his workers from his earlier gubernatorial campaign group. Carroll's base of support came from members of Collins's organization. More than one-third of these 1987 elite workers had not participated actively in the 1983 primary.

In terms of continuity of support, 64 percent of the elite workers who supported Beshear in 1987 (panel members and new participants) stated that they worked actively in his 1983 lieutenant governor's electoral contest. Of those who worked for Stumbo in both primaries, 91.8 percent made up their minds to work again for him in 1987 very early in the campaign.

We have not found that there are some well-defined, clear-cut factional alignments extending over successive primaries in the period from 1979 to 1987. We do not see the Brown-Atkins workers moving en masse to Stumbo, who obviously had to develop his own base of support. We even see some slippage in support for Sloane from 1979 to 1983 and for Stumbo from 1983 to 1987. The continuity of support we find is neither strong nor consistent, and it certainly does not indicate the presence of any underlying factional system.

Table 15. Continuity of Activists' Support, 1983 and 1987 (New Participants in 1987 Study)

	1987 Candidates				
	Beshear (N=48)	Brown (N=58)	Carroll (N=33)	Stumbo (N=45)	Wilkinson (N=132)
1983 Candidates					
Collins	18	23	14	3	53
	37.5	39.7	42.4	6.7	40.2
Sloane	13	8	7	5	26
	27.1	13.8	21.2	11.1	19.7
Stumbo	3	5	—	26	4
	6.3	8.6	—	57.8	3.0
Did not partici-	14	22	12	11	49
pate in 1983	29.2	37.9	36.3	24.4	37.1

Note: The first entry in each cell is the number of activists; the second entry is the percentage of the 1987 candidate's supporters who worked for the 1983 candidates.

We would expect to find even less continuity of support among rank-and-file voters. A study (Goldstein, 1988) of Jefferson County voters in the 1987 Democratic gubernatorial primary suggests that there is also relatively little continuity in their voting patterns between 1983 and 1987. These data, collected in exit polls, are less reliable than the data from political activists because voters would presumably be less likely to remember how they had voted in a primary four years earlier. (The voters' stated preferences in 1987 accurately reflect the actual vote in Jefferson County that year, but their recollections of their 1983 vote seriously overstate the vote for Collins and understate that for Stumbo and Sloane.)

In 1987 John Y. Brown was able to get nearly half of the vote from those who said they had voted for Collins and over 40 percent of the Sloane vote, even though in 1987 Sloane was endorsing Beshear. Beshear won only one-sixth of the former Sloane supporters. Grady Stumbo was able to gain votes from only about one-seventh of those who said they had voted for him in 1983. Wilkinson drew a larger share of former Stumbo supporters than did Brown, even though there had been a clear link between Brown and Stumbo in 1983. In short, there is no evidence that Jefferson County voters were paying any attention to the linkages and endorsements among politicians.

Amateurs and Professionals

We have described Kentucky political activists as professionals because most of those we surveyed have been consistently involved in gubernatorial primaries and have worked frequently in campaigns at other levels. It is true, of course, that each primary election brings new workers into the campaign process. Moreover, candidacies differ a lot in their ability to attract different types of activists. Those candidates who are running for political office for the first time, such as Brown in 1979, Stumbo in 1983, and Wilkinson in 1987, might be expected to rely more heavily on workers having little or no campaign experience. To test that possibility, in table 16 we compare the political experience of workers for the various candidates in the three gubernatorial primaries.

Based on the levels of political activity, there were fairly sharp distinctions among the supporters of the various candidates. Sloane (1979), Brown (1979), and Stumbo (1983 and 1987) attracted workers who had been active in politics for shorter periods of time. In fact, one-fourth of Stumbo's 1983 supporters had been active for less than five years, the highest proportion of any candidate in the three primaries. In 1987 Stumbo's supporters were more experienced but were still more amateur than those supporting any other candidates. At the other extreme almost half of workers for McBrayer and Hubbard in 1979 and for all of the candidates except Stumbo in 1987 had been active for over twenty years (data not in table). Although the new candidates generally had fewer veteran workers than did others, it is important to recognize that all candidates relied heavily on experienced political activists. A majority of the elite workers for each candidate had been active for at least ten years, and this proportion was over two-thirds for Wilkinson in 1987.

About four-fifths of McBrayer and Stovall workers in 1979 and more than three-fourths of Collins's and Sloane's in 1983 and Beshear's activists in 1987 had been active in all or most political campaigns. In contrast, almost 30 percent of Sloane workers in 1979, one-third of Stumbo's in 1983, and more than one-third of Brown's and Stumbo's supporters and more than 30 percent of Wilkinson's in 1987 had been active in few political contests during the last five years.

At least one-third of the supporters of most candidates held local party office, but there were some marked differences among the different candidates' camps. For the 1979 candidates, the proportions were almost one-half for McBrayer and Stovall workers, and both of these groups included a number of local officeholders. Among the 1983 candidate camps, Collins had the highest proportion of supporters holding party office or local elective office, while only one-fourth of Stumbo's workers held local party office. In the 1987 primary, Stumbo was again the only candidate to have much less than one-third of his workers holding party office. Beshear had the most local party committee members, and he and Carroll had the largest proportions of local officeholders.

These 1979, 1983, and 1987 candidates (except for Stumbo) drew most of their support from people with a long record in politics. However,

Table 16. Political Activity of Activists by 1979, 1983, and 1987 Candidate Groups (in Percentages)

1979	Atkins (N=37)	Brown (N=125)	Hubbard (N=30)	McBrayer (N=252)	Sloane (N=98)	Stovall (N=67)
Active 10 years or more	64.8	61.6	70.0	80.5	58.2	76.1
Active in all or most political campaigns (last 5 years)	75.0	76.0	82.7	86.5	70.9	80.6
Political positions held now						
Member local party committee	32.4	38.4	36.7	48.8	28.6	44.8
Elected to local office	8.1	10.4	13.3	24.2	6.1	17.9
1983	**Collins (N=305)**	**Sloane (N=239)**	**Stumbo (N=120)**			
Active 10 years or more	67.6	70.3	55.9			
Active in all or most political campaigns (last 5 years)	78.9	79.8	64.7			
Political positions held now						
Member local party committee	41.3	36.4	25.0			
Elected to local office	23.2	15.9	10.0			
1987	**Beshear (N=129)**	**Brown (N=108)**	**Carroll (N=47)**	**Stumbo (N=77)**	**Wilkinson (N=188)**	
Active 10 years or more	79.8	85.2	80.8	61.1	69.1	
Active in all or most political campaigns (last 5 years)	78.3	64.8	70.3	61.1	66.5	
Political positions held now						
Member local party committee	45.0	30.6	34.0	22.1	33.5	
Elected to local office	24.8	10.2	23.4	3.9	15.4	

maiden statewide candidacies do attract new elites, and Brown in 1979, Stumbo in 1983, and Wilkinson in 1987 did rely on both amateurs and professionals in their campaigns. Generally, these data bear out our assertion that most elite political activists are long-term political professionals with a continuing record of involvement in statewide politics, rather than amateurs who drop into and out of Democratic campaigns as a consequence of new stimuli.

Recruitment

There is a dearth of studies in the literature about the *recruitment* of activists at all levels of the political process. To what degree are gubernatorial activists self-starters? Who are the recruiters—candidates, friends, business associates, incumbent political leaders, or others? Which and how many activists are recruited through interest groups—that is, come into politics through their membership in labor unions, teacher associations, business organizations, or other groups?

In our 1987 survey, we asked the activists (concerning the 1987 and 1983 primaries): "Did some person and/or group contact you to work? If not, please describe what kind of initiative you took." In the 1987 primary, most of the activists were recruited to work in a particular campaign: 161 panel members and 232 new participants. More than one-half of these panel members and one-third of the new participants were recruited by the candidates themselves; another 10 percent of panelists and 20 percent of new participants were recruited by statewide campaign managers. Moreover, activists' friends and relatives contacted 12 percent of the panel members and 17 percent of the new participants to become involved in particular campaigns. Also, early committed campaign workers recruited 11 percent of panelists and 14 percent of new participants; whereas 9 percent of panel members and 10 percent of new participants were contacted by county-level politicians. Few activists in both samples said they were recruited by either state leaders, candidates' friends and relatives, or interest group friends. A much smaller number of activists were "self-starters"—56 panel members and 65 new participants; of these, three-fourths of each sample contacted particular campaigns and volunteered their services. More than one-tenth personally contacted either the candidates or groups with whom they had political ties. The responses concerning recruitment in 1983 were comparable.

An examination of a few of the responses to the open-ended recruitment question reveals the dominant presence of the candidates and statewide campaign leaders in the recruitment process. A Beshear supporter remarked, "I was asked by Steve Beshear to participate." According to a Wilkinson activist, "Wallace Wilkinson and Dr. Poore recruited me." Another Wilkinson supporter noted, "J.R. Miller asked if I would help him in Hancock County." One Carroll worker explained that he was asked by "the candidate, Julian Carroll, a personal friend"; whereas another Carroll worker said, "Rep. Hank Hancock asked me to serve as county chairman." In contrast, one Beshear activist explained that he was recruited "through both individuals in my county and the Kentucky Education Association."

We are looking for some evidence that recruitment occurs through factional leaders or through organized interest groups. In fact, we find that the recruitment process is more individual than institutional. The candidate or a top aide does the recruiting; or else it is done by friends and relatives of the activists. But we must keep in mind that we are dealing with people who have worked often before; they are ready to be asked.

Motivation for Political Activity

The various 1979 and 1983 candidates tended to draw rather differently motivated campaign supporters. In 1979 McBrayer supporters were more solidary oriented than the supporters of all the other candidates. We earlier noted that McBrayer was a "faction" candidate, while Brown, Atkins, and Sloane were all "antipolitics" candidates. In 1983 the workers of Grady Stumbo were significantly less solidary oriented than those supporters of Martha Layne Collins and Harvey Sloane. In 1979 Stovall's supporters were significantly less materialistic than those of McBrayer. There were no significant differences in material motivations among supporters of the other candidates. In 1983 workers of Stumbo were significantly less materially oriented than were those of Collins and Sloane, the leading candidates to the very last moment.

In 1979 Stovall activists were significantly more purposive than those of most other candidates, but there was no significant difference between Stovall's workers and Brown's. But in 1983, in regard to purposive incentives, there were no significant differences among the candidates' supporters. In 1979 Brown supporters were significantly less candidate oriented than workers of the other candidates. In 1983 Collins supporters were significantly more candidate oriented than supporters of Sloane or Stumbo.

There were also differences in 1987 among the motivations expressed by the various candidates' supporters. Beshear, Brown, and Carroll supporters were significantly more solidary oriented than the others; these men had held the highest statewide offices and tended to draw volunteers with close long-term ties to the Democratic party establishment. To many of their rural volunteers, politics was a major part of their social life. Beshear and Brown workers were more materially oriented, presumably because their candidates were front-runners, and they were expecting to reap the spoils of victory. Stumbo and Wilkinson activists were significantly more purposive oriented than the other candidate groups. Stumbo's populist working class message attracted many workers who wanted to elect a candidate who shared their issue concerns. The lottery "no tax increase" stand of Wilkinson tended to draw some workers into the entrepreneur's campaign.

In an open-ended question, each respondent was asked to give the most important reason for his or her involvement in the 1979, 1983, and/or 1987 primaries. More than one-third of the workers in both the 1983 and 1987 gubernatorial ampaigns cited their candidate's personal qualities—e.g., honesty, experience, and integrity—as the primary reason for their involvement. In 1979, however, this response was less common (17 percent) than personal friendship with their candidates (27 percent). Another reason cited most often was "working for issues"—one-fifth of the 1987 volunteers, 17 percent in 1983, and 11 percent in 1979. Material incentives were emphasized by fewer than 1 percent of the respondents.

It is interesting to look at some of the activists' explanations for their involvement in primary campaigns. Some supporters noted their candidate's commendable personal qualities. A Collins volunteer remarked, "Having known Martha Layne Collins since 1970, and having followed her achievements through the years, I felt that Martha Layne Collins was the best qualified candidate for Governor." Another Collins worker commented, "I liked her as a friend. Had really gotten to know her and liked her integrity, honesty, and relationships with people." A Carroll activist responded, "Strong belief that we needed an experienced, handsome governor and believe Julian Carroll was the most knowledgeable Kentuckian with regard to state government." A Wilkinson volunteer added, "I thought Wilkinson was the best candidate and we needed someone qualified after the Collins fiasco."

Other supporters noted their personal friendships with their candidate and key Kentuckian politicos as their primary motive for involvement. A McBrayer worker said, "I was a close friend of Gov. Julian Carroll and Terry McBrayer; they recruited me to be chairman of my county." Another McBrayer activist explained, "Terry McBrayer was a local attorney and neighbor. I knew his parents and family. I wanted a governor to help with roads and bridges in this area." A Stovall activist commented, "Telma Stovall is a good friend. I've worked many years with her in Kentucky politics—and in her successful lieutenant governor race." A Wilkinson worker explained, "Wallace is my neighbor and friend. He asked me to be part of his winning campaign."

Some activists cited "working for issues" as their most important reason for involvement. A Stovall volunteer stated, "I wanted a liberal candidate for the working people of Kentucky and Stovall's labor record proved her beliefs." A Brown supporter commented on the "availability of a man with new ideas and business experience. I thought we had a winner." A Sloane activist in 1983 remarked, "Sloane attracted me from his 1979 campaign and from issues he stood on through his mayoral races; I would have supported Sloane in 1979 had I known him." Another Sloane worker noted, "I have an interest in having some influence in Frankfort regarding educational issues and other favorite 'causes.'" A Wilkinson worker stated, "I want to elect a person who identifies with small business and ordinary working people. Ready for a change in state government." To establish a state lottery was stressed by several Wilkinson workers as their chief motivation for involvement; one supporter explained, "Kentucky needs a lottery and Wilkinson is the man to get it done."

Only a few respondents mentioned material incentives for involvement. A Brown activist in 1979 remarked, "Because John Y. Brown, Sr., had done me a favor in the early 1950s." A Carroll supporter commented, "For the benefit of family and friends." Another Carroll worker said, "Julian Carroll has always been good to my county—plenty of jobs and roads."

Some workers wanted, as their main incentive, to defeat certain opponents. According to a Brown worker in 1979, "We had to defeat McBrayer and Carroll to get rid of corruption in state government." A Wilkinson supporter acknowledged, "Someone to beat John Y. Brown as he was one of the worst. Wilkinson is a go getter and has new ideas." A Stumbo worker in 1983 maintained, "We needed a candidate who could fully understand the economic base of Eastern Kentucky. Also I have become somewhat tired of the controlling Democratic factions of Kentucky and I saw in Stumbo an alternative to Collins and the courthouse group."

Demographics

There were fairly sharp differences among the candidates' supporters in a few of the demographic characteristics previously described in chapter 3. Among the 1979/1983 activists, both Hubbard and Stumbo received significant support from "born again" activists. McBrayer, Stovall, and Collins activists were stronger Democrats than the other candidates' volunteers; we would expect these seasoned candidates to attract long-term, strongly partisan professional workers. Both Brown and Collins supporters were wealthier than the other candidate groups, whereas Stovall and Stumbo activists—many with strong labor union ties—had the least financial resources. In terms of education, Sloane workers ranked the highest, Stovall the lowest. The different candidate groups attracted people from various occupations; McBrayer and Collins had more lawyers and elected or appointed public officials, Sloane had more teachers, and Brown, Atkins, Hubbard, and Collins had more business types. Both

Sloane and Stumbo attracted younger volunteers, whereas McBrayer, Hubbard, Stovall, and Collins attracted older workers; both Sloane and Stumbo had more young political newcomers—amateurs—in their campaign organizations.

Among the 1987 activists, both Beshear and Brown supporters were wealthier than the other candidate groups; more than one-half of Beshear's and Brown's elite volunteers earned over $50,000 a year, and another one-fifth earned over $35,000. In contrast, as anticipated, only one-half of Stumbo's group earned more than $35,000 a year (one-half of these making over $50,000). In terms of education, Beshear supporters ranked the highest, Carroll's the lowest; almost one-half of Beshear's workers had postcollege graduate education. Beshear had more lawyers and teachers, whereas Wilkinson, Brown, and Carroll had more business persons. Beshear has had strong teacher support in all his statewide races, and we would expect the millionaire entrepreneurs, Wilkinson and Brown, to attract more businessmen. Surprisingly, "born again" Christians were not attracted to any one candidate, although Julian Carroll was trying to attract this group. About two-fifths of those in each campaign organization identified themselves as such. In terms of partisan identification, Beshear and Stumbo supporters were stronger national Democrats than were supporters of other candidates; Beshear, Carroll, and Wilkinson workers were stronger state Democrats than were workers for other candidates.

The Impact of Interest Group Involvement in Choice of Candidates

As noted in chapter 3, social and issue groups (i.e., noneconomically based groups such as women's rights, antiabortion, and civil rights groups) are not usually salient in Kentucky party politics, particularly in the gubernatorial nominating process. Do activists become committed to candidates because of their loyalty to interest groups supporting those candidates? Do interest group leaders in Kentucky actively recruit their members to become part of particular candidates' campaigns? Unfortunately, this type of data is not available; but we do know, based on our 1987 survey findings, that very few activists were directly recruited into the different candidates' organizations by their interest group friends.

We find much variation in interest group involvement among the 1979, 1983, and 1987 activists. For example, 25 percent of Stovall's supporters in 1979 and 35 percent of Stumbo's in 1983 mentioned labor union involvement. This helps to explain why labor issues were important to both Stovall's and Stumbo's activists. In both 1979 and 1983 Sloane activists were more likely than others to cite involvement in educational groups; and Sloane's supporters gave greater emphasis to education issues. Even though education was a major issue in both 1979 and 1983 and though teachers were active in the two primaries, their support was widely divided among the candidates in both elections. Business interest group involvement was more important to Atkins (31 percent), Hubbard (31 percent), and Brown (29 percent) activists in 1979 and to Collins supporters (30 percent) in 1983; this finding helps to explain the fairly conservative orientation of these candidates' supporters on tax issues. It is surprising that Collins had relatively few supporters belonging to women's groups.

The 1987 qustionnaire asked activists to list not only the groups in which they were involved but also those in which they were very active. In 1987, as in 1983, Stumbo activists were more involved than other candidates' supporters in labor union activities, even though Beshear won the AFL-CIO statewide endorsement. We note that most of Stumbo's labor union members were very active interest group participants. Almost one-fourth of Beshear activists had educational group ties; the teachers were instrumental in his lieutenant gubernatorial victory in 1983. Brown's supporters led the other candidate groups in their ties to business organizations and other professional groups. At least one-third of every campaign group was involved in church-related organizations. Almost one-fourth of Brown's, Carroll's, and Wilkinson's elite volunteers participated in farm groups, although few were very actively involved. Very few 1987 candidates' activists were engaged in civil rights, women's rights, conservation/environmental, or antiabortion groups—the traditional national Democratic social and issue groups.

Importance of Issues in Activists' Choice of Candidates

Critics of the national presidential nominating system often argue that candidates must make strong commitments on issues or expensive promises in order to satisfy political activists whose support they must have; and these commitments and promises undermine the nominee's chances of winning the general election. Walter Mondale's experience is often cited as an example. Mondale's 1984 presidential campaign was handicapped by the many commitments he had made to a variety of liberal groups in winning the nomination.

In making a choice about a candidate to support, do Kentucky political activists give much weight to the positions taken by candidates on issues? Must a Kentucky gubernatorial candidate take positions on specific issues in order to win the support of activists; if so, can this requirement be a handicap in winning the general election? At the outset, there are several reasons for doubting that this situation arises very frequently in Kentucky. On the one hand, we know that most activists do not have strong commitments to interest groups, and we doubt that many of them have strong ideological convictions. On the other hand, most Democratic nominees do not risk electoral defeat in November. Conventional wisdom suggests that issues are not as important in Kentucky politics as they are in some other states. One reason for doubting that issues affect activists' choices is that activists frequently make a commitment to work for a candidate very early in the campaign before the central issues in a campaign begin to emerge. On the other hand, gubernatorial candidates who have experience in state government may have previously taken positions on issues or made commitments to interests that are well known to political activists. At the start of the 1987 campaign, for example, Beshear was well known as a supporter of education, Stumbo had a record of support for populist positions, and Brown was preparing to run on the record of his previous administration.

It is also very possible that during the primary campaign some candidates may be constrained in defining their issue position on issues because of the types of supporters in their camps. For example, in 1987 Beshear could not afford to alienate the teachers, and Wilkinson could not afford to deviate from the image of being a tax cutter that he had developed from the start.

Before jumping to conclusions about the importance of issues, we need to examine more carefully what political activists say about issues and about their perception of the candidates' issue positions. Our data are drawn from several questions in the surveys of activists: (1) When respondents were asked (in a closed-ended question) what were the reasons for working in the campaign, one answer they could choose was "to work for issues I feel strongly about." (2) They were also asked an open-ended question: "Was there any particular issue (or issues) which caused you to become actively involved?" (3) Respondents were asked their opinion on several issues that played some importance in the primary election. (4) Respondents were also asked their perception of each of the candidates' positions on these same issues.

Consequently, we can determine whether activists assert that issues play a part in their choices, and we can also tell whether activists have clear perceptions about candidate positions and whether they are more likely to support candidates whom they perceive as agreeing with them.

In 1979 and 1983 more than 85 percent of the supporters of all the candidates mentioned (in a closed-ended question) working for issues they felt strongly about as an important reason for involvement in the primaries. In contrast, in response to the open-ended question about particular issues that led them to become involved, there was great variation among the supporters of particular candidates. In 1979 the proportion mentioning a specific issue ranged from 30 percent of the Brown supporters to only 11 percent of McBrayer's activists. In 1983 58 percent of Stumbo's supporters but only about one-third of the Collins and Sloane activists mentioned a specific issue. Some, but not all, of these variations among the major candidates are consistent with conventional wisdom about these candidates. For example, we think of McBrayer as being less issue oriented and more of an administration candidate; and Stumbo was perceived as waging an issue-oriented campaign. But it is surprising to find only a small proportion of Sloane supporters in both 1979 and 1983 citing issues because Sloane was regarded as a more ideological, nonorganization type of candidate.

There are only a few issues that were cited frequently by supporters of particular candidates. In 1979 education was mentioned often by the supporters of McBrayer and Sloane, labor and social issues were stressed by the Stovall activists, and honesty and the reform of government were emphasized by supporters of Atkins and Brown, as well as the few Hubbard supporters who cited issues. In 1983 the most salient issues cited as reasons for involvement were education (particularly by the Collins and Sloane groups) and labor and right-to-work issues (mainly by Stumbo activists). In each case, these issues reflect the positions emphasized by the candidates, and in several cases they are compatible with the interest group loyalties of political activists.

Whether or not activists assert that their support for a candidate was motivated by one or more issues, it is interesting to determine whether various candidates drew support from activists having distinctly different positions on issues that were important during the campaign.

In fact, we find some important variations among the candidate groups in response to closed-ended questions about activists' opinions on major issues. Significantly more Sloane supporters (in both 1979 and 1983) strongly advocated tax support for education than the supporters of any other candidate. Hubbard supporters were more concerned than all other candidate groups in 1979 and 1983 about the importance of coal production to Kentucky (versus modifying environmental regulations). In 1979 Sloane activists were most likely to oppose cutting back services, as an alternative to raising taxes; in 1983, however, the differences among the three candidate groups on this issue were small. Significantly more Atkins and Sloane supporters than other 1979 candidate groups disagreed with the proposition that the political process would work better if there were more patronage available. Generally speaking, there were greater differences on issues among the supporters of various candidates in 1979 than in 1983.

In 1987 the respondents were asked their opinions on a series of issues as well as their perceptions of the different candidates' stands on the same issues. These were all ones that had been pertinent during the campaign: cutting back services as an alternative to raising taxes, increasing funds to get quality education, priority emphasis on teaching morality, more professionalism and less patronage in government, basing increased teacher pay on merit and not on longevity, and paying more attention to the working people.

Despite the importance of these issues and the amount of campaign debate devoted to some of them, there was far from complete consensus among activists in their perception of the views of each candidate. On those issues where the position of a candidate was generally recognized by a substantial proportion of activists, an even larger proportion of that candidate's supporters were likely to recognize it. On some issues the supporters of a candidate were the only ones to have a clear perception of his position. On those issues where the position of a candidate was not clear, other candidates' supporters were usually unsure of his position, whereas the candidate's own workers were likely to attribute their views to their candidate. We can illustrate these conclusions with a number of examples.

On the issue of cutting back services as an alternative to raising taxes, the positions of Wilkinson and Brown were well recognized; more than one-half of all the activists perceived both candidates as agreeing with the necessity of paring down services in order to avoid any tax increases. Wilkinson and Brown workers shared this view about their candidates' stands to an even greater extent. In contrast, there were wide splits, even among their own workers, in the perception of Beshear's and Stumbo's positions on this issue. There is some sign of activists' opinions guiding their perception in the case of both Beshear's and Stumbo's supporters.

On the issue of increasing funding to get quality education, a recognition of Beshear's position stands out among all respondents, and his activists were even stronger (84 percent) in their perception of Beshear's support for education funding. The positions of the other candidates were less well known. Wilkinson was perceived by almost one-third of the activists to be against raising education funding, and this perception was particularly held by those of his supporters who shared that opinion.

The argument that priority emphasis be given to teaching morality was recognized as Carroll's position by 73 percent of all respondents and by 91 percent of his supporters. Wilkinson and Stumbo supporters were much more likely than others to believe these two candidates were strong advocates of teaching morality, and this was particularly true of supporters of that position.

Brown was recognized as an advocate of more professionalism and less patronage in government by 68 percent of all activists and by 90 percent of his workers. Nearly all Stumbo workers and most Wilkinson workers also perceived their candidates as strongly for professionalism in government, and the Wilkinson activists' opinion was strongly related to their own opinions. The perception of Beshear was split on this issue, even for his own supporters, whose perception was correlated with their own opinions.

On the question of basing increased teacher pay on merit and not on longevity, none of the candidates had well-recognized positions, probably because they avoided the issue during the campaign.

Most respondents recognized that the populist issue of paying more attention to the working people had been emphasized by Stumbo, a perception shared by almost all of his supporters. The activists' perception of Brown's stand was split, even in the case of his supporters, where it was related to their own opinions. Carroll and Wilkinson volunteers were both more likely than others to perceive their candidate as supporting a populist position.

In all three elections there were distinct differences among the candidates' support groups on some of the issues. This suggests that the issue position of candidates has some effect on the choices made by political activists. On the other hand, it is likely that some activists choose a candidate for reasons unrelated to issues and subsequently either adopt their candidate's position on an issue or attribute to the candidate their own position. The data from the 1987 race help to clarify this relationship because they also include the activists' perceptions of positions taken by the candidates. When a candidate is prominently identified with an issue, this will be recognized by most activists, but the candidate's supporters are particularly likely to perceive this issue position and also to agree with it. When there is more general uncertainty about a candidate's stand on an issue, his or her supporters are more likely to attribute to the candidate their own issue preferences.

The Impact of Ideology in Activists' Choice of Candidates

Kentucky gubernatorial candidates are rarely described in the media as either liberals or conservatives, and primary voting alignments are not usually defined in clear ideological terms. In 1983 and 1987 the gubernatorial activists rarely mentioned the terms *liberal* and *conservative* in any of their open-ended explanations of the reasons for active involvement for particular candidates.

Although this evidence suggests that these activists do not think of candidates explicitly in liberal/conservative terms, some indirect measures suggest that ideological perceptions are important. First, we would consider that ideology has an influence if there is some consensus among the candidates' supporters about the ideological position of the candidates and some fairly clear distinctions are perceived among them. A second criterion would be whether activists generally prefer the candidate whom they perceive as being closest to their own ideological position. We would posit

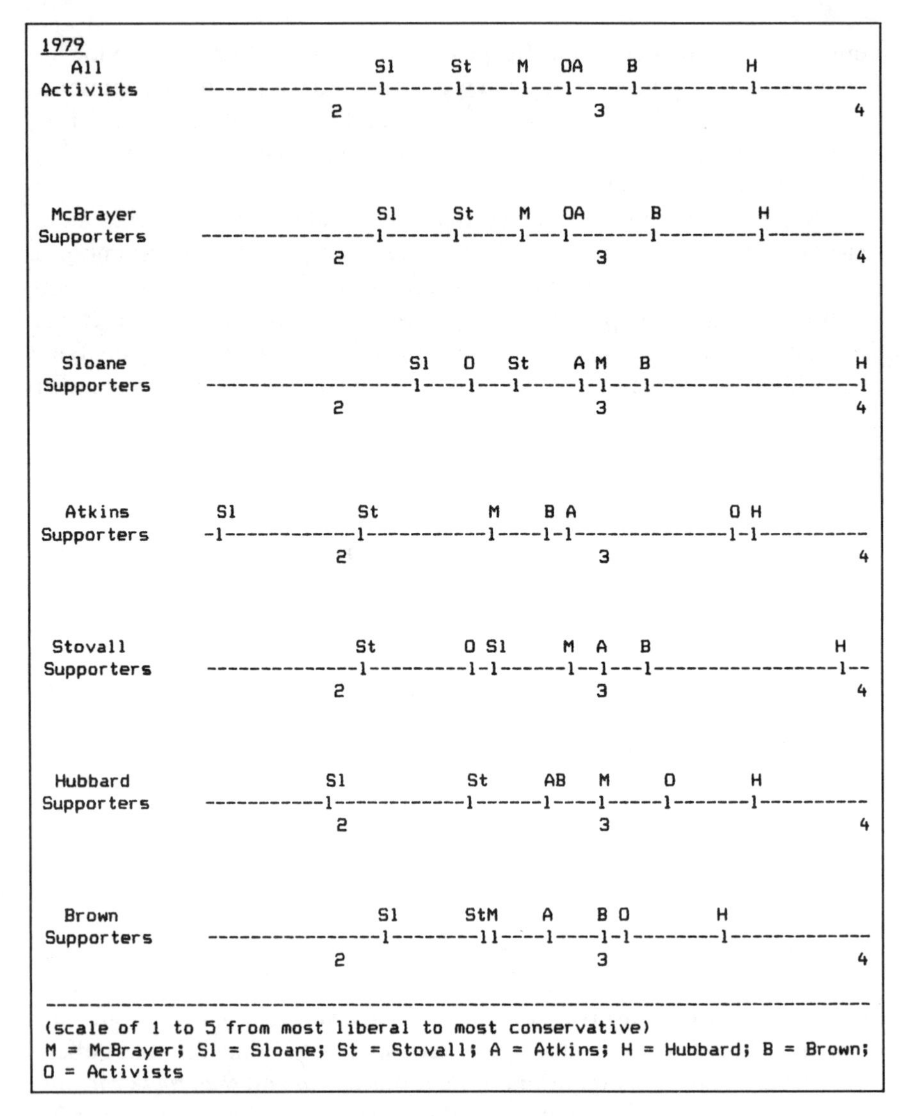

Figure 1. Placements of Candidates and Activists on Liberalism/Conservatism Scale in 1979

that ideology has a strong influence on choice where we find a strong positive relationship.

Figures 1 to 3 show a fairly substantial range in the ideological positions of the candidates from most liberal to most conservative (on a scale of 1 to 5) as perceived by all the activists (mean of the entire sample). When we break down the sample by individual candidate's supporters, for the most part this observation still holds true. There is some tendency for

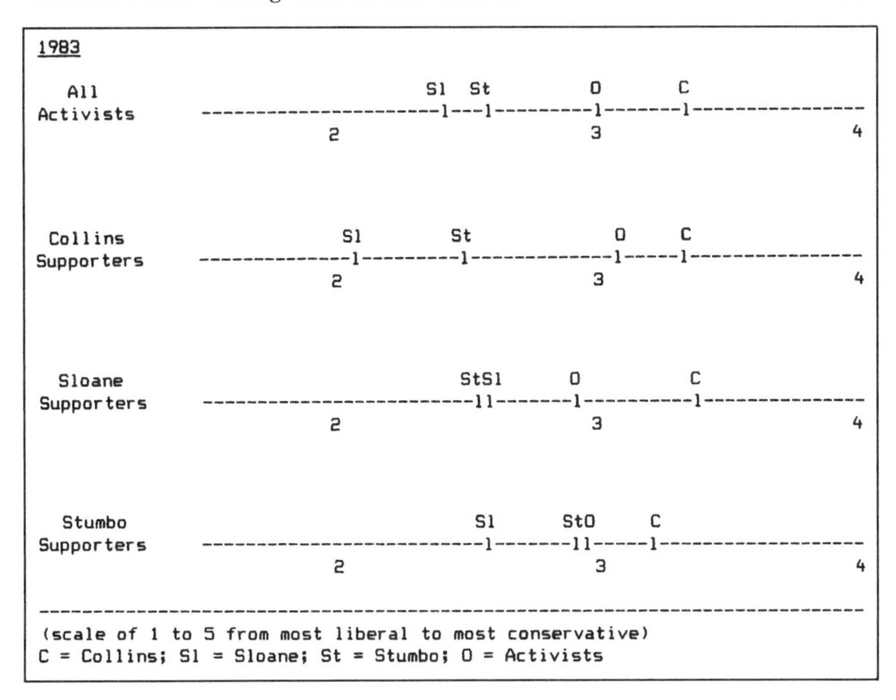

Figure 2. Placements of Candidates and Activists on Liberalism/Conservatism Scale in 1983

supporters of other candidates to perceive an opposing candidate in more extreme terms. For example, in 1979 Hubbard is perceived as more conservative by Sloane activists than by his own supporters; and Sloane is perceived as more liberal by Atkins and Hubbard supporters than by his own. In general, activists supporting candidates at one end of the spectrum tend to perceive candidates at the other end of the spectrum as being more extreme in their ideological views.

In 1983, however, there are not very large differences among the supporters in their own ideological positions, and there are only modest differences in the activists' perceptions of the opposition candidates compared to 1979. There is surprising little difference as to how Collins is perceived by each of the candidates' activists.

In 1987, as shown in figure 3, Beshear is perceived as somewhat liberal to middle-of-the-road by both his own supporters and the activists as a whole, whereas he is viewed as considerably more liberal by some supporters of the more conservative candidates (i.e., Brown, Carroll, and Wilkinson). In contrast, Brown is perceived as middle-of-the-road to somewhat conservative by his own activists and as middle-of-the-road to somewhat conservative by supporters of Beshear and Stumbo.

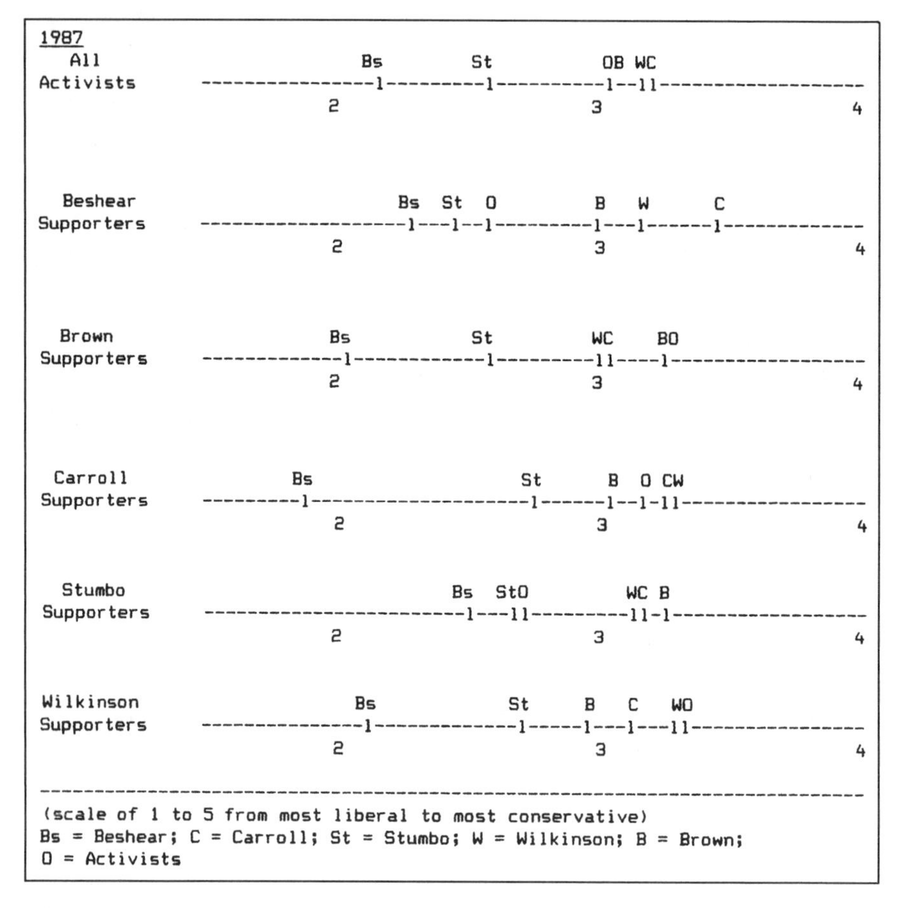

Figure 3. Placements of Candidates and Activists on Liberalism/Conservatism Scale in 1987

The "born again" Carroll is perceived as middle-of-the-road to somewhat conservative by both his own elite volunteers and all the activists. The more liberal candidate Beshear's supporters view Carroll as the most conservative of all the candidates. The populist Stumbo is perceived as somewhat liberal to middle-of-the-road by his workers, all the activists, and the elite volunteers in each of the other candidates' groups. In contrast, Wilkinson, the eventual victor, is perceived as middle-of-the-road to somewhat conservative by his supporters and also by the workers in each of the other gubernatorial campaign groups.

As noted in figures 1 to 3, there is usually a very close relationship between one's own ideological position and one's perception of one's candidate's position (i.e., there is a fairly small distance between where a supporter stands and the perceived stance of his or her candidate). In some cases in 1979 and 1987, the candidate's perceived ideological position is not the closest to that of the candidate's activists. For example, in 1979 McBrayer supporters were closer to Atkins than to their own candidate, and the Atkins supporters were closer to Hubbard than to anyone else. The overall position of the activists was closest to the overall perception of Atkins. Also, in 1987 Beshear workers were closer to Stumbo than to their own candidate. In contrast, in 1983 all of the candidates' supporters were closest to their chosen candidate in political ideology. One probable reason for this finding is the smaller number of candidates in the 1983 primary contest. With six candidates in the 1979 race and five candidates in the 1987 race, it is not surprising that the supporters were not always closest to their chosen candidate.

There is generally only a small gap between the mean ideological preference of activists supporting a particular candidate and their perception of his or her ideological preference. This may mean that activists choose to support candidates whose ideological preferences they agree with. It could also mean that activists attribute to their candidate their own ideological leanings. This is similar to the dilemma we encountered in assessing the influence of perceived issue positions on choice. The data do not permit us to measure the impact of issue positions with any precision. Where most activists, including a candidate's supporters, agree on their perception of his or her ideological posture and where candidates are perceived to have quite different postures, it would seem that ideology plays a part in the choice of a candidate to support. This is the pattern that we find in figures 1 to 3 for most candidates.

An entirely different possibility, suggested by cognitive dissonance theory (Heider, 1958), is that activists may choose a candidate on the basis of factors other than ideological proximity but, having selected their candidate, then come to perceive the candidate as sharing their own political views. Augmenting this tendency toward "assimilation" of the favored candidate may be a "contrast" effect, embodying the tendency to exaggerate the differences between oneself and candidates one opposes (see, e.g., Granberg and Brent, 1974; Sherrod, 1971-72).

Electability and Viability

Prior researchers have argued that candidate choice in conventions and primaries often involves a trade-off between a candidate's ideological position and his or her electability (Abramowitz, McGlennon, and Rapoport, 1986; Jewell, 1984; Stone and Abramowitz, 1986b). However, in Kentucky Democratic politics, this trade-off is usually not very critical, since any nominated Democratic gubernatorial candidate is usually electable. Unlike the party professionals in a strong two-party state, Kentucky activists are not heavily concerned with the strongest candidate in the general election, because the Republicans are usually weak. For example, more than 90 percent of the activists in our 1979/83 sample felt that their primary candidate would very likely win the general election.

In order to gain information about the viability of Democratic candidates, we asked the 1987 activists to assess their candidate's chances of winning the primary election: "When you first became active in the campaign, how did you assess your candidate's chances of winning the primary?" Half of the elite volunteers were optimistic; more than 35 percent thought that their candidate was very likely to win, and another 15 percent felt that their candidate would probably win. In contrast, less than one-fourth of the respondents believed that their candidate would probably or very likely lose the election. The more pessimistic activists were usually those supporting Wilkinson, Stumbo, and Carroll—the candidates generally perceived early in the campaign as least likely to win.

Activists have obvious reasons for wanting to support a winner, and this was clearly a major reason for the support given to Beshear and particularly to Brown in 1987. On the other hand, those activists who started out being pessimistic about the chances of their candidates in the primary (particularly the Wilkinson, Stumbo, and Carroll supporters) clearly did not choose a candidate on the basis of perceived viability.

But changing perceptions of viability caused some activists to shift candidate support late in the campaign. According to polls and political experts, in 1987 there was a last-minute shuffling of voters and activists from certain candidates to the surprise winner, Wilkinson. The collapse of Beshear's campaign, Carroll's failure to generate support, and the polls showing that Wilkinson was gaining all contributed to changes in activists' support. In the last few days of the campaign, there is evidence that a number of activists, particularly Beshear supporters and some Carroll workers in western Kentucky joined the Wilkinson ranks.

Summary of Factors Distinguishing Candidate Groups

In order to have a clearer understanding of the different factors that distinguish the various candidate organizations in 1979, 1983, and 1987, we have summarized the most significant distinctions in table 17. This includes the following factors: continuity of support, professional/amateur status, motivations, demographics, interest groups, issues, and ideology.

Multivariate Analysis of Activists' Choice

In earlier research (1985), based on the survey of 1979 and/or 1983 political activists, Miller used multivariate analysis to measure the variables that

Table 17. Summary of Factors Distinguishing Candidates' Groups

	Continuity	Amat/Prof	Motives	Demogr	Groups	Issues	Ideology
1979							
Atkins		Prof		Business	Business	Honesty	Mid
Brown		Amat/Prof	Less Cand	Business Hi Inc	Business	Honesty	Mid
Hubbard		Prof		Born ag Business	Business	Coal Honesty	Cons
McBrayer		Prof	More Sol More Mat	Lawyers Pub off		Educ	Mid
Sloane		Amat/Prof		Hi educ Young	Teachers	Educ	Lib
Stovall		Prof	Less Mat More Purp	Lo educ Lo inc Older	Labor	Labor	Lib
1983							
Collins	McBrayer	Prof	More Cand	Hi inc Business	Business	Educ	Mid
Sloane	Sloane McBrayer	Prof		Hi educ	Teachers	Educ	Lib
Stumbo	Brown	Amat/Prof	Less Sol Less Mat	Born ag Young Lo inc	Labor	Labor	Lib
1987							
Beshear	Collins	Prof	More Sol More Mat More Cand	Hi inc Hi educ	Teachers Profess	Educ	Lib
Brown	Collins	Prof	More Sol More Mat	Business	Business Profess	No tax Antipatronage	Mid
Carroll	Collins	Prof	More Sol More Mat	Low educ Business Older	Farm	Morality	Mid
Stumbo	Stumbo	Amat/Prof	More Purp	Young	Labor	Populist	Lib
Wilkinson	Collins	Amat/Prof	More Purp	Business	Farm	No tax Lottery	Mid

Factors: Continuity of Support, Amateur/Professional Status, Motivations (Solidary, Material, Purposive, Candidate-Oriented), Demographics, Interest Groups, Issues, and Ideology

bring activists into a particular candidate's primary campaign. (Detailed information concerning the dependent and independent variables is provided in the Appendix.) Table 18 summarizes the results of a discriminant analysis of these data for the 1983 primary campaign. Two discriminant functions were derived, both of which are statistically significant and make major contributions to discriminatory power. The first function, with a

Table 18. Discriminating among Supporters of Collins, Sloane, and Stumbo

	Standardized Discriminant Function Coefficients	
Predictor	Function I	Function II
Motivations for involvement		
Solidary	.221**	−.050
Material	.060	.170
Purposive	−.048	−.109
Candidate-oriented	−.063**	−.224**
Ideological closeness to candidates		
Closeness to Collins	.067***	−.618***
Closeness to Sloane	.619***	.416***
Closeness to Stumbo	−.555***	.098***
Interest group membership		
Labor union	−.534***	.297***
Educational/Teachers group	.037	.003
Business organization	.071	−.122
First worked actively in 1983	−.161*	.111
Candidate supported in 1979 primary		
Atkins	.012	.018
Brown	−.001	.260*
Hubbard	.131*	.150
McBrayer	.310**	.183
Sloane	.469***	.506***
Stovall	−.040	.209
Group centroids		
Collins Supporters	−.030	−.746
Sloane Supporters	.722	.567
Stumbo Supporters	−1.344	.636
Eigenvalues	.537	.443
Canonical correlations	.591	.554
Percent correctly classified	69.7	
Goodman and Kruskal's tau	.521	

*Significant at .05 level; **significant at .01 level; ***significant at .001 level
The significance test was based on the serial deletion procedure described by Sigelman (1984).

canonical correlation only slightly greater than that of the second, explains 54.8 percent of the common variance. The model's discriminatory power is fairly impressive, as indicated by Goodman and Kruskal's tau coefficient of .521, which means that by knowing where the respondents stood on the independent variables we reduce by 52.1 percent the number of errors we would otherwise make in classifying each one as a Collins, Sloane, or Stumbo supporter.

According to the group centroids, the first function distinguishes Sloane supporters on the one extreme from Stumbo supporters on the other, with Collins supporters falling in between but closer to the Stumbo supporters. The second function separates the Collins supporters from the Stumbo and Sloane supporters, who are closely clustered. The central issue, however, is neither overall predictive power nor the alignment of the three groups of volunteers on the two functions but the impact of each predictor in the model, as indicated by the standardized discriminant function coefficients.

Motivations for involvement. Two broad motivational dimensions distinguish between Sloane and Stumbo supporters. Probably because Stumbo was a new candidate with only a regional rather than an established statewide base, activists motivated by solidary considerations were more likely to gravitate to the Sloane campaign. Stumbo's volunteers were more likely to have been drawn to the candidate himself than were Sloane's workers. But the coefficient for the same motivation on the second factor indicates that Collins supporters were significantly more candidate oriented than either Stumbo or Sloane supporters; Collins, a longtime campaigner, had developed close personal ties throughout her political career with many "professional" activists.

Ideological proximity. The ideological closeness between activists and the three candidates had a sizable impact on their choice of a candidate. On both functions all three ideological proximity measures registered significant effects, and the direction of these effects was quite predictable: those whose liberal/conservative self-descriptions were close to their descriptions of a particular candidate were likely to sign on with that candidate's campaign.

In order to examine this effect more closely, let us return to figure 2, which reveals that across all three groups of activists there was a fairly wide range in perceptions of the candidates' political orientations, with Sloane and Stumbo perceived as more liberal than Collins. The same pattern shows up in the perceptions held by each group of activists. Interestingly, though, the three groups were themselves quite similar in terms of their self-perceptions, for all tended to describe themselves as falling very near the midpoint of the ideological continuum. Moreover, figure 2 shows graphic evidence of the point made statistically in table 18: on average the supporters of a given candidate saw themselves as having more in common with that candidate than with either of the other contenders. The clearest case in point is that of the Stumbo supporters; whereas both the Collins and the Sloane workers tended to see Stumbo as being fairly far removed from the Kentucky political mainstream, the Stumbo volunteers, whose ideological self-images were virtually identical to those of their counterparts in the other two camps, viewed their candidate as no less moderate than they themselves were.

Interest group membership. Of the three large interest group constituencies, only one—labor unions—was linked to candidate support in 1983, and Stumbo was the primary recipient of this support. Collins, seen as the most conservative of the three contenders, enjoyed little support within the labor movement, while the UAW, UMW, and AFL-CIO all threw their support to Stumbo after watching Sloane waffle on the right-to-work issue.

Activity in prior primaries. Stumbo, a newcomer to statewide politics, drew significantly greater support from activists who had not previously been involved in a Democratic gubernatorial primary than did Sloane, a repeat candidate. First-time gubernatorial primary activists were less likely to be involved in the Collins campaign.

Continuity of support. The activists who had worked for Sloane in his unsuccessful 1979 campaign tended to line up behind him again in 1983; indeed, more than 77 percent of those who claimed to have worked for Sloane in 1979 joined the 1983 Sloane campaign as well. Sloane also drew significantly more heavily than Stumbo did from the 1979 supporters of Terry McBrayer. Brown's followers were more likely to gravitate to either the Stumbo or the Sloane camp than to the Collins campaign, as evidenced by the significant coefficient for 1979 Brown support on the second function.

Analysis. A multivariate analysis such as this enables us to weigh the relative importance of a number of variables that may explain activists' choice of a candidate to support. One disadvantage is that this may cause us to overlook the importance of a single variable, such as one issue emphasized by one candidate in one election. Moreover, discriminant analysis is an awkward technique for discriminating among supporters of five or six candidates. This is why we have used it only in the 1983 primary election.

Among the variables most helpful in predicting which candidate political activists would support in 1983 were their support for a particular candidate in 1979, their involvement in a labor union, their basic motivation for supporting a candidate, and—above all—their ideological closeness to the perceived position of a candidate.

The fact that Kentucky Democratic activists tend to be longtimers rather than in-and-outers, coupled with the factional tradition of Kentucky politics, also suggests that activists' involvement might be characterized by considerable continuity of support from one campaign to the next. Some such linkages are visible in our data, but all in all the continuity factor is not nearly as strong as might have been expected. Nor do group memberships, other than union membership, appear to have played a very important role in drawing activists into particular campaigns.

It is noteworthy that ideological proximity has so much importance in a discriminant analysis. We have already pointed out, however, that there may be other explanations for the ideological congruence between activists and the candidates for whom they work. In Kentucky Democratic activists tend to work year in and year out with political friends and neighbors, and a shared set of political orientations may underlie these continuing networks. This suggests more of a collective than an individual logic of candidate choice, a possibility premised on group attraction to a given candidate. Moreover, some activists may attribute to candidates their own ideological positions. Unfortunately, our data do not permit us to determine which of these interpretations best accounts for the unexpectedly strong showing of ideological proximity as a factor underlying candidate choice among Kentucky Democratic activists.

Conclusions

Kentucky gubernatorial activists are the heart and core of the state's political nominating process. They are the most active and vital political volunteers; they provide much of the essential manpower and funding that are required to carry out campaigns for nominations. Similarly, they provide much of the effort and funding in the general election campaigns. These elite workers appear to make choices on the basis of material incentives and personal contacts in contrast to ideological, issue-oriented concerns. They tend to be long-term professionals without close ties to interest groups; they pledge their first loyalties to the party and not to significant interest groups. However, we find that their choice of candidates often coincides fairly closely with ideological closeness and certain issues, an apparent anomaly that we discussed above.

In the contemporary political environment, there are some campaigns where political activists play a much smaller role. In these campaigns paid professionals perform the key organizational tasks; professional campaign structures take the place of volunteer activists' organizations. A professionally staffed campaign group, utilizing sophisticated mass media techniques, might be a very successful electoral vehicle in a nominating system that relies largely on primary elections and makes no use of organizational endorsements. The 1979 gubernatorial campaign of John Y. Brown, Jr., was an example of a candidate with considerable financial resources winning by having a professionally staffed media-oriented campaign. Wallace Wilkinson in 1987, however, combined a more traditional organization of activists with an expensive and skillful media campaign.

Perspectives of the Primary Campaign

Reasons for Winning or Losing

Activists were asked to give the most important reasons for the win or loss of their candidates in the 1979, 1983, and/or 1987 primaries. Generally, elite volunteers for victorious candidates stressed reasons such as the commendable personal qualities of the candidate (65 percent), popular issues (51 percent), good organization (38 percent), favorable finances (35 percent), and good media (25 percent). More than 90 percent in 1979, 84 percent in 1983, and 43 percent in 1987 praised their candidate for possessing admirable qualities—e.g., honesty and integrity (John Y. Brown, Jr., 1979; Martha Layne Collins, 1983; and Wallace Wilkinson 1987), experience (Collins), and "nonpolitical status" (Brown and Wilkinson). Almost 90 percent of the Wilkinson supporters cited popular issues for the victory of their candidate—especially the no-tax/lottery stand; in contrast, only 30 percent of Brown's and one-third of Collins's workers stressed popular issues. On the other hand, more than 53 percent of Collins's supporters emphasized good organization, compared to 18 percent of Brown's and 22 percent of Wilkinson's activists. Although the 1987 gubernatorial campaign was, by far, the most expensive in Kentucky's history, with the winning candidate spending almost $4.3 million, only 34 percent of Wilkinson's supporters emphasized financial resources as a major reason for his victory.

A Brown activist in 1979 commented, "John Y. Brown has charisma. He looks good on television. And Phyllis is such an asset." Another Brown worker stated, "He's a millionaire who is going to run Kentucky like a business. He has promised to get rid of the political corruption in Frankfort." A Collins worker in 1983 remarked, "I think it was her 'eyeball to eyeball' contact with the voters and her remarkable memory in calling them by name after meeting only one time." One Collins activist attributed the victory to good organization and enough money: "Martha Layne Collins had the best grass roots organization and ample funds to get her message across."

One volunteer perceived that Wilkinson won because of the "lottery—money—and the skills to communicate to people across Kentucky that he was sincere and not counterfeit." Another Wilkinson worker suggested the victory was due to "well executed campaign strategy, issues, organization. Poor campaign strategies of opponents—especially mud-slinging." One Wilkinson worker's explanation included the candidate's outsider status: "The lottery issue, coupled with commitment not to raise taxes, ample funds to get the message across—good organization—new face not tainted by public's low opinion of Frankfort."

Among the supporters of losing candidates in 1979, 1983, and/or 1987, the most frequently given reasons for the loss were inadequate financial resources (47 percent), negative advertising/bad media (43 percent), unpopular issues (23 percent), and weak organization (1 percent). McBrayer supporters in 1979 stressed his association with the unpopular Governor Carroll and the harmful effects of negative advertising, whereas Sloane activists in 1983 stressed Governor Brown's last-minute endorsement of Stumbo as a major reason for their candidate's loss. Also, Beshear's and Brown's activists in 1987 cited the devasating effects of negative advertising; in contrast, Stumbo's and Carroll's supporters emphasized very inadequate financial resources.

A McBrayer activist in 1979 remarked, "Brown came in at the last minute and bought the election. And his mud-slinging ads against the Carroll administration were very effective." According to one Stovall worker, "Thelma didn't have enough money and the media portrayed her as a loser." A Stumbo supporter in 1983 commented, "I believe the reason Stumbo lost was due to the fact that he was an unknown candidate and his funds were insufficient in comparison to the publicity Collins and Sloane have had over a period of years." One Sloane volunteer in 1983 suggested, "John Y. Brown's support for Grady Stumbo in the last few days took votes away from Sloane and caused him to lose." Another Sloane activist in 1983 stated, "Sloane's loss was in direct relation to his inability to get a bloc vote from organized labor, a group he had done so well with in previous elections. Stumbo won over some 35,000 labor votes that would have voted for Sloane."

One Beshear supporter in 1987 commented, "Beshear followed poor advice, created a perception of a negative campaign, would not endorse the lottery issue, could not explain where new revenue would be found other than growth." Another Beshear volunteer maintained, "Beshear was forced to take on Brown to set Brown's record straight; but the negative campaign had a backlash and Beshear opened up the way for Wilkinson who had avoided any close scrutiny since he was not seen as having a chance of winning." According to a Carroll supporter, her candidate lost because of his political past: "The scandal the last time he was governor and the deal with Hunt." One Carroll worker remarked, "The media repeatedly defamed Mr. Carroll, never gave him any praise—all bad and this made people wonder if and why he was in the race—so he could not raise moneys or hopes." Brown's laziness was noted by one of his volunteers: "John Y. didn't work very hard. He went to a ball game and played golf the last days of the campaign. He gave away the election to Wilkinson."

Divisive Primaries and Party Activists in 1979 and 1983

It has often been asserted that direct primaries undermine political parties by producing, exacerbating, or at the very least publicizing rifts among their supporters. V.O. Key (1964) believed that "the adoption of the direct primary opened the road for disruptive forces that gradually fractionalized the party organization. [T]he primary system . . . facilitated the construction of factions and cliques attached to ambitions of individual leaders" (p. 342). Those who voluntarily commit their time, energy, money, and other resources to a candidate who loses the party primary may be reluctant to transfer their loyalties to the winner (Hacker, 1965). Even if the issue positions of the winning and losing candidates are virtually identical, the experience of losing can sour an activist on further involvement, as can the fact that the winning candidate was the agent of this defeat.

Over the years considerable research has accumulated concerning the effects of divisive primaries on general election outcomes (see Born, 1981; Kenney and Rice, 1984; Piereson and Smith, 1975; Stone, 1984, 1986), but relatively little is known about how activists respond to defeat in primaries. Are they more likely to pitch in and work for the primary worker in the general election campaign or to withdraw, at least temporarily, from the political fray? Just as importantly, what factors shape these responses? A rare glimpse at these issues was provided by Johnson and Gibson's (1974) study of volunteers in the 1970 primary and general election campaigns in an Iowa congressional district. Among those whose candidate did not survive the primary, three-quarters anticipated becoming less active in the general election campaign, nearly half indicated an unwillingness to vote for the primary winner, and one-fifth actually intended to work for the other party in some capacity. But this short-term drop-off in partisan activity seemed unlikely to inflict lasting harm on the party, since most of the activists—losers as well as winners—voiced an intention to participate in future campaigns and to seek higher positions within the party (Johnson and Gibson, 1974: 76-77).

Since the Johnson-Gibson study was limited to a single district during a single year, it seems appropriate to reexamine the response of primary activists to the defeat of their candidate. We use data from our survey of Kentucky gubernatorial workers in the 1979 and 1983 primary campaigns to clarify the impact of divisive primaries on party activists.

A closely contested primary is not necessarily divisive. Rather, divisiveness occurs only when the campaign is characterized by bitterness and ill feelings among the participants—by animosity so palpable as potentially to alienate individuals and groups essential to the party's success in the general election (Westlye, 1985: 5).

Were the 1979 and 1983 primaries truly divisive? Before Brown's entry the 1979 primary was a free-for-all, with the party split along several lines. Then Brown, in an eleventh-hour, media-based campaign, launched a hard-hitting attack against old-style politics in general and the Carroll administration in particular, focusing on corruption as the prime issue in the campaign. Although McBrayer was not named in the ongoing grand jury investigation of the Carroll administration, Brown and others (especially Atkins) capitalized on McBrayer's links with Carroll to tar him with the same brush, and the campaign in its latter stages became uncommonly personalistic and acrimonious. Brown's maverick operating style and public disdain for the party organization also antagonized many party regulars. The Sloane camp, for its part, was embittered by what it perceived as Atkins's sellout to Brown, especially since a Sloane-Atkins linkage had earlier been considered. In the end, all the defeated candidates did back Brown's candidacy in the general election, but the primary battle left long-term scars.

The sheer nastiness of the 1979 primary was not repeated in 1983, but even then ill feelings continued to prevail among the various camps. Sloane was portrayed as a "wimp," a characterization that naturally rankled him and his backers, while Stumbo, who enjoyed support from the labor movement, was pictured by some as a wild-eyed radical. Doubts were also raised about Collins's fitness for the job, with overt references to her background as a beauty queen and home economics teacher and to her close ties to the "courthouse crowd." There were also veiled suggestions that Kentucky was not ready for a female chief executive. Stumbo's labor supporters worked energetically to defeat Sloane. Sloane, the acknowledged front-runner early on, was very upset with his defeat in this very close primary (Collins won with just 35 percent of the vote). Sloane demanded a recount, conceded to Collins only two weeks after the primary, and withheld even his grudging endorsement for several more weeks.

By any standard, then, the 1979 primary would have to be considered highly divisive. The 1983 primary was a less vitriolic and divisive affair. But since the close three-way race generated sharp antagonisms among the three camps, we believe that it, too, can fairly be included in the category of divisive primaries. It should be remembered that in neither of these primaries did any of the losing candidates support the Republican candidate in the general election, as Chandler had done in some previous primaries that he had lost.

How did those who campaigned for losing candidates in the 1979 and 1983 primaries react? It seems likely that responses to a primary loss are shaped by the activist's political experience and commitments. Those who have been involved in politics on a more or less continuous basis and who strongly identify with the party should be less prone to walk away from a general election campaign after their candidate loses in the primary; those whose involvement has been more intermittent or who are less firmly bonded to the party should be more likely to sit out the general election campaign. Johnson and Gibson (1974) noted in this regard that "bolters" were more likely than "nonbolters" to be political amateurs; 80 percent of the bolters had less than five years of political experience, and nearly 50 percent had no campaign experience. Similarly, only 25 percent of the bolters, but 50 percent of the nonbolters, were strong party identifiers (pp. 73-76).

It also seems possible that activists' reactions to a primary loss are shaped by the motivations that led them to become involved in the primary campaign in the first place. In particular, those motivated by a material incentive (e.g., financial rewards or career enhancement) are primarily interested in the "spoils" of victory, in contrast to those whose motivation is more social (solidary) or ideological (purposive) (Clark and Wilson, 1961). Where the materialistic orientation prevails, the activist should be eager to become involved in the general election campaign, for to withdraw after a loss in the primary would be to cut oneself off from the spoils. On the other hand, some of those who enlist in a campaign are motivated mainly by their friendship with or admiration for a candidate, and this type of motivation seems less likely to transfer over to a second candidate.

It is also plausible that activists who invested most heavily in a primary campaign and who derived the greatest satisfaction from their participation in the primary would be most willing to become involved in another candidate's bid for election. We might also anticipate that the willingness to work in the general election would depend on which loser the activists had worked for. Some candidates seem to attract more "professional," long-term activists than others, and these professionals tend to work year in and year out in both primary and general election battles. In the Kentucky context, we would expect, for example, that McBrayer's relatively professional supporters would have been more likely to line up behind Brown than would Sloane's relatively amateur supporters.

Analysis here focuses on the subset of respondents who worked for a losing candidate and who answered every question upon which the analysis is based (N = 284 for 1979 and 262 for 1983). There are obvious difficulties in using recall data of any kind (see Weir, 1975), but political activists might be expected to remember their participation in a campaign much more accurately than the average citizen recalls his or her relatively casual political involvement. On the other hand, the time dimension of this study presents a potential complication. Respondents were asked in 1983 to describe their involvement in the 1983 primary and, where applicable, in the 1979 primary as well. If their memories had faded over four years, they may have based their 1979 responses on their 1983 experiences.

The dependent variable in the analysis is a yes/no response to the question, "In 1979 [1983], did you work for the Democratic gubernatorial nominee in the general election?" The independent variables, based on the propositions outlined above, fall into five categories: personal political characteristics, motivations for involvement in the primary campaign, level of involvement in the primary campaign, positive affect toward the primary campaign, and primary candidate preference.

Four *personal political characteristics* were included in the analysis: a 1 to 5 Likert scale summarizing a respondent's degree of involvement in Kentucky campaigns during the last five years; the number of years the respondent had been actively involved in Kentucky politics; a 1 to 5 liberalism-conservatism scale; and the respondent's party identification (measured on the traditional 1 to 7 scale). *Motivations for involvement in the primary* were measured in a series of thirteen 1 to 4 Likert-type items drawn from prior empirical work o the Clark-Wilson (1961) typology of motivations (see chapter 3 for a detailed explanation). One item ("support of a particular candidate I believe in") was set aside because so many of the respondents highlighted it. Factor analyses of the remaining twelve items uncovered three dimensions in both 1979 and 1983—solidary, material, and purposive. Based on these results, each set of items was combined additively to form a summary score for each respondent on each dimension in a given year. The "personal friendship with a candidate" item was used by itself as an indicator of a candidate-centered motivation for participation in the primary.

Two separate indicators of *level of involvement in the primary campaign* were employed for each year: the number of hours per week and the amount of money the respondent contributed to the campaign. *Positive affect toward the primary campaign* was probed in a series of seven 1 to 5 Likert-type items ("experienced good relationships with the co-workers"; "felt primary deserved my support even if I were unable to participate"; "campaign involvement made me more interested in sticking with politics"; "felt I belonged to a cohesive group"; "cared about what the campaign organization said or did"; "participation increased due to personality of candidate"; and "importance of the primary campaign's purpose"). Since factor analyses uncovered a single underlying dimension for each year, the seven items were combined into a single additive index of positive feelings about the primary campaign. Finally, dummy (0, 1) variables were coded to designate each activist's *candidate preference* in the campaign(s) in which he or she worked.

Of the 284 activists who had worked for one of the losers in the 1979 Democratic gubernatorial primary, 214 (75.4 percent) subsequently joined the campaign of the Democratic nominee, John Y. Brown, Jr. This percentage declined somewhat in 1983, when (probably as a reflection of animosities that developed during the extremely competitive primary) only 67.6 percent of the Sloane and Stumbo supporters decided to work in the Collins campaign. Did the 30 percent or so of the Kentucky activists who did not join in the general election campaign after their favorite lost in the primary differ in any systematic way from the approximately 70 percent who did campaign for the winner of the primary? Table 19 summarizes a pair of discriminant analyses bearing on this question; the two analyses are identical, except that the variables in each were matched to the election at hand.

As the summary statistics at the bottom of table 19 indicate, the performance of these models was fairly impressive. The best gauges of predictive power are Goodman and Kruskal's tau coefficients of .405 and .434 for 1979 and 1983, respectively; this means that the errors in classification based on the discriminating variables were more than 40 percent below what would have been expected had classification been attempted based solely on the marginal distribution of the grouping variable.

The standardized discriminant function coefficients identify the independent variables that do most to distinguish those who remained active in the general election campaign from those who did not. In both 1979 and 1983, two personal political characteristics stood out above all the other predictors in the model. Those who had been involved in political campaigns relatively rarely or only intermittently over the previous five years were significantly more likely to drop out after a primary loss than those who had been involved in Kentucky politics on a more sustained basis. Similarly, the party identification scale (which largely distinguished between strong and less strong Democrats, with some independents and a handful of Republican identifiers) also separated the stayers from the dropouts among supporters of losing primary candidates; those who were more closely identified with the Democratic party were more likely to work for the party's nominee after their preferred candidate had lost in the primary.

The effect of political ideology was significant in 1983 but fell short of significance in 1979. In 1979 Brown ran as a reformer, attacking corruption in state government and old-style patronage politics. He did not adopt any

Table 19. Discriminant Analysis Summary, 1979 and 1983 Activists' Response to Primary Defeat

	Standardized Discriminant Function Coefficients	
Predictor	1979	1983
Personal political characteristics		
Frequency of campaign activity	.581***	.443*
Years of campaign activity	.236	−.100
Party identification	.504***	.464***
Political ideology	−.206	.450**
Motivations for primary involvement		
Solidary incentives	−.239	.029
Material incentives	−.034	.401*
Purposive incentives	−.057	.253
Candidate-centered incentives	.029	−.169
Level of involvement in the primary		
Hours worked	−.089	−.038
Money contributed	−.163	.254
Satisfaction with the primary campaign	.028	.271
Candidate Preference		
Atkins 1979	.401*	
Hubbard 1979	.204	
McBrayer 1979	.403*	
Stovall 1979	.234	
Sloane 1979 (reference category)	—	
Stumbo 1983		.115
Sloane 1983 (reference category)		—
Group centroids		
Nonworkers for the Democratic nominee	−.899	−.641
Workers for the Democratic nominee	.294	.308
Eigenvalues	.266	.199
Canonical correlations	.458	.407
Percent correctly classified	78.200	76.300
Goodman and Kruskal's tau	.415	.456

*p ⟨ .05 **p ⟨ .01 ***p ⟨ .001

identifiable issue positions, except for his refrain that he would "run state government like a business." On the other hand, in 1983 Collins was clearly the most conservative of the three primary candidates, both in her orientation toward reform and the issue positions with which she and her opponents were identified. Thus, the more liberal among the supporters of Sloane and Stumbo were significantly more likely to sit out the 1983 general election campaign than were their more conservative counterparts.

Among the motivations for involvement in the primary campaign, only the material motivation significantly affected the losing primary activists' likelihood of remaining active in the general election campaign, and that only occurred in 1983. Those who participated in a primary campaign for what they hoped to get out of it in a material (largely career-advancement) sense were less hesitant to transfer their loyalties to the primary winner's campaign than those who were less moved by material considerations. In 1979, however, Brown's oft-expressed scorn for old-style patronage politics led to a perception that few tangible rewards, especially jobs, would result from working for him in the general election. By contrast, Collins, an old-line politico and ally of courthouse "professional" activists, was probably seen as more likely to reward her supporters with jobs, personal service contracts, and other forms of patronage.

In 1979 Atkins and McBrayer backers were significantly more likely than Sloane supporters to sign on with the Brown general election campaign. These differences come as no great surprise, considering Atkins's withdrawal from the primary and subsequent endorsement of Brown, McBrayer's heavy reliance on long-term "professional" politicos who would be predisposed to back the party's choice no matter who it may have been, and the predominantly "amateur" character of Sloane's primary workers. By contrast, in 1983 there was no significant difference between Sloane and Stumbo supporters in the decision to work for Collins's election; in both cases the percentage who worked for Collins in the fall campaign fell below the percentage of losing primary activists who had rallied behind Brown in 1979.

We have seen that the decision of activists who backed a losing candidate in the primary to work for the party's standard-bearer in the general election is reasonably predictable. The more active a primary worker has been in recent elections and the stronger his or her sense of identification with the party, the greater the likelihood that he or she will work to elect the winner of the primary. It is also true that backers of some primary candidates are more likely to sit out the general election than are supporters of other primary candidates.

Two points stand out about the willingness or reluctance of Kentucky Democratic party activists to back a party nominee against whom they have campaigned in the primary election. First, the sheer frequency with which Kentucky Democratic activists transfer their loyalties from a candidate who lost in the primary to the party's gubernatorial nominee appears to be considerably higher than was the case in the Iowa congressional district analyzed by Johnson and Gibson (1974). Second, the factors that best predict this tendency relate to the activists' involvement in the party. Together, these two points convey a strong sense that Democratic activists in Kentucky view primaries as intramural contests for which they must choose up sides. When one's side loses the intramural contest, there is relatively little hesitancy—especially on the part of those who identify most strongly with and participate most extensively in the party—to enlist in the extramural battle against the Republicans.

We consider it highly probable that this willingness to campaign for the election of a candidate one originally opposed reflects the decline of traditional factionalism, the fluidity of political alignments, and the non-ideological nature of politics in Kentucky. This interpretation suggests a proposition that can serve as a guidepost for future comparative state analyses: that the willingness of losing primary activists to campaign for the primary winner is greatest in party systems where there are neither deep factional nor ideological divisions.

8

FUNDING POLITICAL CAMPAIGNS

IN ORDER to run a competitive, statewide campaign in Kentucky, a candidate must employ a wide variety of techniques for communicating with at least half a million voters. The candidate must travel back and forth across the state, along with members of the staff, for many months. Campaign literature must be printed and mailed to hundreds of thousands of voters; yard signs and bumper stickers must be purchased and distributed. Many of the jobs that used to be performed by volunteers are now carried out by paid workers, such as those who run the phone banks. A serious candidate for major statewide office must hire political consultants, media experts, and pollsters; and the good ones are expensive. Statewide polls done by professionals are also expensive; cut-rate polls are virtually useless. Most expensive of all is the cost of creating and buying time for television and (to a lesser extent) radio advertising.

The costs of carrying out a competitive campaign are high and are continuously growing. In our analysis of gubernatorial primaries, we have seen that the success of a candidate increasingly depends on the quality and quantity of his or her television advertising. The costs of campaigns are escalating in large part because the importance and cost of television have been growing. They have also escalated because, in recent campaigns for major office, there have been more candidates who were able either to raise large sums of money or to loan large sums to their campaigns.

The High Cost of Campaigns

Campaign costs for statewide and state legislative races have escalated dramatically over the last two decades. In 1967 the thirteen candidates for governor spent a total of just under $2 million in the primary and general election campaigns. In 1987 one candidate for governor spent more than twice that amount in the primary alone. Between 1975 and 1987 the cost of living has slightly more than doubled, but the cost of campaigning has

Table 20. Spending by Statewide Candidates in Democratic Primaries, 1975-87

Office	Total costs for office	Cost of winner	Highest cost
Governor			
1975	$1,548,733	$1,043,884	$1,043,884
1979	5,817,043	1,617,438	1,877,944
1983	6,426,549	2,469,725	2,769,246
1987	12,324,038	4,271,632	4,271,632
Constant $			
1975	1,548,733	1,043,884	1,043,884
1987	5,832,483	2,021,596	2,021,596
Lieutenant Governor			
1975	1,156,827	49,859	638,517
1979	1,469,193	111,306	624,072
1983	1,225,570	370,277	370,277
1987	5,032,810	2,206,379	2,206,379
Constant $			
1975	1,156,827	49,859	638,517
1987	2,381,832	1,044,193	1,044,193
Attorney General			
1975	101,440	46,156	46,156
1979	226,846	128,628	128,628
1983	415,583	142,719	142,719
1987	556,056	454,261	454,261
Constant $			
1975	101,440	46,156	46,156
1987	263,159	214,984	214,984
Auditor			
1975	42,657	37,603	37,603
1979	61,900	16,647	26,156
1983	215,786	113,937	113,937
1987	325,923	294,337	294,337
Constant $			
1975	42,657	37,603	37,603
1987	154,247	139,298	139,298
Superintendent of Public Instruction			
1975	23,308	12,739	12,739
1979	89,650	51,969	51,969
1983	170,918	96,238	96,238
1987	433,522	86,427	181,039
Constant $			
1975	23,308	12,739	12,739
1987	205,169	40,903	85,679

Table 20 (cont.)

Office	Total costs for office	Cost of winner	Highest cost
Commissioner of Agriculture			
1975	80,021	31,516	31,822
1979	80,198	14,805	24,557
1983	204,052	84,512	84,512
1987	232,500	207,184	207,184
Constant $			
1975	80,021	31,516	31,822
1987	110,033	98,052	98,052
Secretary of State			
1975	49,818	46,080	46,080
1979	73,015	65,998	65,998
1983	84,468	20,586	56,582
1987	203,701	58,001	58,001
Constant $			
1975	49,818	46,080	46,080
1987	96,404	27,450	27,450
Treasurer			
1975	45,723	37,461	37,461
1979	31,320	31,320	31,320
1983	193,387	106,396	106,396
1987	299,591	70,643	90,440
Constant $			
1975	45,723	37,461	37,461
1987	141,785	33,433	42,802
Totals for all offices			
1975	3,048,527	—	—
1979	7,849,165	—	—
1983	8,936,313	—	—
1987	19,408,141	—	—
Constant $			
1975	3,048,527	—	—
1987	9,158,112		

Source: Compiled from the records of the Kentucky Registry of Election Finance for each of the years.

risen far more than that (table 20). Just about everyone seems to deplore the spiraling cost of campaigning and the increasing amount of time required for fund-raising. "It's obvious that campaign costs are getting totally out of hand," said Steve Beshear, who raised and spent $2.9 million in finishing third in the 1987 Democratic primary. "We're reaching the point where only the very wealthy will be able to run." Unless candidates have a personal fortune, they have little choice but to accept large donations from special interests. Such donations sometimes come with strings attached—commitments on appointments, contracts, and jobs.

Statewide Elections

Because Democratic primaries are usually more competitive than general elections, they are usually more expensive. Table 20 provides some perspective on the rising expenses of Democratic primaries and what it costs to win. The governor's race, of course, has been by far the most expensive. From 1975 to 1987 the costs of winning the gubernatorial nomination increased by almost four times, and total expenses increased by eight times. In terms of constant dollars, the cost of winning doubled, and total costs increased by three and one-half times.

In 1979 campaign finance in Kentucky was changed dramatically and perhaps permanently. The impetus was the candidacy of John Y. Brown for governor. Realizing that much of the public was disillusioned with the corrupt electoral process, Brown ran as the candidate without political support, who could not be bought; he set out to spend his own money for his election bid. Since there are no limits to the use of personal funds, Brown lent his campaign $1.25 million of his own money, hiring a campaign staff across the state to substitute for a patronage-driven volunteer organization. Brown's four major opponents attempted to spend equal amounts, and in the end over $5.8 million was spent in that primary—almost five times more than any previous Kentucky race.

In the 1983 gubernatorial campaign, personal spending was a smaller factor, but overall expenditures continued to rise. With only three major candidates seeking the Democratic nomination, over $6.4 million was spent. Brown's election had made media more central to the Kentucky campaign process. In order to meet media's insatiable needs, more money was spent. Candidates became more dependent on individual contributions, enhancing the risk of more promises for political favors.

The 1987 primary marked a new phase in the campaign finance process. Candidates running for statewide office in the 1987 primary spent more than $19.6 million, making the election by far the most expensive in Kentucky's history. However, the total cost would be more than $20 million if the tally included expenditures for the political services of independent committees or the in-kind contributions of individuals. In the governor's race, the Democratic and Republican candidates spent $12.5 million, led by Wilkinson, who spent more than $4.2 million in winning the Democratic nomination. Wilkinson spent an estimated $2.09 for every registered voter or about $18.09 for every vote he actually received. In losing efforts, Brown spent $18.38; Beshear, $21.84; Carroll, $23.73; and Stumbo, $8.86 per vote received. For both the general election and primary campaigns, the cost of the governor's race topped $15 million. Wilkinson's bid for governor carried a record $6.8 million price tag (*H-L*, June 27, 1987, p. A10).

While the rising costs of the gubernatorial election have attracted the most attention, financing has also begun to have a major impact on the outcome of the primary for lieutenant governor. In most election campaigns, if there are large disparities in spending, the winner is the candidate who spends the most. But exceptions can occur if the low spender is much better known than the high spender. In 1975 Thelma Stovall, a veteran state officeholder, spent only $50,000 in her successful campaign for lieutenant governor; one of her opponents, a county judge, spent over $600,000. In 1979 Martha Layne Collins, who had been elected once to statewide office, was narrowly nominated lieutenant governor despite being outspent by another candidate by half a million dollars. But in 1987 Brereton Jones, a political newcomer with a budget of over $2 million, defeated several candidates who had more electoral experience but smaller budgets. The total spending in the lieutenant governor's primary was over $5 million, not far behind the total costs of gubernatorial primaries in 1979 and 1983.

There have also been rapid increases in the costs of races for the other state offices, some of which used to be quite inexpensive. It cost ten times as much to be nominated attorney general in 1987 as it did in 1975. In 1979 the winning candidate for auditor spent less than $17,000; in 1987 the winner spent nearly $300,000 and outspent his opponent almost 10 to 1. The cost of winning the job of commissioner of agriculture rose from under $15,000 in 1979 to over $200,000 in 1987.

The contrast between the costs of Democratic and Republican primaries is startling. The total costs of Republican gubernatorial primaries was $250,000 or less in three of the four elections from 1975 through 1987, although in 1979 the price tag rose to over half a million dollars. Generally, these races have not been closely competitive; and even when the race was closer (as in 1987), the candidates have been unable to raise large funds. The costs of Republican primaries for all other statewide offices in the four election years were negligible, largely because the Republicans have rarely had any significant competition.

In the general election campaigns for governor, there have been wide variations in the level of Republican spending, and the Democratic party has generally raised as much money as was necessary to stay ahead. In 1975 Julian Carroll, who enjoyed the advantage of incumbency, spent less than $300,000. Both Louie Nunn in 1979 and Jim Bunning in 1983 spent more

Table 21. Total Spending in Statewide General Election Races, 1975-87

	1975	1979	1983	1987
Governor				
Dem.	286,395	1,863,250	1,394,584	2,610,075
Rep.	233,292	1,225,148	1,364,700	255,788
Lieutenant Governor				
Dem.	15,452	99,359	79,760	913,947
Rep.	15,488	87,469	54,452	6,299
Attorney General				
Dem.	14,493	14,687	57,492	224,003
Rep.	2,641	18,730	12,337	52,389
Auditor				
Dem.	9,509	7,845	916	66,491
Rep.	7,324	2,296	2,878	1,341
Superintendent of Public Instruction				
Dem.	6,210	29,672	153,375	145,574
Rep.	1,631	7,749	9,473	1,850
Commissioner of Agriculture				
Dem.	15,358	30,352	35,100	89,614
Rep.	1,835	5,594	3,847	1,490
Secretary of State				
Dem.	9,605	26,965	14,983	31,072
Rep.	29,443	12,131	8,643	29,759
Treasurer				
Dem.	14,684	10,426	38,662	21,068
Rep.	3,424	3,396	12,133	5,797
Totals	666,784	3,445,069	3,243,335	4,456,557
Dem.	371,706	2,082,556	1,774,872	4,101,844
Rep.	295,078	1,362,513	1,468,463	354,713

Source: Compiled from the records of the Kentucky Registry of Election Finance for each of the years.

than $1 million in their general election bid, and the Democratic candidates spent comparable or higher amounts (table 21).

In 1987 the Republican nominee, John Harper, was not perceived by most Republicans as a competitive candidate. He was able to raise and spend only a quarter of a million dollars, less than any Republican candidate for governor in at least twenty years. Harper's fund-raising effort faced unusual handicaps because he decided to run only after Larry Forgy's surprise withdrawal from the race in January 1987. Forgy had raised more than $750,000 and was expected to be a formidable challenger. The last time a Republican won a gubernatorial election—when Nunn ran in 1967—he raised more than four times what Harper raised before adjusting for inflation. Democrat Wallace Wilkinson, engaging in financial overkill, spent $2.6 million, more than ten times as much as Harper. If primary and general election spending are combined, Wilkinson outspent Harper about 25 to 1.

Legislative Elections

The cost of running for the state legislature has also escalated dramatically. The costs of primary and general election campaigns quadrupled from $722,000 in 1975 to more than $2.8 million in 1986, while the cost of living was approximately doubling (table 22). In addition to summarizing the total spending in legislative races for each year, the table shows the average cost of winning primaries and general elections in which there were contests and the highest amount spent by any winner in these races.

The most obvious finding in the table is that it costs much more to be elected to the Senate than to the House. There are about 100,000 people in the average Senate district and 38,000 in a House district, a ratio of 2.6 to 1. It has generally cost from two to four times as much to run successfully in a Senate primary and about twice as much to run in a Senate general election, though the small number of Senate races in any one category makes precise comparisons impossible.

The most striking finding is the rapidly increasing costs of winning an election. Between 1975 and 1986 the average cost of winning a contested primary has increased by four to five times; the cost of winning contested general elections has increased about seven times. Another way of measuring change is to compare the proportion of expensive races.

Many of the most expensive winning House races are found in the two largest counties; in 1979 and 1981, thirteen of twenty-two House races costing over $10,000 (for primary and general elections combined) were in Jefferson or Fayette counties. In 1984 the most expensive successful House campaign, costing almost $74,000, was in Fayette County (the losing Democrat in the primary and the losing Republican in the general election spent another $70,000). In 1983 the most expensive Senate campaign was in a district largely in Pike County; the winner spent over $84,000 in the Democratic primary (beating a candidate who spent almost $77,000) and another $5,400 in the general election.

In the 1988 primary at least eight candidates spent more than $40,000 each, with Sen. Michael Moloney of Lexington setting a record by raising $99,465 and spending $87,836 to finance his successful reelection bid against his half sister, Mary Moloney Mangione, who raised and spent

Table 22. Spending by Candidates in Legislative Races, 1975-86

	Total costs	Average cost of winning in contested races	Winner's highest cost
House of Representatives			
	Democratic Primaries		
1975	$245,618	$2,375	$13,401
1981	415,744	4,588	15,837
1986	893,057	11,366	67,245
Constant $	437,773	5,571	32,963
	Republican Primaries		
1975	37,105	1,130	1,825
1981	182,247	2,644	17,651
1986	205,948	4,622	15,870
Constant $	100,955	2,266	7,779
	General Elections		
1975	161,629	1,738	8,446
1981	480,051	6,644	28,454
1986	692,663	11,665	40,858
Constant $	339,541	5,718	20,028
Senate			
	Democratic Primaries		
1975	$190,558	$7,661	$26,683
1981	375,339	17,091	31,474
1986	617,725	35,609	68,903
Constant $	302,806	17,455	33,776
	Republican Primaries		
1975	$24,926	4,354	$7,406
1981	24,605	8,627	8,627
1986	151,307	23,964	26,842
Constant $	74,170	11,747	13,158
	General Elections		
1975	54,420	3,701	7,630
1981	217,797	12,196	26,234
1986	349,753	28,391	65,651
Constant $	171,448	13,917	32,182

Source: Compiled from the records of the Kentucky Registry of Election Finance for each of the years.

Constant dollars are 1986 spending controlling for inflation since 1975.

$43,749. The amount raised by Moloney easily eclipsed the previous record of $81,315 by Sen. Helen Garrett in 1986 (*C-J,* July 8, 1988, p. B1).

Political Implications of High Costs

It has become expensive to run a competitive race for the Kentucky Senate and sometimes for the House. Unless they are wealthy, candidates who must raise $15,000 to $20,000 or more must devote considerable effort to fund-raising and in most cases must have the support of local party leaders or other organized groups. The cost of mounting an effective challenge to an incumbent state senator is a serious obstacle to any challenger. When no incumbent is running, the higher level of competition is likely to increase campaign costs.

At the state level the high cost of fund-raising has even more serious implications. Experienced, capable individuals who ought to be taken seriously as candidates for statewide office either decide not to run or to drop out of the race because they are not personally wealthy and are unable to raise large sums or are unwilling to make the commitments that are part of large-scale money raising.

Joe Prather, a former president pro tem of the state senate who dropped out of the Democratic gubernatorial primary early in 1987, said he became frustrated with trying to raise large amounts of money. Prather said that money was not the main reason he quit the race—"it was the only reason." He said he decided not to use his position as the apparent favorite of the Collins administration to raise money from people who hold state contracts. Offering jobs as cabinet secretaries or positions on university boards of regents and trustees will bring "about whatever you want to name," Prather said. But, he added, brokering such important positions hurts the universities and the state. Most of the money going into political campaigns is from people or interest groups who want something, Prather said. "I don't care how sensitive a governor is to the issue," he said. "You are going to end up more obligated than you want to be" (*C-J,* October 14, 1987, p. A1).

Harvey Sloane and Grady Stumbo are examples of major candidates who accumulated large debts during their first gubernatorial campaigns, debts that became an embarrassment and an obstacle when they renewed their quest for the gubernatorial nomination four years later.

Wealthy candidates who can pay their own way have a significant advantage over those of average means. Had Wilkinson been employed in a job that paid $38,000 a year, he would not have won the nomination in 1987. Longtime politicians dropped long-held plans to run for governor—simply because of the tremendous difficulty of competing with the more wealthy candidates. Julian Carroll lent his campaign $250,000, while

Grady Stumbo lent his campaign $150,000; but that is insignificant compared to the more than $2.33 million loaned by Wilkinson to his campaign.

The 1988 Kentucky General Assembly passed new legislation that is supposed to make it impossible to pay back loans by candidates. H.B. 453, which became effective January 1, 1989, prohibits candidates from recouping debts after the primary and general elections. Wilkinson recouped more than $2.33 million, including $144,000 in interest on loans he made to his campaign, after winning the primary. Lieutenant Governor Jones lent his campaign $1.6 million and then tried to recover much of that amount. According to H.B. 453, gubernatorial candidates may not lend more than $50,000 in money, service, or other thing of value to their committee in any one election and be compensated for it. Other statewide elected officers are limited to $25,000, and remaining candidates are limited to $10,000. S.B. 47 prohibits candidates from soliciting or accepting contributions for primary or general election expenses after the dates of the respective elections. The campaign-debt measure also prevents anyone from raising money on a candidate's behalf.

This legislation is expected to reduce campaign costs because candidates will be reluctant to spend their own money or borrow what they cannot recover. This law may also encourage people to get involved in campaigns from the start, since they would not be able to buy into the camp of a winning candidate after an election, and it might eliminate the perception that people who do buy in receive special treatment for doing so. Had such a law been in effect during the 1987 primary season, Wilkinson would have been prohibited from mounting the intense fund-raising drive that recouped his $2.3 million investment in the few months after he won the primary.

Role of Interest Groups in Elections

One of the most important trends in campaign financing in recent years has been the growth of political action groups (PACs) created by interest groups to channel funds to the candidates they favor. Some attention in the literature has been focused on interest groups' financing of legislative and statewide campaigns (see Jacobson, 1980; Patterson, 1982; Malbin, 1984; Alexander, 1984; Sabato, 1984; Giles and Pritchard, 1985; Jones and Borris, 1985; Schlozman and Tierney, 1986; Schneider, 1986; and Sorauf, 1988). We are most interested in the level of PAC contributions in Democratic primaries and general election campaigns for governor, other statewide races, and for the legislature. Which interest groups make significant contributions to political campaigns, and what proportion of campaign funding comes from PACs?

Since 1968 the Kentucky Registry of Election Finance has been the repository of campaign reports for all state and local offices. Campaign treasurers must submit reports on all contributions of individuals and groups of more than $100. Before 1968 the unrealistic legal limitation on contributions and the minimal requirements for reporting prevented the collection of comprehensive and accurate campaign finance data. In July 1986 the maximum contribution an individual can make to a candidate in one state or local election was increased from $3,000 to $4,000. Before 1988 there was no cap on PAC contributions in Kentucky. Individuals, who could give no more than $4,000 to a candidate in any one election, could give unlimited amounts to PACs, which in turn could give as much as they wanted to a candidate. The legislation passed in 1988 limits both the amount that an individual may contribute to a PAC and that a PAC may accept from an individual to $2,000 in any one election; it also limits both the amount that a PAC may contribute to a candidate and that a candidate or a committee may accept from a PAC to $4,000 in any one election.

Interest groups make contributions to candidates for one or both of two reasons. The first is to attempt to make those candidates who are elected indebted to them, more accessible to their lobbyists, and more willing to act in accordance with their wishes on policy issues. The second reason is to assist in the reelection of incumbents or the election of new candidates who appear to be already sympathetic to the viewpoints of the interest group.

For candidates at least willing to lend a sympathetic ear to a special interest group's concerns, PACs constitute a tempting source of money. In part because it is easier to raise money from PACs than from individuals and because of the absence of legal limits on PAC funding before 1988, Kentucky politicians have been increasingly relying on PACs to help fund the growing cost of campaigns.

How much power do special interests have in Kentucky? According to R.G. Dunlop and Richard Whitt, reporting in the *Courier-Journal* (October 11, 1987, p. A1), "the rights of individuals are frequently subordinated to those of special interests who view Frankfort and the county courthouses as their personal fiefdoms and who make contributions to political candidates and parties in return for favors. In an era of skyrocketing campaign costs . . . poorly financed citizens' groups have little chance against big corporations, their lobbyists and political action committees." In addition, state representative Joe Clarke said, "The excessive amount of money in campaigns, and where it's coming from, is perverting the system. It's coming from special interests, not from people saying, 'This person would make a good governor or representative.' The ordinary guy doesn't get a chance to participate except as part of a special interest, and the public interest is rarely served." Because some interest groups have more resources than others to contribute to political campaigns, the growing dependence of candidates on funding from PACs may obviously affect the way decisions are reached and choices are made among competing interests in Frankfort.

The concern about the influence of PACs in Kentucky reflects the fact that their influence in state and local elections has increased significantly in the last decade (Hays, 1987-88). During the period from 1977 to 1987, the number of PACs registered in Kentucky leaped from 93 to 331. The amount of money they gave to political candidates doubled, and the PAC percentage of total donations also rose sharply. PAC outlays to candidates in the state increased from $1.35 million in 1977 to an estimated $2.3 million in 1987. During that ten-year period, PACs contributed a total of $17.8 million to candidates in Kentucky (see Graves, 1987). But, as we shall see, the increases in PAC contributions have been much more dramatic in legislative races than in gubernatorial races.

In this section we discuss PAC contributions to several levels of campaigns: gubernatorial and other major statewide races (1979, 1983, and 1987) and legislative races (in selected years from 1975 through 1986). Several broad questions concerning PAC contributions need to be addressed: What kinds of PACs contribute the most funding to gubernatorial races? Do PACs follow the strategy of concentrating their funds on one candidate or hedge their bets by spreading contributions among several candidates? What choices do PACs make in putting money into the primary and/or general election? Do PACs follow the general strategy of supporting the favored winner, or do they try to change the outcome of a race? Are there certain groups that put their funding primarily in legislative races? Have some groups substantially increased their funding to legislative races since the shift of balance of power from the governor to legislators?

Gubernatorial Elections

Table 23 shows, by type of interest group, how much the PACs spent in the 1983 and 1987 gubernatorial races (data on the 1979 race is also provided in this discussion). We have identified seventeen types of interests and aggregated the money given by PACs within each group. Most of the categories in the table are self-explanatory; the special issues include such things as right to life and gun regulation. The business and industry category excludes groups named in other categories, such as coal and insurance. Although these categories are not exhaustive, they were chosen because of their recognized political and economic power in Kentucky and the frequency and total sums of their giving.

Table 23. Contributions by Categories of Interest Groups to Gubernatorial Candidates in Primary and General Elections, 1983 and 1987

Categories of groups	1983 Primary	1983 General Election		1987 Primary	1987 General Election	
	Dem.	Dem.	Rep.	Dem.	Dem.	Rep.
Education	70,864	2,250	1,190	53,000	—	35,000
Labor	221,366	78,360	1,621	78,000	44,000	—
Public employees	6,000	350	—	6,500	5,000	—
Professionals	7,000	12,700	6,000	90,000	8,000	—
Health & medical	500	1,750	—	13,000	19,000	1,000
Insurance	—	1,000	500	25,500	32,000	1,500
Real estate	5,200	7,000	—	13,000	2,000	—
Construction	1,000	1,000	4,000	12,000	21,000	—
Banking and finance	6,900	21,000	10,500	131,050	13,500	2,500
Business and industry	17,775	16,390	4,100	19,000	41,700	—
Horse industry	1,000	3,000	—	16,300	5,000	—
Transportation	7,500	500	—	16,750	10,000	—
Utilities	1,400	—	—	9,500	7,500	—
Oil and gas	3,000	—	500	16,000	6,000	—
Coal	1,000	500	—	1,000	—	—
Liquor	4,000	2,000	2,000	6,500	—	—
Special issues	3,200	—	—	2,300	—	—
Total group contributions	357,705	147,800	30,411	509,400	214,700	40,000
Total receipts guber. races	4,408,910	1,770,551	1,221,617	12,324,038	2,610,075	255,788
% of guber. receipts from groups	8.1%	8.4%	2.5%	4.1%	8.2%	15.6%

Source: Compiled from the records of the Kentucky Registry of Election Finance for each of the years.

We do not include in our calculations the large group of PACs that are designated "political" by the Kentucky Registry; these PACs do not represent specialized interest groups. In some cases, they are the personal campaign financial vehicles of elected officials to channel funds into the campaigns of targeted candidates—e.g., Sheriff Jim Greene PAC and the Harvey Sloane Committee. In some cases, they represent a cluster of individuals of varied occupations who pool their moneys to enhance the electability of certain candidates—e.g., Kentuckians for Progressive Government PAC (primarily for Wilkinson). And in other cases, they are the political arm of certain state, regional, or county party organizations—e.g., Good Ole Boys of the Grand Old Party.

The size of PAC contributions to gubernatorial candidates grew from 1979 to 1987, but in all three elections PAC contributions constituted a relatively small proportion of total funding for gubernatorial candidates in both primaries and general elections. PAC contributions to Democratic gubernatorial primary campaigns increased from $86,000 in 1979 to $516,000 in 1987; but as a percentage of all funding, PAC contributions increased only from 2 to 4.2 percent (but hit a high of 8.1 percent in 1983).

Only two organized interests—labor and education—consistently made major contributions through PACs to the gubernatorial races. These interests have a tradition of organized campaign efforts in Kentucky Democratic primaries and general elections. Most of the other organized interests made very little use of PACs for these races. In fact, the increase between 1979 and 1983 in PAC spending for primaries was due largely to greater spending by education and labor PACs. The percentage of PAC spending was lower in 1987 than in 1983 partly because labor contributed less but largely because of a huge increase in individual contributions, resulting partly from Wallace Wilkinson's efforts after the May 26 primary to raise money to pay off his loans.

In general election campaigns, PACs contributed about 4 percent of costs in 1979, 6 percent in 1983, and 9 percent in 1987. In each case funding for Democrats outweighed that for Republicans by a margin of about 4 to 1 or 5 to 1. The proportion of Republican funding that came from PACs was unusually high (15.6 percent) in 1987, not because of a large increase in PAC funding, but because funding from individuals dropped by almost $1 million between 1983 and 1987.

In the 1987 Democratic primary, most of the PAC money went to the three leaders. Beshear, who was perceived as the early favorite, received $196,000; Brown, the later favorite, got $130,000; Wilkinson, the eventual winner, got $152,000. Carroll and Stumbo, the two other major Democratic gubernatorial contenders, received minimal PAC moneys.

Nearly one-third of Beshear's PAC support came from the banks and securities firms; Beshear, in his roles as lieutenant governor and attorney general, had wooed these interests as political friends. More than one-fourth of his PAC support came from the Kentucky Education Association and its local affiliates, and he also received substantial funding from labor unions. Both education and labor groups had contributed significant moneys to his earlier campaigns since he had worked hard as a state representative and public official promoting their issues. In 1987 local, state, and international labor groups were courted heavily by both the Beshear and Stumbo forces, and Beshear eventually received the lion's share of labor funding, perhaps because he was perceived as more likely to win (Stumbo, a staunch advocate of labor, had received substantial funds in his 1983 unsuccessful quest for governor). Although Beshear received more funding from PACs than did other candidates, it constituted less than 7 percent of the money he raised.

Brown's PAC support was spread among law firms, banks, utilities, and other businesses, with the largest contributions made by banking and finance PACs ($31,600). Brown was also the recipient of $24,000 from the Kentucky Life Insurance Company PAC. Various transportation PACs were also supportive of Brown's candidacy ($10,250). It is not surprising that the millionaire Brown, with his well-known ties to Kentucky and national corporate interests, received considerable business and banking PAC money. As governor (1979-83), he had striven to "run Kentucky like a business."

The political newcomer Wilkinson's PAC support was spread among many of the categories of specialized interests, with a majority of the PAC contributions coming after the May 26 primary upset. Major PAC contributors included professionals (lawyers, engineers, accountants, and architects), $53,250; banking and finance institutions, $35,700; labor unions, $20,800; and business and industry groups, $14,000. Wilkinson did not receive for his primary campaign committee any PAC support from teachers, public employees, utilities, transportation groups, and special issue groups.

In the 1987 gubernatorial general election, Wilkinson garnered more PAC support than he had received in the primary: $216,200. Those interests that had supported other candidates in the primary had a particularly strong incentive to contribute to Wilkinson's fall campaign. Labor groups contributed more than one-fifth of Wilkinson's total PAC receipts, followed closely by business and industry PACs. Having backed a loser, Brown, in the primary, the insurance industry gave its significant financial assistance to Wilkinson in the general election contest. The health industry PACs also jumped on board Wilkinson's victory train.

Although Republican candidates received token PAC contributions in the primary, the political arm of the Kentucky Education Association gave Republican Harper $35,000 in the general election; it was the largest single contribution he received in his campaign for governor. Harper, the first Republican to be endorse by the KEA, had almost no success in raising moneys from other PACs.

As reported earlier, table 23 does not reflect the contributions of political PACs. In the 1987 gubernatorial primary and general election campaigns, these political PACs did make some significant contributions to targeted candidates. For example, Lieutenant Governor Beshear received $15,000 from a PAC operated in the name of Jefferson County sheriff Jim Greene and an additional $4,000 from the Friends of Mayor

Abramson PAC. After snaring the nomination on May 26, Wilkinson's primary campaign committee also received a $9,000 contribution from the Abramson PAC. Wilkinson was also given $21,000 for his primary committee by a political PAC, Citizens for Better Government—especially established to channel moneys for Wilkinson's campaign expenditures. In the 1987 gubernatorial general election, political PACs contributed more than $25,000 to Wilkinson's landslide victory. County judge executive Harvey Sloane's committee contributed almost $9,000, and Sheriff Greene's PAC gave $4,000. Kentuckians for Progressive Government helped swell Wilkinson's campaign chest with an additional $10,000.

In the 1983 Democratic gubernatorial primary, the leading PAC contributors in the 1983 Democratic gubernatorial primary were labor, education, business and industry, professionals, transportation, and banking and finance. Labor unions, whose money was funneled through national, state, and local PACs, overwhelmingly supported Grady Stumbo ($210,710) with 95 percent of their contributions; the bulk of the funds was contributed by national organizations. The Kentucky Education Association, through its statewide and county PACs, clearly favored Harvey Sloane, giving him more than $63,000, which was 89 percent of what education PACs invested in the race. Martha Layne Collins, who won the primary, was the major recipient of money coming from business and industry PACs.

In the 1983 general election, more than half of the PAC contributions to Democrat Martha Layne Collins came from labor unions. Banking, business, and professional groups were the only other organizations contributing more than $10,000 in the election, in each case more heavily to the Democratic candidate. Surprisingly, education PACs made only token contributions in the gubernatorial race.

We conclude that, despite the dominant role of the gubernatorial race in Kentucky politics and the governor's powerful role in public policy making, most interest groups—other than the labor and education PACs—have contributed little or nothing to gubernatorial races. Candidates for governor must raise most of their funds from individuals.

Other Statewide Races

With a few important exceptions, PACs have not made major contributions to the campaigns of candidates running for other statewide races. By far, the largest contributions were made by the education and labor PACs.

In recent years the most expensive statewide races below the gubernatorial level have been Democratic primaries for lieutenant governor. In 1987, when spending for this race broke all records, PACs contributed less than 2 percent of the more than $5 million total. Education and labor PACs were not viable contributors in this race. Although they leaned toward Armstrong and Jones, education groups neither endorsed nor gave PAC money to any candidate. (They had supported Armstrong generously in his 1983 successful attorney general bid.) Also, since several of the candidates eagerly vied for labor's support, the labor PACs were reluctant to put their valuable financial and manpower resources behind any one candidate. Armstrong was the sole recipient of any labor moneys—a minimal $7,000 total from a few groups. The front-runner, Armstrong, did receive the lion's share (96 percent) of PAC moneys, almost $75,000; this represented 12.7 percent of his total receipts. Armstrong's major PAC support was spread among law firms, housing industry contractors, banking and securities institutions, and labor unions. His largest contributions—more than $30,000 —were from lawyers' PACs; as attorney general, he had worked closely with attorneys from around the state.

In the 1983 Democratic lieutenant gubernatorial primary, PACs contributed 10.6 percent of the nearly $728,000 total, and in 1979 PACs gave only 4.1 percent of the nearly $1.4 million spent by four candidates. By far, the largest contributors in both races were the education PACs, which gave $41,155 in 1983 and $23,500 in 1979 to candidates for lieutenant governor in the primary. There were other significant contributions by labor PACs (almost $15,000 in 1983 and over $9,000 in 1979).

The costs of general election contests for lieutenant governor have been more modest, although in 1987 a record $913,947 was spent by the Democratic victor (a lot of this money was earmarked to help recoup Jones's personal campaign debts). Although Jones had only reaped $2,000 in PAC moneys in his primary battle, he received more than $63,000 from PACs for his general election contest. Specialized interests wanted to support the winning ticket. Jones's major PAC support was spread among banking and finance institutions ($10,800), law firms ($10,025), teachers ($10,000), and businesses and industries ($8,000). The Republican nominee, Webster, received no PAC moneys.

In the 1987 primary election, the most important examples of PAC contributions to statewide candidates below the lieutenant gubernatorial level were the funds contributed to the Democratic candidates for superintendent of public instruction, attorney general, auditor, and secretary of state. In his unsuccessful bid for the top education spot, state representative Roger Noe, chairman of the House Education Committee, received the financial backing of the supposedly powerful teacher groups—$57,000 from the state and local KEPACs. State representative Fred Cowan received important PAC contributions (almost $20,000) in his successful quest for the attorney general's office; the teachers gave him $7,500, along with $3,000 from banking and finance institutions and $2,000 from law firms. Lexington councilman Bob Babbage, in his auditor's race victory, reaped more than $7,500 in small contributions from various specialized interests. In the secretary of state contest, Bremer Ehrler received more than $14,000 in PAC funds; his largest contributions, $12,000, came from public employee groups. In contrast to their primary involvement, special interest groups doled out minimal contributions in the 1987 general election to statewide candidates, other than the top two offices. Before 1987 the most important examples of PAC contributions to statewide candidates below the lieutenant gubernatorial level had been the funds contributed to the candidates for superintendent of public instruction, particularly in Democratic primaries. In the 1983 Democratic primary, education PACs contributed $40,000, which was 39 percent of the total spent in that race.

Legislative Races

The cost of legislative campaigns for all the House seats and half the Senate seats quadrupled between 1975 and 1986, with total campaign receipts increasing from $722,000 to $2,847,000. During the same period the amount of funds received from PACs grew more dramatically, from about $40,000 to nearly $900,000, with the proportion of money contributed by PACs increasing from 5.6 to 31.5 percent. In 1986 PACs contributed 30.6 percent of the total receipts of legislative primaries and 32.5 percent of the total receipts of legislative general elections. The rapid increase in the rate of PAC contributions to legislative campaigns reflects the growing power of the legislature vis-à-vis the governor, a trend that a number of the interest groups have clearly recognized.

The leading PAC contributors to House and Senate electoral campaigns have been education, health and medical, labor, horse industry, banking and finance, business and industry, and real estate interests. The education lobby, through its statewide and county PACs, has clearly concentrated most on legislative races. Health and medical PACs contribute more heavily to legislative races than to statewide races. As the costs of health care rise and the available funds fail to keep pace, health and medical PACs have a greater stake in legislative decisions and more reason to invest in legislative races. Labor has also substantially increased its funding of legislative races, with most of its funds going to Democratic candidates in targeted House and Senate races.

The horse industry has also discovered the legislature. In the past most of the contributions were made by individuals rather than PACs and were given to gubernatorial candidates. The Kentucky Horsemen's Benevolent Protective Association (including trainers and small owners) took the lead in forming a PAC and contributing to legislative races. Subsequently, the Kentucky Thoroughbred Association (primarily breeders and large owners) has followed its lead.

During the 1988 session of the General Assembly, PACs donated nearly $50,000 to the campaign funds of several legislators. Although many legislators said privately that the practice is unseemly, most said there is no easy way to restrict such contributions before and during a session. "Political contributions are a fact of life for those of us who are not wealthy," stated House majority leader Greg Stumbo, D-Prestonsburg. "I think if you look most of those PAC donations are less than $300 or $400. In this day of high-cost politics, you're not going to find many people who would be swayed by $300 or $400." Two legislators, Rep. Bill McBee, D-Burlington, and Rep. J.R. Gray, D-Benton, held a joint fund-raiser the night before the session began (*C-J,* April 19, 1988, p. A1).

Most Kentucky PACs usually support incumbent legislators and seldom support challengers. There are very good reasons for such tactics. Incumbents in Kentucky are seldom defeated. The domination of most districts by one party has always made it difficult to defeat incumbents in general elections. As incumbent legislators have gained greater visibility and seniority, they have also become less vulnerable to defeat in primary elections.

Comparing Group Contributions to Legislative and Gubernatorial Candidates

The rate of PAC contributions to legislative campaigns has been growing more rapidly than PAC contributions to gubernatorial campaigns. In 1979 PAC contributions to gubernatorial races exceeded those to legislative races by about $100,000. In 1986/87 the gross amount of contributions from PACs had been reversed; PACs gave about $120,000 more to legislative than to gubernatorial races. In proportional terms the contrast is even greater, partly because the costs of gubernatorial races have been rising so rapidly and partly because of the persistence of self-financed campaigns. In 1986 31 percent of all legislative campaign funding came from PACs. If PACs had provided 31 percent of the funding for the 1987 gubernatorial race, they would have contributed about $4.7 million instead of about $770,000.

It is difficult to calculate the exact percentage of PAC contributions to gubernatorial campaigns because winning gubernatorial candidates have been able to recover the sizable sums that they have loaned their campaigns. For example, in 1979 John Y. Brown at first paid personally for huge amounts of campaign expenditures; PAC contributions were artificially low because a large percent of the total funds came from Brown himself. During the course of his administration, Brown recouped all of his electoral investments from grateful supporters, though only a small proportion of this came from PACs. In contrast, it did not take any time at all for Wilkinson to recover the funds he loaned his 1987 primary campaign. He did it immediately, chiefly from individual contributors who wanted to do business with the state or receive jobs, appointments to commissions, or other benefits. In other words, he got paid back before the official books were closed on the primary election, partly from PACs, but largely from individual contributions of $4,000 each. Why have PACs in recent years given such a high priority to legislative races, compared to gubernatorial races? The obvious answer is that the legislature has been gaining a much stronger role in policy making, and the governor's domination of legislative decision making has faded. Interest groups recognize that, in order to pass or defeat legislation, it is at least as important to win supporters in the legislature as to win the support of the governor. There is another explanation that may not be so obvious. A large proportion of the increasing funding for gubernatorial races comes from individuals who want some tangible benefit from state government: a job, an appointment to a board, a chance for their firm to do business with the state. It is the governor's office, and not the legislature, that controls those benefits.

Abuses and Reforms of PACs

During the last decade PACs were not perceived to be a problem by many politicians in Frankfort, where two modest proposals to impose some restraints on PACs fell flat. In 1983 and again in 1984, the Registry recommended to a legislative subcommittee that PAC donations to political candidates be subject to the same limitations as those governing individuals. Both times, the recommendation got nowhere. But the high level of spending during the 1987 Democratic primary and the attention given to the problems of PAC contributions by the *Courier-Journal* (in a series written by R.G. Dunlop and Richard Whitt and published in mid-October 1987) brought the issues of PAC spending onto the high-priority agenda of the 1988 General Assembly.

Two examples from the Wilkinson campaign illustrate the problem caused by the absence of limitations on PAC contributions and spending. Four days before the 1987 May primary, four Lexington residents gave a total of $21,000 to a PAC called Citizens Committed to Better Government. One of the group gave $8,000; another gave $6,000. The PAC turned around and passed the money on to the campaign of Wilkinson, who won the Democratic gubernatorial nomination. Only after the *Courier Journal* (July 18, 1987, pp. B1, B9) brought the matter to the attention of the Registry of Election Finance was the PAC asked to retrieve some of the money from Wilkinson and return it to the original contributors. The

Registry made its request—which it had no power to enforce—on the grounds that the PAC had been used in an attempt to disguise contributions in excess of the $4,000 limit for individual donations.

Another Wilkinson PAC, Kentuckians for Progressive Government, raised $120,000 from a handful of individuals and paid for more than $100,000 of Wilkinson's campaign expenses. One contributor—beer distributor Ronald J. Plattner of Fort Mitchell—gave the PAC $35,000, and four others gave a total of $50,000. All the contributions were apparently legal under existing state law, since there were no limits on how much individuals could give to a PAC (*C-J,* October 16, 1987, pp. A1, A8). The Registry did investigate Kentuckians for Progressive Government to see whether it supported more than one candidate or was merely a campaign fund for Wilkinson. The Registry concluded, much to the consternation of PAC watchdog opponents, that the PAC's activities were legal. Although Wilkinson's campaign did not report these expenditures, the director of the Registry explained that Wilkinson would not be penalized because PACs "are pretty loosely controlled."

It remains to be seen how future Kentucky statewide and legislative elections are affected by the 1988 legislation on PACs, which limits the amount that a PAC may contribute to $4,000 per candidate per election and limits contributions to a PAC to $2,000 per individual in any one election. There is also a provision that names of PACS must now "reasonably identify" the group's sponsorship and purpose, a requirement intended to allow the public to know what PACs such as Kentuckians for Progressive Government stand for.

The Role of Individual Contributors in Political Campaigns

We have noted earlier that, despite the dominant role of the gubernatorial race in Kentucky politics and the governor's powerful role in public policy making, most interest groups—other than the labor and education PACs—have contributed little or nothing to gubernatorial races. Candidates for governor must raise most of their funds from individuals; some of these contributors are actively involved in interest groups, but their contributions seem designed more to advance their own concerns than the goals of the organized groups.

In the case of many organized interests, the contributions of individuals dwarfed those made by PACs. Because campaign finance reports list the occupations of contributors, it is possible to calculate individual contributions of specific occupational groups, and such data for 1983 have been summarized for several groups by O'Keefe (1986). In the 1983 Democratic gubernatorial primary, for example, coal operators contributed $111,803;

Table 24. Comparison of Contributions to Beshear, Brown, and Wilkinson in 1987 Gubernatorial Primary

	Beshear	Brown	Wilkinson
Total amount raised	$2,905,699	$3,476,058	$4,271,632
Total contributors	5,928	2,877	4,484
Number of giving $4,000 legal maximum	106	257	295
Number giving $300 or less	3,694	738	1,943
Total contributions $300 or less	$373,515	$102,819	$133,432
Number giving over $300	2,234	2,139	2,541
Total contributions over $300	$2,280,197	$3,234,171	$3,641,933
Donations from PACs of 17 interest group categories	$196,100	$129,850	$151,950
From architects/engineers & family members	$248,300	$193,305	$336,656
From lawyers & family members	$265,621	$185,318	$274,610
From coal operators & family members	$41,500	$107,500	$157,684
From state employees & family members	$36,577	$4,500	$48,550

Source: Courier-Journal, May 10, 1987, pp. A1, A13.
Candidate Reports at Kentucky Registry of Election Finance

Note: Some of the figures may be incomplete because the candidates' official election finance reports for contributions do not list specific or correct occupations for each donor.

The total amount raised for each candidate does include in-kind contributions and other receipts.

The totals for PAC contributions do not include moneys from "political PACs"—e.g., $15,600 to Beshear's campaign from the Sheriff Jim Greene PAC.

These accounts have not been audited; therefore, sometimes the figures are understated or overstated because of the method of reporting.

farmers gave $63,540; insurance agents gave $42,421; and bankers gave $39,490—in each case a much larger figure than was contributed by the corresponding PACs. In the 1983 general election, data on individual contributions in several interest areas show much larger contributions than those made by PACs. For example, individuals in the construction business gave $162,000; coal operators gave $87,000; and bankers gave $73,000. There were also significant contributions by persons in the horse business, insurance agents, and farmers (O'Keefe, 1986). In nearly all cases, a large proportion of the funds went to the Democrats.

In the 1987 gubernatorial primary, millionaire businessman John Y. Brown, Jr., was heavily financed by Kentucky's corporate community and wealthy large contributors. More than 250 people donated the $4,000 legal maximum to Brown's campaign (table 24) and thus contributed 30 percent of the money raised by Brown. Steve Beshear had both broad individual support and financing from a variety of special interests. Beshear received just slightly more than 100 contributions of $4,000 apiece.

Beshear, who liked to contrast himself to Brown by stressing his broad appeal and his ties to the average voter, received contributions from far more people than Brown, and many more people gave him $300 or less (3,694 to 738)—lending considerable credence to the lieutenant governor's claim of greater grass-roots support. However, Beshear's small givers donated a total of only $373,515, which constituted only about 13 percent of the total he raised. That means the remaining 2,234 givers to Beshear donated more than $2.2 million, 75 percent of his total receipts, an amount nine percentage points lower than Brown's (*C-J,* May 10, 1987, pp. A1, A13).

Beshear appeared to be the candidate preferred by representatives of special interest groups that often do business with state government. Those groups have traditionally given generously to candidates in the hope of later being able to win contracts or jobs, get favorable treatment on regulatory matters, or simply have a receptive ear in Frankfort. Architects, engineers, lawyers, and their relatives gave Beshear nearly 18 percent of the total he raised. Donations from those sources constituted about 11 percent of Brown's total and 14 percent of Wilkinson's.

Coal operators have traditionally given generously to the state's politicians. But donors who could be identified as coal operators and members of their families gave surprisingly little to the gubernatorial candidates (about $107,500 to Brown, $41,500 to Beshear, and $157,684 to Wilkinson). Industry representatives say the main reason for the relatively low level of donations is the depressed market that has left few operators' profits unscathed (*C-J,* May 10, 1987, pp. A1, A13).

Since state employees (and their families) viewed Beshear as the early front-runner, he received the majority of their financial support compared to Brown: $36,577 to $4,500. After his primary victory, Wilkinson took in the bulk of receipts from this bloc of givers: almost $50,000.

Once Wilkinson won the primary, there was an outpouring of money from contributors—engineers, architects, "businessmen," lawyers, contractors, bankers, coal operators, and so on—who wanted access to the next governor. Wilkinson's campaign committees raised about $2.4 million during the summer—enough to repay the $2.3 million loans he had made to his main primary election committee. Therefore, as depicted in table 25, the winner reaped $4,271,632 in total amount raised for the primary campaign, the major bulk after the May 26 election. By designating earlier committees as primary committees and creating a new committee to finance the general election, the Wilkinson campaign was able to maximize contributions from big givers. Soon after the primary some people,

Table 25. Individual Contributions by Occupational Group to Wilkinson Primary Campaign

Occupational group	Total contributors	Number giving $4,000	Total $ raised
Accountants	74	7	$99,201
Agriculture	48	4	$64,400
Architects	28	5	$41,190
Attorneys	219	15	$274,610
Banking & finance	92	10	$125,450
Business	1,268	148	$1,847,740
Coal operators	97	17	$157,684
Contractors	152	23	$259,550
Consultants	23	4	$36,990
Doctors	48	2	$48,362
Education	19	—	$18,050
Elected officials	25	2	$19,540
Engineers	167	35	$295,466
Health industry	18	1	$23,900
Horse racing & breeding	22	2	$26,500
Insurance	70	2	$85,000
Real estate	56	2	$55,837
Retired	30	1	$25,538
State employees	34	2	$48,550
Others	51	12	$88,376
Totals	2,541	294	$3,641,934

Source: Compiled from the records of the Kentucky Registry of Election Finance.

Note: Some of the figures may be incomplete because the candidate's official election finance reports do not list specific or correct occupations for each donor.

Contributions include family members.

many of whom had earlier made maximum $4,000 contributions to Brown or Beshear, gave the maximum $4,000 individual contribution to the Wilkinson primary committee and then gave another $4,000 later to the general election committee.

After the primary several of Wilkinson's biggest donors were from out of state. Almost 10 percent of Wilkinson's money came from people who were not able to vote for him in the general election, a total of over $500,000 in donations from people in twenty other states and the District of Columbia. The contributors included engineers, contractors, developers, bond-finance specialists, and coal company executives. Two of Wilkinson's out-of-state contributors, Robert C. Kanuth, Jr., of Washington, D.C., and William E. Roberts of Columbus, Ohio, had put $450,000 into Collins Investments Inc., a company founded by Dr. Bill

Collins shortly after his wife, Martha Layne Collins, was elected governor in 1983. Both men are executives with Cranston Securities, which became senior underwriter or comanager of the sale of more than $1 billion in state bonds, earning $1.35 million in commissions (*C-J,* October 24, 1987, p. A6).

Table 25 provides a detailed breakdown of individual contributions ($300 or more) by occupational groups (and their family members) to Wilkinson's primary campaign. For each category information is given for (a) the number of contributors; (b) the number contributing the $4,000 legal maximum; and (c) the amount raised. Two-thirds of the money ($2,394,850) was raised after the May 26 election. Wilkinson received $4,000 maximum donations from almost 300 individuals representing diverse occupational groups. Almost 50 percent of the 2,541 givers fall into the catchall "businessperson" category; this constituted 43 percent of the total primary receipts. Raymond Wallace, the executive director of the state Registry of Election Finance, said that overly broad descriptions of occupations have been a "sore spot" with the Registry, but (as of then) the agency "hasn't taken any exception to it." S.B. 268, passed by the 1988 legislature, requires that occupations of contributors must be specific; general terms such as *businessman* are prohibited.

John Harper, the Republican gubernatorial nominee in 1987, had great difficulty raising money for the simple reason that he was not perceived as a possible winner. Contributors to a gubernatorial race who hope to get some kind of return on their investment have no reason to contribute to a losing cause. Harper's largest donors were four individuals who gave in both the primary and general election: Harold Hardy, a Shepherdsville businessman; GOP chairman Robert Gable; and John Tarrant and A. Robert Doll, both Louisville lawyers. Because Harper, too, formed separate committees for the primary and the general election, the four were able to surpass the usual limit of $4,000 in contributions per individual per candidate. At least one of Harper's biggest contributors, Doll, also gave to Wilkinson after his primary victory. Much of Harper's large financial support appeared to be from executives and professionals (*C-J,* October 14, 1987, p. A1).

When individuals contribute to a gubernatorial candidate, they may be hoping to gain either collective or individual benefits. Instead of giving to a PAC, for example, business or professional persons may contribute directly to a gubernatorial candidate in an effort to get favorable consideration for a particular interest.

Because he wanted the racing industry to have the ear of the man likely to be the next governor, in July 1987 Churchill Downs president Thomas Meeker sent out a fund-raising letter, on Churchill Downs letterhead, to help raise the $2.3 million that Democratic nominee Wilkinson lent his own campaign. Meeker wrote, "We at Churchill Downs are in active support of Mr. Wilkinson, since we firmly believe he will provide the thoroughbred industry with his personal support and assistance before the General Assembly. . . . Please join me and others who make their living in the thoroughbred industry in supporting Wallace Wilkinson, our next governor." Meeker sent the letter to about ten people who have businesses allied with thoroughbred racing and who have an interest in protecting the industry. Meeker received several checks that he passed on to the Wilkinson campaign (*C-J,* July 15, 1987, pp. B1, B3).

It is not always possible to determine the motives of contributors by knowing about their business interests. Does a prominent coal mine operator donate to the gubernatorial campaign in the hope that strip mining regulations will generally be relaxed or in the hope that permits for his own mining operations will be expedited? In cases like this, it is obvious that both motives may be involved.

But when large contributions are made by the persons in those businesses and professions that most often do business with the state, it is reasonable to assume that their primary goals are individual rather than collective. In reality, those who raise funds for gubernatorial candidates concentrate their attention on the business and professional groups that are most likely to seek state contracts.

One common use of gubernatorial patronage power is the granting of personal service contracts. State personal service contracts are big business; during the 1985-86 fiscal year alone they were worth approximately $74 million. Engineers and architects received over $100 million worth of these contracts from 1980 to 1987, more than 25 percent of all personal service contracts (awarded for such projects as road and bridge design, building construction, and reclamation of abandoned strip mines) and far more than any other profession. "State contracts for professional services, including those provided by engineers and the architects who often work closely with them, are not awarded through a competitive bidding process. Rather they are granted under subjective 'professional selection' guidelines that sometimes result in decisions influenced by politics" (*C-J,* October, 15, 1987, pp. A1, A10).

Personal service contracts are not awarded to the lowest bidder; fees are negotiated once a firm or an individual is selected for the job. To get a contract, a firm must send information about itself to the state, which accepts the application without requiring documentation. State officials review the firms and compile three top choices. The list is given to the secretary of finance or the secretary of transportation to make the final decision. Every step of the way, state officials concede, a call from the governor's office or from Democratic party headquarters can make a big difference. And as Floyd Poore has admitted, when suggesting a firm to award a contract, "you pick one favorable to you. I don't think there is any question about that (*C-J,* October 15, 1987, p. A10).

"There is no evidence that unqualified firms are regularly awarded state personal service contracts. Indeed, even the system's harshest critics concede that firms doing business with the state generally are at least competent. But some firms that get contracts also happen to be the most generous contributors to successful candidates for governor and the Democratic Party. Conversely, some who do not give don't get" (*C-J,* October 15, 1987, pp. A1, A10).

The act of giving as a prerequisite for getting is particularly prevalent in the case of architects, engineers, and others who do business with the state under personal service contracts. Although state officials say these nonbid contracts are bestowed on merit, evidence abounds that the process is in fact highly politicized. A survey by the *Courier-Journal* (October 15, 1987, pp. A1, A10) of roughly seventy architects and engineers in 1987 showed that more than two-thirds of those who would voice an opinion—31 of 45—believe political favoritism influences contract awards. While the National Society of Professional Engineers prohibits political contributions where there is even an appearance of a quid pro quo, Kentucky's legislation merely prohibits making a political contribution for "specific work." As a result, there are many cases like engineer Wesley Witt, who gave an unsolicited $3,000 to Beshear and later a solicited $2,000 to Wilkinson, explaining it was "in keeping with the political aspect of business in politics." Among those firms who have never received contracts, many blame the failure on their lack of political connections. Engineer William Cassidy, whose firm has applied for twenty state jobs in the past ten years but has never received one, claimed, "If you are going to do work in Kentucky, you are going to donate."

An examination of state contracts gives credence to these opinions. It is no coincidence that almost 60 percent of the more than two hundred members of the Democratic party's Century Club are architects and engineers. Five engineering firms that received more than $50 million worth of personal service contracts under the Collins administration donated a total of at least $85,000 to Collins' 1983 campaign or to the Democratic party in the ensuing years. All five regularly purchase at least one Century Club membership (*C-J,* October 11, 1987, p. A14; October 15, 1987, p. A10).

Even in the face of budget cuts totaling $250 million, the amounts spent on personal service contracts rose dramatically under the Collins administration, allowing her to "take care" of people who made substantial donations. While Brown—who depended less on campaign contributions in his race—spent $33.8 million on average each year of his term, Collins spent $47.4 million a year. Payments to attorneys rose from $1.9 million a year to $2.2 million, while state attorneys could have handled much of the load at costs far less to the state (*C-J,* October 14, 1987, p. A11).

Promising state jobs and appointments in exchange for political contributions has always been a common occurrence in Kentucky politics. When a new governor is elected, his or her first few months in office are devoted to making appointments to task forces and committees, filling state jobs, and awarding personal service contracts. Although the growth of the merit system has reduced the proportion of state patronage jobs, the governor makes a large number of appointments to boards and commissions. Most of these are party-time positions and may pay very little beyond expenses, but they often carry great prestige. An obvious example is an appointment to the Board of Trustees of the University of Kentucky and the boards for the other state universities.

It is expected that the new governor will allot his or her patronage to friends and to those who helped win the election. It is a traditional practice for a gubernatorial candidate to promise a prospective supporter a position or a contract in exchange for a campaign contribution. For example, shortly after Gov. Martha Layne Collins took office in December 1983, then Transportation Secretary Floyd Poore, one of the top fund-raisers in her campaign, submitted a lengthy list of supporters who were in line to get state positions. Poore's memorandum to the staff in the governor's office, dated February 16, 1984, stated, "Following is a list of commitments to the following boards, councils or commissions for March, April, May and June, 1984. . . ." The final page of the memo listed twenty-five of the thirty-one names under the heading, "COMMITMENTS THAT MUST BE MADE." According to state records, Collins honored only twelve of the commitments—nine from the so-called must list. Among those appointed included Jerry Stricker, a Collins fund-raiser, who was named to the University of Kentucky Board of Trustees, and Jack Moreland, a large contractor, who was named to the advisory council on vocational education. Warren Shovert was promised by Poore that he would be named to the Northern Kentucky University Board of Regents in exchange for a $2,500 contribution, but he never received it. Four years later Poore promised Shovert the same appointment for a $6,000 contribution (from Shovert and his wife) to the Wilkinson campaign (*C-J,* October 14, 1987, pp. A1, A10).

In a move that could reduce the number of the governor's political appointments, a state court ruled in June 1987 that the state's Department of Personnel must redefine its rules regarding state workers paid with federal money. If this ruling stands past appeal, 300 of 515 jobs would be brought under the state's merit system, limiting the number of political appointments. This decision has the potential of limiting some of the political abuses that are so apparent, but the governor's patronage powers remain great.

Implications of the Campaign Financing System in Kentucky

What difference does it make how much it costs to win elections and how the money is raised? There are implications for both the government and politics of Kentucky. Despite the growth of legislative power, the governor remains the single most powerful decision maker in Frankfort. Thus, it seems ironic that the majority of money raised in gubernatorial campaigns comes from persons who want personal benefits from the state rather than from those who are trying to influence state policy making.

If contracts are granted only to those firms that have made campaign contributions, there is the risk that the state will pay more for poorer goods and services than it would in a patronage-free system. If campaign contributions are a prerequisite to service on important boards and commissions, obviously the state will lose the services of talented individuals who are unwilling to pay this price. As the demands on state government increase and the problems it must solve grow more difficult, the real costs of the gubernatorial campaign financing system to the commonwealth continue to escalate.

It is more difficult to evaluate the governmental implications of legislative campaign financing. Because most races are relatively uncompetitive and inexpensive, most legislative candidates do not have to depend on PACs for a large amount of financial aid. But, if the trend toward more expensive races and higher PAC financing continues, there is a greater likelihood that some legislative decisions will be influenced by the relative financial strength of the various interest groups.

In the political realm, as long as most legislative campaigns are relatively uncompetitive and inexpensive, it seems unlikely that candidates are often discouraged from running because campaign funds are unavailable. The fact that incumbents can raise money more easily is only one of many advantages that they usually have over challengers. Those challengers, in either primaries or general elections, who are perceived to have a serious chance of winning are usually able to raise enough money to be competitive. Campaign financing at the state legislative level has not yet become the all-consuming force that it is in congressional politics.

The political impact of campaign financing on gubernatorial elections is far more dramatic and discouraging. The skyrocketing cost of political campaigns has placed serious constraints on potential gubernatorial candidates. There are only two possible routes a candidate can follow in order to be competitive. The first is to be wealthy and willing to give or loan millions of dollars to the campaign. The second route is to gain enough political strength to be perceived as a plausible winner and then to make whatever commitments are necessary to raise millions of dollars. Candidates like John Y. Brown and Wallace Wilkinson have combined these two approaches. They have started out by loaning large sums to their campaigns and then have recovered all or most of these funds by following the second route to success. This technique for making and repaying loans will not work if the legislation passed in 1988 is successful.

The campaign financing system, as it has operated in recent years with escalating costs and greater emphasis on television advertising, gives an obviously huge advantage to the wealthy candidate who is willing to invest in a political future. It places certain other types of candidates under an equally large disadvantage. One is the political newcomer or underdog who might be a highly successful campaigner if he or she had enough funds for a television campaign. If Brereton Jones or Wallace Wilkinson had not been wealthy, how could they have gained the visibility needed to capture public attention? If Grady Stumbo had been as well financed as his opponents in 1983 or 1987, might he have won the nomination? If John Harper had been taken seriously by Republcan fund-raisers, could he have won as many votes as Nunn in 1979 or Bunning in 1983?

Another type of person who is seriously handicapped is the non-wealthy candidate who refuses to solicit funds from those who would do business with the state or to make promses to those who want jobs and board appointments. Larry Forgy asserted that one reason he abandoned the Republican campaign for governor in 1987 was his unwillingness to make the promises and commitments sought by many potential contributors. "If you're willing to sell positions, you can raise a lot of money," according to former state senator Joe Prather, who made an abortive run for the Democratic nomination for governor in 1987. Although state law prohibits a candidate from paying money for political support, it apparently permits promises of jobs, contracts, and board appointments in exchange for financial support. "The big attraction of giving," according to Sen. Ed O'Daniel, D-Springfield, "is what everyone gets when the cookie jar is opened" (*C-J,* October 14, 1987, p. A1).

The fact that most contributors to gubernatorial campaigns want something in return is nothing new; it is a familiar reality in Kentucky politics. But some things have changed: the escalating costs of gubernatorial politics and the growing number of wealthy political amateurs. Because the ground rules have changed and fund-raising has assumed greater importance, serious candidates for governor are under greater pressure to pay any price and make any necessary commitments in order to be competitive. If one were inventing an electoral system designed to produce the best possible governor, it seems unlikely that it would resemble the present system.

9

REPUBLICAN ORGANIZATION AND FRAGMENTATION

IN MANY respects, Kentucky is a competitive two-party state. The Republican party has won seven of nine presidential elections starting in 1956. It held both U.S. Senate seats from 1957 to 1972 and regained one in the 1984 election. In the U.S. House the Republicans have consistently held the mountain Republican seat; since the mid-1960s they have consistently held at least one seat in the suburbs of Louisville and northern Kentucky; and since 1978 they have held a Bluegrass seat centered in Lexington. The Republican majority exceeded 60 percent in Sen. John Sherman Cooper's race in 1966 and in the 1972 and 1984 presidential elections.

But in state elections the Republican party has failed to capitalize on its success in national races. Kentucky has elected only one Republican governor since the 1943 race: Louie Nunn in 1967. In recent years the Republican party has consistently won between 20 and 30 percent of the state legislative seats—approximately the same number it held during the 1940s and 1950s and considerably less than it held during the administration of Louie Nunn (1967-71). Despite some success in metropolitan and urban counties and cities, the Republican party has not made significant inroads into local offices in Democratic counties. Almost inevitably, an analysis of the Kentucky Republican party must focus on the question: "What has gone wrong?"

The administration of Louie Nunn appears to have been the golden age of the modern Republican party. After defeating Jefferson County judge Marlow Cook in a bitter primary, Louie Nunn was elected with a margin of 51.6 percent and with the support of dissident Democrats led by "Happy" Chandler. Nunn, having run for governor previously and having managed statewide campaigns, understood electoral politics and believed strongly in building the party organization. Governor Nunn also understood the importance of patronage; it was handled in the governor's office and was used to build the party organization at the state and local levels.

During Nunn's administration there was a close working relationship between his office and the state party headquarters. Nunn selected John

Kerr to serve as state party chairman, and he remained in office throughout the administration. The state party had an executive director with several assistants and an annual budget of about $100,000. The governor encouraged the party to run registration drives. He helped the party to raise funds and consistently attended the dinners and other events held for that purpose.

Nunn also worked to unify the Republican party. In the 1968 Senate race, after backing another candidate in the primary, he supported his former opponent, Marlow Cook, in the general election. Nunn raised money for Cook and threw the full weight of his administration behind him, and Cook was elected. The state party chairman also served as campaign chairman in 1968 in an effort to coordinate activities on behalf of the entire congressional and presidential ticket. In addition, Nunn worked vigorously to help the party carry the state for Richard Nixon. With the governor's support, extensive efforts were made to recruit strong legislative candidates, though they failed to prevent some slippage in the unusually high proportion of Republicans in the legislature.

After polling leaders of his administration and the Republican party, Nunn decided that Tom Emberton would be the strongest candidate for governor. Emberton's campaign was well financed, but he did not prove to be a strong campaigner and lost the election to Wendell Ford, polling 44.3 percent of the vote. The golden age was over, and the decline of the state Republican party had begun.

One person who was very active in the state Republican party during the 1970s, after Nunn's administration, described that period as the "wilderness years" for the Republican party. Republicans were damaged by the repercussions from the Watergate scandal, but in Kentucky they were damaged even more by the political successes of Governors Wendell Ford and Julian Carroll. Both men were able to unite the Democratic party after their primary victories, and both gave attention to maintaining the effectiveness of the state and local Democratic parties. The Republican party lost governmental control of Louisville and Jefferson County in 1969, although in 1977 Republicans recaptured the Jefferson County judge executive's position with Mitch McConnell's victory.

In 1975 the Republican gubernatorial candidate, Robert Gable, got only 37.2 percent of the vote, running against incumbent Julian Carroll. In 1979 Louie Nunn won only 40.6 percent of the vote in his comeback effort against John Y. Brown. In 1983 the Republican party leadership had great difficulty finding an experienced, well-known Republican who was willing to run for governor. One after another of the leading officeholders and other prominent Republicans considered and then declined the offer. Finally, Jim Bunning, a state senator from northern Kentucky (and former major league pitcher), agreed to run. But he entered the race too late and with too little financial support, and he lost to Martha Layne Collins with 44.2 percent of the vote, just shy of the Republican percentage in 1971.

It appeared that in 1987 the Republicans would finally have a strong, well-financed candidate who would get an early lead in the campaign and have wide support within and outside the party. But that candidate, Larry Forgy, withdrew from the race early in January 1987, too late to find a replacement who could be a serious contender. John Harper, a relatively obscure state representative, emerged from the primary with 41 percent of the vote. But he was not taken seriously by Republican leaders, had great difficulty raising money, and polled only 36 percent against Wallace Wilkinson, the lowest proportion of votes cast for a Republican candidate for governor since 1868.

The State Republican Party Organization

The responsibility for developing organizational strength, supporting local parties, raising funds, recruiting and assisting candidates, and registering and mobilizing voters rests with the state party organization. When a party does not control the governorship, the resources for carrying out these duties and rewarding party workers are limited. The longer a party has been in the minority, the more difficult—and the more important—it becomes to run an effective party organization. The question is what has the state Republican organization done, and what can it do, to rebuild the Republican party?

During the 1970s a number of persons served as state party chairman, but none of them stayed in office long enough to have any major impact on the party organization. Some continuity was provided, however, by Larry Van Hoose, who was executive director of the state Republican party from 1972 to 1979. The party organization made some effort to recruit more and better statewide, legislative, and local candidates; while the party leadership claimed some success, there continued to be serious shortages of viable Republican candidates, particularly at the legislative and local levels. The fact that elections are held annually in Kentucky may be an obstacle to a minority party in trying to recruit candidates; because a new election is always just around the corner, there is never enough time for long-range planning and the development of candidates.

During the period when Van Hoose was executive director, some efforts were made to modernize the state party headquarters. The annual budget was raised to about $200,000 during this period, with as many as six staff members. The headquarters acquired a computer for word processing and mailing lists. While some efforts were made to strengthen local Republican organizations, there was little indication of any success. In the heavily Republican Fifth District, the local parties did not believe that a high level of organization was necessary, while in the much larger number of heavily Democratic counties, the Republican party was often virtually nonexistent. Someone familiar with local politics has estimated that during this period the Republican organization existed only on paper in 95 percent of the counties.

During the 1980s the Republican state chairmen included Liz Thomas, who had been on the staff of Congressman Gene Snyder; Gordon Wade, another northern Kentucky leader; and Robert Gable, a Lexington businessman (and former gubernatorial candidate), who took office in November 1986.

On paper the Republicans have a large and elaborate party structure. The state convention meets in even numbered years, its members chosen at county mass meetings. The Republican state central committee (RSCC) is a huge body, including, among others, the chairman and vice-chairman of each county committee, all Republican legislators, state and congressional officeholders, the heads of various party organizations, and twenty at-large members chosen by the convention. The RSCC holds one regular meeting a year and selects the chairman and other offices. But most of the work of the RSCC is carried out by its executive committee, which is scheduled to meet almost every month and which consists of the twenty elected members plus nineteen ex officio members.

Activities of the Republican State Party

The Republican state party has an annual budget of about half a million dollars. The party headquarters is located in a house in Frankfort, not far from the capitol. It has a staff of four: the executive director, a political director, a finance director, and an administrative assistant. The headquarters has a computer, used primarily for maintaining various mailing lists. It publishes a newsletter, maintains contacts with local organizations as well as with the national party, runs fund-raising campaigns, and carries out the other kinds of activities that would be expected for a state party headquarters. The state Republican party organization carries out the fund-raising efforts necessary to finance its $500,000 a year budget, though about $65,000 of the budget comes from the state government under the taxpayer check-off plan. Though the state party provides a number of services that may be helpful to candidates, it provides only very limited and occasional funding to help candidates running for public office. For the most part state, legislative, and local candidates must raise their own money.

One of the fundamental problems facing the state Republican party has been the weakness of local organizations in a large proportion of the rural counties outside the Fifth District. The small proportion of registered Republicans, the shortage of viable local candidates, and the absence of local party activists undermine the best efforts at party building. In July 1987 the state party instituted what it called the Four-Star Program, designed to provide incentives to the county party organizations to become more active. The plan was to evaluate the success of local parties in twenty-two areas of activity, ranging from voter registration to filling all the precinct positions and organizing women's and young Republican organizations. In the area of registration, for example, points would be awarded for increases in Republican registration over a year. Counties achieving the highest scores would be recognized annually and would be given a modest financial award.

The obvious purpose of the program is to encourage counties to improve their organizations and to increase their level of political activity. One by-product is to give the state organization a more accurate picture of the level of organization and activity in the various local parties. When the program was inaugurated in the summer of 1987, only 60 percent of the county parties filled out the surveys sent out by state headquarters to measure the initial level of activity. In the first year only one-third of the local organizations qualified for any points under the program; most of them were in larger and middle-sized counties, and they included only a dozen of the twenty-nine counties that have a majority of voters registered Republican. Obviously, much work remains to be done in building viable local organizations throughout the state.

One of the most serious weaknesses of the Republican party in Kentucky is its failure to run candidates for a large number of legislative seats, including some in districts where a strong candidate should have a reasonable chance of winning. In the four elections from 1979 through 1986, the Republicans contested an average of only 53 of 100 House seats and 11 of 19 Senate seats. In 1988 the number of seats contested by Republicans fell to 41 in the House and 9 in the Senate.

From time to time the Republican state party has made some effort to recruit a larger number of legislative candidates. In 1967, the year of Louie Nunn's election, the Republicans contested 78 House and 16 Senate seats. During the Nunn administration the state party organization made serious efforts to recruit and support legislative candidates, particularly in districts where the party had some realistic chance of winning. It sought out persons to run, raised funds for both incumbents and challengers, and ran training programs for legislative candidates. In the two elections held during the Nunn administration, 1969 and 1971, the Republicans had 70 and 68 House candidates and 11 and 16 Senate candidates.

In the years that followed, the state party organization continued to make efforts to recruit and finance candidates, but the results were disappointing. The proportion of House seats that were contested dropped to little more than half, and from 1973 through 1981 there were 36 House districts that had a Republican candidate only once or not at all in five elections.

Following the 1986 election the state party organization developed a targeting plan in order to identify the legislative districts where the party had the best chance of winning. The party collected precinct-level data on recent elections from the county courthouses and contracted with the national Republican party to aggregate these data and prepare an index for each legislative district. The index was based on Reagan's presidential victory in 1984 (weighted double) and two Senate races, McConnell's winning effort in 1984 and Jackson Andrew's losing effort in 1986. The resulting index, called the "optimum Republican voting strength," measured the proportion of votes in each legislative district that might be cast for a Republican candidate who was running a serious campaign. (The choice of these three elections produces a statewide index of 49 percent.)

The index, like any targeting system, enables the party leadership to determine where the party should make the greatest effort to recruit candidates and where it should concentrate its resources, including funds raised or services provided to a candidate. In districts where the index is 50 percent or more (or perhaps even 45 percent), the data can be used to encourage potential candidates to run. The index based on the 1984 and 1986 statewide elections was 50 percent or better in 50 House districts, suggesting that Republican candidates should have a realistic chance in at least half of the districts. But in reality only 41 Republicans, 27 of them incumbents, ran for House seats in 1988. The targeting system may have helped the party to distribute resources, but it failed to encourage candidates to run in a number of seats that, in theory, were winnable. Of course, some of these uncontested seats may have been held by entrenched Democrats who were perceived to be unbeatable.

One of the most valuable resources in political campaigns is computerized lists of individuals who have made previous donations to political candidates. The state Republican headquarters has such lists of contributors, but there is contradictory evidence about its willingness to share such lists with Republican candidates. In 1987 the Harper organization believed that the contributor lists it received from the state party were incomplete and did not include some of the best prospects. The Harper organization was also concerned that, while it was struggling to raise funds for its campaign, the state Republican organization was carrying on its own competing fund-raising operation. The state party headquarters apparently does not have a policy of making statewide lists of contributors available to every state Republican candidate or making local lists available on request to those running for legislative or local office. When the party targets state legislative districts as important, it sometimes contacts proven contributors and asks them to contribute to these campaigns.

Criticisms and Limitations of the State Party

Republicans around the state differ in their judgments about the priorities and the accomplishments of the state party organization. Those who criticize the RSCC also differ in their prescriptions for the party. Some critics charge that a small group maintains control over the state central committee, a charge that is difficult to evaluate from the outside and one that is probably inevitable in a party that has often suffered from factionalism. The rules now provide that the executive committee will nominate a slate of officers—chairman, vice-chairman, secretary, and national committeeman and committeewoman—and that the central committee must vote for or against the entire slate. This rule is criticized as a device used by the leadership to stay in office.

The argument is often made that the party organization, at both the state and local levels, does not try hard enough to attract new members. The issue came to a head in 1988 when supporters of Pat Robertson tried to win seats on various state and local party committees. Under present party rules a person who wants to shift party membership cannot participate in Republican party affairs until he or she has shifted registration (and state law prohibits shifting between the general election and the primary). In 1988 some efforts were made, unsuccessfully, to permit newcomers to participate in party affairs before they were able to shift their party registration.

Some critics argue that the Republican party should devote more attention to developing potential state and local candidates. They distinguish between recruiting, which is done—often in desperation—at the last moment, and development, which is a long-term process. This may be a more appropriate task for local organizations, which are in a better position to identify new talent. Some have suggested that the state party should run long-term training programs (on the model of Leadership Kentucky) for Republican activists identified by local parties as being particularly promising.

The state party organization can provide a few services that should benefit any Republican running for office. For example, from time to time the state party organizes voter registration drives or, less frequently, campaigns to convert Democrats to Republican registration. In reality, however, the success of such efforts depends almost entirely on the vigor of local organizations.

The management of political campaigns has become a complex and sophisticated business, and serious candidates for major office must rely on experts in polling, television and radio advertising, mass mailing, and computer technology. By offering such services to candidates, state party organizations in some states have been able to strengthen the party's competitive position and at the same time enhance the effectiveness and influence of the state organization.

The Kentucky state Republican party could carry out public opinion polls and make the results widely available. It could provide analyses of county and precinct returns to state, congressional, legislative, and local candidates; and it has very recently provided such data on a limited basis to legislative candidates. The state party could use its computer resources to provide candidates with various kinds of lists, such as registered voters, active Republican workers, and financial contributors, and it has apparently done so on a selective basis.

The state Republican party could provide more extensive services to a larger number of candidates, but to do so would cost money; and the state party seems to have difficulty raising enough funds to maintain its existing level of operations and services. The approximately $65,000 it receives from the state government, under the taxpayer check-off plan, is less than 15 percent of its annual budget.

If the state party organization were to engage in a much more aggressive fund-raising operation, it would be competing for funds directly with individual candidates and particularly with the senatorial and congressional officeholders, who have been very successful in building large campaign chests. Because its resources are limited, the state party is selective in providing even minimal help to Republican candidates. The purpose of targeting legislative races is not only to recruit more candidates but to distribute limited resources wisely. The state party has provided little assistance to those Republican challengers for congressional seats whose campaigns appeared hopeless.

Local Republican Party Organizations

Though a comprehensive analysis of local Republican organizations is beyond the scope of this book, the organizations in Jefferson County (Louisville) and Fayette County (Lexington) deserve particular attention. These are counties with large numbers of voters who frequently vote for Republican candidates, though a majority of them are registered as Democrats. These are counties that Repulican candidates for statewide office must win if they are to be seriously competitive. Consequently the organizational effectiveness of these county parties is of great importance to the state Republican party.

Louisville

The modern Jefferson County Republican party organization developed in the late 1950s when a new generation of leaders, headed by William Cowger and Marlow Cook, gained control of the organization. The old guard had been dominated by businessmen and fund-raisers rather than active party workers. The new leadership reorganized the executive committee to include the chairmen of the city wards and county districts. (It was not until 1974 that the organization was organized along legislative district lines.) Steps were taken to encourage broader participation in the party.

Once the organizational groundwork had been laid, the party won control of both the Louisville and Jefferson County governments in 1961. After easily winning primary contests, William Cowger was elected mayor of Louisville, and Marlow Cook became county judge. The organization quickly capitalized on its position of power. It hired a full-time organizational chairman, and by the late 1960s there were nine salaried employees working at headquarters on a year-round basis. As long as the Republicans controlled both the city and county, they had approximately two thousand patronage jobs to dispense, and the patronage workers were assessed 2 percent of their salaries to support the party. From this and other sources, the party raised enough funds to support this operation and to provide assistance to candidates. Persistent voter registration drives substantially narrowed the gap between Democratic and Republican registration totals in the county. The availability of patronage jobs provided one strong incentive for registering as a Republican.

The party leadership continued the established practice of endorsing candidates for legislative and local office. The executive committee appointed a candidate selection committee, which solicited recommendations from ward and precinct leaders and investigated potential candidates. The candidates endorsed by the executive committee for local and legislative office were frequently unopposed and were rarely defeated in primaries. The party then provided strong support for these candidates in the general election.

In 1965 Marlow Cook was reelected county judge; Mayor Cowger (who could not serve a second term) was succeeded by Republican Kenneth Schmid. The next year Cowger was elected to Congress from the Third District, and Republican Gene Snyder was elected from the Fourth District. During the 1960s the Republicans usually won majorities, occasionally large majorities, in the legislature. They were aided by the 1963 reapportionment that provided more seats primarily in suburban areas.

The Republican success in Jefferson County did not breed harmony, however. There was a split between the relatively liberal Cowger-Cook faction and the deeply conservative Gene Snyder. Snyder, who had been elected in 1962 and defeated in the 1964 landslide, had to defeat a candidate from the Cowger-Cook faction in the 1966 primary before winning the election, and this was a source of continuing bitterness. The first step in Louie Nunn's gubernatorial election in 1967 was a bitter primary battle with Marlow Cook, which inevitably damaged relations between the county and state Republican organizations.

In 1969 Republican control of Jefferson County and Louisville came to an end. Cook was elected to the Senate in 1968; his appointed successor as county judge died in an automobile accident, and his replacement lost the 1969 election to a Democrat. The Louisville Republicans lost control of the board of aldermen in 1967 and the mayor's office in 1969. And in 1970 Representative Cowger was narrowly defeated by Democrat Ron Mazzoli.

The 1970s was a period of factional turmoil on the executive committee. Because it lacked officeholders and patronage, the organization had fewer resources and a smaller staff, and it lacked the ability to maintain as strong a precinct organization as in the past. In the early 1970s the party organization abandoned the practice of endorsing candidates for nomination to local and legislative office.

In 1977 the Jefferson County Republican drought ended when Mitch McConnell was elected county judge. McConnell was a former aide to Marlow Cook who had been active in Jefferson County Republican party affairs for several years. He was reelected in 1981, completing seven years in the post before his election to the Senate in 1984.

The seven years of Republican control in Jefferson County did not restore the party to the position of strength it had enjoyed in the 1960s. This was in part because Mitch McConnell did not devote much attention to party-building activities, and he gave little priority to recruiting local and legislative candidates. He was willing to lend his name and appearance to fund-raising events for the party. But many Republicans believed that McConnell's fund-raising efforts were focused primarily on his own campaign for reelection and subsequently on his campaign for the U.S. Senate. McConnell's priorities have frequently been criticized by other Republican leaders in the county. But McConnell, like some other Republican officeholders in the state, believes that successful candidates must be self-reliant, raising their own funds and mobilizing their own supporters.

Another reason why the Jefferson County Republican party benefited less from McConnell's tenure as county judge was that the party failed to win control of the mayor's office in Louisville, as it had in the 1960s. There may also have been less patronage available at the county level than had been the case a decade earlier. The disappearance of party organizational endorsements in primaries may also have weakened the party.

During the 1980s the Jefferson County Republican party has not been as well organized as it was in the 1960s or as the Democratic party has been in recent years. The lack of patronage has made it more difficult to provide incentives for workers at the precinct and district levels. Candidates for local and legislative office find that some precincts are well organized and in others they must recruit their own workers.

The county party organization faces several handicaps in raising funds. It cannot rely on patronage workers for funds. Some of the business and professional persons who might be expected to support the Republican party have preferred to make campaign contributions to the Democrats who hold office in the city and county, notably Mayor Abramson and county judge executive Sloane. The decline in financial resources has inevitably led to reductions in the party headquarters operation; in the late 1980s it has had only three paid staff members.

In recent years the county party organization has become more active in recruiting local and legislative candidates. In 1986 and 1988, for example, it tried very hard to find someone to run in every legislative district. It succeeded in finding a candidate, though not necessarily a viable one, in nearly every district in 1986; but in 1988 there were a number of gaps in the slate. The county organization is selective in the amount of assistance it provides to local and legislative candidates. Those who demonstrate the ability to raise funds and recruit volunteer help, and thus prove that they have some potential for winning, are most likely to receive some tangible assistance from the organization. The party has recently provided candidates with voter registration lists and organized seminars in campaigning run by Washington consultants. Another resource made available to some candidates is a phone bank at party headquarters. The party has not, however, provided them with lists of financial contributors.

The factional divisions that once plagued the Jefferson County Republican party appear to be a thing of the past perhaps because, for the party out of power, there is less to fight over. On several occasions during the 1970s, there had been competing slates for party office, but during the 1980s the pattern has been for a single slate of candidates to be elected to the county committee without opposition.

Lexington

The Republican party in Fayette County was one of the first to capitalize on the popularity of national Republican candidates in the late 1950s and the 1960s. It developed a relatively active grass-roots organization, and in

1965 it won temporary control of the county judgeship. In the mid-1960s the increase in representation for Fayette County enabled the party to start winning legislative seats, particularly in the higher-income suburban districts.

Some of those active in the Fayette Republican party believe that since that time there has been a decline in the level of organizational effort. Some attribute it to the growing importance of television, which makes the candidates more independent and reduces the importance of old-fashioned organizational work. The party has had success in running telephone banks and working the polls on election day. Less than two-thirds of the precinct offices have been filled in the late 1980s. In recent years, however, the party has had some success in raising money and has been able to maintain an office for party headquarters. By 1988 the local party had a budget of about $15,000 a year.

From time to time the Fayette County party has tried to recruit more candidates for local and legislative office. In 1981, for example, it ran a number of candidates for courthouse offices but without success. From 1971 through 1988, in elections for each of the two Senate seats entirely in Fayette County, the Republicans consistently held one seat and contested the other only two of five times. In the nine elections for the five House seats entirely in the county, the Republicans always won the seventy-eighth; contested the seventh-ninth seven times, winning it once; contested the seventy-sixth six times, winning it once; and contested the seventy-seventh only five times and the seventy-fifth only four times. Only in 1971 did it contest all the seats, while in 1979 it contested only the seat it won.

The strongest component of the Fayette Republican organization is that led by Rep. Larry Hopkins, who first sought legislative office in 1971. State senator John Trevey and state representative Pat Freibert have worked closely with Hopkins, and each holds a legislative position formerly held by Hopkins. Though none of the three often face a serious challenge, they have a network of supporters who can be mobilized when necessary. Persons close to the Hopkins organization argue that it gives strength and vitality to the entire county organization. Critics argue that the Hopkins group works principally for its own candidates and does not contribute enough to the county organization.

There has been some fluidity in leadership of the party; during the 1980s four different persons chaired the local organization. The entry of Robertson supporters into the Fayette County organization (discussed later) raised the possibility of more instability of leadership as well as factional rivalries within the party.

Fragmentation in the Republican Party

Political Fiefdoms

The minority party in any state faces the necessity of winning votes from independents and majority party voters in order to win elections. The Republican party in Kentucky faces the reality that only 29 percent of voters are registered as Republicans. Republican candidates for statewide or congressional office (outside the Fifth District) face the same problem. They must win both Democratic and Republican votes, and in some congressional districts they must win more Democratic than Republican votes in order to put together a majority coalition.

A Republican candidate who seeks statewide or congressional office in Kentucky is, for the most part, on his own. The state party organization can provide very little assistance. The candidate must raise his own campaign funds, recruit his own political workers, build his own political organization, and develop issues that will appeal to both Republican and Democratic voters. It is true of course that, in raising funds and recruiting volunteers, the candidate will draw largely from a pool of Republican contributors and workers. But to be successful, the candidate must develop and maintain his own organization, including persons who have not been active in the Republican party and often including Democrats as well.

Once a Republican candidate has been elected to office, the strategy for winning reelection remains the same. The incumbent builds as large a bank account as possible for the next campaign. He tries to maintain and strengthen his political organization. He publicizes his service to the people of the district or state. He tries to develop a record that will be acceptable to a majority of constituents. He tries to broaden the base of his political support among Democrats as well as Republicans. And when he runs for reelection, the radio and television commercials and the billboards do not emphasize his affiliation with the Republican party.

In addition to Sen. Mitch McConnell, elected in 1984, there are three Republican members of the U.S. House. When Larry Hopkins was elected in 1978, he became the first Republican in modern times to represent the Sixth District, which encompasses Lexington and the surrounding Bluegrass area. Jim Bunning was elected to the Fourth District seat in 1986, replacing the retiring Republican congressman Gene Snyder, who had represented the district since 1966. The Fourth District includes the suburbs of Louisville, the suburban area south of Cincinnati, and the rural counties along the Ohio River between these two areas. The only truly Republican district is the Fifth, in the hill country of southeastern

Kentucky. Since 1980 it has been represented by Harold Rogers.

The Republican members of Congress have developed their own power bases that are independent of the Kentucky Republican party. These congressmen believe that they were originally elected because of their own efforts, and they are convinced that they must maintain this independence if they are to be reelected. If they are perceived as partisan Republicans by Democratic and independent voters, their reelection is jeopardized. If they work actively for, or campaign with, Republican candidates for other offices, their bipartisan image may be damaged. If they share their organizational resources, such as lists of financial contributors, with other candidates, their own electoral prospects may be weakened.

The best example of an independent Republican congressman is Larry Hopkins. In 1978, when the incumbent Democratic congressman in the Sixth District was upset in a primary, Republican leaders persuaded the Republican candidate, who was perceived as too weak, to withdraw and selected state senator Larry Hopkins in her place. He won his first race by a 51 to 46 percent margin. In subsequent elections the Democratic candidates have become weaker, and Hopkins's margin has grown—to 71 percent in 1984 and 74 percent in both 1986 and 1988.

The voter registration in the Sixth District is 77 percent Democratic and 20 percent Republican. When Hopkins won 71 percent of the vote in 1984, he must have gained nearly two-thirds of his votes from registered Democrats (assuming he won nearly all the Republican votes and taking into account a slightly higher turnout among Republicans). Hopkins's ability to win the votes of most Democratic voters is not unique, of course. In the 1984 election Ronald Reagan carried the Sixth District by 62 percent and probably got at least 60 percent of his votes from Democrats.

The Democratic party rarely wins a contested statewide election by a margin as large as its 7 to 3 advantage in registration, and Democratic candidates for Congress and the legislature who have more than token opposition rarely win a share of the vote equivalent to the Democratic share of registration in their district. In other words, a substantial proportion of registered Democrats regularly vote Republican, and an even larger percentage are potential Republican voters in any election. Nevertheless, Republican candidates like Larry Hopkins are always very conscious of the disadvantage that they face in terms of voter registration, and thus they are conscious of the need to build and maintain a bipartisan voting coalition.

Larry Hopkins has developed that coalition by his untiring attention to his constituents. He does everything that the textbooks say a congressman should do to win reelection. Hopkins pays careful attention to the needs of his district, and his staff handles casework diligently. Hopkins visits the district every weekend and makes excellent use of his time. Hopkins makes sure that constituents know about his activities and his accessibility. If he spends a Saturday afternoon at a shopping mall to meet constituents and listen to their concerns, postcards are sent out in advance, and a story appears in the press the next day, reporting on his appearance. He sends out newsletters regularly to constituents in general and to specialized groups. He appears frequently on television commenting on legislation and public issues.

Hopkins has a conservative voting record in Congress and a record of strong support for a Republican president. But he has demonstrated enough independence in his voting record to satisfy many moderate and conservative Democrats. He is skillful in becoming identified with issues that will appeal to a bipartisan constituency. As a member of the subcommittee of the Armed Services Committee that visited Lebanon to investigate the tragic bombing of the Marine barracks, he was the only Republican to join in the majority report attacking the military leadership for negligence. He has vigorously supported residents of Richmond, in the Sixth District, in their fight against the army's plan to build an incinerator on a nearby base to dispose of nerve gas stores, a plan that they believe is fraught with danger.

Hopkins's game plan and his hard work have paid off. Potential Democratic candidates who might be tough adversaries have declined to run, and in recent years Hopkins has faced only little-known candidates who had few resources and little support fro the Democratic party. Consequently, he has not had to run a vigorous or expensive campaign. In recent years Hopkins has not found it necessary to establish a formal campaign headquarters or to mobilize an army of volunteers. In part because of this, Hopkins has not had to run for office as a partisan Republican. Instead, he runs as an incumbent congressman. He is the most successful Republican vote getter in the history of the Sixth District, but he accomplishes this by using a strategy that makes it easy for Democrats and independents to vote for him.

Without a doubt, Hopkins's bipartisan strategy is perfectly designed to win reelection comfortably in a district that is Democratic in registration and bipartisan in its voting patterns. The question is whether this strategy damages the efforts of Republicans to build a stronger state party in Kentucky. If Hopkins were more openly a Republican and used his position as an incumbent to engage in party-building activities, would it make a significant difference—or would it simply increase the risk that the Sixth District seat would be lost to the Democratic party?

Those Republicans who speak disparagingly of the congressional "fiefdoms" may criticize all of the Republican incumbents, but Larry

Hopkins is more often a target because he has been in office longer and because it is he who has perfected the bipartisan strategy. Some of these critics speak in general terms, focusing on Hopkins's bipartisan style and asserting that he is "not a strong party person." Some criticisms are more specific.

There are charges that Hopkins has built his own organization in Fayette County and uses it for his own campaigns but has been unwilling to use his resources and workers to build a stronger Republican organization in Fayette County. Those who work closely with Hopkins, on the other hand, assert that it is the Hopkins campaign group that has energized the Fayette County organization and has provided a large proportion of the volunteers who have worked in other local campaigns. They claim that, because Hopkins is so strong and rarely has serious challenges, his supporters are free to devote more time to other campaigns in Fayette County and the other counties in the Sixth District.

Critics argue that Hopkins has raised a campaign chest larger than he needs and continues to raise funds, even during gubernatorial campaigns, but is unwilling to participate in fund-raising efforts for other Republicans. Hopkins has taken the position that candidates must raise their own funds; he will not donate to other candidates funds that have been contributed to his own campaign. He does not usually speak at fund-raisers for other candidates nor provide other tangible assistance to candidates. Moreover, Hopkins does not share his lists of contributors with other Republican candidates, probably in part because he raises some of his funds from Democrats, who would be less likely to contribute if Hopkins provided their names to other Republican candidates. Supporters of Hopkins argue that other candidates do not need lists of contributors because the names of any contributors over $300 are a matter of public record at the Registry of Election Finance.

Supporters and critics of Hopkins do not disagree about the reality of his campaign style. Larry Hopkins raises his own funds and campaigns independently of other Republican candidates. He appeals to Democrats, independents, and Republicans, and he does not emphasize his Republican affiliation. He campaigns on his record as a congressman and particularly his long record of service to the district and its constituents. Supporters and critics disagree about whether this independent strategy harms the Republican party. Hopkins and his supporters argue that the greatest contribution he can make to the Republican party is to keep on winning reelection by the largest margin possible. He argues that the presence of a strong Republican on the ticket, one who is able to win votes from Democrats as well as Republicans, is a major asset to other Republicans running for state or local office in the Sixth District.

The issue of campaign fund-raising is one of the major sources of dissension among congressional officeholders and candidates. As the cost of campaigning has increased, money raising has become a year-round preoccupation of most senators and representatives. Even those who have rarely had strong opposition, like Larry Hopkins, believe it is necessary to keep building a larger campaign war chest because the next election may produce a stronger challenger. Mitch McConnell's election to the Senate in 1984 was barely over when he started raising money for the 1990 race, and by mid-1988 he had raised $1.2 million and had $1 million in the bank.

Friction arises among Republican leaders over the timing, the boundaries, and the style of fund-raising efforts. Candidates for Congress never stop raising funds, and this arouses resentment from gubernatorial candidates trying to raise funds in a noncongressional election year. John Harper was also upset that during his gubernatorial campaign the state Republican party was raising funds for its own treasury and using his name in the campaign. Congressional candidates may object if a statewide, or another congressional, candidate comes into their district to raise funds. Mitch McConnell agreed to travel with John Harper in 1987 and introduce him to audiences but held his own fund-raising events at the same time. When McConnell campaigned on Nunn's behalf in the 1979 gubernatorial race, he used the occasion to distribute sign-up sheets to those in the audience and to use these lists for his own fund-raising efforts.

Other Sources of Dissension

Through the years there have been a number of other factors that have caused dissension in the party. The wide diversity among areas of Republican strength within the state is one source of disagreement. In the Appalachian Fifth District lie most of the counties of traditional Republican control. The Republican leaders and activists in these counties may be more interested in winning and holding county office than they are in the statewide fortunes of the Republican party. As we have noted, the Republican party in some of these counties is divided into factions sometimes based on family loyalties. The main concern of a Republican congressman from the Fifth District is to maintain this political base and to avoid challenges in the primary.

The second major base of Republican strength is in the major metropolitan centers of Louisville, Lexington, and northern Kentucky. All three are areas where congressional and local races are potentially competitive though not always closely contested. The Republican bases of metropolitan power are greatest in the congressional seats and in local government of Jefferson County and sometimes Louisville. The social and economic interests and the issue priorities of Republican constituents in metropolitan areas are quite different from those in the Republican Appalachian areas.

Bitterly contested primaries within Republican ranks are not a cause of discord, because they are so rare. The last primary for major office that might be described as bitterly divisive was the 1967 gubernatorial primary in which Louie Nunn defeated Marlow Cook. Ironically, it also produced the last candidate able to win a gubernatorial election.

In the years since his administration, Louie Nunn has from time to time been a controversial figure within the party. Despite Nunn's support for Cook in his successful race for the Senate in 1968, relations between these two figures remained uneasy as long as Cook was active in politics. Surprisingly, when Nunn ran for governor again in 1979, he had only minor opposition in the primary. Nunn is an outspoken man, in public and in private; and for many years his brother Lee, a skillful campaign manager, was also a source of controversy. Some other Republican leaders who have appeared on the scene more recently seem to resent Nunn's continuing efforts to wield some influence behind the scenes. There has been friction between Louie Nunn and both of the recent Republican congressmen from the Fourth District: Gene Snyder and Jim Bunning.

From time to time the state's active Republicans have been divided in their loyalties to presidential candidates. That was the case, for example, in 1976 when Pres. Gerald Ford narrowly and somewhat surprisingly defeated Ronald Reagan in the presidential primary. In 1988 there were some sharp conflicts between the supporters of George Bush and Robert Dole. There has been little evidence, however, that these differences have caused any lasting splits in the Republican party.

In 1988, however, the supporters of Pat Robertson added a new dimension to Republican factionalism. In the primary election Robertson got only 11 percent of the votes (less than 14,000 votes in a light turnout), but his campaign enlisted a number of workers, many of whom were new to Republican politics. Some had been Republican voters, though not politically active; some had been Democrats, who changed party registration; and some had not even been registered. Once the campaign was over, the Robertson supporters in some parts of the state turned their attention to trying to win a place in the Republican party. They were led by Philip Thompson, who had served briefly in 1985 and 1986 as executive director of the state Republican party.

In the spring of 1988 (after the primary), the Robertson supporters attended Republican county meetings in a small number of counties and tried to win seats on the county committees, with mixed success. Their most dramatic success occurred in Fayette County, where a large number of Robertson loyalists attended the county convention. (One party regular, looking at the newcomers, asked, "Who are these people?") Voting as a bloc, they elected a slate of candidates to the county executive committee that included a number of new Robertson supporters and a number of veteran conservatives who were acceptable to them (*National Journal*, June 26, 1988, p. 824).

Among the other counties where Robertson supporters won control of local committees were Madison and Franklin; they also made some inroads in Jefferson County meetings. In some of the county and district meetings, Robertson supporters or delegates were challenged by veteran Republicans who questioned whether they had shifted their registration to the Republican party early enough to meet the deadline. Some of the fights over credentials had to be settled at the state level.

By the time the state convention was held in April, compromises had been worked out between the party leadership and the Robertson forces. Six Robertson supporters, including Thompson, were among the twenty at-large members elected to the forty-member state central committee. The attitude of established Republican leaders and veteran activists to the newcomers loyal to Robertson is varied and sometimes ambivalent. On the one hand, Republicans understand that the party needs to expand its ranks, and it needs the enthusiasm and commitment that characterize many of the newcomers. On the question of issues, the difference between the two groups is one of priorities, not principles. Some Republicans doubt whether these converts will maintain their commitment to the party when and if Robertson fades from the political scene and whether they will demonstrate equal enthusiasm in working for other Republican candidates.

Some of the Republicans who have controlled local party organizations are less than enthusiastic about sharing their power with any new group of political activists. Some critics believe that the conflicts over the Robertson group are symbolic of a broader problem in the Republican party. Those who hold state or county Republican office, it is claimed, are too often content to keep the status quo and to take advantage of whatever patronage or benefits come from Republican control of the White House, rather than sharing power and trying to enlarge the Republican base of support.

The problems faced by the Republican party organization are not unique to Kentucky. They are typical of the problems that have been faced by the minority Republican party in most southern states. It is not unusual for those Republicans who win election to state or local office to give higher priority to their own reelection than to state party-building efforts. In Texas, for example, the Republican party has developed relatively slowly, given its potential electoral base, and former senator John Tower and Gov. William Clements have both been criticized for their lack of support for the party organization.

It is easy to blame state party chairmen and members of the state Republican committee for failing to recruit more aggressively and to provide more tangible assistance to the party's candidates. But the state party needs substantial financial resources to provide significant amounts of support; and the minority party has very little leverage in raising funds and runs the risk of competing directly with its officeholders if it makes vigorous efforts to raise funds. If there is any prescription for Republican success, it would be to elect a governor who is deeply committed to party-building activities, a point we will return to in the next chapter.

10

NOMINATING AND ELECTING REPUBLICANS

Republican Registration and Primary Elections

In order to vote in Republican primaries, a voter must be registered as a Republican; and during the gubernatorial primaries from 1979 through 1987, the percentage of registration that was Republican remained steady at 28 percent (down from 30 percent in 1975).

Registered Republican voters are distributed unevenly across the state, even more so than are the Democrats (chapter 3). In 1987 the largest proportion of Republican registrants (37 percent) was found in 29 counties where they constituted a majority of those registered; 29 percent were in the four major metropolitan counties, where they constituted 29 percent of registered voters; and 24 percent were in 29 other counties where Republicans were between 21 and 50 percent of the total (table 26). In the remaining 58 counties, including most of western Kentucky and scattered counties in the rest of the state, Republicans had less than 20 percent of the registration total and comprised only 10 percent of the statewide Republican registration total.

In the 1987 gubernatorial primary, the distribution of Republican votes approximated the distribution of registered Republicans, except that a larger proportion of the primary turnout (44 percent) came from the counties with a majority Republican registration. In other words, voters who were registered as Republicans were more likely to participate in the gubernatorial primary if they lived in heavily Republican counties. Among the major metropolitan counties, the level of voting in Republican primaries was considerably higher in Fayette than in the other three.

A voter might be expected to register as a Republican in order to participate in primary elections at the state level, or the county level, or both. In reality, highly competitive Republican primaries at the state level are rare, and the winners of those primaries are usually defeated in the

Table 26. Republican Patterns of Registration and Turnout in 1987 Gubernatorial Primary

Counties (N)	Total Rep. regis. (000s)	Total Rep. regis. (%)	Total Rep. prim. vote (000s)	Total Rep. prim. vote (%)	Rep. gen. elect. vote (000s)	Rep. gen. elect. vote (%)	Rep. prim. vote as % of Rep. regis.	Rep. prim. vote as % of Rep. gen. elect. vote
Jefferson 28% Rep. regis.	102	18.5	14	15.6	63	23.2	14.1	22.6
Fayette 29% Rep. regis.	26	4.7	5	5.7	23	8.3	21.3	24.2
Campbell & Kenton 30% Rep. regis.	30	5.5	4	4.1	16	5.9	12.5	23.6
Major metro 29% Rep. regis.	158	28.6	24	25.4	102	37.4	15.3	23.6
Rep. regis. under 10% (34)	14	2.6	3	3.0	22	8.2	19.0	12.3
Rep. regis. 10-20% (24)	43	7.7	6	6.9	46	16.7	14.7	13.7
Rep. regis. 21-50% (29)	131	23.7	18	19.7	58	21.4	13.8	30.9
Rep. regis. over 50% (29)	205	37.2	41	44.2	45	16.3	19.7	90.9

Source: Calculated from data compiled by the State Board of Elections.

general election. While Republican candidates for the U.S. Senate or House are more likely to win, there is seldom serious primary competition if the incumbent is running. The voters who have the strongest incentive to register as Republicans are those living in counties where local government is under Republican control. Not only are there likely to be competitive primaries, but the winners frequently win the November election.

The importance of local Republican primaries can be illustrated by looking at the figures for turnout in the 1985 Republican primaries, when only local races were contested (table 27). Two-thirds of all the votes cast were in the counties where the Republicans held a registration majority, in most of which it is likely that Republicans held some or all of the local offices. In these 29 counties almost 64 percent of the registered Republicans voted. By contrast, only 11 percent of the primary vote came from the four major metropolitan counties, which contained 28 percent of the

Table 27. Republican Patterns of Registration and Primary Turnout in Local Races, 1985

Counties (N)	Total Rep. regis. (000s)	Total Rep. regis. (%)	Total Rep. prim. vote (000s)	Total Rep. prim. vote (%)	Rep. prim. vote as % of Rep. regis.
Jefferson 28% Rep. regis.	108	18.1	13	6.3	12.3
Fayette 29% Rep. regis.	30	5.0	6	2.8	19.4
Campbell & Kenton 30% Rep. regis.	31	5.2	4	1.9	13.2
Major metro 29% Rep. regis.	169	28.3	23	11.0	13.7
Rep. regis. under 10% (33)	14	2.4	1	0.7	10.1
Rep. regis. 10-20% (25)	48	8.1	3	1.4	6.2
Rep. regis. 21-50% (29)	143	24.0	43	20.1	29.7
Rep. regis. over 50% (29)	222	37.3	141	66.8	63.5

Source: Calculated from data compiled by the State Board of Elections.

registered voters; in these counties 14 percent of the registered Republicans voted.

Registered Republicans are much more likely to vote in local primary elections than they are in statewide contests. In each of three years with only local (or legislative) elections on the ballot (1977, 1981, and 1985), at least 200,000 registered Republicans participated in primary elections. The highest Republican primary turnout in a gubernatorial election year during the 1979-87 period was in 1979 when 142,000 voters cast a vote, 132,000 of them in the gubernatorial contest. Even the presidential primary in 1988 attracted only 122,000 Republican voters. In years with only senatorial or congressional races on the ballot during this period, there was no Republican turnout higher than 70,000 (table 28).

The relatively low proportions of Republicans voting in primaries for statewide office have several implications. The most obvious point is that a small proportion of voters are able to determine who the party's nominees will be. In 1987 only 90,000 participated in the primary selecting John Harper to run for governor, though he eventually won three times that many votes in the general election. In 1984 only 50,000 participated in the senatorial nomination, though Mitch McConnell, the winning candidate, eventually received 645,000 votes in the fall election.

There are two major reasons for this large disparity between voting in the Republican primary and in the general election. A relatively small proportion of Republicans participate in primaries, and a substantial number of registered Democrats usually support the Republican candi-

Table 28. Republican Statewide Primaries for Major Offices, 1978-88

Year	Office	Total vote	Vote as % of Rep. regis.	Winning percentage	Winning candidate
1978	Sen.	30,114	6.1	47.2	Louis Guenther
1979	Gov.	132,125	27.9	80.2	Louie Nunn
1980	Pres.	94,795	19.4	82.4	Ronald Reagan
1980	Sen.	61,280	12.4	42.0	Mary Louise Foust
1983	Gov.	97,836	19.0	74.4	Jim Bunning
1984	Sen.	49,817	9.5	79.2	Mitch McConnell
1986	Sen.	41,592	7.5	39.0	Jackson Andrews
1987	Gov.	90,370	16.4	41.4	John Harper
1988	Pres.	121,644	22.0	59.6	George Bush

date in the general election. In 1984, for example, less than 10 percent of registered Republicans voted in the senatorial primary, but 69 percent of them went to the polls in the November election (though probably not all voting in the Senate race). In that general election race, McConnell received 246,000 more votes than the total registered Republicans who went to the polls.

The disparity between turnout in the primary and general elections also gives greater influence on the outcome of the primary to the areas of highest turnout. In the 1987 election, for example, the 29 counties with a majority of registered Republicans cast 44 percent of the vote in the gubernatorial primary but only 16 percent of the Republican vote in the general election. The four major metropolitan counties cast 37 percent of the Republican general election vote but only about one-fourth of the primary vote for governor.

In theory, the disparities in registration and turnout in Republican primaries should give an advantage to a candidate who runs well in the counties that have heavy turnout in the primaries. These counties might choose a candidate who had less political strength in the counties that had a larger vote in the general election. For example, primary voters in the strong Republican counties of the Fifth District might be able to select a candidate who was unable to appeal to potential Republican voters in the metropolitan counties and thus unable to be elected. In reality, this problem seldom arises, largely because so few statewide Republican primaries are seriously contested.

The most important close Republican primary in modern times was the 1967 gubernatorial race in which Louie Nunn defeated Marlow Cook by only 5,000 votes (two percentage points). Marlow Cook, county judge of Jefferson County, carried that county with 76 percent of the two-candidate vote (there was a minor third candidate); Louie Nunn won 62 percent in the rest of the state. Both Jefferson County and the most heavily Republican registered counties had larger proportions of the primary vote than of the general election vote. Nunn's weakness in Jefferson County did not prevent him from winning the general election.

In the 1987 primary we have noted that the turnout was low. Harper got half the vote in the four largest metropolitan counties and only 35 percent of the vote in the heavily Republican counties that had a disproportionately high turnout. While this disparity contributed to Harper's small margin, it did not prevent his being nominated.

In 1967 a total of 179,000 Republicans, about one-third of those registered, voted in the gubernatorial primary. Louie Nunn defeated Marlow Cook, 50.4 to 48.3 percent, and went on to win the election. At that time it was the third largest number for a Republican gubernatorial primary in history (the higher turnouts being in 1927 and 1939). Over the next five elections, the highest turnout in a gubernatorial primary was 132,000 (27.5 percent of party registration), and the average was 101,000 (20 percent of registration).

The major reason for this low turnout was a lack of close competition in the primary; in some races there was probably also a perception that none of the candidates stood a chance of winning in November. In 1971 Louie Nunn's handpicked candidate, Tom Emberton, had no difficulty winning 84 percent of the primary vote against three opponents. In 1975 Robert Gable won 54 percent of the vote against three opponents but was never perceived to have a good chance against incumbent Julian Carroll. In 1979 Louie Nunn easily won the nomination with 80 percent of the vote against three minor opponents. In 1983, despite his late entry into the race, Jim Bunning won three-fourths of the vote, which was ten times the vote of his closest opponent. The 1987 race was considerably closer; John Harper won 41 percent, compared to 25 percent for the second-place finisher. But none of the candidates were well known or generated enough interest to produce a higher turnout. After twenty years the Republican primary had still not produced another close contest between strong candidates.

Can the Republican Primary Be Revived?

Encouraging More Competition

The absence of close competition among serious candidates in gubernatorial primaries hurts the Republican party in several ways. The short-run effects are most obvious. During the primary campaign season, Democratic candidates dominate the media and gain public attention and name recognition. Because the primary campaign generates little interest, turnout in the primaries is low and is likely to be unrepresentative of Republican registered voters. Republican voters who have paid little attention to the campaign and have failed to vote in the primary have not developed any sense of commitment to a Republican candidate. Whoever wins the primary becomes the nominee without having been forced to test the effectiveness of his campaign skills and of his issues before large numbers of voters.

There are also some long-run implications. Because there is seldom serious competition in statewide Republican primaries, voters who identify with the Republican party have little incentive to register as Republicans and to get in the habit of primary voting—unless they live in one of the counties where local politics is dominated by the Republican party. Voters who have no strong commitment to either party, but are dissatisfied with the administration in office, tend to look for a candidate they can support in the Democratic primary rather than looking for a good Republican candidate.

There are, of course, some advantages to the Republican party in avoiding primary battles. The most obvious advantage is that the party avoids bitter primary fights that can divide the party and make it difficult to unite behind the victor and win the general election. The morning after Louie Nunn's bruising primary victory over Marlow Cook, the press analysis suggested that it would be very difficult for Nunn to reunify the party in time to win the November election; but he succeeded, thanks in part to a factional split in the Democratic party. Despite this example, it is highly possible that a divisive Republican primary could be damaging enough to undermine the prospects of a nominee who might otherwise be competitive.

A second and perhaps more serious problem is a financial one. Republican candidates for statewide office have had difficulty raising enough funds to compete effectively in the general elections (a problem we discuss in more detail below). These problems would be compounded by a competitive primary because the candidates would have to raise funds from the same types of persons, and often the same individuals, who would contribute to a general election campaign. Assume that it would cost a candidate $2 million to run a vigorous, closely contested race for the Republican nomination and $3 million to run such a race in the November election. If there were one strong candidate, uncontested in the primary, Republican fund-raisers would have to raise $3 million; if there were two strong Republican candidates, they would have to raise $4 million for the primary, making a total of $7 million. And if most of the available Republican sources were exhausted in the primary election, it might not be possible to raise enough money to beat the Democrats in the fall.

Most Republican leaders agree in theory that, despite the costs and risks, the Republican party would benefit from having competitive primaries for major office when there is no incumbent Republican running and when the party has some realistic prospect of winning the general election. They do not see any advantage in encouraging several weak candidates to run or in finding a primary challenger if one strong candidate is in the race.

In practice it is much more difficult to persuade two strong candidates to enter a race. In both 1983 and 1987, the party had difficulty recruiting one reasonably strong candidate. Bunning agreed to run in 1983 only after an extensive search had produced no other viable candidate; it is difficult to believe he would have agreed to battle for the nomination against a strong challenger. In 1987 Larry Forgy's somewhat reluctant campaign was based on the assumption that he would have no challenger in the primary; and when he dropped out, the party could not even produce one strong candidate as a replacement.

Expanding the Primary Electorate

All Republican leaders seem to agree on the necessity of increasing the number of Republicans who participate and who are eligible to participate in the primary. Obviously, the best way to get registered Republicans to participate and to encourage Republican registration is to have more competitive primaries. If Kentucky continues to hold presidential primaries, leaders hope that more voters will be persuaded to shift registration in order to vote in those contests. Some Republican leaders are also exploring a variety of ways to make more voters eligible to vote in Republican primaries. These would require a change in state law and/or party rules. Three changes have been suggested, moving from the simplest to the most drastic: (1) shortening the lead time required for changing party registration, (2) permitting independents to vote in Republican primaries, and (3) adopting open primaries.

State law provides that an individual who wants to change party registration in order to vote in a primary must make the change before the preceding general election. This means that a registered Democrat who wanted to vote in the May 1987 Republican primary had to change by early October 1986. Similarly, Democrats who wanted to support Pat Robertson in the March 1988 primary had to shift registration by October 1987. Voters are most likely to be attracted to the Republican primary by a candidate whom they particularly want to support; but by the time such a candidate files for office, it is too late for Democrats to change party registration.

In 1988 supporters of Pat Robertson who wanted to change party registration challenged the Kentucky law in federal court. The judge rejected their challenge, citing a U.S. Supreme Court decision upholding a New York law that set such a deadline. Republican legislators have tried in vain to get the Democratic majority in the legislature to reduce the lead time required for changing registration.

In 1966 the U.S. Supreme Court ruled (*Tashjian* v. *Republican Party of Connecticut*) that the Connecticut Republican party had the right to permit registered independents to vote in its primary despite a state law requiring that primary voters be registered with the party. Early in 1987 the Republican leaders in Kentucky debated the desirability of capitalizing on this decision and inviting independents into their party. But the executive committee of the state party was split down the middle on the question, and the proposal was dropped. Only 3 percent of registered voters are independents, but this is approximately 10 percent of Republican registration. If many of these decided to vote in a Republican primary, it might have a modest effect on the outcome. A decision by the Republican party to open the primary to independents might have a greater symbolic value, demonstrating that the Republican party is open to new voters. Independents who voted in the Republican primary might be more likely to vote for the party's candidates in November.

There appear to be several reasons why the Republican executive committee did not adopt a policy of permitting independents to participate in the primary. The number of voters registered as independents is too small to have any dramatic effect on the party's primary. Some Republicans in the Fifth District were apparently concerned that Republicans in their counties might shift their registration to independent, retaining the right to vote in the primary. Rural Republicans might also have recognized that their influence in the primary might be eroded by an influx of independents. Over 70 percent of the independent registrants are found in eight counties that are in or near metropolitan areas; in these counties the independents constitute 6 percent of total registration.

Most Republican leaders agree that the party would benefit much more from the adoption of an open primary law that would permit all registered voters to participate in either party's primary. Mitch McConnell, for example, has said that closed primaries are "the single biggst inhibiting factor to the growth of the Republican party in Kentucky." If primaries were open, in those years when the Republicans had more competitive primaries, voters who often support Republican candidates would be more likely to vote in the Republican primary. Such voters would presumably be more likely to support Republicans in November than if they had voted in the Democratic primary. Perhaps more important, in a competitive primary the choice would be made by a larger electorate, and the winner would be a candidate who should be better able to appeal to a broader range of voters in the general election. The same reasons that make Republicans enthusiastic about an open primary, of course, make Democratic legislators unwilling to adopt it.

While the argument that an open primary would help the Republican party is plausible, there are equally plausible arguments on the other side. Whether the primary is open or closed, the Republican primary will only attract substantial numbers of voters if and when it becomes competitive. In an open primary system, voters could cross over to the Republican primary when it offered interesting choices but could just as easily return to the Democratic primary in years when there were no significant Republican contests. If the Republican party consistently had important contests, a significant number of voters would probably shift registration in a closed system. Among the eleven southern states, only two, Florida and North Carolina, have closed primaries; but the Republican parties in those states have made as much progress in recent years as those in other southern states. In the period from 1965 to 1982, Florida and North Carolina ranked second and third among the southern states in the proportion of voters in gubernatorial primaries voting in the Republican primary (Jewell, 1984: 215).

The 1987 Republican Gubernatorial Primary

On May 26, 1987, John Harper won the Republican gubernatorial primary with 41 percent of the vote; he finished seventeen percentage points and 15,036 votes ahead of his nearest competitor, Joe E. Johnson III. State representative Harper defeated three opponents in a race that drew little enthusiasm among the state's Republicans. His opponents were Johnson, a former Fayette County judge; tractor-pull promoter Leonard "Buck" Beasley; and perennial candidate Thurman Jerome Hamlin.

Why were there so few Republican votes cast? Why was there so little interest and so much apathy in the race? Why did Larry Forgy, the party's all-but-anointed nominee, drop out of the race in early January 1987? Just six months before the primary, Forgy was expected to have an excellent chance of wresting the governor's office from the longtime domination of the Democrats. In an effort to answer these and other questions, we will examine the 1987 campaign in some detail: the candidates, their campaign strategies and resources, the development of issues, and the use of television.

The 1987 campaign deserves attention because it is one of the most unusual in recent years—finally a Republican candidate had a chance of beating the Democrats, yet he dropped out of the primary electoral battle. But it also deserves attention because in many ways it is typical, in its last five months, of recent Republican gubernatorial primaries—low turnout, minimal campaign funds expended, and very limited use of television and radio advertising. The last five months of the Republican gubernatorial primary were in stark contrast to those of the Democratic counterpart (discussed in detail in chapter 4). The three top GOP gubernatorial hopefuls spent less than 1 percent of the $12 million spent by the five major Democratic hopefuls. Unlike the costly, exciting Democratic primary, the Republican campaign did not begin in earnest until May 1987.

The Candidate Who Withdrew from the Race

Larry Forgy, aged forty-seven, was a Republican loyalist who began working in politics at age sixteen in his native Logan County, where he grew up in a family of "blue-belly Republicans." Forgy received a B.A. and law degree from the University of Kentucky. He became a partner in a Louisville law firm and also developed coal business interests. He moved to Lexington in the late 1970s, partly to broaden his exposure to more Kentuckians.

For years Forgy "carried the presumption that some day he would run for governor and quite possibly be elected. . . . Some of Kentucky's most powerful political figures were his patrons. He was, as one Republican observed, almost the surrogate son of such influential Kentuckians as former U.S. Senator John Sherman Cooper and former Governors Louie B. Nunn and Bert Combs." He served in Nunn's administration as state budget director and was a partner in Wyatt, Tarrant & Combs law firm. His political and legal affiliations placed him close to Kentucky's powerful coal and tobacco interests; and twice he had managed Ronald Reagan's presidential campaigns in Kentucky (*C-J,* January 18, 1987, p. D1).

Forgy was, in short, a real possibility to be governor, a phenomenon not known by Republicans in Kentucky for twenty years. He had started early enough, had an appeal that "crossed party lines in urban and rural areas alike," and had a style agreeable to reporters and editorialists. He seemed in a position to engage any of the Democratic candidates who were well known at the time. "Former Governor Julian Carroll would be easy pickings . . . because of his exposure to a federal grand jury investigation. Parts of Lieutenant Governor Steve Beshear's record as a legislator and attorney general might put him at risk if he were the Democratic nominee. A John Y. Brown victory would leave the party divided and allow Forgy to reap a harvest of dissident Democrats" (*C-J,* January 11, 1987, pp. A1, A12).

Forgy launched his campaign in the fall of 1985 and began spending most of his time raising money. He expected to raise far more than the $1.5 million that Bunning did in 1983. No primary opposition surfaced for him, although in the early stages Sixth District congressman Larry Hopkins refused to rule himself out of the gubernatorial race. By January 1987 Forgy had raised almost $750,000—from individuals (e.g., attorneys, coal industry executives, doctors, business executives, etc.) and PACs (e.g., banking interests, law firms, tobacco groups, horse interests, etc.). Most of the contributions came from within the state—from both Democrats and Republicans. Moreover, it was generally acknowledged that Forgy would be able to count on large contributions from major Republican donors outside Kentucky because of his close relationship with the Reagan forces.

In announcing his surprise decision to withdraw from the race in January, "Forgy said that after having spent more than 20 years in politics, working for other candidates and causes, he found it difficult to do for himself what he had done for others. He found himself unwilling to make personal sacrifices and compromises; fund-raising was especially distasteful. He told some people that he had made the greatest mistake of his life by entering the campaign" (*C-J,* January 18, 1987, p. D1).

"Politicians in both parties were skeptical that Forgy, a veteran of 30 years in politics, pulled out solely because of his distaste for the campaign, especially the fund-raising side of it. Almost unanimously, they felt his decision was prompted by the precipitous decline in President Reagan's popularity in the wake of the Iran-Contra affair. . . . Forgy stuck to his contention that he found he did not have the stomach for the burdens of his first race and his role as his own major fund-raiser. . . . He also said he was troubled by the need to keep silent about what he said are Kentucky's critical budget and revenue problems: "How do you campaign across the state and be frank about that without committing political suicide?" [*C-J,* January 11, 1987, p. A14]

According to political writer Bob Johnson, "Given Forgy's knowledge of politics and government, it is inexplicable that he could play the role of governor-in-waiting for as long as he did and go all the way to the starting gate before scratching himself from the race" (*C-J,* January 18, 1987, p. D1).

Almost one year after his startling withdrawal, Forgy acknowledged that he was on the brink of setting up a "laundering operation" to conceal large illicit cash contributions when he decided in January to drop out of the race instead. "I was confronted with a fundamental decision of whether I would continue to operate as I had been . . . or whether I was going to have operatives in the 'black-bag sense.' And I decided that simply wasn't for me." Forgy estimated that he rejected $200,000 or more in cash (*H-L,* October 17, 1987, pp. B1, B10).

The Last-Minute Candidates

When Forgy shocked the state with his decision not to run, Republican party leaders made brave statements about finding someone to fill the void in the seven weeks before the February 25 filing deadline. The best Republican prospects had already assessed the odds and rejected the opportunity. With Forgy on the bench, the 1987 gubernatorial race looked like the start of another of Kentucky's political mismatches. Democrats had every reason to expect that the winner of the May gubernatorial primary would sweep past nominal Republican opposition in November. Four loyal Republicans came forth, for various reasons, to seek the state's highest office.

John Harper, born in Chicago in 1931, spent most of his boyhood in Louisville, where his family owned a construction business. After two years at the University of Louisville and service in the air force, he returned to Louisville after his father's death to take charge of the family business, which was sold four years later. After establishing his own engineering and manufacturing firm in Chicago in 1956, Harper set up a second household in the mid-1960s in Bullitt County on what had been the farm of his wife's grandmother. In 1976 he sold his business and returned to his Kentucky farm. Harper, a practicing engineer, a licensed towboat operator, a part-time sod farmer, and an amateur historian, has traveled the world to supervise the installation of the equipment he designed as an engineer.

In 1952 Harper became involved in Eisenhower's campaign by walking into a GOP office in Louisville and offering to help; he was named a precinct captain and began going door-to-door. People in Bullitt County, which is overwhelmingly Democratic, watched Harper revive and take charge of the local Republican party in the late 1970s. He lost his first bid for elected office in 1981, when he ran for Bullitt county judge executive. In 1984 he was elected state representative over an incumbent Democrat, becoming Bullitt County's first Republican legislator despite the 7 to 1 Democratic registration advantage. As a legislator, Harper was responsive to local people but made few legislative waves (*C-J,* March 15, 1987, pp. D1, D4).

Joe E. Johnson III attended first the University of Virginia and then the University of Kentucky, where he received his B.A. and law degrees; then he returned to Perry County to take over the family coal business. His feuds with roving union pickets were well publicized at the time. Johnson finally moved back to Lexington, and in 1963 he and two other young Republicans swept three of four Fayette County seats in the state House, where he served one term. Johnson headed Barry Goldwater's 1964 presidential campaign in Kentucky and a year later won the Fayette County judgeship. During his four-year term, he clashed with the University of Kentucky over its purchase of Maine Chance Farm, conducted a court of inquiry that led to the indictment of two local officials on bribery charges, and tangled with the Lexington newspapers and the late financier Garvice D. Kinkaid, among others. Johnson was defeated for reelection in 1969 by Robert Stephens, now the chief justice of the state Supreme Court. Since then, he has been practicing law and tending to his coal and thoroughbred business interests.

In January 1987, after Forgy's withdrawal, Johnson broke his self-imposed political exile to assure a Republican primary. "I wasn't even thinking about it," Johnson said in an interview, "until Forgy said he wouldn't run and I saw all those Republicans on television saying that there was no hope for the Republican Party because Forgy didn't run. I think we really need a primary to rejuvenate the party" (*C-J,* March 22, 1987, pp. D1, D4).

During the very low-key campaign, the fifty-seven-year-old Lexington native espoused a simple message: The state's problems are tied to a chain of Democratic administrations that have spent the state into massive financial problems. Johnson ran a lackluster campaign; because of business financial woes, he had to devote his major energies to keeping the Kentucky Horse Center (a corporation in which he was the major stockholder) solvent. Johnson, who placed second, reported $26,141 in spending. His major contributors included friends in the coal and horse industries. His campaign emphasized direct mail. He did not use television, and his only radio advertising was targeted spots on stations in London and Hazard.

Leonard "Buck" Beasley, age forty-three, a native of Louisville, studied engineering and political science at the University of Louisville for about eighteen months, finally dropping out because work and service in the Kentucky National Guard took up too much time. Over the years he has been successful in several careers—from selling insurance to running the Kentucky Farm Machinery Show in Louisville. Residing in Washington County, he currently operates a convenience store and a small thoroughbred horse farm that complements Pro Shows, Inc., which promotes tractor pulls across the nation.

The political newcomer did not jump into the 1987 race until Larry Forgy dropped out. Polls indicated, from the start, that Beasley's bid was a long shot. In a *Courier-Journal* poll in March 1987, none of the Republican voters surveyed supported Beasley; Harper and Johnson each received support from 14 percent of those polled. But 71 percent of the voters were undecided, and it was this group that Beasley thought he could capture through personal appearances across the state and a few television commercials. The affable tractor-pull promoter felt that his work on past campaigns, his diverse business experience, and his ability to understand all types of people would be enough to win the nomination.

Beasley believes the state should spend more money promoting its businesses, its farms, and its tourist attractions in other states. He proposed building an $80 million domed stadium to attract entertainment events to Kentucky to raise money; the stadium would be built with private dollars and leased to the state. Beasley, who finished third, just 1,229 votes behind Johnson, spent $13,559; he received very few outside contributions. He lent his campaign $12,880, none of which was repaid. Since he is familiar with broadcast advertising, he made more use of the medium than his opponents, running some television spots and radio commercials (*C-J*, April 12, 1987, pp. B1, B7).

Thurman Jerome Hamlin, of London, Kentucky, has run for public office every year except one since 1951. The perennial candidate finished last, with less than 10,000 votes. The former educator had a memorable slogan, urging voters to "vote for Hamlin before Hamlin dies." During his very limited campaign, he stressed that he supported raises for teachers but opposed raising taxes.

The Harper Campaign

Like Joe Johnson, John Harper entered the race early in January 1987, and he also had no illusions. He did not really expect to become governor of Kentucky, nor did he have great hopes for the GOP after Forgy's withdrawal. He focused on the long-range goal of ending Democratic domination of Kentucky politics: "You've got to do what you can—spread the gospel that there is an alternative." Harper said he did not enter the race "as a sacrificial lamb or with reluctance, but to get into it enthusiastically. There was no reluctance whatsoever." He said "his decision arose from a flash of inspiration, a sense of duty, and a belief in his own ability." His candidacy was viewed by Republicans with a certain amount of skepticism (*H-L*, March 8, 1987, pp. A1, A12).

His campaign staff was skeletal, consisting of a paid consultant, his wife, who is an elementary schoolteacher and his "guiding light," and several volunteers. Harper drove himself wherever he went. And he went just about everywhere during the primary, to Lincoln Day dinners across the state, to shopping malls, and to school campuses.

Harper campaigned much the same way he conducts himself as a state representative—he "gets to the point." At political forums he never wandered from his script, nor was the script typically political. Instead of generalities, he read from or stayed close to his prepared position papers. At informal gatherings Harper reflected his measured approach, often explaining that he feared that he might embarrass himself, his family, or his party. He kissed no babies and slapped no backs, literally or figuratively; "yet Harper undertook the task of campaigning with a sense of humor that offsets his serious demeanor." For people who read about politics, who talked about it every day, he provided an image to respect and enjoy. But the apathy of the voter was very real in the 1987 primary, and Harper was not very good at whipping up emotions among primary voters (*H-L,* March 8, 1987, p. A12).

Harper tried, with limited success, to set up local organizations. He was successful in his organization-building efforts in about twenty to twenty-five counties, mostly urban and Fifth District counties. But there were some Fifth District counties that clearly were not going to support him—Perry, Clay, and a few others; he was told that these counties had already been bought and sold. Organizational efforts were also undertaken in certain areas of western Kentucky—Owensboro, Bowling Green, Glasgow; he did not try to build a strong base in Paducah. He visited Somerset a dozen times and campaigned somewhat in northern Kentucky. Harper targeted the Louisville area since he had previously been a resident of Jefferson County for a long time; Bullitt County is just on the edge of Jefferson County. Harper's candidacy was helped by the support of top Republican officials in Jefferson County. Although he tried to get some minority votes, he was never able to crack the west end vote in Jefferson County. And he claimed the support of most of the state's Republican representatives and senators.

None of the GOP gubernatorial candidates wanted to spend much money in the primary because they were saving what little they had largely for the general election. Harper reported spending the most of the GOP final competitors—$33,265; he lent his campaign $13,000, then converted it to a donation to close out the books for his successful primary-election effort. His major expenses were for a direct mail campaign and limited television advertising. In the last two weeks when he was running in a dead heat with Johnson and Beasley, he began targeting mailings to Republican voters and used a few television advertisements. Free media attention was good in the Lexington area, but the Louisville media paid little or no attention to the Republican gubernatorial primary race, probably because of the assumption that the Republican candidate was doomed.

Just nine days before the May primary, the three top Republican candidates were locked in tie for the lead, with the majority of voters undecided and little interest generated by the race. Although some Republican county officials saw Harper as the likely nominee, they all agreed that none of the candidates had a stranglehold on the nomination and that any one of them could emerge the winner. Harper and Johnson early on were considered the major candidates, but Beasley made surprising advances, especially with the assistance of a statewide television campaign. All the GOP candidates' races began late and were hampered by a shortage of money and interest. On May 26, 1987, John Harper emerged the Republican gubernatorial nominee after a very lackluster contest.

The 1987 Gubernatorial General Election

On November 3, 1987, Democrat Wallace Wilkinson trounced Republican John Harper, winning the governorship by a record margin of 65 to 35 percent. The previous record was set by former governor Julian Carroll, who got 62.8 percent in 1975. About 40 percent of the state's 1.9 million registered voters—about 777,000 people—went to the polls, one of the lowest turnouts in decades. Voter turnout was lower than the 1,041,649 votes cast in the 1983 governor's race and the 958,158 cast in 1979. In fact, it was the lowest percentage of the voting-age population cast for a governor's race in this century. Twice as many voters stayed at home as voted for Wilkinson. Although Wilkinson carried 115 of the state's 120 counties, compared with the 90 former governor Martha Layne Collins won in 1983, he lost in Fayette County, where he lives. Wilkinson blamed his poor showing there on "negative press."

Wilkinson's support was strongest in rural areas, where he received 69 percent of the vote, compared to 59 percent in urban areas across the state. Wilkinson did well in western Kentucky and in the traditionally Republican Fifth Congressional District, his boyhood home. His largest margin of victory was in the First Congressional District of far western Kentucky, where he polled about 76 percent of the vote. He carried the Fifth Congressional District with 62 percent. In counties with a heavily Democratic registration, Wilkinson received about 81 percent of the vote. In counties with a heavy Republican registration, he received 59 percent. Wilkinson received a record percentage of the vote obviously because Harper did not draw the traditional Republican support (*H-L,* November 4, 1987, pp. A1, A16).

In the primary and general election, Wilkinson raised about $6 million and spent nearly all of it; in contrast, Harper raised and spent about $250,000. For every dollar Harper raised since the primary, Wilkinson had raised at least $40. Money alone was not the only difference: Wilkinson brought to the campaign enormous energy and an incredible work ethic. He was tireless in pressing his antiestablishment themes, particularly in the smaller, rural counties. During the primary and general election campaigns, he had visited every county seeking out voters, talking to and touching them. Wilkinson also developed other themes, notably promoting a state lottery, a proposal that gave credibility to his pledge to raise no taxes while spending the money required to bring economic development, jobs and wealth, to town after town across a frustrated state. As election day approached, Wilkinson called on supporters to help him fight one more battle against the political establishment in Frankfort. His appeal in the Republican Fifth District, his home region, was particularly direct. In speeches there he told crowds that their time had come and that "a 5th District boy" was going to Frankfort to run the state (*H-L*, November 4, 1987, pp. A1, A11).

Above all, Wilkinson had money; and money produced consultants, commercials, computers—and the staff to implement decisions and penetrate the public consciousness from one end of the state to the other. There was also "the presumption of inevitable success that usually comes with winning the Democratic gubernatorial nomination in Kentucky." In contrast, Harper had only his position papers, his own energies, and those of the hard-core Republican party. He did not have the funds to compete in any way with Wilkinson; and the Republican party did not deliver him an organization or any conduit to the voters. Nor did the GOP offer Harper any enthusiasm, hope, or concern. Throughout the general election, the polls never changed; from beginning to end, Wilkinson dominated the race (*C-J*, October 11, 1987, p. D1).

Harper tried to conduct a statewide campaign on the thinnest of shoestrings and without any experience in running a modern statewide campaign. Lacking Wilkinson's helicopters and campaign buses, Harper drove himself from stop to stop in a black Oldsmobile. Because he had no alternative, he tried to sell himself to voters at retail, reaching them in small groups. But the game is won by making the sale in wholesale lots.

Harper's campaign management style involved getting the most done with the fewest people at the least cost. His shoestring budget dictated a much smaller staff than Wilkinson's. Most of his help and advice came from friends and interested Republicans in addition to those who joined after he won the primary. Like Wilkinson, the Republican nominee depended on his staff to organize his campaign, deal with the news media, and handle day-to-day tasks that the candidate cannot do while keeping a hectic travel schedule. Harper depended mainly on the help of four people who made up the core staff in his campaign: Bob Rowland, Jon Ackerson, Carolyn Davis, and Helen Kendall.

After experimenting unsuccessfully with other consultants, the Republican nominee found among his primary campaign group a good, trusting "quasi campaign manager"—Bob Rowland—who was employed in the minority leadership office of the legislature. Rowland was among the first to ask Harper to replace Forgy in the Republican gubernatorial primary, and he was involved with Harper's campaign from the beginning. Harper and Rowland, who had no statewide campaign experience, worked well together; Rowland was sensible, helpful, understood what was happening, and knew how to treat the press. Rowland spent four days a week helping to run the Louisville campaign office and three days on the road with Harper. The candidate attributes any campaign successes to Rowland's efforts. Another key member of Harper's original support base was state representative Jon Ackerson from Louisville. Ackerson was a volunteer with several roles—general campaign adviser, Jefferson County chairman, chair of the statewide group of campaign advisers, and negotiator for the two televised debate formats.

Another valuable Harper staffer was Carolyn Davis, the statewide campaign coordinator. Davis did not get involved in the Harper campaign until the primary election victory because of her position as executive director of the Jefferson County Republican party. Davis helped coordinate mass mailings, scheduling, volunteer activities, and office management in the state headquarters in Louisville. A former chairperson of the Fayette County Republicans, Helen Kendall was in charge of Harper's central Kentucky headquarters. Kendall has been active in Republican party politics at the state level for years and in 1984 was the state executive director of the Reagan-Bush campaign (*H-L*, October 11, 1987, pp. E1, E3, E8).

After his primary win, Harper was told by the Republican state chairman that the agenda of the state party was not necessarily the same as Harper's. The message was that the state party had to be there permanently, while candidates come and go. Harper was informed that he needed the expert advice of Washington consultants, and several were produced. He was reluctantly given $6,000, voted on by the executive committee of the Republican Party of Kentucky (RPK). There would be two separate payments—$5,400 at first and another $600 once he produced his contributors' list. A condition was placed on the money—it had to be used to engage a consultant selected by the RPK, at a rate of $1,000 a day. According to Harper the consultant afforded him no assistance and spent his time serving the needs of the state party headquarters. Consequently, after the first month, Harper terminated the arrangement with this consultant.

Harper found that the Republican state party headquarters was often more of an obstacle to him than an asset. On the same day that he held a major press conference on his economic development plans, for example, Harper was upstaged by state party chair Gable who decided to launch a personal attack on Wilkinson. The RPK gave Harper only a partial financial contributors' list, which he did not think contained the best prospects. (In contrast, Forgy provided him with a complete list.) Harper was also upset because during his campaign the state party used his name to raise funds for its own needs. Unfortunately, Harper did not discover what was happening until his organization began to call these contributors and found that they thought they had already contributed to Harper's candidacy.

Of course, during the gubernatorial race, Representative Hopkins, Senator McConnell, Vice-President Bush, and other Republicans were raising money for their electoral pursuits. Congressman Bunning refused to assist in Harper's campaign because of Harper's stand against the lottery, which Bunning had endorsed in his 1983 campaign for governor. Former governor Nunn was the only major leader who worked hard for Harper; Nunn toured the Fifth District with Harper and was very insightful.

Sen. Robert Dole campaigned for Harper a couple of times in Kentucky, and Harper subsequently supported Dole in his presidential campaign in the state, which was rather abortive. At the state GOP picnic in August 1987, with 400 Republicans in attendance, Harper received support from several prominent Republicans, including Dole, Republican national chairman Frank Fahrenkopf, former U.S. senator John Sherman Cooper, and Louie Nunn. State party chair Robert Gable used the occasion to assail Democratic nominee Wilkinson's character and integrity.

Harper was impressed by the effectiveness of many of the local party organizations during his general election contest. About two-thirds of the county groups were fairly active; Harper's group could contact them, and they would get things set up for Harper's campaign visit to their counties. Even in some counties that are heavily Democratic, the local Republican groups were responsive to Harper's candidacy. Local election headquarters were established, voter education and registration drives were conducted, in county after county. Harper especially commended the local party groups in the lower tier of counties near Tennessee for their strong campaign efforts on his behalf.

Harper found that campaigning in the Fifth, Seventh, and even lower Second congressional districts was quite an experience; it was totally foreign to what he had been accustomed. In a number of the counties, local political leaders asked him, "How much walking-around money have you got?" When Harper told them that he did not do that, they told him that he could forget their counties.

Harper's utilization of paid media was in direct contrast to that of Wilkinson's. The Republican nominee was able to purchase much less television time, and he clearly did not have top professional assistance in preparation of his few political commercials. As in the primary, Wilkinson's expert consultants produced a plethora of sophisticated, well-targeted television and radio spots during the general election contest. Harper paid slightly more than $20,000 for television ads that were aired just before the election, whereas Wilkinson paid more than $100,000 for ads that were on the air by the end of September. Harper's low-budget campaign relied on polling and media assistance from the Republican National Committee.

Although Harper received few endorsements and meager campaign funds, the political arm of the Kentucky Education Association (KEA), which represents more than 30,000 teachers statewide, contributed $35,000 to his struggling campaign. Harper became the first Republican gubernatorial candidate in history to be endorsed by the KEA. David Allen, KEA's president and the chairman of KEPAC, said the size of the contribution reflected "a sincere commitment" to Harper's candidacy and "a definite desire to fully work toward the man's election." KEA was most unhappy with Democrat Wilkinson, who, unike Harper, said he felt no obligation to finance previous education programs. The 1985 education package largely favored teachers with higher salaries, bonuses for experienced teachers, smaller classes, and teacher aides. Wilkinson also angered KEPAC members by not meeting with them for an endorsement interview (*C-J,* September 27, 1987, p. B1).

Upon receiving the endorsement of the 190,000-member AFL-CIO, the state's largest labor organization, Wilkinson claimed that the labor group's support was "six times more important" than the KEA's. Harper, a longtime friend of labor in the General Assembly, had tried to capture the AFL-CIO endorsement for himself. The Democrat nominee had earlier received the support of the state's United Mine Workers, United Auto Workers, and the Teamsters Union (*H-L,* October 4, 1987, p. B1).

The Debates

It became obvious to Harper in the last few months that there was a tide rolling in Wilkinson's favor that could not be stopped. Harper considered the use of television debates to be valuable because debates would put both candidates on an equal footing. In August Harper recommended six debates throughout the state. In contrast, Wilkinson wanted two debates—one in eastern Kentucky and one in western Kentucky. Wilkinson was reluctant to hold debates because he wanted to attract as little attention as possible; this would be the only vehicle by which Harper could get an equal arena to play on. It was finally agreed that there would be two debates, one in Owensboro and one in Richmond.

During the first sit-down debate held in Owensboro on October 4, the candidates sparred over the lottery and finances. Harper accused Wilkinson of trying to dupe the public with his claims about a lottery as "the panacea to all ills" and the alternative to more taxes. He asserted that the lottery is a regressive tax because poor people spend proportionately more of their income on lottery tickets. Harper claimed that Wilkinson was overestimating the money a lottery would produce. In rebuttal, Wilkinson continued to maintain that the lottery was one way to pay for state services—that it would bring in $70 million. During the hour-long, often confrontational exchange, Harper tried to demonstrate his knowledge of state affairs and legislative activities.

Wilkinson emphasized the theme that he would not raise taxes, while saying that Harper would. The Democratic nominee said state conformity to the new federal tax code, which Harper supports, would amount to a tax increase. Harper asserted that he had talked to legislative budget leaders and considered conformity one way to tackle the state's expected $450 million budget shortfall.

Wilkinson also disagreed with Harper concerning large incentive packages to lure new businesses to Kentucky, such as the one given to Toyota ($125 million incentive package). Wilkinson claimed that he favored instead "county-by-county economic development." Harper replied that the Collins administration ought to be commended for attracting Toyota Motor Corporation to Scott County because it meant 2,000 to 3,000 jobs at the plant and as many as 10,000 others at satellite industries.

During a question-and-answer period, the candidates attacked each other for conducting negative personal campaigns. Wilkinson said that in recent weeks Harper had called him "a Nazi," "a little weasel," and "sleazy." Harper denied using the first epithet, apologized for the second, and reiterated the "sleazy" description; he charged Wilkinson and his campaign with slandering his family (*H-L*, October 5, 1987, pp. A1, A15).

On October 19 in Richmond, the second televised debate was held. Harper gained in a hard-won agreement that the second debate be a stand-up one (Harper is a much larger man than Wilkinson). When he found that one of the podiums had been placed closer to the cameras and was apparently intended for Wilkinson, Harper got to the auditorium first and claimed that podim so that the camera angles would increase, rather than decrease, the apparent differences in size.

In the second debate the candidates repeated many of the points they had made in the first. Both candidates agreed on the necessity of reforms in election practices. They clashed over Wilkinson's release of income tax records. The high point, or low point, of the debate occurred when Harper refused to retract his assertion that Wilkinson was a "wild card" who would "pluck the state clean like a chicken."

The Development of Issues

During the general election campaign, the Republican nominee released platforms dealing with education, transportation, tourism, and economic development; periodic press conferences gained his program some attention in the free media. The Harper and Wilkinson campaigns tackled the same themes but took different approaches to them. Most notable was Wilkinson's proposal for a constitutional amendment that would allow the establishment of a state lottery. Wilkinson presented the lottery as an alternative to taxes for raising $70 million a year for education and senior citizens. Harper called it "Wallace in Wonderland economics," but he did not object to putting a lottery amendment on the November 1988 ballot. Harper favored applying the provisions of the new federal income tax code to state tax law; it would reduce or eliminate many state income tax deductions. In contrast, Wilkinson was adamantly opposed to adopting the federal code.

Harper and Wilkinson differed sharply over financing and improving Kentucky's impoverished schools. Wilkinson angered education advocates and state legislators by declaring that he would not commit himself to preserving the education programs enacted in the 1985 and 1986 sessions of the General Assembly. In contrast, Harper promised to keep most of these programs. Harper refused to rule out a tax increase to help education; Wilkinson offered the lottery as an alternative to higher taxes. Wilkinson's innovative educational plan included spending $5 million each year on fifteen "benchmark schools" across the state where new methods could be implemented. Wilkinson also proposed a $70-million-a-year incentive fund to reward individual schools for improvement, rather than focusing on teacher evaluations and teacher merit pay. Harper described his education priorities as preventing dropouts, continuing reductions in class size, attracting and retaining good teachers, and providing free textbooks. Both Harper and Wilkinson agreed they would protect higher education from cuts when it came time to deal with the state's revenue shortfall (*C-J,* October 19, 1987, pp. A1, A15).

A Question of Money

Have Republican gubernatorial candidates been losing elections because they cannot raise enough money? Or are they unable to raise enough money to be competitive because they are widely perceived as having little or no chance of winning elections? The answer to both questions might appear to be yes, but in reality the answer is more complicated. In 1979 Democrat John Y. Brown outspent Republican Louie Nunn by a 3 to 2 margin and won almost 60 percent of the vote. In 1983 Martha Layne Collins outspent Jim Bunning by only about $30,000 and won about 55 percent of the vote. In 1987 Wallace Wilkinson outspent John Harper by a margin of over 10 to 1 and won 65 percent of the vote.

It can be argued that a Republican gubernatorial candidate actually needs to outspend a Democrat in order to overcome other factors, including the Democratic advantage in registration and the assistance often provided to Democratic candidates by the incumbent administration. A better argument is that a comparison of spending ought to take into account the primary election. Most of the money spent by candidates in both primaries and general elections—whether it is on various forms of advertising, the cost of personal campaigning, or the expenses of staff and consultants—has the effect, directly or indirectly, of creating identification and an image for the candidates. To put it more simply, a candidate must spend money to become well known.

When the primary campaign is over, the Democratic nominee is usually much better known than the Republican because he or she has spent much more money. The Democrat is more successful in raising large amounts of money and must do so in order to win the primary. The Republican nominee has frequently faced only limited primary opposition, has had fewer sources of campaign funds, and has often hoarded these funds for the fall campaign. If we combine primary and general election spending for the Democratic and Republican gubernatorial nominees, we find that in both 1979 and 1983 the Democratic candidate outspent the Republican by roughly a 7 to 3 margin; and in 1987 Wilkinson outspent Harper by about 25 to 1.

In both the 1979 and 1983 races, the Republican gubernatorial candidates were perceived as underdogs but not hopeless underdogs. Nunn was a former governor, while Brown's political strength was hard to predict. Bunning was taken seriously, despite his late start, because the Democratic race had been very close and there were doubts about the electorate's willingness to vote for a woman. For these reasons the Republican candidates were able to raise enough funds to buy a substantial amount of advertising and appear competitive. If the Republican candidate in either of these races had been able to spend another half million dollars, the race might have been closer, although it seems likely that both Brown and Collins would have been able to match that increase if necessary.

The case of John Harper's campaign in 1987 is very different. Harper entered the race in January after Larry Forgy's unexpected withdrawal, and he had to defeat three other candidates to reach the November election. It is obvious that Republican fund-raisers and contributors did not believe that Harper had a serious chance of winning, and thus they did not raise and contribute enough money to enable Harper to run a competitive campaign. He had only a quarter of a million dollars to spend for his campaign, far less than would be necessary to run even a modest television advertising campaign. There is no way of telling whether the result would have been much closer if Harper had had a million dollars at his disposal. He was relatively unknown, with a minimum of political experience, and without personal magnetism; thus, it was unlikely that he could have beaten Wilkinson or even come very close if the financial playing field had been level. But it is certain that Harper had no realistic chance in part because he lacked the funds needed to buy enough advertising to overcome his obscurity and to present himself to the voters of Kentucky.

How difficult is it for Republicans to raise the sums of money necessary for statewide campaigns? Republicans who have played leading roles in statewide races give contradictory answers. Some Republicans claim that their party faces an especially heavy burden in raising funds, particularly for a governor's race, because they are in the minority. They argue that many business and professional people who can afford to make substantial contributions and who are sympathetic to the Republicans do not give because they fear retaliation from a Democratic administration in Frankfort. They would be unable to do business with the state, or their businesses would suffer from unusually strict regulation.

Robert Gable, the Republican party chairman, has publicly asserted that the laws on public disclosure of the names of campaign contributors (giving over $300) damage the competitive political system. These laws "in effect, are steps toward totalitarianism in that they give a powerful chief executive a list of enemies, or at least his opponents. . . . If you fear that the present governor or the likely governor may be vindictive, you may fear to give money to his opponent" (*H-L*, March 8, 1987). He argues that a large number of potential donors work in businesses or professions that are affected by state government. He asserts, for example, that most lawyers work in law firms where at least one lawyer has a personal service contract or represents a client whose firm is doing business with or is regulated by the state. Coal operators may be hurt economically if it takes an unreasonably long time to get a permit from the state.

Republican fund-raisers have found that some potential donors are willing to make large, anonymous (and thus illegal) contributions in cash but only small contributions in checks. If this is a widespread practice (and it is impossible to confirm), it would support the argument that many persons are intimiated by the possibility of retaliation from a Republican administration.

When Larry Forgy suddenly dropped out of the 1987 race for governor, he gave as one of his reasons the difficulty he would face in trying to raise the $3 to $4 million necessary for a race, after having spent a year raising less than $1 million. Some observers thought that Forgy was discouraged by the demands of various kinds made on him by those whose contributions he was soliciting. Gable has said that many persons wanted to know how they could contribute to the Forgy campaign without its being reported, despite the fact that Forgy was perceived as a plausible winner and Martha Layne Collins was not perceived as being a vindictive governor (*H-L*, June 14, 1987, p. 81).

There are other experienced Republicans who deny that fund-raising is a fundamental obstacle to Republican success in a statewide race. One leader said, "There is plenty of money out there if you know how to raise it." He argued that large sums could be raised in relatively small amounts by using mass-mailing techniques. One Republican leader who is sometimes mentioned as a possible gubernatorial candidate said that he would have no difficulty in raising $4 or $5 million if he got an early start. In his view, "A good Republican candidate who is perceived by potential donors as good can raise all the money that is needed for a race." He also made the interesting argument that fund-raising by Republican congressmen does not really compete with gubernatorial fund-raising because potential contributors to the latter effort have different motivations.

In our discussion of campaign financing (chapter 8), we demonstrated that a large proportion of funding for a gubernatorial race comes from business and professional persons who hope to benefit directly from contributing to the wnning candidate. Such persons have no particular interest in the ideology, the issue positions, or the party affiliation of the candidates; but they do not want to waste money on a loser. Obviously, there are loyal Republican donors who want to see a Republican elected governor, but much of the funding for a gubernatorial campaign must come from persons who are betting that they have chosen a winner.

This line of argument leads us inescapably to the conclusion that Republican gubernatorial candidates will be able to raise adequate funds for a gubernatorial race only when and if they are widely perceived to be potential winners. It is equally obvious that one of the best ways a candidate can demonstrate that potential is to prove that he or she can raise funds. One of the great ironies of Larry Forgy's abortive campaign was that he was widely perceived as a potential winner, but he concluded that he was unable or unwilling to raise enough funds to be a credible candidate.

Is There a Strategy for Republican Success?

Most party leaders have a prescription for achieving Republican success in state elections. Their suggestions differ, and some seem to be incompatible. Some we would judge to be more promising and realistic than others.

One veteran participant-observer in Republican politics, when asked "How do you turn things around?" replied simply, "Candidates turn things around." You need a candidate with enough "fire in the belly" to run, to recruit supporters, and to raise money. It is argued that this is the way the party has won congressional and senatorial elections, by finding a strong candidate who was willing to make the commitment to a vigorous campaign.

What should be the role of the party in recruiting good candidates? A frequent answer to the question is that the party should be developing and encouraging promising candidates early in their careers. Someone suggested that the Republican party should develop an inventory of potential candidates, for races at all levels in all of the counties, and then should provide more encouragement and assistance to them. The Republican party in recent years has lacked the resources and often the determination to carry out such efforts. But a Republican party operating under a Republican governor should have not only more resources but more incentive.

Some Republicans emphasize that an effective party organization should be able to recruit and develop strong candidates; others insist that the first step must be the emergence of a strong candidate, who can build his or her own campaign, raise enough money, get elected, and then help to build a strong party organization. This debate often has all the characteristics of a chicken-and-egg controversy.

But the issue is a serious and a difficult one. A Republican candidate capable of being elected governor might come from one of two sources. A wealthy, charismatic businessman (a Republican John Y. Brown) might appear on the scene and be able to win election with little help from the party organization. The alternative would be a candidate who had gained experience, visibility, and credibility as an officeholder at other levels (as Mitch McConnell and Larry Hopkins did). The better organized the state party is, the more help it can give to the second kind of candidate. Moreover, if the state party gave greater priority to the nurturing of good candidates at the lower levels, there would be a greater supply of potential gubernatorial candidates. Either approach is a plausible way to win the governorship, and neither one has been successful in recent years.

There is evidence from other states that the key to rebuilding a minority party is often one or two strong, successful candidates. In the 1950s Edmund Muskie revitalized the Democratic party in Maine, and Hubert Humphrey did the same in Minnesota. More recently, in southern states Jesse Helms boosted (but also divided) the North Carolina Republican party; William Brock, Howard Baker and Lamar Alexander breathed life into the Tennessee Republicans; and Strom Thurmond (by conversion) personified the new Republican party in South Carolina.

The strongest, most durable Republican officeholder in Kentucky in modern times was John Sherman Cooper, who was senator (with some interruptions) from 1947 to 1972. But Cooper was a highly independent senator and an unorthodox Republican, qualities that enabled him to win Democratic and independent voters. But Cooper was never governor, though he often toyed with the idea of running.

To make the Republican party truly competitive in Kentucky, the party must win the governorship. The impact of U.S. senators and representatives is primarily felt in Washington. A skillful governor who is committed to party building has greater opportunities than any other elected official. He or she can use patronage to strengthen the organization, can raise large sums of money for campaigns, and can recruit both talented administrators and candidates for other offices. Moreover, that person has the opportunity to build a public record of accomplishment as governor that will make it easier to elect Republicans to high office in the future.

To have the maximum impact, the Republicans must control the governorship for at least two successive terms. That much time is needed to rebuild the party, to have a long-term impact on public policy, and to impress the voters with what Republicans can accomplish in the governorship. As long as the constitution bars gubernatorial succession, no Republican governor—no matter how charismatic and skillful—can hold that office for more than four years. Consequently, the party needs two strong gubernatorial candidates who can be elected in succession. Or else it needs one successful candidate who can use the governor's office to build a stronger party and also to develop a number of capable candidates who can run competitively for governor and for other offices.

There are also those who believe that the Republican party needs to develop a stronger, more identifiable position on issues, a position that is distinctly different from that of the state Democratic party. Those advocating this position usually mean that the Republican party should be more conservative, and they usually believe that a strongly conservative stance will appeal to Kentucky voters. That issue has not been directly tested in a recent gubernatorial race.

Some of those who urge that the party take a stronger conservative stand want it to focus attention on moral issues, or family issues. This is obviously the position of the new activists in the party who supported Pat Robertson in the 1988 campaign. It is a strategy designed to attract Democratic and independent voters in the Bible Belt, the geographic base of which is usually defined as the western part of the state.

An alternative strategy would be to seek new supporters primarily in the larger urban centers of the state, such as Louisville, Lexington, and northern Kentucky. These are areas that have elected Republican congressmen and often voted Republican in statewide and presidential races. These voters are more independent and more diversified. Some may be attracted by emphasis on moral issues, and others give greater priority to a conservative position on economic issues; still others are moderate voters, less likely to be attracted by a conservative ideology than by such issues as improvements in education and reforms in Frankfort.

A third approach might be called an inclusive strategy: not overlooking any voter, but trying to arouse the interest and deal with the concerns of voters in all parts of the state. This is sometimes described as the Larry Hopkins model. By definition, such an approach must be flexible and personal rather than heavily ideological. It is the kind of strategy appropriate for a televised campaign built around an appealing candidate.

Whose responsibility is it to develop a strategy with regard to issues? Some have argued that the state party chairman should speak out more forcefully and frequently on issues, but the chairman often lacks the visibility and credibility on issues to attract much attention. Republicans in the legislature have greater opportunities to develop a platform for the party and to speak out against the failures of Democratic administrations. The Republican legislative party seldom plays that role with enough vigor or unity to gain public interest. Moreover, the legislature is out of session for long periods of time. There is a serious question about whether any single leader can speak authoritatively for the party on policy questions, without fear of contradiction by other Republicans.

In the last analysis, of course, it is the gubernatorial candidate who defines the issues for the party, with little regard for the party's legislative record or the stands of previous standard-bearers. John Harper, for example, in opposing Wallace Wilkinson's lottery proposal, was directly contradicting the position that the last Republican gubernatorial candidate, Jim Bunning, had taken. It is difficult for the party and its candidates to define issues clearly because the two parties do not stand for well-recognized differences on major issues. To the extent that political leaders disagree on important issues, the differences are more likely to be fought out in the Democratic primary than in the general election.

11

PATTERNS OF VOTER TURNOUT

The conventional wisdom is that the turnout of voters in Kentucky elections is relatively low, and that impression is accurate. In the presidential elections from 1972 through 1988, Kentucky ranked between thirty-fourth and fortieth in voter turnout. In gubernatorial elections from 1960 through 1986, Kentucky ranked thirty-second among the forty-two states electing governors in nonpresidential election years. On the other hand, in gubernatorial primaries from 1951 through 1982 (when both primaries were contested), Kentucky ranked nineteenth out of thirty-six nonsouthern states.

It is important to understand why, and in what types of elections, voting turnout is low. Under what types of conditions do Kentuckians go to the polls? What would be required to raise the level of turnout in primary and general elections?

Tables 29 and 30 on general and primary elections from 1978 through 1988 provide a starting point for our analysis, showing turnout as a proportion of the registered vote and, for general elections, as a proportion of the

Table 29. Voting Turnout in Kentucky General Elections, 1978-88

Year	Voting-age population	Number registered	Number voting	Voters as percentage of	
				Population	Registered
1978	2,528,000	1,666,104	557,608	22.1	33.5
1979	2,562,000	1,728,631	958,158	37.4	55.4
1980	2,596,000	1,821,417	1,291,929	49.8	70.9
1981	2,624,000	1,875,231	1,036,014	39.5	55.2
1982	2,652,000	1,825,954	740,504	27.9	40.5
1983	2,675,000	1,852,353	1,041,649	38.9	56.2
1984	2,697,000	2,017,756	1,379,735	51.2	68.3
1985	2,711,000	2,102,765	924,857	34.1	43.9
1986	2,724,000	1,998,899	781,995	28.7	39.1
1987	2,735,000	1,952,202	821,062	30.0	42.0
1988	2,746,000	2,026,307	1,322,517	48.2	65.3

Source: Calculated from data compiled by the State Board of Elections.

Table 30. Voting Turnout in Kentucky Primary Elections, 1978-88

	Democratic Primary			Republican Primary		
Year	Number registered	Number voting	Percentage	Number registered	Number voting	Percentage
1978	1,163,800	126,519	10.8	489,002	39,532	8.0
1979	1,161,621	573,925	49.4	473,421	141,910	29.9
1980	1,199,836	250,922	20.9	489,990	105,060	21.4
1981	1,269,969	650,156	51.1	515,518	200,616	38.9
1982	1,225,579	193,722	15.8	517,981	65,612	12.6
1983	1,263,869	659,735	52.1	513,768	118,043	22.9
1984	1,304,758	278,119	21.3	524,665	63,027	12.0
1985	1,418,241	735,478	51.8	569,917	211,406	35.4
1986	1,349,382	251,024	18.6	570,767	70,159	12.2
1987	1,319,078	639,516	48.4	550,978	118,546	21.5
1988 (P)	1,302,066	320,391	24.6	549,631	121,085	22.0

Source: Calculated from data compiled by the State Board of Elections.
Note: (P) = presidential primary.

voting-age population. Voting as a percentage of the population is the best way of measuring turnout in general elections; but to measure separately turnout in Democratic and Republican primaries, it is necessary to measure voting as a percentage of registration.

The proportion of persons who are registered tends to increase for those elections that are perceived as more important by the voters, such as presidential races. Between 1978 and 1988 for each type of election year (such as presidential and gubernatorial), there has been an increase of a few percentage points in the proportion of the voting-age population that is registered.

Tables 29 and 30 report the total number of persons going to the polls each year, not simply the total voting for the highest statewide race. Turnout has been heaviest in the presidential races (about one-half of the voting-age population). Turnout was nearly 40 percent in the gubernatorial elections of 1979 and 1983 but dropped to 30 percent in 1987 when the race was perceived to be lopsided. It is surprising to find that turnout was almost 40 percent in 1981 when only local and legislative races were on the ballot, though this figure dropped to 34 percent in 1985, perhaps because legislative races were moved to even-numbered years in 1984. Turnout has been lowest (less than 30 percent) in congressional election years, because most U.S. House and Senate and (since 1986) state legislative races are not very competitive.

The pattern is different in primary elections (table 30). In the Democratic party turnout has been close to 50 percent of registration in years with gubernatorial or local elections. It has been barely 20 percent in even-numbered years, either presidential or congressional, because there are very few seriously contested U.S. Senate or House primary races. Turnout was very low in the 1980 presidential primary because the race had been decided by late May; in 1984 Kentucky did not have a presidential primary; but in 1988 the turnout in the presidential primary rose to nearly one-fourth of registered Democrats.

In the Republican primary turnout has been highest (from 35 to 39 percent of registration) in local primaries, where there is frequently close competition. Gubernatorial primaries have been less competitive, and turnout has dropped from 30 percent in 1979 to less than 23 percent in 1983 and 1987, perhaps in part because state legislative races are no longer held in odd-numbered years. Turnout in presidential and congressional election years has been very low (13 percent or less) except in the two years with presidential primaries (1980 and 1988).

There is a clear explanation for the patterns of turnout in both general and primary elections. Voters are more likely to participate in elections that are competitive and that they perceive to be important. Presidential elections are obviously important, well publicized, and sometimes close in Kentucky. By contrast, congressional elections are usually one-sided, and the only close senatorial election held during this period—the McConnell-Huddleston race—occurred in 1984, a presidential year.

Kentucky Democratic primaries are highly competitive in years with gubernatorial elections and also in years with local races—at least in the counties with heavy Democratic registration; and turnout is relatively high in both election cycles. Republican primary competition is high in local elections in heavily Republican counties, but it is low in gubernatorial races; thus, Republican turnout is much higher in local primaries. Neither party has close congressional primaries very often, and so turnout is light.

The close relationship between turnout and competition in Kentucky is not a recent phenomenon, as we can demonstrate by adopting a historical perspective. From 1896 through 1932 the percentage of eligible voters who voted in presidential elections was higher in Kentucky than in the nation as a whole. Since 1936 the proportion of voters in Kentucky has been lower than the national average in presidential elections (table 31). The 1896 election inaugurated a period of regionalism in American politics, with southern states continuing to be dominated by the Democratic party and most northern states dominated by Republicans. The drop in state-level competition led to a decline in levels of national voting turnout that lasted until the 1928 and 1932 elections and the New Deal realignment.

In Kentucky, on the other hand, the 1896 election marked the begin-

Table 31. Kentucky and U.S. Voters in Presidential Elections as Percentage of Persons Eligible to Vote, 1892-1988

Year	Kentucky	U.S.	Kentucky Lead or Lag
1892	72.6	76.1	− 3.5
1896	88.0	79.6	+ 8.4
1900	86.0	73.6	+12.4
1904	76.7	65.4	+11.3
1908	83.0	65.5	+17.5
1912	73.7	60.7	+13.0
1916	81.7	59.0	+12.7
1920	71.2	49.3	+21.9
1924	60.5	48.8	+11.7
1928	66.6	56.7	+ 9.9
1932	67.1	57.0	+10.1
1936	59.7	61.4	− 1.7
1940	59.0	62.8	− 3.8
1944	53.1	56.0	− 2.9
1948	49.5	53.0	− 3.5
1952	58.8	63.1	− 4.3
1956	58.6	60.4	− 1.8
1960	60.5	63.7	− 3.2
1964	53.3	61.7	− 8.4
1968	51.2	60.1	− 8.9
1972	48.4	55.5	− 7.1
1976	48.0	54.4	− 6.4
1980	49.8	52.6	− 2.8
1984	50.8	53.4	− 2.6
1988	48.2	50.1	− 1.9

ning of a period of intense two-party competition, in both national and state elections. A substantial number of conservative Democrats, upset by the "radical" policies of William Jennings Bryan, joined the Republican ranks, and many of them never returned. Although the Democrats carried Kentucky in most presidential elections from 1896 through 1928, the margin was always small and often less than a majority. Moreover, the Republican party won five of nine Kentucky gubernatorial elections from 1895 through 1927 (including the disputed election of 1899). Because the two parties were competitive in Kentucky, the level of turnout remained remarkably high. The New Deal realignment, which undermined regionalism and enhanced two-party competition at the national level, led to the reestablishment of Democratic dominance in Kentucky. As turnout levels rose nationwide, they fell in Kentucky, never to recover.

Table 32. Voting Frequency of Registered Voters in General Elections and Primaries (in Percentages)

Frequency of Vote	All Elections	Primary Elections		General Elections		
	All voters	Dem.	Rep.	Dem.	Rep.	All
0	0.0	15.4	27.8	3.4	2.1	3.0
1	9.2	28.5	33.6	13.2	13.0	13.2
2	10.5	27.3	19.3	16.2	16.3	16.3
3	12.2	15.7	11.5	20.4	21.9	20.9
4	13.6	8.9	5.5	22.3	22.3	22.3
5	14.0	4.2	2.3	24.5	24.4	24.4
6	13.1					
7	10.8					
8	8.0					
9	5.5					
10	3.0					

Source: Sigelman and Jewell, 1986.

Individual Patterns of Voting

We can gain more insights into voting turnout in Kentucky by looking at patterns of individual turnout from two sources. The first is an examination of individual records of voting and nonvoting maintained on computer by the State Board of Elections. We examined these records of voting in the five primaries and five general elections from 1978 through 1982. The second source of data is a telephone survey of a sample of registered voters in the state conducted in mid-1983.

We were interested in finding out what proportion of voters went to the polls consistently over a five-year period and what proportion voted only occasionally or rarely. To make this estimate, we included in our calculations only those persons who were registered to vote over the five-year period in this study (Sigelman and Jewell, 1986). We used a 10 percent sample of registered voters (totaling over 100,000).

These data on individual voting (table 32) show that a relatively small proportion of registered voters cast votes consistently over the five-year period. Just over one-fourth voted in at least seven of ten elections; at the other extreme one-fifth voted only once or twice.

Five of the ten elections included in this survey are primary elections; and in some counties during some years, we know there is little or no competition in one or the other party primary. When there is no state or local contest in a party primary, no election is held in the county, and obviously a citizen of that county cannot gain a perfect voting record. In other counties the only contests may be very lopsided. We can gain a more realistic picture of turnout by looking separately at individual voting in general and primary elections.

We find that the proportion of persons voting in most general elections is much higher than those voting in most primaries; almost one-half of the registered voters voted in four or five of the general elections, but only 13 percent of Democrats and 8 percent of Republicans voted in four or five primaries. There was greater Democratic participation in primaries but virtually no partisan differences in general elections.

We know from aggregate data (table 30) that in most elections a higher proportion of registered Democrats than of Republicans votes in primaries; thus, it is not surprising to find that individual Democratic voters are more likely than Republicans to participate in primaries. It is noteworthy that more than one-fourth of the Republicans and only 15 percent of the Democrats participated in no primaries. This results largely from the higher level of competition in statewide Democratic primaries. The reason the contrasts are not larger is that many of those who register as Republicans live in counties where local primaries are highly competitive.

Critics of Kentucky politics frequently ask, "Why is voting turnout so low?" One answer, as we have seen, is the low level of competition often found in primaries and general elections. This problem is compounded by the frequency of elections, which results in elections being scattered thinly over the four-year cycle.

What other factors affect voting turnout in the state? Is turnout low, for example, because education levels are low in Kentucky? Are certain voters more likely to stay home on election day: those who are poorly educated, those who have a lower income, or younger voters? Is turnout affected by voters' attitudes toward politics or parties? These are all variables that have proved to be important in other states (Wolfinger and Rosenstone, 1980; Crotty, 1977). Finally, is it possible that state election laws and procedures make registration and voting difficult (as indicated by Wolfinger and Rosenstone, 1980)?

Data on individual patterns of voting and nonvoting in Kentucky come from two statewide surveys conducted in mid-1983. One was a survey of 1,468 persons who were registered voters, stratified (based on the voter registration files) to include voters with various levels of voting participation. The second survey included 632 respondents who were not registered to vote. This made it possible, by merging the two samples, to measure the characteristics and attitudes of individuals, ranging from those who were not even registered to those who voted most frequently. A probit analysis was used to measure the relative effect of a number of variables.

In this survey the best predictor of whether, and how frequently, a

Kentuckian would vote was age. For example, if we compare typical Kentuckians (those who were average in all other respects), less than half of those twenty-six years old were registered and voted at least once in the five years, while only one-fifth of average citizens who were sixty years old failed to vote at all in five years. It may often be true that younger persons have other characteristics that make them less likely to vote; for example, they may be more mobile geographically and have less interest in politics. But we have found that age has a major effect on registering and voting even when all of these other variables are controlled (Sigelman, Roeder, Jewell, and Baer, 1985).

Several other variables had a considerable effect on voting. Those voting more frequently were likely to be better educated, to have lived in the state and the county for a longer period, and to be married. Not surprisingly, the frequent voters were more likely to have a strong sense of civic duty and an interest in politics. There was also some tendency for males and persons who strongly identified with a party to vote more often.

Assessing the Obstacles to Registration and Voting

Some research on voting and nonvoting in the fifty states has suggested that registration and voting are higher in those states where election laws and procedures make it easier for citizens to register as voters and to cast their votes. Kentuckians must register thirty days before a primary or general election, unlike a few states where election day registration is permitted. One way of determining whether legal rules contribute to the low turnout of voters in Kentucky is to ask why individuals do not register and often do not vote.

Reasons for Not Registering

In the 1983 survey nonregistered respondents were asked why they have never registered or why they failed to register after being dropped from the rolls or after moving to Kentucky. Two-thirds (68 percent) of the respondents said that they were not interested in politics; 11 percent said they were too busy or did not have enough time; 9 percent claimed not to have enough information about politics or expressed distrust of the political system or politicians; 4 percent seemed to think that they were unqualified to be registered; and 4 percent mentioned reasons of age, health, or the need to travel frequently.

If these answers accurately reflect the attitudes of nonregistrants, it is difficult to believe that more flexible registration rules would produce much more registration. Almost 90 percent of the nonregistrants appear to be uninterested, uninformed, distrustful, or simply too busy to bother with registering.

Nonregistrants were also asked a series of specific questions about the requirements for registration and, where appropriate, were asked whether these requirements accounted for their failure to register. The factors that were mentioned most frequently as reasons for not registering were the use of registration rolls to draw jury panels, the 6:00 P.M. closing time for voting, the requirement of party registration to vote in a primary, and uncertainty about whether one was entitled to take time off from work to vote. Although these were the most frequently mentioned reasons, none were mentioned by more than 10 percent of the nonregistrants, and none had been volunteered by more than a handful of nonregistrants in answering our earlier open-ended questions about their reasons for not registering.

The survey also found, however, that half of the nonregistrants had been registered at some time in the past, either in Kentucky or in some other state. When they were questioned about how they had lost their voting registration, about half said they had been purged from the rolls for nonvoting, while the other half said that they had moved. A substantial proportion of those who had moved claimed to have voted fairly often when they were registered.

Obviously, people who have much interest in political affairs and elections can renew their registration relatively easily after moving to another county or state. Those with a marginal interest in politics, however, are likely to forget about the need for reregistering. Recent research on voting and nonvoting has shown that persons who have recently moved are significantly less likely to vote; and a major reason for this is the necessity of changing registration (Squire, Wolfinger, and Glass, 1987). This is apparently one of the less obvious reasons why younger persons vote less often.

Proposals have been made in Congress to deal with this problem by requiring post offices to hand out reregistration forms to persons who fill out a change-of-address form. If the state of Kentucky were serious about encouraging those who move to reregister, it could use a variety of similar techniques, such as making registration forms available to those who renew driver's and automobile licenses. It is difficult to predict how much voting could be increased by making registration easier. But the nonregistrants who have the greatest potential for voting are probably those who used to be registered before they moved; thus, a reform of registration procedures aimed at them would probably be productive.

Reasons for Not Voting

There are many reasons why people do not vote, including lack of interest in politics in general or in the candidates running in a particular election;

personal circumstances that make it inconvenient or impossible to vote; and lack of electoral competition, particularly in local elections or some primaries. Changes in the requirements for voting would presumably have little effect on those uninterested in politics or those who live in counties with little competition. They might have some effect on persons who have some interest in voting but find it difficult or inconvenient to get to the polls.

In the 1983 survey all registered voters were asked how often they voted. Their answers differed markedly from the actual record because of the widespread tendency to exaggerate one's level of political activity. In fact, slightly over 40 percent claimed that they always voted—a figure at considerable variance from reality. All the rest (those who did not claim to always vote) were asked, "When you do not get a chance to vote, what is the main reason?" Although these explanations for nonvoting are not completely reliable, they may provide some clues to the variety of reasons for low turnout.

The wide variety of answers to this open-ended question included the following most common groups: 36 percent, by far the largest group, expressed a lack of interest in politics or in particular elections or candidates; 20 percent said they did not get a chance to vote because of their job; 14 percent said they were too busy, did not have time, or found it inconvenient to vote; 11 percent said they sometimes had been unable to vote because of poor health or age; and 8 percent claimed that travel prevented them from voting.

It seems unlikely that those who are uninterested, distrustful, or poorly informed would vote if the process were made easier. Those who find it inconvenient to vote might vote more frequently if procedural changes were made. Those who say they are deterred from voting by work, travel, or poor health might be the most likely to take advantage of changes in voting procedures.

One way of evaluating these reasons for not voting is to determine which ones are expressed most often by those persons who actually vote with some frequency or who show some interest in politics. It is obvious from table 33 that persons who say that health, age, or travel sometimes prevents them from voting are more frequent voters and are more interested in politics than are people who cite other reasons for not voting. On the other hand, people who say they do not vote because of work conflicts are much more similar to those who cite lack of time or interest.

Three-fifths of those who mentioned health as an excuse for not voting knew that persons who are disabled or ill can get an absentee ballot, though only 8 percent in this group had ever voted absentee. Among those mentioning travel as an excuse for not voting, 84 percent knew they could obtain an absentee ballot if they were going to be out of the county, but only 14 percent of them had used the absentee ballot.

Table 33. Reasons Given for Not Voting by Those Voting Frequently and Those Very Interested in Politics

Excuse for not voting	Proportion voting in at least half of elections	Proportion very interested in politics
Health or age	43	34
Travel	29	30
Lack of time	23	18
Work	22	18
Lack of interest	22	13
Other excuses	10	10

More than two-thirds (69 percent) of the registered voters knew they must be registered with a party to vote in its primary. Over half (53 percent) preferred to be able to vote in a party's primary without being registered with the party, while 35 percent favored party registration for primary voting. Less than 2 percent knew the deadline for changing party registration.

Based on these answers, there is some reason to believe that those persons who are interested in politics and vote more than occasionally would be likely to vote with greater regularity if it were easier for them to use the absentee ballot when they were ill or were traveling.

An Assessment of Nonvoting

Almost every characteristic of Kentucky politics contributes to depressing turnout in elections. The average level of education in the state is low, and less well-educated persons are less likely to vote. There is so seldom competition in the Republican primary, except in local races in Republican counties, that registered Republicans often have little incentive to vote and sometimes literally have no contests in which to vote. In many rural counties a single party is so strong that there is often no serious two-party competition for local and legislative offices. Several congressmen are so well entrenched that they do not face serious challenges in either the primary or the general election. For many voters the only opportunity they have to make a choice between reasonably competitive candidates is in some statewide and presidential races. When there is little or no serious competition, it is not surprising that turnout is low.

The state has established a schedule of annual elections, which increases the burden on the voters and reduces the number of offices on the ballot at any one time—thus reducing the likelihood that some of the races on the ballot would be competitive. There would be higher turnout in congressional elections in nonpresidential years, for example, if the governor and other statewide offices were elected at the same time, as is the pattern in most states. There would also probably be higher turnout in primary elections if the state were to adopt an open primary law. This might or might not have the effect of making the Republican party more competitive and thus indirectly of increasing turnout.

Until a few years ago, Kentucky law required that, in order to vote, a person must have lived in the state one year, in the county six months, and in the precinct for sixty days. A lifelong resident of the state who had voted in every election could have temporarily lost the right to vote by moving across town a few weeks before the election. The law, which was on the books for many years, reflected a lack of understanding by political leaders that voting should be a fundamental right of Kentuckians.

The current election laws and procedures now make it possible for almost everyone who is determined to register and vote to do so, but they do not always make it convenient for less-motivated persons to register and vote. More persons would register and fewer would be dropped from the registration rolls if registration procedures were made easier, though the increase in registration would not be accompanied by a proportionate increase in voting turnout. More persons would presumably vote if the polling places closed an hour or two later than 6:00 P.M. There is evidence that voting would increase if it were made easier to vote by absentee ballot. A few states have gone so far as to permit anyone to vote absentee without having to provide the excuse of illness or travel.

In some Kentucky counties political leaders have found the absentee ballot to be a useful vehicle in their efforts to buy or otherwise control votes. Legislators seeking to end election fraud have periodically tightened the restriction on the use of absentee ballots. When the *Courier-Journal* in 1987 published a series of articles about vote buying, there was some serious discussion about abolishing the absentee ballot. Instead, the legislature in 1988 placed additional restrictions on the use of absentee ballots. The absentee ballot is important partly because, in its absence, citizens who are well informed, interested in politics, and highly motivated will lose the right to vote. If the General Assembly is seriously interested in expanding voter turnout, it must devise some method of encouraging use of the absentee ballot by those who are legitimately entitled to use it.

12

PARTISANSHIP AND VOTING PATTERNS IN GENERAL ELECTIONS

Partisan Trends in State Elections

Kentuckians think of their state as fundamentally Democratic, but this has not always been true in the past, and it is not an accurate description of modern politics. From the mid-1890s until 1932, Kentucky had one of the most competitive two-party systems in the country. The Democratic party had a 6 to 3 margin in presidential victories from 1896 to 1928, but its electoral margin was usually small and often less than a majority. The Republican party won five of nine gubernatorial elections from 1895 through 1927, including the disputed election of 1899. The legislature, however, with rare exceptions remained under Democratic control. Despite the closeness of races at the state level, most counties voted consistently for one party or the other.

Franklin Roosevelt's election in 1932 launched two decades of Democratic control of Kentucky politics. From 1932 through 1952 the Democrats won every race for the presidency in Kentucky, won every gubernatorial race except in 1943, and won every senatorial contest except for victories by John Sherman Cooper (in 1946 and 1952). On the other hand, the Democrats rarely won lopsided victories in these major races. Republican candidates won at least 40 percent of the vote in every race for president except 1932 and 1936, every race for governor, and every senatorial race except for 1936 and 1938. Democrats controlled all of the U.S. House seats except the traditional Republican southcentral seat and (after 1946) the seat in Louisville. The legislature remained heavily Democratic.

Since 1956 the pattern of elections in Kentucky has become more complicated. Republican candidates have been very competitive in national elections and much less successful in state and local races. Republican presidential candidates have carried the state in every election except

Table 34. Partisan Percentages and Votes Cast in Statewide Elections, 1966-88

Year	Type of race	Percentage of Vote		Votes Cast		
		Dem.	Rep.	Dem.	Rep.	Other
1988	Pres.	43.9	55.5	580,368	734,281	
1987	Gov.	64.9	35.1	504,674	273,141	
1986	Sen.	74.4	25.6	503,775	173,330	
1984	Pres.	39.4	60.0	539,539	821,702	
1984	Sen.	49.5	49.9	639,721	644,990	
1983	Gov.	54.6	44.2	561,674	454,650	
1980	Pres.	47.6	49.1	616,417	635,275	31,127
1980	Sen.	65.1	34.9	720,861	386,029	
1979	Gov.	59.4	40.6	558,088	381,278	
1978	Sen.	61.0	36.9	290,730	175,766	
1976	Pres.	52.8	45.6	615,717	531,852	
1975	Gov.	62.8	37.2	470,159	277,998	
1974	Sen.	53.5	44.1	399,406	328,982	
1972	Pres.	34.8	63.4	371,159	676,446	
1972	Sen.	50.9	47.6	528,550	494,337	
1971	Gov.	50.6	44.3	470,720	412,653	
1968	Pres.	37.7	43.8	397,541	462,411	193,098
1968	Sen.	47.6	51.4	448,960	484,260	
1967	Gov.	48.0	51.2	425,674	454,123	
1966	Sen.	35.5	64.5	266,079	483,805	

Note: Only the most important other presidential candidates are listed: John Anderson in 1980 and George Wallace in 1968.

1964 and 1976. The Republican party won all six senatorial races from 1956 through 1968, but the Democrats won five of six from 1972 through 1986. The Republican party has repeatedly won elections in three of the seven U.S. House races. In nine gubernatorial elections from 1955 through 1987, however, the Republican party won only once, in 1967. In the legislature the Republican minority during the 1980s was smaller than it had been in the late 1960s.

In order to understand this new pattern of competition in Kentucky, we must obviously examine more closely how Kentuckians have been voting. A starting point is to review the vote cast for Democratic and Republican candidates, and the parties' percentage of the total vote, in presidential, senatorial, and gubernatorial elections from 1966 through 1988 (table 34).

By far the greatest Republican success has been in presidential elections; the party won five of six elections from 1968 through 1988, and its candidates averaged almost 55 percent of the vote in the last five (excluding the three-party contest in 1968). Two candidates, Nixon in 1972 and Reagan in 1984, passed the 60 percent mark. In presidential politics it is now accurate to say that Kentucky is normally a Republican state. The Republican party in Kentucky, as in most border and southern states, is most successful when the Democratic opponent is a liberal from a northern state.

The Republican party has not achieved comparable success running against Democratic candidates from Kentucky in senatorial or gubernatorial elections. The Democratic party averaged almost 55 percent of the vote in eight senatorial races (1966-86) and almost 57 percent of the vote in six gubernatorial elections (1967-87).

The most striking conclusion to be drawn from an examination of senatorial races is that differences in the quality of candidates lead to huge variations in Democratic and Republican votes. During this time period the Republicans won three senatorial races, but only once did they poll at least 52 percent of the vote—in 1966 when John Sherman Cooper won almost 65 percent of the vote in his final campaign. Before the period covered in table 34, Cooper ran six times for the Senate. From 1946 through 1956 he ran five races, winning three and losing two, with margins from 46 to 53 percent (being forced to run frequently because he was elected three times for short terms). Finally, in 1960 he won by a comfortable margin of 59 percent. Without Cooper on the ballot, the Republican party has been limited to narrow senatorial victories. The other three Republicans elected to the Senate since 1946, Thruston Morton, Marlow Cook, and Mitch McConnell, all had margins of less than 53 percent.

The Democratic party, on the other hand, in recent years has benefited from strong senatorial candidates and from a shortage of Republican opponents with enough experience, political skill, and funding to make a serious challenge. In 1974 Democratic governor Wendell Ford defeated Republican senator Marlow Cook and won 54 percent of the vote. In the next two races, Ford faced increasingly weak candidates and won with margins of 65 and 74 percent. (The latter margin was the largest for any senatorial or gubernatorial candidate since 1868.) The other successful Democratic candidate during this period, Walter Huddleston, narrowly defeated Louie Nunn in 1972, won 61 percent against a weak opponent six years later, and very narrowly lost to McConnell in 1984.

During the 1966-86 period, the Democratic percentages in senatorial elections have ranged from 35 to 74 percent, and the Republican percentages have ranged from 26 to 65 percent. Clearly, there are large numbers of voters who have been voting "for the man, not the party" in senatorial races over a number of years. On occasion, presidential coattails have helped Republican senatorial candidates. This was almost surely the case in 1984 when Reagan won with a 60 percent majority and Mitch McConnell had a margin of 0.4 percentage points. But Reagan's coattails were not strong enough to help Republican Mary Louise Foust in 1980, nor were Nixon's coattails enough in 1972 to elect Louie Nunn to the Senate.

There is, of course, no exact way to measure split ticket voting from aggregate voting figures (in the absence of survey data on ticket splitting). It is particularly difficult to make estimates when the turnout is much lower in one race than in the other. Nevertheless, it is possible to make some estimates that suggest how much ticket splitting has gone on in years when presidential and senatorial races have coincided. In 1984 Senator Huddleston polled about 100,000 more votes than Walter Mondale, and McConnell polled about 177,000 fewer votes than President Reagan; at least 100,000 voters probably split their ticket for Huddleston, not quite enough to reelect him. In 1972, when Huddleston led the presidential ticket by 158,000 and Nunn trailed his ticket by 182,000, at least 160,000 (nearly one-fourth of those voting for Nixon) probably split their ticket for Huddleston. In 1980 Wendell Ford must have benefited from 100,000 ticket splitters, in addition to more than 170,000 voters for president, who cast no senatorial ballot, many of them probably ignoring the weak Republican candidate.

During the period since 1978, the State Board of Elections has compiled data on the turnout of Democratic and Republican registrants at the polls. These data show that in most statewide elections the level of turnout was approximately the same for voters registered in each of the parties. The greater Republican success in national elections and greater Democratic success in state elections was not caused by variations in partisan turnout. One exception occurred in the 1987 governor's race, when Republican turnout was six percentage points less than Democratic turnout.

The Republican party elected Louie Nunn as governor in 1967 with 51.2 percent of the vote, but Democratic candidates won the next five gubernatorial elections with majorities ranging from 50.6 percent to 64.9 percent. Nunn's election resulted in part from factional divisions in the Democratic party. But since that time the old factions have disappeared, and each of the five Democratic nominees from 1971 through 1987 had the support of the other Democratic candidates for the nominations. The size of Democratic majorities has depended less on party unity than on the political skills and experience of the two parties' candidates.

In 1971 the Republican nominee, Tom Emberton, had the backing of the Nunn administration but lost to Lt. Gov. Wendell Ford by more than six percentage points. After Ford's election to the Senate in 1974, Julian Carroll succeeded to the governorship and thus ran as an incumbent in his highly successful race (a margin of over twenty-five percentage points)

Figure 4. Partisan Voting of Counties in Statewide Elections, 1920-1966

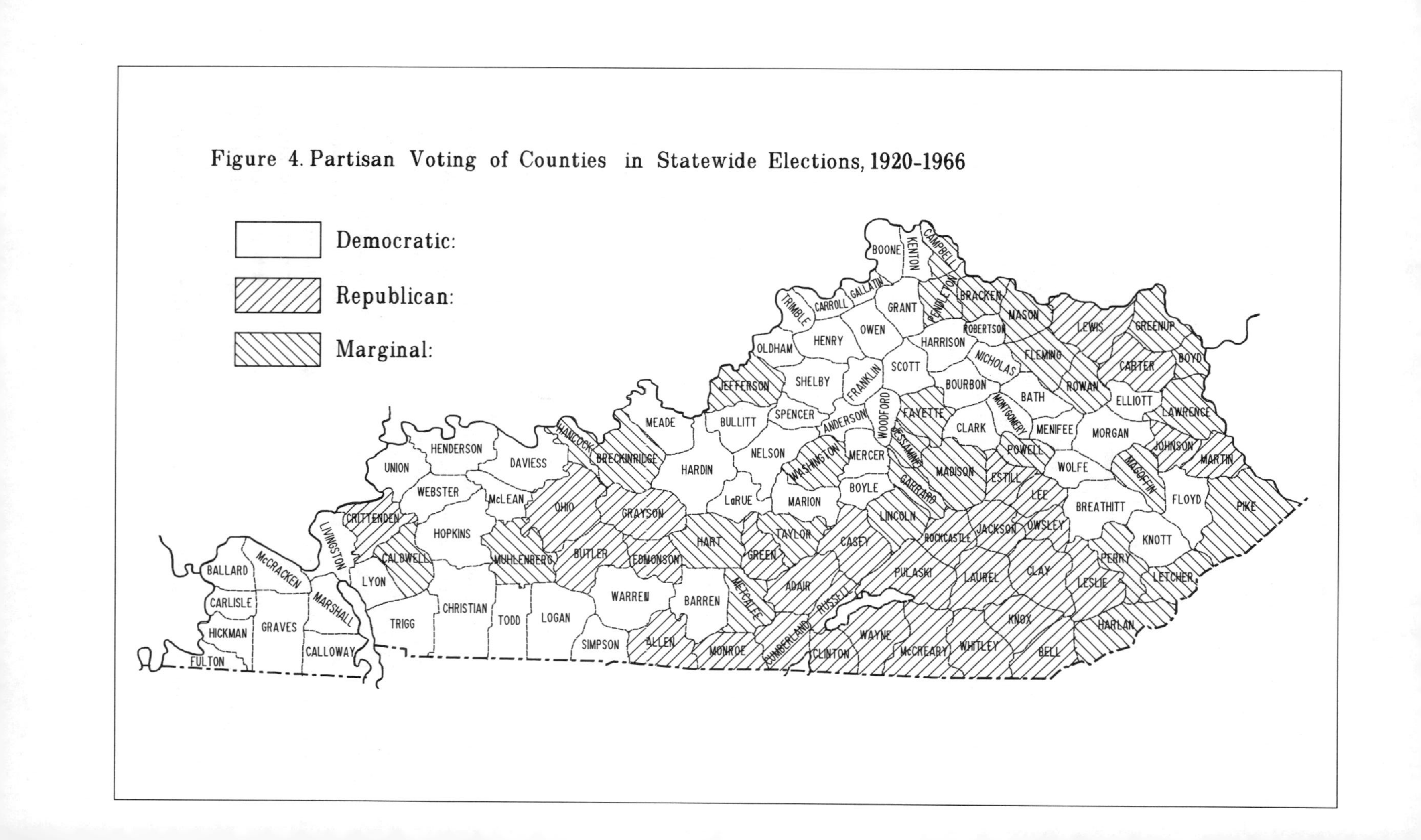

against Robert Gable. In 1979, after narrowly winning the primary with a late surge, John Y. Brown coasted to victory (almost twenty points) over former governor Nunn. In 1983 many observers believed that the Democratic candidate, Martha Layne Collins, was beatable because her primary margin had been tiny and because Kentucky voters had never elected a woman governor or senator. But the Republicans had great difficulty finding a viable candidate, and state senator Jim Bunning, the eventual nominee, was handicapped by a late start and limited financing. Collins won by more than ten percentage points. In 1987 Republican prospects were severely damaged by Larry Forgy's late withdrawal from the race. The nominee, state representative John Harper, had little visibility, poor campaign skills, little financing, and almost no support from party leaders. It was no surprise when Wallace Wilkinson defeated John Harper by a margin of nearly 2 to 1.

Regional Voting Patterns in State Elections

There are traditional regional and county patterns of voting in Kentucky that date back at least to the turn of the century and often further back. In the last three decades, as we have seen, some of these patterns have been changing, at least in presidential and some other national elections. We will illustrate these patterns of both continuity and change with maps and with statistical summaries, emphasizing differences between national and state elections. We will also pay particular attention to voting trends in the larger, more urbanized counties, because of their greater numerical importance and also because such counties are often more volatile and less bound by traditional voting patterns.

The simplest way to describe regional and county voting patterns is by using maps, though these obviously understate the importance of the large, urbanized counties. The first map (figure 4) illustrates traditional voting patterns in the counties. It covers all presidential, senatorial, and gubernatorial elections from 1920 through 1966. In those counties labeled as Democratic or Republican, the median of the average votes for the three types of elections was at least 55 percent for that party. All other counties are considered marginal. The traditional Democratic counties include most of those in western Kentucky, most of the Bluegrass, and much of the northern and northeastern counties. The single largest concentration of Republican counties is in the southcentral area, roughly equivalent to the present Fifth Congressional District. There are, however, some Republican outposts in the west (particularly the cluster of Ohio, Grayson, Butler, and Edmonson) and in the northeast (Lewis, Carter, Johnson, and Martin). Some of the marginal counties are along the borders between Repub-

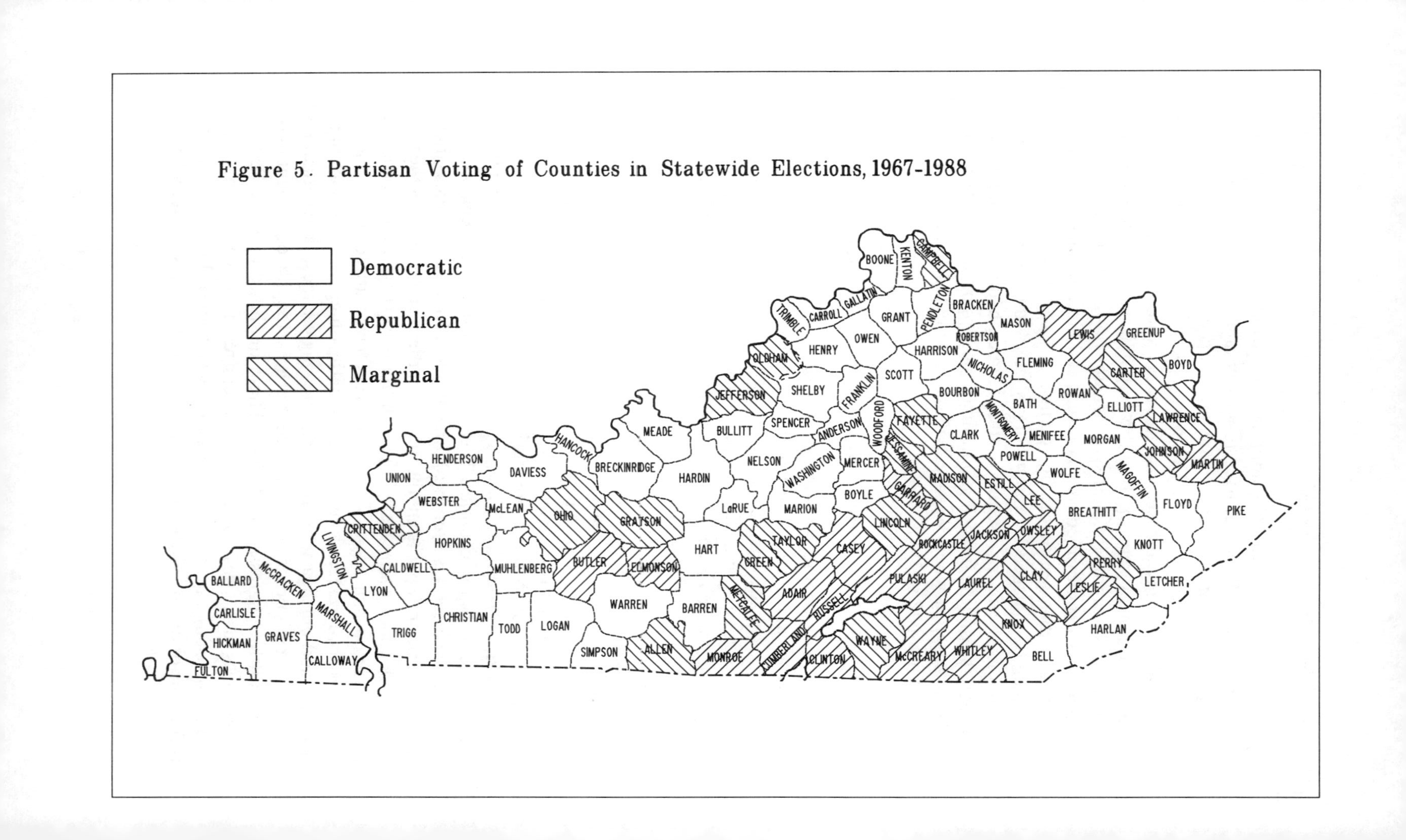

Figure 5. Partisan Voting of Counties in Statewide Elections, 1967-1988

lican and Democratic areas, and some are in the northeast and southeast. Of the eleven counties with the highest voting totals that we will be examining, five were traditionally in the marginal category (Jefferson, Fayette, Campbell, Boyd, and Pike) and six were Democratic (McCracken, Daviess, Hardin, Warren, Kenton, and Franklin).

The second map (figure 5) shows the counties that voted most consistently Democratic or Republican in statewide elections during the period from 1967 through 1988. A similar technique, based on the median of averages for the three types of elections, is used, with 55 percent being the criteria for Democratic or Republican counties (see Blanchard, 1982). While some counties have shifted from one time period to the next, the general geographical patterns of party strength are similar. The Democrats remain strong in the west and much of the Bluegrass, northeast, and southeast; the only solid bloc of Republican strength is in the southcentral counties. Compared to the map covering the 1920-66 period, there are more consistently Democratic counties and fewer marginal counties. (The method of measuring voting consistency that is employed, however, does not fully reflect the recent growth of Republican votes in presidential elections.)

County voting in gubernatorial elections continues to follow the traditional patterns that we have seen. Most of the changes in voting patterns have occurred in national and particularly in presidential elections. The next map (figure 6) covers voting patterns in the 1979 and 1983 gubernatorial races, which are the closest ones since 1971. It shows the counties voting consistently Democratic or Republican in the two races, as well as seventeen counties that voted inconsistently. The only large bloc of consistently Republican counties is in southcentral Kentucky. Almost all of the counties in this region that were inconsistent, including several further east, were carried by Nunn but not by Bunning. The only other bloc of consistently Republican counties is Butler, Grayson, and Edmonson in the westcentral area. Because he was a resident (and county judge) in Barren County, Nunn was also able to carry several counties close to that bloc, including his own. The only significant group of counties carried by Bunning and not by Nunn were those along the Ohio River, most notably Campbell, Kenton, and Boone, which was Bunning's home base. It is noteworthy that all of the large urban counties except Campbell and Kenton voted Democratic, although the margins were small in 1983 in Jefferson and Fayette (and Fayette voted Republican in the 1987 race).

The county pattern of voting is quite different in presidential races. The Republican party is much stronger, having averaged 55 percent in the last five presidential races, compared to 43 percent in the last six gubernatorial races. That means that the Republican party has been able to carry

Figure 6. Partisan Voting of Counties in 1979 and 1983 Gubernatorial Elections

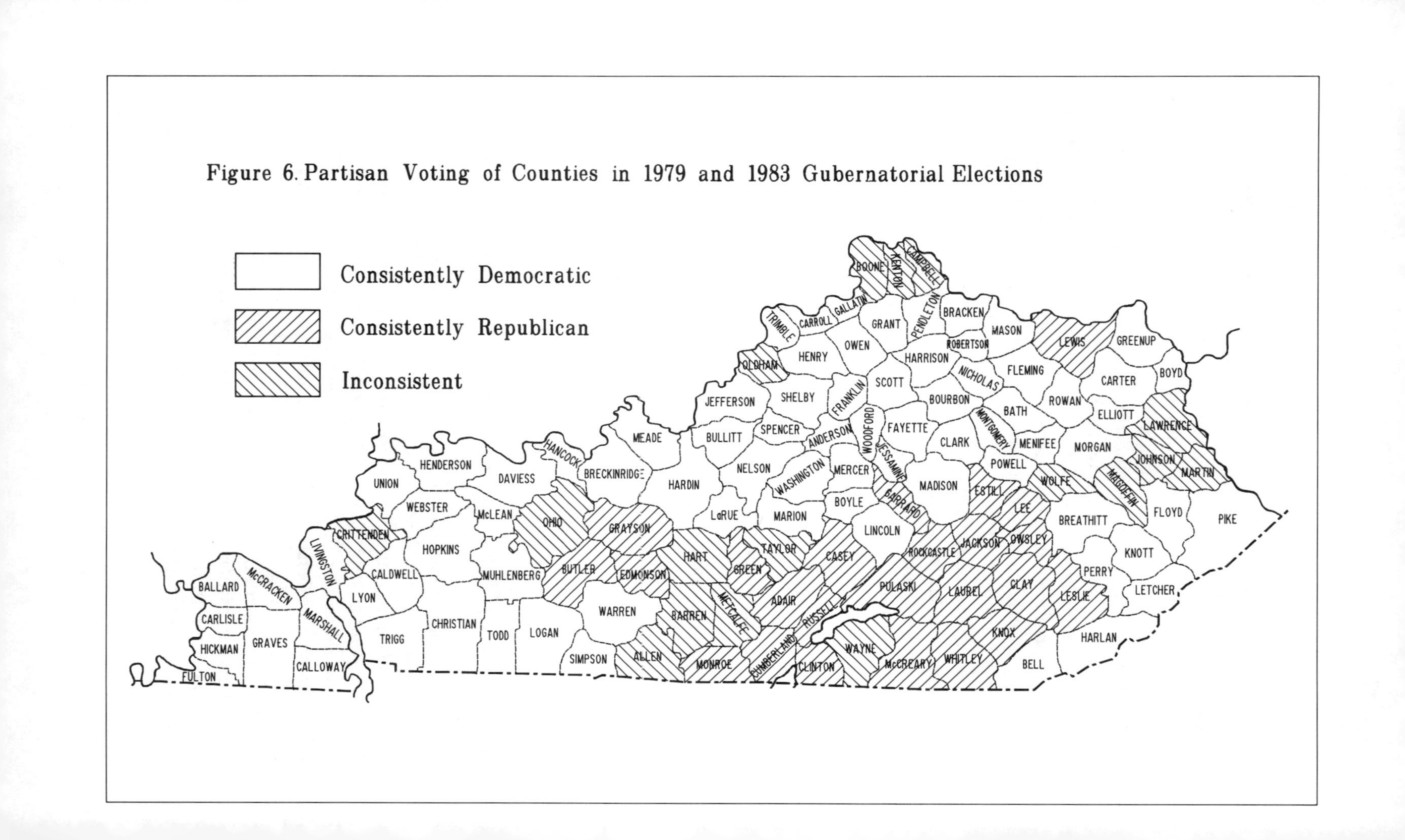

a much larger proportion of the counties in some presidential races than in most gubernatorial races. In examining the maps of county voting, we will concentrate on the last four presidential races, 1976 through 1988. The presidential map for 1976 (figure 7), the only one of these four won by the Democrats, is very similar to the map of recent gubernatorial races, with most of the Republican strength being concentrated in the southcentral counties and the small westcentral bloc. The major difference is that the Republicans also carried the four largest urban counties: Jefferson, Fayette, Campbell, and Kenton.

The strongest Republican showing was in 1984. The map (figure 8) shows that Walter Mondale, the Democratic candidate, was able to carry only a cluster of twelve eastern and southeastern counties and seven of the most heavily Democratic rural counties in the far west. All of the other counties that have normally consistently voted Democratic in most gubernatorial races voted Republican in the 1984 presidential race. Although Michael Dukakis won a larger minority of the vote in 1988 than Mondale had done in 1984, the pattern of county voting in 1988 was quite similar. By comparison with 1984, in 1988 the Democrats picked up six counties in the northeast, a cluster of five counties between Jefferson and Boone counties in the north, traditionally Democratic Marion County, and nine more counties in the far west.

The closest presidential race during this period was in 1980, when Reagan defeated Carter by a margin of one and one-half percentage points. The map for that year (figure 9) therefore illustrates well the balance of counties in presidential elections. Generally speaking, those counties voting Democratic are more Democratic than the state as a whole, and the remainder are as much or more Republican than the whole state. That map shows that, in addition to the traditional southcentral counties, the Republicans carried a larger bloc of westcentral counties, a few counties in the northeast, and the urban counties of Jefferson, Fayette, Campbell, and Kenton.

In recent years most Kentucky counties have cast a larger proportion of votes for Republican candidates in presidential races than in gubernatorial races. But the difference is particularly strong among certain categories of counties. We can see these differences if we rank order every county in an election from the largest to the smallest percentage for one party and then compare the vote in each county with the state average. For example, in the 1983 governor's race, when the statewide Democratic average was 55.3 percent, the percent in Elliott, the strongest Democratic county, was almost 24 percent higher, while it was almost 29 percent less than the state average in Clinton, the least Democratic county.

We can compare voting in two of the more closely contested races, for

Figure 7. Partisan Voting of Counties in the 1976 Presidential Election

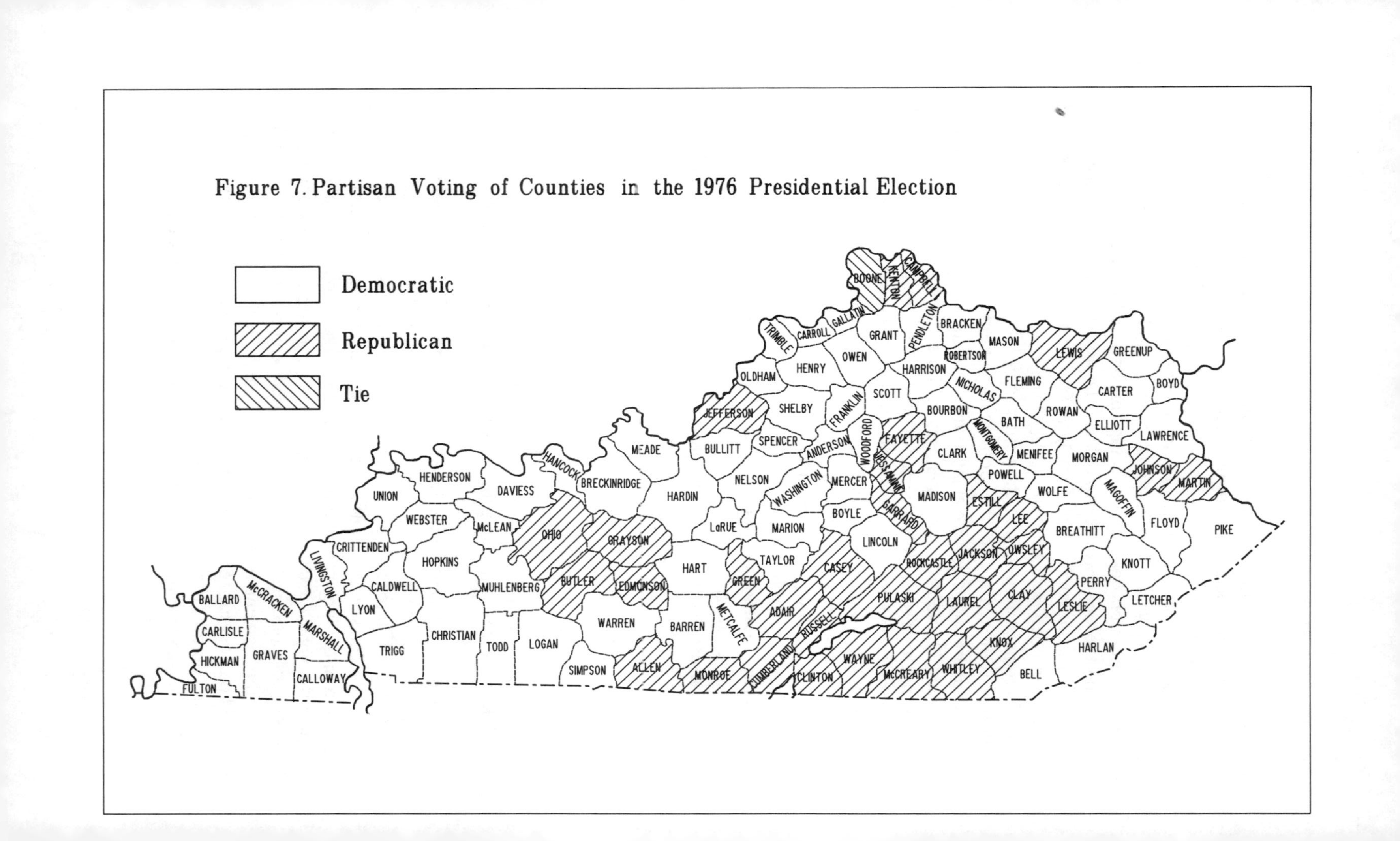

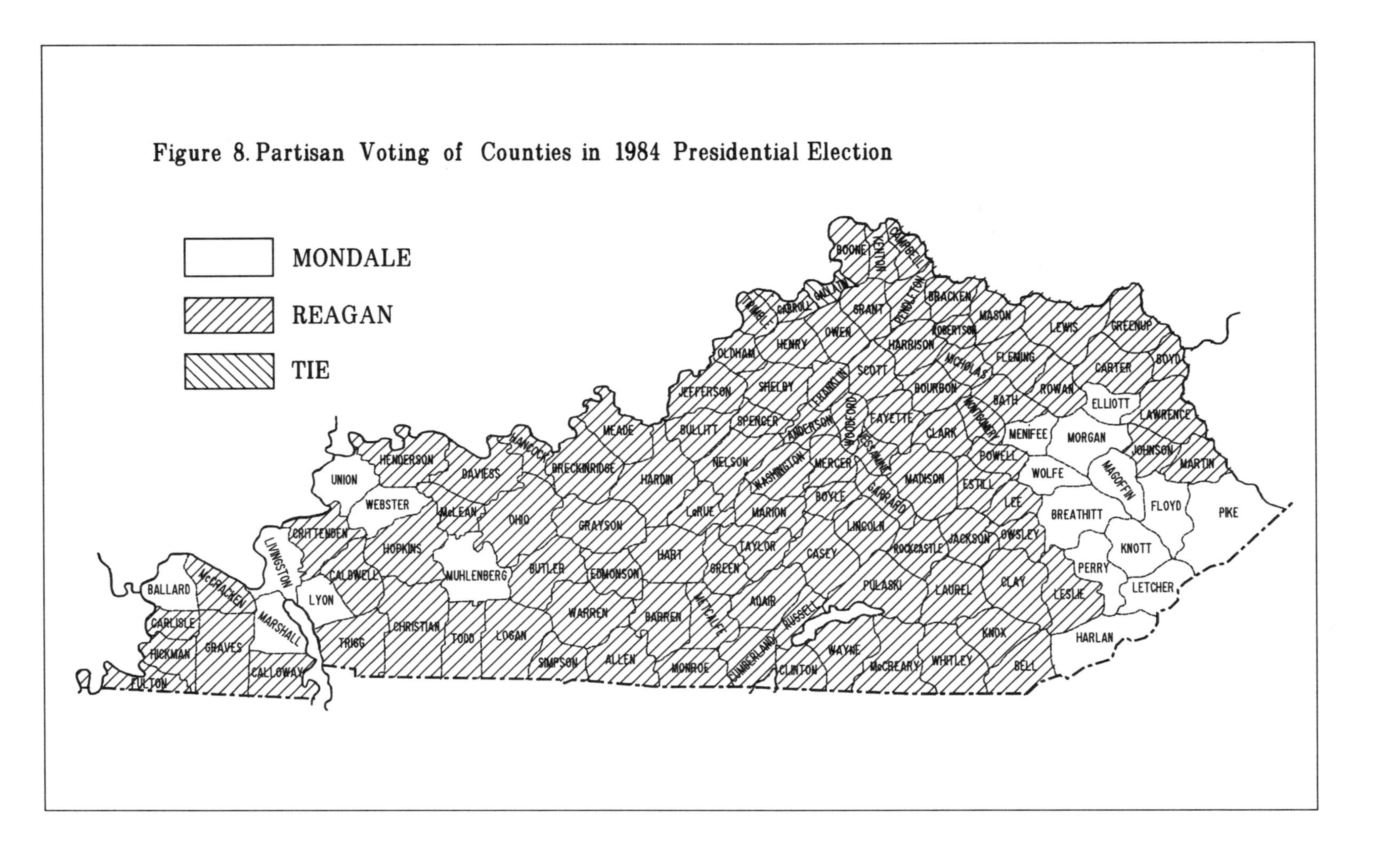

Figure 8. Partisan Voting of Counties in 1984 Presidential Election

Figure 9. Partisan Voting of Counties in 1980 Presidential Election

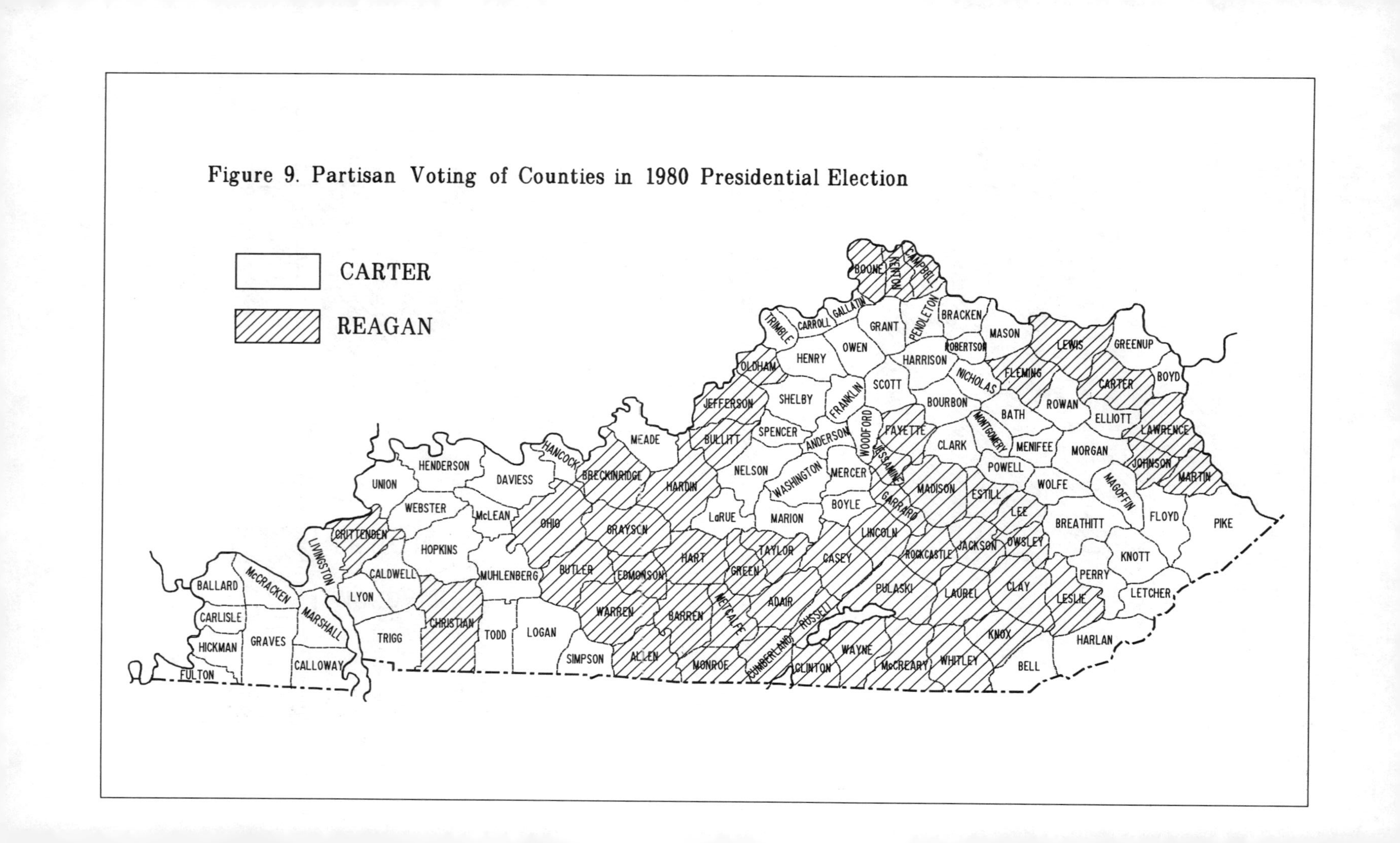

governor in 1983 and for president in 1980. Most of the counties that were above the state Democratic average in one race were also above it in the other, but in some counties there were sharp differences. Woodford County voted 71 percent Democratic for governor in 1983 (sixteen points above the state average) and just over 50 percent Democratic in 1980 (only one point above). Relative to the state average, Woodford was fifteen percentage points more Democratic in the governor's race than in the presidential race, the largest gap (in that direction) in the state. Nelson County, on the other hand, was thirteen percentage points more Democratic in the presidential race.

Using this measure, we find forty-four counties that were at least three percentage points more Democratic in gubernatorial than in presidential races. About three-fourths of these counties are ones that remained loyal to the Democratic party in the state election but shifted further toward the Republican party than did the state as a whole in the presidential election. The largest proportion of these counties is in western and westcentral Kentucky, but some are in the Bluegrass and northern area. The other one-fourth are counties that voted Republican in the governor's race but more heavily Republican (compared to the whole state) in the presidential race. This latter group is concentrated almost entirely in the traditionally south-central region.

There were sixteen counties that were at least three percentage points more Democratic in presidential races (or more precisely, lagged at least three points behind the statewide shift to the Republicans in such races). All of these were counties that voted Democratic in the governor's race. They were scattered around the state but included several Democratic counties in the southeast, several in the west (in and around Henderson), and several central counties like Marion and Nelson that have traditionally been loyal to national Democratic candidates in part because of their Catholic population.

Clearly, most of the rural counties have maintained their traditional partisan loyalties in gubernatorial races and presumably in other races for state office. The pattern of voting for state legislators in rural counties follows these same traditional patterns (Jewell and Miller, 1988: 22-25). These voting patterns have frequently been broken in recent presidential elections, in which traditionally Democratic counties have been voting Republican. This is particularly the case in the southwestern counties of the state, which have the reputation of being particularly conservative and where the liberal policies of national Democratic candidates have the least appeal.

The eleven counties with the highest number of voters deserve more careful attention for two reasons. In recent years they have cast about 45

Table 35. Voting in Urban Counties in Gubernatorial and Presidential Elections, 1976-88

	Average Democratic Percentage of Vote		Average Democratic Percentage of Vote Compared to Statewide Average		
County	Gubernatorial	Presidential	Gubernatorial	Presidential	Difference
McCracken	73	56	+13	+ 9	+ 4
Franklin	71	55	+11	+ 8	+ 3
Pike	63	60	+ 3	+13	−10
Boyd	62	51	+ 2	+ 4	− 2
Daviess	63	47	+ 3	0	+ 3
Warren	65	41	+ 5	− 6	+11
Jefferson	58	48	− 2	+ 1	− 3
Hardin	61	41	+ 1	− 6	+ 7
Fayette	53	42	− 7	− 5	− 2
Campbell	55	37	− 5	−10	+ 5
Kenton	45	38	− 6	− 9	+ 3

percent of the total vote in the state. Moreover, in most of these counties, voting patterns are determined less by tradition than is the case in most rural counties. Compared to the other counties, most of these counties have demonstrated stronger Republican leanings in presidential than in gubernatorial races.

Table 35 shows for each of these counties the average Democratic percentage of the two-party vote in three gubernatorial races (1979-87) and four presidential races (1976-88). All of the counties except Kenton have averaged more than 50 percent Democratic in gubernatorial races, but only four counties (McCracken, Franklin, Pike, and Boyd) have averaged more Democratic than Republican in presidential races.

The table also shows the average difference between the Democratic vote in each county and the statewide percentage. Most counties remain above the state Democratic average in gubernatorial races; the exceptions are Kenton, Campbell, Fayette, and Jefferson. But only five counties—McCracken, Pike, Franklin, Boyd, and (narrowly) Jefferson—are more Democratic in presidential races.

Seven of the counties (all but Jefferson, Fayette, Campbell, and Kenton) have much in common. They are located in traditionally Democratic parts of the state. They have continued to deliver comfortable Democratic margins in most gubernatorial races. But they differ in presidential races. Only Pike County has stayed nearly as strongly Democratic at both levels of elections. McCracken's strong Democratic commitment in state races has eroded but not quite disappeared in presidential contests. The other counties have moved to varying degrees toward Republican presidential support, particularly Warren and Hardin counties.

Campbell, Kenton, and Fayette counties are the most Republican of the major urban counties. The gubernatorial races are usually very competitive, but Republican presidential candidates can depend on substantial margins in all three counties. In fact, in the 1984 and 1988 elections, the Republican majority was at least two-thirds in Campbell and Kenton. These are high-income counties, with large areas that are suburban in character and that are obviously attracted to conservative candidates for national office.

Jefferson County is the largest county, producing over one-fifth of the total state vote. The average vote in both gubernatorial and presidential elections is close to the statewide vote, though the Jefferson County electorate is also volatile. The city of Louisville, with significant labor union and black voting strength, is more Democratic; and the suburban areas of Jefferson County are more Republican. Jefferson County voters were less Democratic than the state average in the 1987 and 1983 gubernatorial elections when the Republican candidates may have been perceived as more urban in their orientations. They were more Democratic in 1979 (when John Y. Brown ran against Louie Nunn). Jefferson County has tended to be slightly less Republican in presidential elections than the rest of the state. The presidential race has been very close in Jefferson County in three of the last four elections, excluding only the 1984 Reagan landslide.

The major urban counties are increasingly important battlegrounds in both state and national elections, not only because they are growing in population, but because they are becoming more competitive and more volatile. In most of these counties, the local parties have at least a minimum of organizational strength, and the campaigning is usually more vigorous than in many rural counties.

Urban voters tend to cast their ballots more independently than rural voters, but this is not consistently true. In the seven presidential and gubernatorial elections from 1976 to 1988, there was a gap of twenty-five percentage points from the lowest to the highest Democratic vote in statewide totals. In seven of the urban counties, that gap was larger, ranging from thirty-two to thirty-eight percentage points. In Jefferson and Fayette, however, the gap was the same as the state average (twenty-five points), because of less enthusiasm for Wallace Wilkinson in 1987, the year when the state Democratic percentage was highest. In Boyd County the gap was only seventeen points; and in Pike County, which seems to vote Democratic whoever is running, the gap was only fifteen points. In other words, a substantial proportion of Kentucky voters has become independent in most counties, but this trend is particularly evident in some of the urban counties.

Patterns of Party Identification

Since the development of modern survey research techniques in the 1950s, political scientists have used the concept of party identification as an important instrument for understanding political behavior and individual voting. They have found that a large proportion of persons identify themselves as either Democrats or Republicans, this identification is relatively stable over a period of years, and party identification helps to predict how persons will vote. For years pollsters have been asking voters whether they consider themselves to be Democrats, Republicans, or independents; those who name a party have often been asked if they were "strong" or "weak" partisans, while independents have been asked if they "lean" toward either party. In recent years there has been some growth in the proportion of independents and some decline in the proportion of partisans who vote consistently for candidates of their party, but party identification remains an important tool of political analysis (Shively, 1980).

Stability of Party Identification

Obviously, we do not have survey data on party identification in Kentucky during the first half of this century. But throughout this period voting patterns were so stable, at both the county and the state levels, that we can assume a large proportion of voters were loyal to one party and usually voted for its candidates. The fact that politics in most counties was dominated by a single party must have reinforced these partisan loyalties. Clearly, a majority of Kentuckians were Democrats, while the Republicans predominated in southcentral Kentucky and a few other counties.

Since the early 1950s, however, the Republican party has won most presidential elections in the state, has won a number of Senate races, and has gained control of three congressional seats. Obviously, a large number of Kentucky voters, frequently a majority, have been voting Republican in these races while many of them have been electing Democrats to the governorship, the legislature, and local offices in many counties.

The fact that so many Kentuckians have been splitting their ticket, in specific elections or at least over a period of several years, raises doubts about the stability and the impact of party identification in Kentucky. Are more voters becoming Republicans or independents? Do their party loyalties have less effect on how they vote? Or is it possible that some voters identify with one party at the national level and another at the state level?

Our best evidence about party identification of Kentuckians comes from the semiannual statewide polls conducted by the Survey Research Center of the University of Kentucky (UKSRC) from 1979 through 1988. These surveys enable us to measure trends over time, as well as to measure the relationship between party identification and party registration, standard demographic variables, and respondents' attitudes on issues. Because most questions have been asked more than once, we can pool the data and thus enlarge the sample.

Voters were asked their party identification repeatedly from 1979 through 1988 (with a break in 1984). To simplify the presentation and the comparison with other variables, we will concentrate on the three-way classification of identification (Democrats, Republicans, independents) but will break these down into more categories where it is useful to do so. (We will omit from the analysis the small number of those who failed to respond with an identification in one of the three categories.)

Figure 10 shows the trend in party identification from 1979 through 1988; in most years the question was asked in both the fall and the spring, and data from the two surveys have been averaged to reduce variations caused by sampling error. The chart reveals a surprising pattern of consistency over the eight-year period. Partisan identification has ranged between 51 and 54 percent for Democrats, between 22 and 28 percent for Republicans, and between 20 and 24 percent for independents. (For a more detailed analysis of these trends, see Jewell and Roeder, 1988.)

There is no clear trend favoring either party but rather a cyclical pattern of small variations linked to the state and national elections. Republican identification was lowest in 1979, 1983, and 1987, years of gubernatorial primaries and elections. Republican identification was highest in 1980 and 1988, during presidential years, as well as in the 1985-86 period. (Data were lacking for the 1984 presidential election year.) Republican gains have come largely at the expense of independents rather than of Democrats.

A study of party realignment in southern states (Swansbrough and Brodsky, 1988) provides evidence of Republican gains in party identification that are greater in almost every southern state than we have found in Kentucky. (In a few states there has been a gain in independent, rather than Democratic, identification, a trend also missing in Kentucky.) For whatever reason, party identification in Kentucky has remained remarkably steady for a decade, except for variations tied to the electoral cycle.

An examination of the seven-way breakdown of party identification (available for the 1980-86 period) also shows remarkable consistency over time. When the data for the years 1985-87 are pooled, they show the following breakdown: 24 percent strong Democratic; 28 percent weak Democratic; 7 percent independent, leaning Democratic; 9 percent inde-

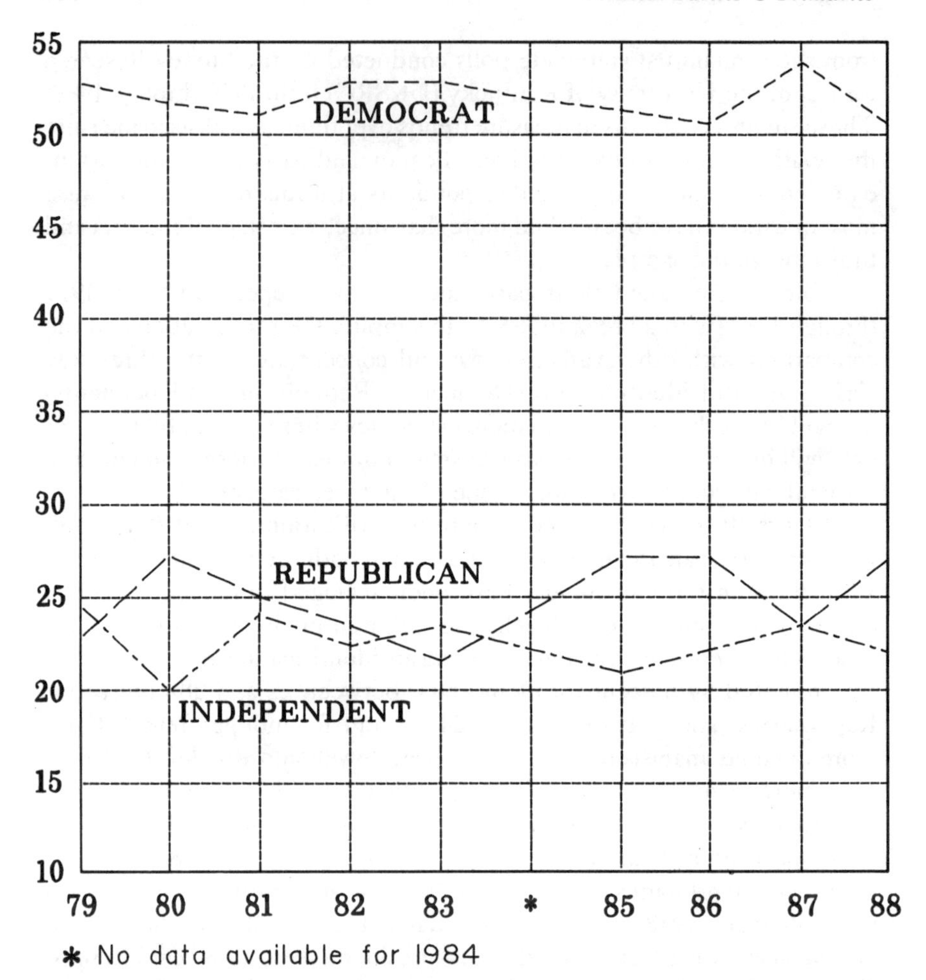

Figure 10. Trends in Party Identification in Kentucky, 1979-1988

pendent; 6 percent independent, leaning Republican; 15 percent weak Republican; 11 percent strong Republican. These are almost identical to the figures for 1980, with slight losses for strong Democrats and slight gains for strong Republicans. The conclusion from these data is unmistakable. Over nearly a decade, there has been no significant change in the party loyalties of Kentucky voters. About half remain Democrats, about one-fourth Republicans, and about one-fourth independents.

Effect of Party Registration on Identification

From 1979 through 1988 the proportion of voters registering as Democrats has ranged from 67.2 percent to 68.8 percent; the proportion of Republi-

Table 36. Comparison of Party Identification and Party Registration, 1982, 1983, 1987

Party identification	Percentage of Total			Party Registration Percentage Across				Percentage Down		
	Dem.	Ind.	Rep.	Dem.	Ind.	Rep.	Tot.	Dem.	Ind.	Rep.
Dem.	56	0	1	97	1	2	100	82	11	3
Ind.	10	4	5	52	23	25	100	15	87	17
Rep.	2	0	2	9	1	91	101	3	2	80
Total								100	100	100

Source: Jewell and Roeder, 1988.

cans has ranged from 27.8 percent to 29.4 percent; and the proportion of independents and others has stayed close to 3.5 percent. Democratic registration inches up in years of gubernatorial races, while Republican registration is slightly higher in presidential years. The proportion of voters registering as independents, while very small, is comparable to that in those other border and southern states that have closed primaries.

Roughly two-thirds of the voters register as Democrats, and nearly one-third are Republicans; but half identify as Democrats, one-fourth as Republicans, and one-fourth as independents. What is the relationship between party identification and party registration in Kentucky? Do most of those who identify as partisans register that way? How do independent identifiers register? Does partisan identification cause party registration, or is it the reverse?

Table 36 provides a cross tabulation of party identification and registration, averaged for the years 1982, 1983, and 1987. (Because some respondents are not registered, the totals are less than those for all identifiers, increasing the proportion of Democrats and decreasing the proportion of independents.) Almost all Democratic identifiers are registered as Democrats, and over 90 percent of Republican identifiers are registered as Republicans. Those who identify as independents are twice as likely to register Democratic than Republican, while one-fifth of them register as independent—virtually the only voters to do so.

There are basically two reasons for a person to register as a Democrat or as a Republican. The first is a sense of loyalty, and the second is a desire to vote in the Democratic or Republican primary. In Kentucky, as in most other southern and border states, the Democratic statewide primaries are often close and exciting, while the Republicans rarely have closely contested statewide primaries. We might expect to find Republican identifiers registering as Democrats in order to vote in state primaries, but our survey suggests that only about 9 percent of Republicans do so.

Locally, the party with a majority in a county frequently has close primaries, while the minority party seldom has contests and sometimes does not even run candidates. Consequently, registration patterns (particularly in rural counties) are affected by the party balance at the county level. In 1987 (as noted in table 3 of chapter 3), there were thirty-four counties (out of 120) where the Democrats had at least 90 percent of the partisan registration, but in most of them the normal Democratic vote in statewide races was at least twenty percentage points less. It would appear that about 20 percent of the voters in these counties were registered Democratic but were usually voting Republican. There were also nine counties where 75 to 86 percent of the two-party registration was Republican though the normal Republican vote was approximately twenty points less than that.

Given these registration patterns, we might expect to find that the relationship between party identification and registration is different in various types of counties. Table 37 shows this relationship for four types of counties: rural Republican, rural Democratic, rural strongly Democratic, and metropolitan (Jewell and Roeder, 1988). The partisan categories for rural counties are based on voting in statewide races. (All Republican counties are combined to generate enough respondents. The data only include two surveys in 1983.)

An examination of the data shows that about 13 percent of Republicans in strongly Democratic and metropolitan counties register Democratic, but (particularly in strongly Democratic counties) the absolute numbers of these voters are very small. Much more important are the differences in registration by those who identify as independent. They are much more likely to register Republican in Republican counties and to register Democratic in the other three categories of counties. In all four types of counties, it is largely the independents who account for the gap in partisan balance between registration and identification. Consequently, it is presumably the independents who largely account for the difference between voting patterns and registration.

What do these data tell us about the meaning of party identification to voters in Kentucky? One possible explanation is that some voters do not think of themselves in terms of party identification until asked to do so by an interviewer. Some of them may confuse identification with registration and give the same answer for both; others, who recognize a contradiction between how they register and participate in primaries and how they vote in general elections, may decide on the spur of the moment to tell an interviewer that they are independents (Finkel and Scarrow, 1985).

There are also substantive explanations for this phenomenon. More than half of those voters identifying as independents are registered as

Table 37. Comparison of Party Identification and Party Registration in Various Types of Counties, 1983

Party identification	Number of Persons			Party Registration Percentage Across				Percentage Down		
	Dem.	Ind.	Rep.	Dem.	Ind.	Rep.	Tot.	Dem.	Ind.	Rep.
Rural Republican counties										
Dem.	51	1	5	89	2	9	100	91	14	6
Ind.	5	6	12	22	26	52	100	9	86	13
Rep.	0	0	72	0	0	100	100	0	0	81
Total								100	100	100
Rural Democratic counties										
Dem.	178	2	5	96	1	3	100	85	18	6
Ind.	26	8	15	53	16	31	100	12	73	17
Rep.	5	1	67	7	1	92	100	3	9	77
Total								100	100	100
Rural strongly-Democratic counties										
Dem.	248	0	2	99	0	1	100	80	0	3
Ind.	55	11	16	67	13	20	100	18	100	26
Rep.	6	0	44	12	0	88	100	2	0	71
Total								100	100	100
Metropolitan counties										
Dem.	210	2	2	98	1	1	100	76	8	1
Ind.	52	20	21	56	21	23	100	19	83	20
Rep.	13	2	81	14	2	84	100	5	8	79
Total								100	99	100

Source: Jewell and Roeder, 1988.

Democrats and presumably vote in the Democratic primary. But, as we will demonstrate later, many of them frequently vote Republican. In fact, among independent identifiers, those registered as Democrats are just as likely to vote Republican as are those who register independent. It appears that a number of voters think of themselves as independents because they are registered Democratic and vote in that primary but frequently vote Republican—at least in national elections. If such voters did not have to register with a party and were not limited to voting in one party's primary, many of them might think of themselves as Republicans.

Characteristics of Party Identifiers

National surveys have shown that Democratic identifiers are likely to have lower socioeconomic levels, including incomes and education; they are much more likely to be black and somewhat more likely to be female.

Table 38. Demographic Characteristics Related to Party Identification, 1982-86

Characteristics	Percentage Down	Percentage Across		
		Dem.	Ind.	Rep.
Education				
Less than high school	26	54	20	26
High school	38	53	24	23
College	35	47	25	28
Age				
18-24	10	49	26	26
25-40	38	48	27	25
41-65	35	55	21	25
Over 65	14	55	16	30
Income				
Less than $10,000	23	56	21	24
$10,000 to $20,000	29	51	24	25
$20,000 to $30,000	25	50	25	26
Over $30,000	23	51	21	27
Gender				
Male	46	50	25	25
Female	54	53	20	27
Race				
White	94	51	23	27
Black	6	69	20	11
Total	100	52	23	26

Source: Jewell and Roeder, 1988.

Until recently younger voters were more Democratic, but there has been a trend of younger voters to be more independent or (most recently) Republican.

We find some of these differences among partisan differences in Kentucky, but the differences are quite small (Jewell and Roeder, 1988). Data from surveys in the 1982-86 period show that there is a slightly higher proportion of Democrats among the less well-educated, older, poorer, and female Kentuckians. There are a few more Republicans among the older and wealthier persons. And there are slightly more independents among those who are better educated and male and considerably more among younger persons (table 38). The reason why most demographic differences are so small is that, particularly in rural areas, many voters develop a loyalty to the dominant party in the county, without regard to their socioeconomic status. A poor farmer in a traditionally Republican county is more likely to be Republican than a prosperous lawyer or business person in a traditional

Table 39. Comparison of Party Identification and Ideology, 1981-87 (in Percentages)

Party identification	Ideology: Liberal		Middle-of-the-Road			Conservative		
	Strong	Weaker	Leans liberal		Leans conser.	Weaker	Strong	Total
Dem.	9.4	12.2	13.0	16.9	18.8	16.2	13.5	(2208)
Ind.	6.9	10.5	9.2	21.8	19.3	19.8	12.5	(1035)
Rep.	4.5	8.6	6.5	15.0	19.6	22.9	22.9	(1150)

Democratic county. When we isolate rural from metropolitan areas, we find that in rural counties income levels are about the same among each group of partisans (although independents have more income in strongly Democratic counties). But in metropolitan counties Republicans have substantially higher income levels than Democrats or independents.

Attitudes of Party Identifiers

National surveys consistently show Democrats to be more liberal than Republicans, although the differences are smaller than those between political activists in the two parties. Surveys in Kentucky conducted by the UKSRC from 1981 through 1987 show that Democrats are somewhat more liberal, Republicans are more strongly conservative, and independents have a slight preference for the ideological center (table 39). Just about half of the Democrats and independents are middle-of-the road, while almost half of the Republicans are conservative. One reason why the ideological contrasts are not sharper is the traditional local base of much party identification. More specifically, many Democratic respondents come from rural areas, particularly in western Kentucky, where conservative attitudes predominate.

There are also moderate differences among the various partisan groups in their viewpoints on policy issues (table 40). Respondents were asked on three separate occasions (1981, 1983, and 1985) about whether more, less, or the same amount of money should be spent by state and local governments on programs for the poor, public schools, and environmental programs. Democrats were slightly more willing than Republicans to support spending for the poor and for public schools, while independents were more likely to support environmental programs. Surprisingly, there were almost no differences among the three groups in their judgment about whether state and local taxes were too high or about right.

Independents were more likely, and Republicans least likely, to sup-

Table 40. Partisan Differences in Viewpoints on Policy Issues

	Percentages Down		
Policy question	Dem.	Ind.	Rep.
Spending priorities			
Aid to poor			
Spend more	55	50	45
Spend same	34	32	35
Spend less	11	18	20
Funding for schools			
Spend more	67	67	58
Spend same	30	29	38
Spend less	3	4	4
Environmental protection			
Spend more	38	43	31
Spend same	50	45	53
Spend less	12	12	16
State/local taxes			
Too high	35	40	36
About right	59	54	54
Too low	2	2	5
Equal rights amendment			
Favor	58	67	49
Oppose	42	33	51
Making abortion illegal			
Yes	60	45	56
It depends	14	18	20
No	26	37	24

port passage of the Equal Rights Amendment (in 1981). A majority of both Democrats and Republicans believed that abortion should be made illegal, while independents were more evenly divided on the issue, possibly because more of them are located in metropolitan areas. There is also evidence (not shown in the table) that Democrats were less supportive of the death penalty for convicted murderers and more supportive of laws regulating handguns than the other two groups.

On balance, we can conclude that the differences among partisans on policy issues are relatively small, compared to what we would expect to find in other states. This is probably because so many Kentuckians remain loyal to a party for traditional reasons and also because the state political parties have not consistently taken opposing stands on most of these issues.

Party identification in Kentucky clearly affects the evaluation of political leaders. In the 1985 and 1986 spring surveys, for example, respondents

Table 41. National and State Party Identification: 1987 Kentucky Survey

National party ID	Percentages of Total				State Party ID Percentages Across				Percentages Down		
	Dem.	Ind.	Rep.	Tot.	Dem.	Ind.	Rep.	Tot.	Dem.	Ind.	Rep.
Dem.	46	4	1	51	91	8	1	100	85	16	3
Ind.	6	19	3	28	21	70	9	100	11	73	13
Rep.	2	3	16	21	9	14	77	100	4	11	84
Total	54	26	20	100					100	100	100

Consistent = 81.8%
Inconsistent = 18.2%
National party ID more Rep. = 10.8%
National party ID more Dem. = 7.4%
Total N = 705

were asked to evaluate the job that Ronald Reagan was doing as president. On the average, for the two years, Reagan's performance was rated as good or excellent by 35 percent of Democrats, 59 percent of independents, and 82 percent of Republicans.

Partisanship has had a much smaller effect on the evaluations of the Kentucky governor. Averaging four gubernatorial evaluations from 1981 through 1986 (two each of Democratic governors Brown and Collins), we find that excellent or good rankings were given by 50 percent of Democrats, 44 percent of independents, and 40 percent of Republicans. Brown, in particular, was evaluated almost as favorably by Republicans as by independents.

Dual Party Identification

Research conducted in other states, particularly in the South, has suggested that some voters have dual partisanship, identifying with one party in national politics and with another party in state or local politics (Hadley, 1985; Niemi, Wright, and Powell, 1987). One plausible explanation for recent voting patterns in Kentucky would be that a substantial number of voters think of themselves as Republicans in national politics and as Democrats in state and local politics.

The best evidece on this question comes from the spring 1987 statewide poll conducted by the UKSRC. After being asked the standard question on party identification, respondents were asked, "When it comes to national politics, do you consider yourself a Democrat, Republican, or independent?" and then "When it comes to state and local politics, do you consider yourself a Democrat, Republican, or independent?"

The results (table 41) show that 18 percent of the respondents an-

Table 42. National and State Party Identification: Fayette, Jessamine, and Woodford Counties in Kentucky, 1986

National party ID	Percentages of Total				Percentages Across State Party ID				Percentages Down		
	Dem.	Ind.	Rep.	Tot.	Dem.	Ind.	Rep.	Tot.	Dem.	Ind.	Rep.
Dem.	23	5	0	28	82	17	1	100	66	11	2
Ind.	6	34	4	44	14	77	9	100	18	76	19
Rep.	5	6	17	28	19	21	60	100	15	13	79
Total	34	45	21	100					99	100	100

Consistent = 73.6%
Inconsistent = 26.4%
National party ID more Rep. = 17.2%
National party ID more Dem. = 9.2%
Total N = 511

swered inconsistently. Only 3 percent, however, identified with the Democratic party at one level and with the Republican party at the other; the rest identified with a party at one level and were independent at the other. Those who were inconsistent were slightly more likely (by an 11 to 8 margin) to be more Republican at the national level.

We might expect dual party identification to be stronger in the metropolitan areas, where the Republican party has been particularly successful in national and congressional races and less successful in state and local races. The evidence is mixed. The subsample of respondents in Jefferson County is large enough for separate analysis. Only 16 percent of them were inconsistent in their identification; and by a 2 to 1 margin, they were more Democratic at the national level.

In a survey conducted in 1986 in Fayette County (Lexington) and two adjoining counties, Jessamine and Woodford, respondents were asked the same series of questions about levels of party identification. The proportion answering inconsistently was much higher (26 percent), with almost two-thirds of these being more Republican in national politics (table 42). Although most of these were independent at one level, 5 percent were national Republicans and state Democrats. One other major difference is that 34 percent of the respondents in these three counties were independents (at both levels) compared to 23 percent in the statewide sample.

It is commonly assumed that many Kentucky voters are registered with the Democratic party and vote in that party's primary but usually vote Republican, particularly in national elections. If this is so, we might expect that party registration would be more closely correlated with state than with national party identification.

A close examination of the data shows a more complex pattern, partly because there are so few who register as independents. Almost everyone consistently identifying as a Democrat registered Democratic, and 91 percent of consistent Republicans registered Republican. Of the consistent independents, 54 percent registered Democratic, 25 percent independent, and 21 percent Republican. Almost everyone who identified with a party at one level and as an independent at the other level regstered with that party (rather than as an independent). Most of the few who were national Republicans and state Democrats registered as Democrats (and there was only one person who was a national Democrat and a state Republican).

These surveys suggest that dual identification results when voters' political beliefs conflict with their state or local identification. In the survey of the Lexington area, state Democrats who identified with the Republican party at the national level were more likely than consistent Democratic identifiers to approve of Reagan and have a conservative ideology. State independents who adopted a national Republican identification were more likely than consistent independents to approve of Reagan and reject liberalism, while those with a national Democratic identification were less likely than consistent independents to approve of Reagan and were more liberal. The 1987 statewide survey of dual party identification also showed that the ideological differences between Democrats and Republicans were slightly greater at the national level of identification than the state level.

Party Identification and Voting

Party identification is a useful tool of analysis primarily if it helps to predict and explain voting patterns. We lack comprehensive data on voting patterns of party identifiers in Kentucky. The data that are available from the UKSRC surveys should be treated cautiously for several reasons. These were not exit polls or surveys conducted immediately after the election but were carried out over a longer period of time. (The data on the 1984 presidential race are even more tentative because they were collected a year before the election.) Not all of the preelection surveys contain questions designed to identify those most likely to vote, and postelection survey respondents may exaggerate their support for the winner.

Despite these limitations, we can see evidence (table 43) that, as we would expect, partisan identifiers are more likely to vote for the candidate of that party, and varying defection rates help to explain the outcome of the elections. These defection rates are comparable to those occurring at the national level in each election. In 1980, when Reagan narrowly carried Kentucky, he won support from nearly one-fourth of Democrats, a major-

Table 43. Party Identification and Vote, 1979, 1980, 1984, 1987

	Party Identification (Percentages Down)		
	Dem.	Ind.	Rep.
1980 Presidential			
Carter	73	31	12
Reagan	24	55	85
Anderson	3	14	3
1984 Presidential			
Mondale	63	29	12
Reagan	37	71	88
1979 Gubernatorial			
Brown	89	68	21
Nunn	11	32	79
1987 Gubernatorial			
Wilkinson	84	71	48
Harper	16	29	52

ity of independents, and over four-fifths of Republicans. Four years later, when Reagan's margin was larger, he won votes from more than one-third of Democrats, over two-thirds of independents, and 88 percent of Republicans.

There are data on only two of the gubernatorial races. In 1979 John Y. Brown, running against Louie Nunn, had most Democratic votes, two-thirds of the independents, and one-fifth of the Republicans. Eight years later Wallace Wilkinson, running against an unusually weak Republican, John Harper, had 84 percent of the Democratic votes, 71 percent of independent votes, and almost half of the Republican votes.

One way of making these data on party identification more meaningful is to translate them into aggregate voting totals. For the 1980 presidential

Table 44. Estimate of Voting by Party Identification in 1980 Presidential Election

Party identification	Vote Cast (in 000's)				Percentage Across				Percentage Down		
	Dem.	Rep.	Ind.	Tot.	Dem.	Rep.	Ind.	Tot.	Dem.	Rep.	Ind.
Dem.	500	167	12	679	73.6	24.6	1.8	100	81.2	26.3	38.7
Rep.	39	314	6	359	10.9	87.5	1.6	100	6.3	49.4	19.4
Ind.	77	154	13	244	31.6	63.1	5.3	100	12.5	24.3	41.9
Total	616	635	31	1,282					100	100	100

election, we have estimated (table 44) the total number of votes cast by Democratic and Republican identifiers and by independents for Jimmy Carter, Ronald Reagan, and John Anderson. (This estimate is based on the actual turnout of party registrants and survey data on the voting preferences and registration of party identifiers. It is impossible to rely only on the survey data, which appears to exaggerate the Anderson vote.) This estimate suggests that half of Reagan's vote came from Republican identifiers, and the other half came almost evenly from Democrats and independents; almost three-fourths of Carter's vote came from Democrats. Because Reagan won the 1980 election in Kentucky very narrowly, this suggests that—to be successful—a Republican presidential candidate must draw at least half of his vote from outside his own party and needs the support of at least one-fourth of the Democrats and about two-thirds of the independents.

Unanswered Questions about Kentucky Voters

The conventional methods for describing voting behavior fall short of explaining voting patterns in Kentucky. Analysis of aggregate voting data by county shows that a large proportion of Kentuckians retain their party loyalties in most state and local elections, but they act much more independently in national—and particularly presidential—elections. This means that a substantial proportion of the voters in recent years has cast votes for both Democratic and Republican candidates. The inability of the Republican party to become fully competitive in state, legislative, and local races results from a shortage of politically experienced, well-funded candidates, not from a shortage of potential voters.

There has been no in-depth study of political attitudes and voting behavior in Kentucky; the only available data are standard questions on party identification and views on ideology and issues asked periodically in statewide surveys. No panel studies have been conducted to measure the consistency of voting from one election to the next or from the primary to the general election.

The concept of political identification, conventionally used by political scientists to categorize voters and to explain their voting behavior, is of limited use in explaining voting patterns in Kentucky. Although it is possible that significant numbers of persons identify with one party at the national level and one at the state level, the available voting surveys fail to demonstrate this convincingly, except in some metropolitan areas. About one-fourth of the voters describe themselves as independents, and we need to understand better how these individuals perceive the political parties and what factors motivate their voting decisions.

Because primary elections continue to be important in the Democratic party (and in some local Republican parties) and because there is little change in party registration, most Democrats and some Republicans vote consistently within the primary of one party while voting more independently in general elections. We know little about how the political parties are perceived and evaluated by those persons who vote in Democratic primaries and frequently vote Republican in general elections.

Kentucky politics is in a stage of transition, and these changes affect voters in many ways. Many Kentucky voters now living in metropolitan counties grew up in rural counties dominated by one party, while others have moved in from other states. A new generation of voters has few, if any, memories of Kentucky political traditions. They do not know or care how rural partisan loyalties were shaped by the Civil War and its aftermath or by family loyalties and feuds. They have never heard of the factions in the Democratic party; they are unaware of Earle Clements; and they know Happy Chandler not as a colorful and controversial politician but as the state's number one sports fan.

Today the voters' perceptions of state candidates are shaped largely by television, a medium that encourages independence in voting because it reaches across party lines. Republicans as well as Democrats are subjected to news coverage and advertisements in the Democratic primary as well as the general election campaigns. The advertising campaigns of incumbent congressmen (particularly Republicans) emphasize constituent service and accessibility rather than partisanship. Television is a medium that gives an advantage to the candidate who has mastered its techniques rather than to the candidate with an established record of office holding. Because most voters no longer have strong loyalties to either parties or candidates, they can be very volatile and easily swayed by effective advertising campaigns, as we saw in the 1987 Democratic primaries.

Kentuckians are proud of their traditions, and we have been slow to recognize that these political traditions are changing. The trends that have affected political parties, campaigns, and voters in the rest of the country have begun to have an impact in Kentucky. These trends have increased the potential for two-party competition, even though this development has not been fully realized in Kentucky. They have changed the character of campaign organization, without ending its importance. More significant has been the growing importance of television as the forum for political communication and television advertising as the vehicle for publicizing the candidate's message. Because of these trends, the Kentucky voter has changed, becoming more independent and unpredictable in the choice of parties and candidates.

APPENDIX

Description of Independent Variables*

Variable	Description
Motivations for involvement in primaries	Four separate scores, based on responses to a series of 13 Likert-type items. Factor analysis was used to reduce the 13 items to three underlying dimensions. "Support of a particular candidate I believe in" had to be excluded from the factor analysis since most respondents so strongly emphasized this reason, thus creating very little variability. The first dimension, on which the highest-loading items included "certain group-political ties," "social contacts," "excitement of campaign," and "work with friends and relatives," clearly tapped solidary motivations. The high loadings of "help my own political career," "make business contacts," and "obtain local/state job" on the second factor pointed to material motivations. Four other items ("work for issues," "influence policies of government," "civic responsibility," and "interest group goals") formed the third dimension of purposive motivation. On the basis of the factor analysis, sets of items were combined aditively to form a summary scale for each respondent on each dimension. Since the "personal friendship with a candidate" item did not load highly on any of the three dimensions, it was used by itself as an indicator of a fourth type of motivation—attraction to or linkage with a candidate.
Ideological proximity to a candidate	Derived by subtracting a respondent's self-identified position on a five-point liberal conservative scale from the respondent's own position on the same scale.
Interest group membership	Separate dummy variables indicating respondent's membership in a labor union, teacher/educational group, or business organization (each coded 1 for membership, 0 otherwise).
First-time campaign activity	A dummy variable coded 1 if the respondent's first active political involvement was in the 1983 primary campaign, 0 otherwise.
Continuity of support	Separate dummy variables identifying which, if any, of the 1979 Democratic gubernatorial contenders the respondent had supported—George Atkins, John Y. Brown, Jr., Carroll Hubbard, Terry McBrayer, Harvey Sloane, or Thelma Stovall.

*The dependent variable, candidate choice, was tapped via responses to the following question: "In 1983, did you support a gubernatorial primary candidate? Which one?"

REFERENCES

Abramowitz, Alan I., John McGlennon, and Ronald B. Rapoport. 1986a. "An Analysis of State Party Activists." In Ronald B. Rapoport, Alan I. Abramowitz, and John McGlennon (eds.), *The Life of the Parties: Activists in Presidential Politics*. Lexington: University Press of Kentucky.

———. 1986b. "Incentives for Activism." In Ronald B. Rapoport, Alan I. Abramowitz, and John McGlennon (eds.), *The Life of the Parties: Activists in Presidential Politics*. Lexington: The University Press of Kentucky.

Alexander, Herbert E. 1984. *Financing Politics: Money, Elections, and Political Reform*. 3d ed. Washington, D.C.: Congressional Quarterly.

Bass, Jack, and Walter DeVries. 1977. *The Transformation of Southern Politics*. New York: New American Library Basic Books.

Beck, Paul A. 1977. "Partisan Dealignment in the Postwar South." *American Political Science Review* 71: 477-96.

Bell, Julie Davis. 1985. "The Decline of Party Revisited: Motivational Change among Political Party Activists." Presented at the American Political Science Association Meeting.

Black, Earl, and Merle Black. 1982a. "Successful Durable Democratic Factions in Southern Politics." In Laurence W. Moreland, T.A. Baker, and R.P. Steed (eds.), *Contemporary Southern Political Attitudes and Behavior*. New York: Praeger.

———. 1982b. "The Growth of Contested Republican Primaries in the American South." In Laurence W. Moreland, T.A. Baker, and R.P. Steed (eds.), *Contemporary Southern Political Attitudes and Behavior*. New York: Praeger.

———. 1987. *Politics and Society in the South*. Cambridge: Harvard University Press.

Blanchard, Paul D. 1982. "Continuity and Change in Kentucky Voting Behavior." Presented at the annual meeting of the Kentucky Political Science Association.

Born, Richard. 1981. "The Influence of House Primary Election Divisiveness on General Election Margins: 1962-1976." *Journal of Politics* 43: 640-61.

Bowman, Lewis, Dennis Ippolito, and William Donaldson. 1969. "Incentives for the Maintenance of Grassroots Political Activism." *Midwest Journal of Political Science* 13: 126-39.

Boynton, G.R., Ronald Hedlund, and Samuel Patterson. 1969. "The Missing Links in Legislative Politics: Attentive Constituents." *Journal of Politics* 31: 700-21.

Bryan, Frank M. 1974. *Yankee Politics in Rural Vermont*. Hanover, N.H.: University Press of New England.

Campbell, Angus, Philip E. Converse, Warren E. Miller, and Donald E. Stokes. 1960. *The American Voter*. New York: John Wiley and Sons.

Campbell, Bruce A. 1977. "Change in the Southern Electorate." *American Journal of Political Science* 21: 37-64.

Carney, Francis. 1958. *The Rise of the Democratic Clubs in California*. Eagleton Foundation Case Studies in Practical Politics. New York: Henry Holt and Company.

Clark, Peter B., and James Q. Wilson. 1961. "Incentive Systems: A Theory of Organization." *Administrative Science Quarterly* 6: 129-66.

Conway, Margaret M., and Frank B. Feigert. 1968. "Motivation, Incentive Systems, and the Political Party Organization." *American Political Science Review* 60: 1159-73.

Costantini, Edmond, and Joel King. 1984. "The Motives of Political Party Activists: A Factor-Analytic Exploration." *Political Behavior* 6: 79-91.

Crotty, William J. 1967. "The Social Attributes of Party Organizational Activists in a Transitional Political System." *Western Political Quarterly* 20: 669-81.

———. 1977. *Political Reform and the American Experiment*. New York: Thomas Y. Crowell.

Eldersveld, Samuel J. 1964. *Political Parties: A Behavioral Analysis*. Chicago: Rand McNally.

Finkel, Steven E., and Howard A. Scarrow. 1985. "Party Identification and Party Enrollment: The Difference and the Consequence." *Journal of Politics* 47: 620-42.

Forthal, Sonya. 1946. *Cogwheels of Democracy: A Study of the Precinct Captain*. New York: William-Frederick Press.

Francis, John G., and Robert C. Benedict. 1986. "Issue Group Activists at the Conventions." In Ronald B. Rapoport, Alan I. Abramowitz, and John McGlennon (eds.), *The Life of the Parties: Activists in Presidential Politics*. Lexington: University Press of Kentucky.

Giles, Michael W., and Anita Pritchard. 1985. "Campaign Expenditures and Legislative Elections in Florida." *Legislative Studies Quarterly* 10: 71-88.

Goldstein, Joel. 1988. "The Continuity of Factional Support among Rank and File Democrats: Kentucky, 1987 Primary Election." Paper presented at the annual meeting of the Southern Political Science Association.

———. 1989. "The Continued Decline in the Rate of Participation in the Kentucky Political Party Income Tax Check-Off." Unpublished paper.

Gosnell, Harold F. 1937. *Machine Politics: Chicago Model*. Chicago: University of Chicago Press.

Granberg, Donald, and Edward Brent. 1974. "Dove-Hawk Placements in the 1968 Election." *Journal of Personality and Social Psychology* 63: 687-95.

Graves, James, S. Yuill, and L. Shier. 1987. "Campaign Financing in Kentucky: A Ten-and-a-Half Year Study of PACs." Paper presented at the annual conference of the Council on Governmental Ethics Laws.

Grupp, Fred. 1971. "Personal Satisfaction Derived from Membership in the John Birch Society." *Western Political Quarterly* 24: 79-83.

Hacker, Andrew. 1965. "Does a Divisive Primary Harm a Candidate's Election Chances?" *American Political Science Review* 59: 105-10.

Hadley, Charles D. 1985. "Dual Party Identification in the South." *Journal of Politics* 47: 254-68.

Hadley, Charles D., and Susan E. Howell. 1980. "The Southern Split Ticket Voter, 1952-76: Republican Conversion or Democratic Decline." In Robert Steed, L. Moreland, and R. Baker (eds.), *Party Politics in the South*. New York: Praeger.

Hauss, Charles S., and L. Sandy Maisel. 1986. "Extremist Delegates: Myth and Reality." In Ronald B. Rapoport, Alan I. Abramowitz, and John McGlennon (eds.), *The Life of the Parties: Activists in Presidential Politics*. Lexington: University Press of Kentucky.

Hedges, Roman B. 1984. "Reasons for Political Involvement: A Study of Contributors to the 1972 Presidential Campaign." *Western Political Quarterly* 37: 257-71.

Heider, Fritz. 1958. *The Psychology of Interpersonal Relations*. New York: John Wiley and Sons.

Hirschfield, Robert S., Bert E. Swanson, and Blanche D. Blank, 1962. "A Profile of Political Activists in Manhattan." *Western Political Quarterly* 15: 489-506.

Hofstetter, Richard C. 1973. "Organization Activists: The Bases of Participation in Amateur and Professional Groups." *American Political Science Quarterly* 1:244-76.

Huckshorn, Robert J., 1976. *Party Leadership in the States*. Amherst: University of Massachusetts Press.

Jacobson, Gary C. 1980. *Money in Congressional Elections*. New Haven: Yale University Press.

Jewell, Malcolm E. 1984. *Parties and Primaries: Nominating State Governors*. New York: Praeger.

Jewell, Malcolm E., and Everett W. Cunningham. 1968. *Kentucky Politics*. Lexington: University of Kentucky Press.

Jewell, Malcolm E., and Penny M. Miller. 1988. *The Kentucky Legislature: Two Decades of Change*. Lexington: University Press of Kentucky.

Jewell, Malcolm E., and Phillip W. Roeder. 1988. "Partisanship in Kentucky: 1979-1986." In Robert H. Swansbrough and David M. Brodsky (eds.), *The New South's Politics: Realignment and Dealignment*. Columbia: University of South Carolina Press.

Jewell, Malcolm E., and Lee Sigelman. 1986. "Voting in Primaries: The Impact of Intra- and Inter-Party Competition." *Western Political Quarterly* 39: 446-54.

Johnson, Donald Bruce, and James R. Gibson. 1974. "The Divisive Primary Revisited: Party Activists in Iowa." *American Political Science Review* 68: 67-77.

Jones, Ruth S., and Thomas J. Borris. 1985. "Strategic Contributing in Legislative Campaign: The Case of Minnesota." *Legislative Studies Quarterly* 10: 89-106.

Kemple, Arlon. 1980. "Changes in Competitiveness and Evolution of the Party Role in Southern Republican Parties." Paper presented at the Citadel Symposium on Southern Politics.

Kenney, Patrick J., and Thomas W. Rice. 1984. "The Effect of Primary Divisiveness in Gubernatorial and Senatorial Elections." *Journal of Politics* 46: 904-15.

Kent, Frank R. 1923. *The Great Game of Politics*. New York: Doubleday Doran.

Key, V.O., Jr. 1949. *Southern Politics in State and Nation*. New York: Random House.

———. 1956. *American State Politics: An Introduction*. New York: Alfred A. Knopf.

———. 1964. *Politics, Parties, and Pressure Groups*. 5th ed. New York: Thomas Y. Crowell

Kirkpatrick, Jeane. 1976. *The New Presidential Elite: Men and Women in National Politics*. New York: Russell Sage.

Lamis, Alexander P. 1984. *The Two-Party South*. New York: Oxford University Press

Malbin, Michael J. (ed.). 1984. *Money and Politics in the United States*. Chatham, N.J.: Chatham House.

Margolis, Michael, and Raymond E. Owen. 1985. "From Organization to Personalism: A Note on the Transmogrification of the Local Political Party." *Polity* 2: 313-28.

Marshall, Thomas R. 1981. "Minnesota: The Party Caucus-Convention System." In Gerald Pomper (ed.), *Party Renewal in America*. New York: Praeger.
Marvick, Dwane. 1968. "The Middlemen of Politics." In William J. Crotty (ed.), *Approaches to the Study of Party Organization*. Boston: Allyn & Bacon.
Milbrath, Lester. 1965. *Political Participation*. Chicago: Rand McNally.
Miller, Penny. 1984. "Motivations of Political Activists in Gubernatorial Primaries: A View of Kentucky's Politics." Paper presented at the annual meeting of the Southern Political Science Association.
———. 1985. "Choosing a Candidate: Political Activists in Kentucky Democratic Gubernatorial Primaries." Paper presented at the annual meeting of the American Political Science Association.
———. 1986. "Motivations and Continuty of Support of Political Activists in Gubernatorial Primaries." Ph.D. dissertation, University of Kentucky.
Miller, Penny M., Malcolm E. Jewell, and Lee Sigelman. 1987. "Reconsidering a Typology of Incentives among Campaign Activists: A Research Note." *Western Political Quarterly* 40: 519-26.
———, 1988. "Divisive Primaries and Party Activists: Kentucky, 1979 and 1983." *Journal of Politics* 50: 459-70.
Moe, Terry. 1980. *The Organization of Interests*. Chicago: University of Chicago Press.
Niemi, Richard G., Stephen Wright, and Lynda Powell. 1987. "Multiple Party Identifiers and the Measurement of Party Identification." *Journal of Politics* 49: 1093-1103.
O'Keefe, Dennis. 1986. "Interest Group Contributions in Kentucky's 1983 Gubernatorial and Senatorial Elections." Paper presented at the annual meeting of the Kentucky Political Science Association.
Olson, Mancur, Jr. 1965. *The Logic of Collective Action*. Cambridge, Mass.: Harvard University Press.
Patterson, Samuel C. 1963. "Characteristics of Party Leaders." *Western Political Quarterly* 16: 332-52.
———. 1968. "The Political Cultures of the American States." *Journal of Politics* 30: 187-209.
———. 1982. "Campaign Spending in Contests for Governor." *Western Political Quarterly* 35: 457-77.
Patterson, Samuel C., and G.R. Boynton. 1969. "Legislative Recruitment in a Civic Culture." *Social Science Quarterly* 50: 243-63.
Pearce, John Ed. 1987. *Divide and Dissent: Kentucky Politics 1930-1963*. Lexington: University Press of Kentucky.
Peirce, Neal, and Jerry Hagstrom. 1983. *The Book of America*. New York: W.W. Norton.
Piereson, James E., and T.B. Smith. 1975. "Primary Divisiveness and General Election Success: A Re-examination." *Journal of Politics* 37: 555-62.
Pomper, Gerald. 1965. "New Jersey County Chairmen." *Western Political Quarterly* 18: 186-97.
Rapoport, Ronald B., Alan I. Abramowitz, and John McGlennon. 1986. *The Life of the Parties: Activists in Presidential Politics*. Lexington: University Press of Kentucky.
Roback, Thomas H. 1974. *Recruitment and Incentive Patterns among Grassroots Republican Officials: Continuity and Change in Two States*. Beverly Hills, Calif.: Sage Publications.
———. 1980. "Motivation for Activism among Republican National Convention Delegates: Continuity and Change, 1972-1976." *Journal of Politics* 42: 181-201.
Rosenthal, Alan, and Maureen Moakley (eds.). 1984. *The Political Life of the American States*. New York: Praeger.

Sabato, Larry J. 1984. *PAC Power.* New York: W.W. Norton.
Salter, J.T. 1935. *Boss Rule: Portraits in City Politics.* New York: McGraw-Hill.
Schlesinger, Joseph A. 1965. "Political Party Organization." In James G. March (ed.), *Handbook of Organizations.* Chicago: Rand McNally.
Schlozman, Kay L., and John T. Tierney. 1986. *Organized Interests and American Democracy.* New York: Harper & Row.
Schneider, Sandra K. (ed.). 1986. *Campaign Finance, Ethics, and Lobby Blue Book 1986-87.* Lexington, Ky.: Council of State Government.
Sherrod, Drury. 1971-72. "Selective Perception of Political Candidates." *Public Opinion Quarterly* 35: 554-62.
Shively, W. Phillips. 1980. "The Nature of Party Identification: A Review of Recent Developments." In John C. Pierce and John L. Sullivan (eds.), *The Electorate Reconsidered.* Beverly Hills, Calif.: Sage Publications.
Sigelman, Lee. 1984. "Doing Discriminant Analysis: Some Problems and Solutions." *Political Methodology* 10: 67-80.
Sigelman, Lee, and Malcolm E. Jewell. 1986. "From Core to Periphery: A Note on the Imagery of Concentric Electorates." *Journal of Politics* 48: 440-49.
Sigelman, Lee, Phillip W. Roeder, Malcolm E. Jewell, Michael A. Baer. 1985. "Voting and Nonvoting: A Multi-Election Perspective." *American Journal of Political Science* 29: 749-65.
Sindler, Allan P. 1956. *Huey Long's Louisiana.* Baltimore: Johns Hopkins Press.
Sorauf, Frank J. 1988. *Money in American Elections.* Glenview, Ill.: Scott, Foresman/ Little, Brown.
Squire, Peverill, Raymond E. Wolfinger, and David P. Glass. 1987. "Residential Mobility and Voter Turnout." *American Political Science Review* 81: 45-65.
Stanley, Harold W., and David S. Castle. 1988. "Partisan Change in the South: Making Sense of Scholarly Dissonance." In Robert H. Swansbrough and David M. Brodsky (eds.), *The South's New Politics: Realignment and Dealignment.* Columbia: University of South Carolina Press.
Stone, Walter J. 1984. "Prenomination Candidate Choice and General Election Behavior: Iowa Presidential Activists in 1980." *American Journal of Political Science* 28: 361-78.
———. 1986. "The Carry-over Effect in Presidential Elections." *American Political Science Review* 80: 271-79.
Stone, Walter J., and Alan I. Abramowitz. 1986. "Ideology, Electability, and Candidate Choice." In Ronald B. Rapoport, Alan I. Abramowitz, and John McGlennon (eds.), *The Life of the Parties: Activists in Presidential Politics.* Lexington: University Press of Kentucky.
Swansbrough, Robert H., and David M. Brodsky (eds.). 1988. *The South's New Politics: Realignment and Dealignment.* Columbia: University of South Carolina Press.
Theodoulou, Stelle. 1986. *The Louisiana Republican Party, 1948-1984: The Building of a State Republican Party.* New Orleans: Tulane University Studies in Political Science.
Verba, Sidney, and Norman Nie. 1972. *Participation in America.* New York: Harper & Row.
Weir, Blair T. 1975. "The Distortion of Voter Recall." *American Journal of Political Science* 19: 53-62.
Westlye, Mark C. 1985. "The Effects of Primary Divisiveness on Incumbent Senators, 1968-84." Paper presented at the annual meeting of the American Political Science Association.

Wiggins, Charles W., and William L. Turk. 1970. "State Party Chairmen: A Profile." *Western Political Quarterly* 32: 321-32.
Wilson, James Q. 1962. *The Amateur Democrat: Club Politics in Three Cities*. Chicago: University of Chicago Press.
———. 1973. *Political Organizations*. New York: Basic Books.
Wolfinger, Raymond E., and Steven J. Rosenstone. 1980. *Who Votes?* New Haven: Yale University Press.

Newspapers and Magazines

The Courier-Journal (Louisville) (*C-J*).
The Lexington Herald-Leader (*H-L*).
The National Journal, June 26, 1988.

INDEX